CENSORED 2020

THROUGH THE LOOKING GLASS

The Top Censored Stories and Media Analysis of 2018–19

Andy Lee Roth and Mickey Huff
with Project Censored

Foreword by
Sharyl Attkisson
Cartoons by
Khalil Bendib

Seven Stories Press

New York • Oakland • London

Seven Stories Press
140 Watts Street
New York, NY 10013
www.sevenstories.com

ISBN 978-1-60980-960-7 (paperback)
ISBN 978-1-60980-961-4 (electronic)
ISSN 1074-5998

Book design by Jon Gilbert

Printed in the USA

9 8 7 6 5 4 3 2 1

Finding Strength in Community
Gilda L. Ochoa

Thinking of teachers

Regardless of whether they carry that name

Inside our schools and far away from those rooms

Who every day

See our full humanity

Show their own vulnerability

Name the realities of inequality

Unmask erased histories

Deconstruct prevailing ideologies

Build spaces showing another way

Inspiring us to continue another day

GILDA L. OCHOA is a professor of Chicana/o-Latina/o Studies at Pomona College. She is the author of three books, including *Academic Profiling: Latinos, Asian Americans, and the Achievement Gap*, which has received several awards. Most recently, she has turned to poetry to more personally convey her thoughts on identity, schooling, and immigration policies.

Contents

Down the Rabbit Hole of "Media Literacy" by Decree

Sharyl Attkisson

Never before have there been so many well-organized, well-funded efforts to root out so-called "fake news." To separate fact from fiction. To educate us on how to be media literate. To learn what—and whom—to believe.

Third parties are stepping up on the public stage and generously offering to "curate" our information for us. Sometimes they're pressed into service behind the scenes by advocacy groups or politicians. *They'll* decide what appears on the information landscape and what is made to disappear, as if it never even happened. Governments, in some cases, promote or demand these efforts through new laws, proposed here in at least a dozen states so far—and through new laws passed around the globe in countries like France and Brazil.

The self-appointed curators, often wielding proprietary algorithms, summarily dispense with facts and ideas that they determine to be false—or maybe just dangerous to their agendas. Thanks to them, we will hardly have to do any of our own thinking. They'll take care of it for us.

Information by popular consensus. Or so we're led to believe.

But what if this movement is, at its heart, actually an attempt by powerful interests to prevent us from becoming aware of particular facts, information, and ideas? What if some of the efforts that bill themselves as a way to sort out fake news are actually ways to shape information—and make us like it?

First, they had to create a demand for their actual product: Censorship. Only they couldn't call it *that*. (This is America, after all.) So they took a page from George Orwell. You'll recall that in Orwell's dystopian novel *1984*, Oceania's war department was named the "Ministry of Peace." Today, some efforts to debunk fake news may actually be ruses designed to push information that is not true. From New Knowledge to PropOrNot and First Draft, many of the most prominent would-be watchdogs have engaged in censorship in the name of fighting fake news.

Then came the hard sell. We need this censorship—er, curating and literacy, we're told—because we simply cannot trust ourselves to sort through it. Something this important is best left to the professionals.

The irony seems lost upon the self-appointed censors: they include media outlets and organizations, such as the *New York Times* and NBC News, that themselves have promoted some of the most notable false reporting in the past few years. Although they deemed the falsehoods in their own reporting fit for publication, they would "curate" away opposing views and publications.

For a reality check, one need only consult the genuine media literacy efforts promoted since the mid-1970s by a small nonprofit called Project Censored. By their definition, "Censorship is anything that interferes with the free flow of information." It's not complicated. Their brand of *critical* media literacy promotes getting all the information into the public sphere. Not shaping, funneling, curating, or censoring. Just the simple noninvasive act of letting it be.

If you choose to let Facebook, Google, the media, or the government curate your information—if you trust them to do so—that's your choice. But it should be just that: a choice. Not a government mandate. Not an uninvited intrusion by a self-appointed third party.

Some might say that in 2019, we—as a nation—have gotten serious about our information. I would argue that we've moved a step closer to societies that we historically abhorred for their dearth of a free press and for their government censorship. And we've done it with barely a whimper, freely inviting the Trojan horse into our midst, in some cases even demanding it, convinced by propaganda to embrace it.

For me? I'll take my information straight up.

Now, more than ever, press freedom is at stake. In opposition to the undemocratic censorship of information, I proudly stand with Project Censored.

SHARYL ATTKISSON is an Emmy Award–winning investigative journalist and host of *Full Measure with Sharyl Attkisson*. She is the recipient of the Edward R. Murrow Award for investigative reporting and author of two *New York Times* bestsellers, *Stonewalled* and *The Smear*, which address the topics of news censorship and bias. For 24 years she worked at CBS, CNN, and PBS, where she enjoyed a great deal of reportage freedoms, received more than a dozen Emmy nominations and awards, and also observed her share of censorship challenges.

Introduction

Mickey Huff and Andy Lee Roth

> *"I ca'n't believe that!" said Alice.*
> *"Ca'n't you?" the Queen said in a pitying tone.*
> *"Try again: draw a long breath, and shut your eyes."*
> *Alice laughed. "There's no use trying," she said: "one ca'n't*
> *believe impossible things."*
> *"I daresay you haven't had much practice," said the*
> *Queen.*
>
> —Lewis Carroll, *Through the Looking-Glass*[1]

Welcome to the looking-glass world of contemporary politics and media in the United States. Every day, powerful entities—including Donald Trump, in the role of a mad-hatter president; the leaders of Facebook, Google, and other tech giants; not to mention the corporate press—challenge us to take a deep breath, close our eyes, and believe the impossible.

Trump would have the country imagine that the greatest threat it faces is immigration, which only a wall and tariffs can stop. Pundits insist that Russia poses a greater threat to election integrity than does the dark money of a corporate oligopoly.[2] Facebook and Twitter seek expert advice on regulating free speech from the leader of a known hate group.[3] A celebrity hosts a party based (loosely) on Hulu's adaptation of Margaret Atwood's *The Handmaid's Tale*, as women's reproductive rights are under attack and the most popular TV programs regularly feature violence against women as entertainment.[4] Nonviolent activists calling for action on catastrophic climate change and the sixth mass extinction are repressed and criminalized as "eco-terrorists."[5] And those seeking justice for police killings of African Americans are labeled "Black Identity

Extremists."[6] The clocks run backward in this looking-glass realm—as evidenced by vicious resurgences of nationalism, racism, sexism, and homophobia. Social media accelerate and amplify the spread of hateful values, while Facebook, Twitter, and a ratings-hungry corporate media profit from sowing division and the public controversy it entails.[7]

As a result, many in the United States see only distorted or even inverted representations of reality through the magic mirrors of clickbait-driven reporting, pundits' 24/7 "hot takes," and social media feeds governed by secret algorithms. By contrast, much like Alice responding to the Queen's wild claims, many of us recognize and oppose these distortions, defying calls to renounce a factually-grounded world in favor of a wonderland where narrow self-interest would serve as truth's primary arbiter. For both groups, *Censored 2020* challenges the corporate news media's looking-glass logic and, as antidote, it presents some of the past year's most exemplary *independent* news reporting and media analyses.

INDEPENDENT ALTERNATIVES TO "NEVER JAM TODAY"

> *"The rule is, jam to-morrow and jam yesterday—but never jam to-day."*
>
> *"It* must *come sometimes to 'jam to-day,'"* Alice objected.
>
> *"No, it ca'n't," said the Queen. "It's jam every other day: to-day isn't any other day, you know."*
>
> *"I don't understand you," said Alice. "It's dreadfully confusing!"*
>
> —Lewis Carroll, *Through the Looking-Glass*[8]

Perverse distortions and mystifying reversals do not capture the full scope of looking-glass logic. Substitute "real news" for "jam" and—in line with the Queen's twisted temporal reasoning—you get a stark rendering of the corporate media's shortcomings when it comes to reporting the full scope of what is newsworthy. (If this assessment strikes some as too harsh a judgment of the establishment press, we invite skeptical readers to jump ahead to Chapter 2, "'Curiouser and Curiouser': A Mad Hatter's Tea Party of Junk Food News," and

Chapter 3, "Comforting the Powerful, Ignoring the Afflicted: News Abuse in 2018–2019.")

For example, in 2018–2019, the corporate news media failed to cover how unconscionable conditions in immigrant detention centers have been worsened by flawed investigations of sexual assaults on detained children, how the right to peaceful protest is threatened by the Department of Defense's plan to systematically surveil citizens' social media accounts, and how the oil and gas industry is set to unleash a devastating 120 billion tons of new carbon pollution by the year 2030. Each of these stories, and more like them, have in fact been reported as news—by independent news reporters and outlets, as documented in Chapter 1 of this book.

Although some may debate whether the marginalization of these stories by the corporate press is intentional, there is no doubting that, on a daily basis, the best independent journalists and news outlets make sure that this jam—fact-based news that serves the public interest, news that serves to "tell the truth and shame the devil"[9]—is available to those with an appetite for it.

This includes, especially, constructive news stories that serve to empower and inspire, as highlighted by Kenn Burrows, Amber Yang, and Bethany Surface in Chapter 9. By covering not only abuses of power and their consequences but also community-based remedies and time-tested solutions, independent reporters and news outlets promote informed public understanding, discussion, *and* engagement.[10]

PUNISHMENT BEFORE TRIAL

"What sort of things do you remember best?" Alice ventured to ask.
"Oh, things that happened the week after next," the Queen replied in a careless tone. "For instance, now," she went on [. . .], "there's the King's Messenger. He's in prison now, being punished: and the trial doesn't even begin till next Wednesday: and of course the crime comes last of all."

—Lewis Carroll, *Through the Looking-Glass*[11]

Those taking up the charge of a responsible fourth estate, which would hold the powerful to account, are on a hero's journey, similar to Alice's. But, as in Alice's descent into Wonderland, too often logic and proportion are turned on their heads. Thus, for example, on Memorial Day in 2019, President Trump pushed to pardon US troops who had committed war crimes, while whistleblower Chelsea Manning was back in prison for her refusal to testify against WikiLeaks's Julian Assange.[12]

Recall that in early 2010 Manning had provided Assange and WikiLeaks with gunsight video footage documenting a US strike on civilians in Baghdad, Iraq—only after establishment media, including the *Washington Post* and the *New York Times*, failed to respond to Manning's attempts to submit the material to them for publication.[13] WikiLeaks published the video of the Baghdad airstrike, titled "Collateral Murder," in April 2010. No US military personnel were held accountable for these clearly-documented war crimes, but the US government prosecuted Manning under the Espionage Act and sentenced her to 35 years in prison. If that is not looking-glass logic, what is?

Similarly, in 2013, when Edward Snowden revealed highly classified information regarding wanton National Security Agency (NSA) surveillance of the US public, the corporate media initially refused to assist Snowden. Instead, they attacked him viciously, even as major corporate media outlets subsequently accepted awards and accolades for reporting based on the very materials that Snowden had leaked. The director of national intelligence at the time, James Clapper, lied under oath to Congress about the NSA's mass surveillance program.[14] Snowden subsequently cited Clapper's congressional testimony as "the breaking point" in his decision to reveal the NSA documents.[15] Snowden was publicly pilloried as a traitor, while Clapper's perjury went unpunished. Yet more political Jabberwocky.

This history is especially important now, as Manning's and Assange's fates hang in the balance, along with the future of press freedoms, according to more than a few notable commentators.[16] As Trevor Timm, executive director of the Freedom of the Press Foundation, stated in April 2019,

While the Trump administration has so far not attempted to explicitly declare the act of publishing illegal, a core part of its argument would criminalize many common journalist–source interactions that reporters rely on all the time. Requesting more documents from a source, using an encrypted chat messenger, or trying to keep a source's identity anonymous are not crimes; they are vital to the journalistic process. Whether or not you like Assange, the charge against him is a serious press freedom threat and should be vigorously protested by all those who care about the First Amendment.[17]

On the same day as Timm's warning about threats to press freedoms, the British government forcibly removed Assange from the Ecuadorian embassy in London, where he had found asylum for seven years. In May 2019, the US Department of Justice indicted Assange for multiple violations of the Espionage Act—making him the first publisher to be charged under the World War I–era law. The US government seeks to extradite Assange from the United Kingdom for trial in the United States, while Manning is once again imprisoned, this time for refusing to testify before a grand jury about her association with Assange. Thus, both Assange and Manning—not to mention others like them—are punished for what Daniel Ellsberg of *Pentagon Papers* fame has called "civil courage."[18] They are the messengers of war crimes and financial malfeasance, who made available to the public cables, communications, and policies that expose the callous inhumanity of the so-called "war on terror" and the neoliberal austerity agenda. Their acts were selfless, driven by the desire to inform the public of the truth and to hold those responsible to account. As Timm noted, the ability of sources to share documents and other information with reporters is "vital" to journalism. In cases like Manning's and Assange's, the messengers of truth have committed no real crimes, but—by looking-glass logic—they have already been, and continue to be, punished.[19]

INSIDE *CENSORED 2020*

A primary goal of Project Censored is to improve media coverage of important social issues. Chapter 1 of *Censored 2020* presents the 25 most important but underreported news stories of 2018–2019 as determined by Project Censored's judges, faculty evaluators, and student researchers. The chapter simultaneously highlights exemplary reporting by independent reporters and news outlets and holds the corporate news media to account for failing to inform the public adequately of these significant news stories. This year's list includes coverage of how survivors of sexual abuse and trafficking are frequently criminalized for acts of self-defense (story #6), the Department of Justice's use of secret rules to evade First Amendment limitations on government surveillance of journalists (story #1), and grassroots efforts to make school lunch programs more equitable (story #23). Despite their remarkable newsworthiness, these stories, along with the rest of the reports that comprise this year's list, have been either marginalized or ignored altogether by the establishment press. Chapter 1 aims to break the corporate blockade on coverage of these issues, by bringing the stories—and the independent journalists and news outlets that deserve credit for covering them—to wider public attention.

In Chapter 2, "Curiouser and Curiouser," Izzy Snow, Susan Rahman, and students at the College of Marin present a Mad Hatter's tea party of Junk Food News. Their chapter starkly contrasts the sensational, titillating, and often trivial stories promoted by corporate news outlets with important topics and issues that were overlooked and underreported. From the "discourse on diapers, crown-jeweled pacifiers, and royal bibs" in anticipation of the birth of Prince Harry and Meghan Markle's baby, to the Notre-Dame Cathedral fire, and the flame war between Kim Kardashian and fashion retailer Fashion Nova, corporate media pushed a wonderland of escapism—while neglecting real news on "birth-striking" as a response to the climate crisis, the arson of African American churches in Louisiana, and the Yellow Vest movement in France. As Snow and Rahman write, "During the 2018–2019 news cycle, logic and proportion fell sloppy dead, torn apart by headlines that spread disinformation, propaganda, and utter nonsense."

Chapter 3, by John Collins, Nicole Eigbrett, Jana Morgan, and Steve Peraza, takes stock of another form of corporate media propaganda, News Abuse. "News Abuse" is the term that Project Censored uses to describe genuinely newsworthy topics that the public is nevertheless unlikely to appreciate or understand due to slanted coverage provided by corporate news outlets. Examining establishment media's hagiographic reports of Senator John McCain's death, the debate surrounding Brett Kavanaugh's Supreme Court nomination, the migrant "caravan" traveling from Central America to the United States, and the election to Congress of a group of women of color dubbed "the Squad," Collins, Eigbrett, Morgan, and Peraza critique the corporate press for its "heavy reliance on tropes, frames, and narratives that served to shield elite groups and the US empire itself from critical scrutiny while marginalizing or casting doubt on the voices of the relatively powerless."

After reading the chapters on Junk Food News and News Abuse, readers might feel much like Alice in Wonderland did when she found herself "up to her chin in salt water," only to realize that it was a pool of her own tears.[20] Chapter 4, "Media Democracy in Action," presents antidotes to the tear-inducing potions of Junk Food News and News Abuse. Compiled by Steve Macek, this year's installment of Media Democracy in Action highlights engaged journalism at its best, including contributions by Kathryn Foxhall of the Society of Professional Journalists on how public information officers serve as censors; Russ Kick, the founder and manager of AltGov2, a website dedicated to increasing government transparency; Matthew Crain and Anthony Nadler, on Silicon Valley's "digital influence machine"; Brendan DeMelle and Ashley Braun on DeSmogBlog's work countering the fossil fuel industry's PR and lies; Alexandra Bradbury on Labor Notes and grassroots union activism; and Aaron Delwiche and Mary Margaret Herring on Propaganda Critic, a website that engagingly educates members of the public about how to defend themselves from media manipulation and propaganda. The contributors to this year's Media Democracy in Action chapter provide useful information and reality-based inspiration to activists and others who believe a better world is possible.

Adam Bessie and Marc Parenteau's "What's Burning?" (Chapter 5) examines the ubiquitous influence of smart devices and social media, through the lens of the Camp Fire, which destroyed the town of Paradise, California, in November 2018. As smoke from the catastrophic fire darkened skies across the San Francisco Bay and the Central Valley, impacting the health of millions of people, filter mask selfies trended on social media. Bessie and Parenteau consider the packaging of crises as social media content, drawing on insights from E.M. Forster's classic dystopian science fiction story, "The Machine Stops" (1909), which imagined instant messaging and video conferencing in a world where industrialization has made the terrestrial environment uninhabitable.

A world apart from San Francisco, Kashmir seldom makes global headlines. When it does, news coverage typically focuses on violence, depicted in terms of border disputes between India and Pakistan, while failing to mention pervasive human rights violations or the region's long history of resistance to occupation. In "Kashmir Uncensored" (Chapter 6), Ifat Gazia and Tara Dorabji document how India, the world's largest democracy, "attempts to use media to control the narrative, military to control the ground, and torture to control the psyche of the Kashmiri people, all in hopes of smashing the independence movement." Based on interviews conducted in

Kashmir in 2017 and 2018 with local journalists and members of the independence movement, Gazia and Dorabji show that, despite the prevalence of torture and other extreme forms of persecution, the resistance "continues to evolve and take on new forms."

Since they took office, President Donald Trump and Vice President Mike Pence have ushered in a new era of intolerance toward the LGBTQ community, rolling back many of the protections established or strengthened under the Obama administration. In Chapter 7, April Anderson and Andy Lee Roth report on the findings from their detailed content analysis of four major establishment newspapers and a variety of independent news publications between January 2016 and November 2018. Anderson and Roth find that both corporate and independent news outlets consistently treated spokespersons for the leading LGBTQ organizations as newsworthy sources of information and opinion, but that corporate outlets focused almost entirely on two controversial topics—so-called "bathroom bills" and Trump's transgender military ban—whereas independent news organizations covered a wider range of issues affecting the LGBTQ community. Their chapter also addresses how news representations of opposing viewpoints can avoid overtly defamatory rhetoric but nonetheless indirectly promote prejudice and discrimination, as exemplified by corporate media's consistent reliance on Tony Perkins, the president of the Family Research Council, as a favored news source.

In Chapter 8, Emil Marmol and Lee Mager show how big tech firms and social media companies are taking advantage of widespread calls to "fight fake news" by legitimizing censorship of online content, de-platforming critical voices on the Right and Left. This censorship effectively highjacks efforts to promote media literacy by making control of the online flow of news and information a matter of "artificial intelligence" (in the form of proprietary algorithms). When it comes to protecting the integrity of the news we receive, though, we need less "A" and more "I." Marmol and Mager delve into the controversies and media distractions of Russiagate as well as the deep state and military–industrial complex involvement in social media companies' fact-checking and content restriction policies, noting significant conflicts of interest. They conclude that we must speak out against the weaponization of "fake news" as a concept, while supporting a free press focused on the public good and promoting support for whistle-blowers as vital sources of truth.

Censored 2020 concludes with Kenn Burrows, Amber Yang, and Bethany Surface's chapter on constructive journalism. At its best, Burrows, Yang, and Surface write, journalism "catalyzes and informs conversations and helps us consider possibilities for a wiser, more creative world." But, they note, the prevalence of negative news inadvertently contributes to cycles of personal cynicism and public disengagement. As a "creative antidote to an exclusive focus on problem-based news," Burrows, Yang, and Surface call for constructive journalism, which highlights "community-generated news, solutions-based journalism, and the power of the arts to spark innovative thought and shared (positive) values." Their chapter provides specific examples of how solutions-based and engaged journalism—founded on mindful inquiry, collective gathering, the power of art and play, and storytelling—provide crucial counterbalances to conventional journalism's longstanding focus on negative news.

BEYOND THE MIRROR

> *There was truth and there was untruth, and if you clung to the truth even against the whole world, you were not mad.*
>
> —Winston Smith in George Orwell's *1984*[21]

Lewis Carroll composed *Alice's Adventures in Wonderland* and *Through the Looking-Glass* in the late 19th century, but we imagine that Alice might have understood and appreciated the perspective of another classic fictional character, Winston Smith, the truth-seeking protagonist of George Orwell's dystopian novel, *1984*, first published in 1949. Alice and Winston hold firm to the truth despite the madness of looking-glass logic, propaganda, and historical revisionism.

We face similar challenges today. But—unlike Alice and Winston—we are not so isolated. Community networks, including face-to-face and digital connections, link us in ways that would have made Alice and Winston envious. We also benefit from the clear-sighted efforts of a robust independent press, as nearly every page of *Censored 2020* shows.

Mirror metaphors frame the adventure in Lewis Carroll's *Through the Looking-Glass*. The mirror has also been a popular, if flawed, metaphor for describing the role of journalism in democratic societies. According to this perspective, which is frequently articulated by journalists themselves, the news is a simple reflection of the real world. However, as critical media scholars have noted, no mirror can reflect the whole world; and, furthermore, the "objects" reflected in the mirror are hardly passive.[22] This means that news—whether reported by corporate or independent outlets—is never the simple "truth." Instead, news is the result of social processes through which reporters, editors, and other media personnel decide which events, people, and viewpoints they consider newsworthy.

This view of news is difficult and challenging—especially at a time when the country's president displays a brazen disregard for the First Amendment and routinely demonizes the press as "the enemy of the people."[23] But to acknowledge that news is a human product is not equivalent to accepting either Donald Trump's dizzying contempt for the truth or the corporate media's frequent complicity in misinforming the American public. Instead, recognition that definitions of newsworthiness depend not only on conventional practices and institutional pressures within journalism as a field but also on the distribution of power and status in the broader society should help to sharpen our judgment when it comes to evaluating news, or claims to truth more generally.

When we say that "truth is a set of agreements," that it is a "social consensus," these agreements and that consensus are, nonetheless, constrained by the conditions of reality—to be deemed true, these agreements must "correspond to what we know or think we know about an external world."[24] When we assess a news story—whether it originated from the corporate press or an independent outlet—we have to consider how propaganda, profits, and prejudices may have shaped its reporting and interpretation.[25] This is a fundamental truth of critical media literacy education as championed by Project Censored and its allies. Like Alice, we must be ever vigilant when the powers that be, acting in accord with the looking-glass logic of Lewis

Carroll's Queen, encourage us to shut our eyes and accept the impossible.

Censored 2020: Through the Looking Glass is Project Censored's effort to make a case, based on verifiable evidence, that we should employ some of Alice's skepticism toward the Queen when we turn to social media or the establishment press as the sources of our news. Put more positively, a guiding theme in all the diverse contributions to *Censored 2020* is that the public's interests are best served by independent reporters and news outlets. We may still need to take a deep breath to ground ourselves, but the practice we advocate—contrary to the demands of Carroll's looking-glass Queen—is to keep our eyes open while envisioning what is distinctly possible: a better world, based on inclusive communities and equitable values, safeguarded by reasoned deliberation and democratic institutions, including a robust and independent free press.

Notes

1. Lewis Carroll, *The Annotated Alice: Alice's Adventures in Wonderland & Through the Looking-Glass by Lewis Carroll; with Illustrations by John Tenniel*, Definitive Edition, ed. Martin Gardner (New York: W.W. Norton, 2000 [Carroll's *Through the Looking-Glass and What Alice Found There* was first published in London by Macmillan and Co. in 1871]), 199.
2. See, e.g., Moira Feldman and Rob Williams, "Russiagate: Two-Headed Monster of Propaganda and Censorship," in *Censored 2019: Fighting the Fake News Invasion*, eds. Mickey Huff and Andy Lee Roth with Project Censored (New York: Seven Stories Press, 2018), 54–56, https://www.projectcensored.org/6-russiagate-two-headed-monster-of-propaganda-and-censorship/.
3. On Tony Perkins and the Family Research Council, see Kirsten Grind and John D. McKinnon, "Facebook, Twitter Turn to Right-Leaning Groups to Help Referee Political Speech," *Wall Street Journal*, January 8, 2019, https://www.wsj.com/articles/facebook-twitter-solicit-outside-groups-often-on-the-right-to-referee-political-speech-11546966779; Alex Bollinger, "Facebook & Twitter are Getting Advice on Free Speech from a Hate Group Leader," LGBTQ Nation, January 10, 2019, https://www.lgbtqnation.com/2019/01/facebook-twitter-getting-advice-free-speech-hate-group-leader/; and Chapter 7 in this volume, April Anderson and Andy Lee Roth's "Stonewalled: Establishment Media's Silence on the Trump Administration's Crusade against LGBTQ People."
4. Arwa Mahdawi, "Kylie Jenner's Handmaid's Tale Party was Tasteless, but is the TV Show Any Better?" *The Guardian*, June 11, 2019, https://www.theguardian.com/commentisfree/2019/jun/11/kylie-jenner-handmaids-tale-party-tasteless-arwa-mahdawi.
5. Heather Alberro, "Radical Environmentalists are Fighting Climate Change—So Why are They Persecuted?" The Conversation, December 11, 2018, https://theconversation.com/radical-environmentalists-are-fighting-climate-change-so-why-are-they-persecuted-107211. See also story #14, "FBI Surveilled Peaceful Climate Change Protesters," in Chapter 1 in this volume.
6. See Hailey Schector and Jeff Simmons, "FBI Racially Profiling 'Black Identity Extremists,'" in *Censored 2019*, 63–65, https://www.projectcensored.org/10-fbi-racially-profiling-black-identity-extremists/; see also Michael Harriot, "The FBI Admits Black Lives Matter Was Never a Threat,"

It's White People You Should be Worried About," The Root, June 11, 2019, https://www.the-root.com/the-fbi-admits-black-lives-matter-was-never-a-threat-i-1835417043.

7. E.g., Chris Hedges, "The Mass Media is Poisoning Us with Hate," Truthdig, May 27, 2019, https://www.truthdig.com/articles/the-mass-media-is-poisoning-us-with-hate/.

8. Carroll, *The Annotated Alice*, 196. As Martin Gardner notes, in this passage Lewis Carroll is playing on the Latin word *iam*, which means "now" in the past and future tenses, but not in the present tense.

9. Walter Lippmann, *Liberty and the News* (Princeton, New Jersey: Princeton University Press, 2008 [first published in New York by Harcourt, Brace and Howe in 1920]), 7.

10. In addition to Burrows, Yang, and Surface's chapter, see Chapter 1 of this volume for five exemplars of constructive journalism, including story #3, "Indigenous Groups from Amazon Propose Creation of Largest Protected Area on Earth"; story #18, "Humanitarian Groups Promote Solutions to Extreme Violence in West Africa"; story #20, "Scientists Accelerate Coral Reef Regrowth with Electricity"; story #21, "Court Ruling Provides 'Blueprint' to Reform Excessive, Discriminatory Policing in Schools"; and story #23, "New Programs Make School Food Systems More Equitable."

11. Carroll, *The Annotated Alice*, 196–97.

12. Alexander Rubinstein, "Trump Pardoning War Criminals, Prosecuting Whistleblowers," Mint-Press News, May 29, 2019, https://www.mintpressnews.com/trump-pardoning-war-crimi-nals-prosecuting-whistleblowers/258845/.

13. See Brian Covert, "Whistleblowers and Gag Laws," in *Censored 2014: Fearless Speech in Fateful Times*, eds. Mickey Huff and Andy Lee Roth with Project Censored (New York: Seven Stories Press, 2013), 65–84.

14. Carlo Muñoz, "GOP's Amash: Clapper Should Resign," The Hill, June 12, 2013, https://the-hill.com/policy/defense/305031-rep-amash-calls-for-dni-clapper-to-resign.

15. Edward Snowden, interviewed by Hubert Siebel, "ARD Interview with Edward Snowden," ARD (German TV), conducted January 23, 2014, broadcast January 26, 2014; transcript online at https://edwardsnowden.com/2014/01/27/video-ard-interview-with-edward-snowden/.

16. See, e.g., Sharmini Peries, interview with Daniel Ellsberg, "Daniel Ellsberg on Assange Arrest: The Beginning of the End for Press Freedom," The Real News Network, April 11, 2019, https://therealnews.com/stories/daniel-ellsberg-on-assange-arrest-the-beginning-of-the-end-for-press-freedom; and Chris Hedges, "The Martyrdom of Julian Assange," Truthdig, April 11, 2019, https://www.truthdig.com/articles/the-martyrdom-of-julian-assange/.

17. "The Trump Administration's Indictment of Julian Assange Threatens Core Press Freedom Rights," Freedom of the Press Foundation, April 11, 2019, https://freedom.press/news/trump-administrations-indictment-julian-assange-threatens-core-press-freedom-rights/.

18. Daniel Ellsberg, "On Civil Courage and Its Punishments," in *Censored 2014*, 208–213.

19. See, for example, Amy Goodman and Denis Moynihan, "Say Goodbye to the First Amendment," Truthdig, June 13, 2019, https://www.truthdig.com/articles/the-chilling-crusade-against-julian-assange-and-chelsea-manning/.

20. Carroll, *The Annotated Alice*, 24–25.

21. George Orwell, *1984: A Novel* (New York: Signet Classics/New American Library, 1977 [first published in London by Secker and Warburg in 1949]), 179.

22. See, e.g., David Croteau and William Hoynes, *Media/Society: Technology, Industries, Content, and Users*, 6th ed. (Thousand Oaks, California: SAGE Publications, 2019), 172–73.

23. Mickey Huff and Andy Lee Roth, "The Free Press as 'Enemy of the People,'" Project Censored, August 2, 2017, https://www.projectcensored.org/the-free-press-as-enemy-of-the-people/. See also "In 869 Days, President Trump Has Made 10,796 False or Misleading Claims," *Washington Post*, June 7, 2019, https://www.washingtonpost.com/graphics/politics/trump-claims-database/.

24. Michael Schudson, "Belgium Invades Germany: Reclaiming Non-Fake News—Imperfect, Professional, and Democratic," in *Why Journalism Still Matters* (Medford, Massachusetts: Polity Press, 2018), 81–95, 85.

25. For more on this theme, see Chapter 8 in this volume, "'Fake News': The Trojan Horse for Silencing Alternative News and Reestablishing Corporate News Dominance," by Emil Marmol and Lee Mager.

CHAPTER 1

The Top *Censored* Stories and Media Analysis of 2018–19

Compiled and edited by Andy Lee Roth

INTRODUCTION

Assured Access to Facts

In *Liberty and the News*, Walter Lippmann proposed "no higher law" for journalism than "to tell the truth and shame the devil."[1] A leading political journalist of his era, Lippmann made this judgment in 1920. His basic insight holds true a century later.

The devils Lippmann had in mind were not figurative. At least some of them included the "propagandists and censors" who would "put a painted screen where there should be a window to the world," in service of what Lippmann—in an original formulation that has been mighty in its influence—described as "the manufacture of consent."[2] Without a "steady supply of trustworthy and relevant news," he warned, democracy would degenerate into "incompetence and aimlessness, corruption and disloyalty, panic and ultimate disaster."[3]

The correctives that he proposed in *Liberty and the News* were multifaceted, but each aimed to promote and safeguard what he described as "assured access to the facts."[4] The strength of Lippmann's conviction on this point is evident in how he specified "the task of liberty"—which in his view required protecting news sources and making news comprehensible.[5] "The administration of public information toward greater accuracy and more successful analysis," Lippmann wrote, "is the highway of liberty."[6]

Breaking the Blockade

Accurate reporting and insightful analysis, in service of informing the public, are hallmarks of the independent news stories highlighted in this chapter. From an article in *YES! Magazine* about a California state court decision that provides a blueprint for reforming excessive, discriminatory policing in schools (story #21), to reports by Common Dreams and the *Guardian* on indigenous efforts to create a "corridor of life and culture" in the embattled Amazon (story #3), and coverage by *In These Times* of the fossil fuel industry's concerted efforts to enlist state governments and co-opt law enforcement in criminalizing its critics (story #14), the independent journalists and news organizations whose work is featured here deserve credit and recognition for providing the public "assured access to the facts" and trustworthy, relevant news on these topics.[7] They tell the truth and shame a cast of devils.

In addition to the high quality of journalism evident in these stories, a second attribute unites and distinguishes them. Each of them has been "blockaded" (to adapt another of Lippmann's vivid images) by the corporate news media.[8] Despite their remarkable newsworthiness, the topics and issues addressed in these stories have been either marginalized or ignored altogether by the establishment press. As a result of this corporate blockade, most residents of the United States are unlikely to be informed on these important public issues.

Project Censored's annual listing of independent news stories that the corporate media have failed to cover adequately should be understood as an affirmation of Lippmann's observation that "whether one aspect of the news or another appears in the center or at the periphery makes all the difference in the world."[9] The corporate press has, one way or another, decentered each of the news stories reported here. This year's Top 25 *Censored* stories represent the best efforts of more than 283 student researchers and 24 faculty evaluators from 15 college and university campuses across the United States to draw greater attention to these stories, and to center them as public issues.

Censored Story Themes

Although each news story featured in this chapter is certainly deserving of recognition on its own, the list of this year's top stories can also be examined for news themes that connect different stories. Indeed, as we have contended in past editions of the *Censored* yearbook, identifying these unifying themes is one significant way to gauge the systemic blind spots, third rails, and "no go" zones in corporate news coverage.[10] From that perspective, this year's story list highlights crucial independent news reporting on the following topics:

THE ENVIRONMENT—including story #3, Indigenous Groups from Amazon Propose Creation of Largest Protected Area on Earth,
> #4 US Oil and Gas Industry Set to Unleash 120 Billion Tons of New Carbon Emissions,
> #13 Corporate Food Brands Drive Massive Dead Zone in Gulf of Mexico,
> #15 Trump Administration Threatens Endangered Species Act,
> #16 Underwater Avalanches Heighten Risks of Oil Catastrophes, and
> #20 Scientists Accelerate Coral Reef Regrowth with Electricity;

CRIMINAL JUSTICE, INCLUDING PRISONS AND DETENTION—including story #6, Survivors of Sexual Abuse and Sex Trafficking Criminalized for Self-Defense,
> #7 Flawed Investigations of Sexual Assaults in Children's Immigrant Shelters,
> #8 US Women Face Prison Sentences for Miscarriages,
> #17 More Than 25 Percent of Formerly Incarcerated People are Unemployed,
> #21 Court Ruling Provides "Blueprint" to Reform Excessive, Discriminatory Policing in Schools, and
> #22 Violence Rises after End of Mandated Monitoring in California's Juvenile Detention Centers; and

CORPORATE MISCONDUCT—including story #2, Think Tank Partnerships Establish Facebook as Tool of US Foreign Policy,

- #4 US Oil and Gas Industry Set to Unleash 120 Billion Tons of New Carbon Emissions,
- #9 Developing Countries' Medical Needs Unfulfilled by Big Pharma,
- #13 Corporate Food Brands Drive Massive Dead Zone in Gulf of Mexico,
- #16 Underwater Avalanches Heighten Risks of Oil Catastrophes,
- #23 New Programs Make School Food Systems More Equitable, and
- #25 Google Screenwise: Consenting to Surveillance Capitalism.

Additional themes showcased in this year's list include *technology* (story #2, #10, #12, and #25), *gender inequalities* (story #5, #6, and #8), *press freedoms* (story #1, #2, and #19), and *surveillance* (story #1, #14, and #25). As this brief summary shows, any one story can belong to multiple news themes—as seen, for example, in story #2, on Facebook's think tank partnerships, which brings together the themes of compromised press freedoms, corporate misconduct, and technology. Of course, careful readers may identify additional story themes beyond those noted here.

During this year's voting, several judges observed that the ballot suffered from a deficit of independent news coverage on the topics of organized labor and LGBTQ rights. While other chapters in this volume address these important subjects (see Chapter 4 for labor, and Chapter 7 for LGBTQ rights), we note these gaps in this year's story list to encourage story nominations focused on these themes for the Project's next volume.

Positive News

We are pleased to note that this year's list does include a number of positive news stories, including reports on indigenous efforts to protect the embattled Amazon rainforest (story #3), solutions to extreme violence in West Africa (#18), efforts to stimulate the regrowth of damaged coral reefs (#20), a California court ruling that provides a model for reforming excessive and discriminatory policing in schools (#21), and new programs to make school food systems more equitable (#23). These stories remind us that not all hard-hitting journalism draws public attention to "bad news." Indeed, these stories can be seen as exemplars of constructive journalism, which Kenn Burrows, Amber Yang, and Bethany Surface describe in Chapter 9. Journalism that advocates solutions to social problems might seem at odds with Walter Lippmann's strenuous imperative that journalists and the public not lose contact with "objective information."[11] But Lippmann did not rule out opinion; he objected to opinion that was not based on verifiable evidence.[12] Instead, "the really important thing," he wrote, "is to try and make opinion increasingly responsible to the facts."[13] The positive news stories highlighted in this year's Top 25 story list fulfill that responsibility even as some of their authors are players and stakeholders, rather than disinterested observers, in relation to the issues they cover.

The chief purpose of news, Lippmann wrote in *Liberty and the News*, is to enable humankind "to live successfully toward the future."[14] From news reports that alert us to grave threats to the planet, the impacts of government and corporate surveillance, and inequalities in the criminal justice system, to stories that bring to public attention solutions to violence and ways to protect ecosystems, the news stories presented here serve that purpose, functioning like a compass that, if followed, can point us in the direction of a more humane and democratic future.

ACKNOWLEDGMENTS: Geoff Davidian, Elsa Denis, Nicole Wolfe, and Mischa Geracoulis provided invaluable assistance and welcome camaraderie in helping to prepare this year's slate of several hundred Validated Independent News stories for the Top 25 vote by our panel of judges. Elsa Denis, Troy Patton, Dasha Bukovskaya, Sierra Kaul, and Katy Nguyen helped with the final vetting of this year's top *Censored* stories. The chapter's introduction benefited from insightful suggestions by John Roth.

A NOTE ON RESEARCH AND EVALUATION OF *CENSORED* NEWS STORIES

How do we at Project Censored identify and evaluate independent news stories, and how do we know that the Top 25 stories that we bring forward each year are not only relevant and significant, but also trustworthy? The answer is that every candidate news story undergoes rigorous review, which takes place in multiple stages during each annual cycle. Although adapted to take advantage of both the Project's expanding affiliates program and current technologies, the vetting process is quite similar to the one Project Censored founder Carl Jensen established more than forty years ago.

Candidate stories are initially identified by Project Censored professors and students, or are nominated by members of the general public, who bring them to the Project's attention.[15] Together, faculty and students vet each candidate story in terms of its importance, timeliness, quality of sources, and corporate news coverage. If it fails on any one of these criteria, the story is not included.

Once Project Censored receives the candidate story, we undertake a second round of judgment, using the same criteria and updating the review to include any subsequent, competing corporate coverage. Stories that pass this round of review get posted on our website as Validated Independent News stories (VINs).[16]

In early spring, we present all VINs in the current cycle to the faculty and students at all of our affiliate campuses, and to our panel of expert judges, who cast votes to winnow the candidate stories from several hundred to 25.

Once the Top 25 list has been determined, Project Censored student interns begin another intensive review of each story using LexisNexis and ProQuest databases. Additional faculty and students contribute to this final stage of review.

The Top 25 finalists are then sent to our panel of judges, who vote to rank them in numerical order. At the same time, these experts—including media studies professors, professional journalists and editors, and a former commissioner of the Federal Communications Commission—offer their insights on the stories' strengths and weaknesses.[17]

Thus, by the time a story appears in the pages of *Censored*, it has undergone at least five distinct rounds of review and evaluation.

Although the stories that Project Censored brings forward may be socially and politically controversial—and sometimes even psychologically challenging—we are confident that each is the result of serious journalistic effort, and therefore deserves greater public attention.

1.

Justice Department's Secret FISA Rules for Targeting Journalists

Trevor Timm, "Revealed: The Justice Dept's Secret Rules for Targeting Journalists with FISA Court Orders," Freedom of the Press Foundation, September 17, 2018, https://freedom.press/news/revealed-justice-depts-secret-rules-targeting-journalists-fisa-court-orders/, republished by Common Dreams, September 17, 2018, https://www.commondreams.org/views/2018/09/17/revealed-justice-depts-secret-rules-targeting-journalists-fisa-court-orders.

Ramya Krishnan, "Targeting Journalists under FISA: New Documents Reveal DOJ's Secret Rules," Knight First Amendment Institute (Columbia University), September 17, 2018, https://knightcolumbia.org/news/targeting-journalists-under-fisa-new-documents-reveal-dojs-secret-rules.

Cora Currier, "Government Can Spy on Journalists in the U.S. Using Invasive Foreign Intelligence Process," The Intercept, September 17, 2018, https://theintercept.com/2018/09/17/journalists-fisa-court-spying/.

Jessica Corbett, "The US Government's Secret Rules for Spying on Journalists are 'Terrifying,'" MintPress News, September 18, 2018, https://www.mintpressnews.com/journalists-government-surveillance/249471/.

"US Can Spy on Journalists Domestically Using FISA Warrants, Declassified Guidelines Show," RT, September 19, 2018, updated September 20, 2018, https://www.rt.com/usa/438785-fisa-spying-journalists-declassified/.

Student Researcher: Andrea Blado (Sonoma State University)

Faculty Evaluators: Brent Mortensen (Healdsburg High School) and Peter Phillips (Sonoma State University)

A pair of 2015 memos, from former attorney general Eric Holder to the Department of Justice's National Security Division, show how the government could use court orders under the Foreign Intelligence Surveillance Act (FISA) to monitor the communications of journalists and news organizations. The Knight First Amendment Institute at Columbia University and the Freedom of the Press Foundation obtained the documents through a Freedom of Information Act (FOIA) request and a lawsuit challenging the lack of disclosure that request yielded.[18]

Since 1978, the Foreign Intelligence Surveillance Court has processed requests by federal law enforcement and intelligence agencies for electronic surveillance, physical searches, and other forms of investigative actions for foreign intelligence purposes. Holder's pair of memos spell out the circumstances for processing FISA applications that target "known media entities" or "known members of the media." As Cora Currier reported for the Intercept, the secret rules "apply to media entities or journalists who are thought to be agents of a foreign government, or, in some cases, are of interest under the broader standard that they possess foreign intelligence information." Ramya Krishnan, a staff attorney with the Knight Institute, told the Intercept, "There's a lack of clarity on the circumstances when the government might consider a journalist an agent of a foreign power." For example, because RT America registered with the Department of Justice as a "foreign agent" in November 2017,[19] reporters working for RT America—and their sources—could be subject to FISA court-ordered surveillance. For its part, RT reported that the details specified in the memos suggested that it was "highly likely" that both the Trump and Obama administrations had surveilled journalists that they considered to be "foreign agents."

The revealed memos raise three "concerning" questions about the government's surveillance of news organizations and journalists, according to Trevor Timm, director of the Freedom of the Press Foundation. First, how many times have FISA court orders been used to target journalists, and are any journalists currently under investigation? Second, why did the Justice Department keep these rules secret when it updated its "media guidelines" in 2015? And, third, is the Justice Department using FISA court orders—along with the FBI's similar rules for targeting journalists with national security letters (NSLs)—to "get around the stricter 'media guidelines'"?[20]

Historically, the First Amendment has limited surveillance of journalists, as well as efforts to determine their sources. As Cora Currier reported for the Intercept, in January 2015, after the Obama administration secretly seized phone records from the Associated Press and named a Fox News reporter as a co-conspirator in a leak case, Attorney General Eric Holder revised the set of procedures, known as the "media guidelines," for when government officials could subject journalists to surveillance. Though the secret 2015 memos specify that FISA applications must be presented to the attorney general or the deputy attorney general for approval before they are submitted to the Foreign Intelligence Surveillance Court, the memos allow for exceptions and, as Trevor Timm and others noted, FISA rules are "much less stringent" than the Justice Department's media guidelines for obtaining subpoenas, court orders, and warrants against journalists. The procedures governing FISA surveillance and national security letters allow government officials to circumvent the media guidelines' requirements that the information sought is "essential" to a successful investigation, that "reasonable alternative attempts" have been made to obtain the information, and that the government inform the journalist and negotiate with them.

Although reporters are probably aware that they may be subject to surveillance, their sources may not be. The unredacted portions of the Justice Department memos do not specify how to handle information that is gathered, or how to mitigate risks posed by exposing journalists' sources.

Corporate news outlets reported little to nothing in September 2018 when the Freedom of the Press Foundation and the Knight First Amendment Institute made public the two secret memos on targeting journalists and news organizations. In Spring 2019, a flurry of news stories and editorials, triggered partly by the *Mueller Report*, focused on Carter Page—a petroleum industry consultant who served as Donald Trump's foreign-policy adviser during his 2016 presidential election campaign.[21] In October 2016, the FBI had wiretapped Page under authority of a FISA warrant based on evidence that he was operating as a foreign agent on behalf of Russia.[22] However, controversy over the use of a FISA warrant to surveil a former Trump campaign adviser has done nothing at all to raise awareness of the threats posed by FISA warrants that target journalists and news organizations.

Ramya Krishnan, the staff attorney for the Knight Institute, summarized the stakes: "National security surveillance authorities confer extraordinary powers. The government's failure to share more information about them damages journalists' ability to protect their sources, and jeopardizes the newsgathering process."

2.

Think Tank Partnerships Establish Facebook as Tool of US Foreign Policy

Adam Johnson, "Media Ignore Government Influence on Facebook's Plan to Fight Government Influence," Fairness & Accuracy In Reporting (FAIR), May 21, 2018, https://fair.org/home/media-ignore-government-influence-on-facebooks-plan-to-fight-government-influence/.

Elliott Gabriel, "Facebook Partners with Hawkish Atlantic Council, a NATO Lobby Group, to 'Pro-tect Democracy,'" MintPress News, May 22, 2018, https://www.mintpressnews.com/facebook-partners-hawkish-atlantic-council-nato-lobby-group-protect-democracy/242289/.

Jake Johnson, "'Alarming': Facebook Teams Up with Think-Tank Funded by Saudi Arabia and Military Contractors to 'Protect' Democracy," Common Dreams, May 18, 2018, https://www.commondreams.org/news/2018/05/18/alarming-facebook-teams-think-tank-funded-saudi-arabia-and-military-contractors.

Jonathan Sigrist, "Facebook Censorship and the Atlantic Council," Global Research, October 14, 2018, https://www.globalresearch.ca/facebook-censorship-and-the-atlantic-council/5656896.

Kevin Reed, "Facebook's Partnership with the Atlantic Council," World Socialist Web Site, Sep-tember 8, 2018, https://www.wsws.org/en/articles/2018/09/08/atla-s08.html.

Alan MacLeod, "That Facebook Will Turn to Censoring the Left Isn't a Worry—It's a Reality," Fair-ness & Accuracy In Reporting (FAIR), August 22, 2018, https://fair.org/home/that-facebook-will-turn-to-censoring-the-left-isnt-a-worry-its-a-reality/.

Alan MacLeod, "Facebook's New Propaganda Partners," Fairness & Accuracy In Reporting (FAIR), September 25, 2018, https://fair.org/home/facebooks-new-propaganda-partners/.

Kevin Gosztola, "How CNN Led Facebook to Censor Pages of Russia-Backed Video Company and Manufactured News Story," Shadowproof, February 16, 2019, https://shadowproof.com/2019/02/16/cnn-manufactured-story-about-russia-video-company-facebook-censorship/.

Alexander Rubinstein, "How a Small Team of Journalists Overcame Neocon-Cheered Facebook Censorship," MintPress News, March 1, 2019, https://www.mintpressnews.com/how-a-small-team-of-journalists-overcame-neocon-cheered-facebook-censorship/255789/.

Student Researchers: Mikhaela Alcasabas (Sonoma State University), Cem Ismail Addemir (North Central College), and Troy Patton (Diablo Valley College)

Faculty Evaluators: Peter Phillips (Sonoma State University), Steve Macek (North Central College), and Mickey Huff (Diablo Valley College)

Under the guise of fighting "fake news" and protecting US democ-racy from "foreign influence," in 2018 social media giant Facebook established partnerships with the Atlantic Council, a NATO-spon-sored think tank, and with two US government creations from the Cold War era, the National Democratic Institute and the International Republican Institute. As a number of independent news organiza-tions reported, despite lofty rhetoric about safeguarding Western democracies, these partnerships have resulted in what amounts to state censorship, with Facebook serving as a tool of US foreign policy.

On May 17, 2018, Facebook announced that it would join forces with the Atlantic Council in order to "identify emerging threats and disinformation campaigns around the world" and to "fight abuse on our platform."[23] According to Facebook's director of global politics and government outreach, Katie Harbath, the partnership with the Atlantic Council's Digital Forensic Research Lab would "increase the number of 'eyes and ears' we have working to spot potential abuse on our service—enabling us to more effectively identify gaps in our systems, preempt obstacles, and ensure that Facebook plays a positive role during elections all around the world."[24]

As Jake Johnson reported for Common Dreams, "While Facebook's statement fawned over the Atlantic Council's 'stellar reputation,' critics argued that the organization's reliance on donations from foreign oil monarchies and American plutocrats puts the lie to the project's stated mission of shielding the democratic process from manipulation and abuse."

The Atlantic Council is a Washington, DC–based think tank funded by the US Department of State, the US Navy, Army, and Air Force, and major multinational corporations—including Chevron, ExxonMobil, Royal Dutch Shell, global asset management firms and banks, and top military contractors. According to a 2014 *New York Times* article, between 2008 and 2013 "at least 25 countries" donated tens of millions of dollars to the council.[25] Its conservative-leaning board of directors includes former CIA directors, retired US generals, and hawkish former State Department officials like Henry Kissinger and Condoleezza Rice. In a May 2018 article, FAIR's Adam Johnson noted that, although there is "some diversity of opinion" within the Atlantic Council, "it is within a very limited pro-Western ideological framework—a framework that debates how much and where US military and soft power influence should be wielded, not if it should in the first place."

As Johnson wrote, it is troubling that Facebook would rely on advice from an organization that has advocated on behalf of Turkish dictator Recep Tayyip Erdoğan, one of its previous funders, and which presented former President George W. Bush—who was directly responsible for "the illegal invasion of Iraq that killed between 500,000 and a million people"—a Distinguished International Leadership award.

In the name of fighting the scourge of "fake news," Facebook altered its proprietary algorithms in ways that significantly reduced traffic to progressive websites such as Common Dreams and Slate.[26] Without formal warning, Facebook shut down left-wing, Venezuela-linked Facebook pages such as teleSUR English and Venezuelanalysis (although both were reinstituted after protests about their removal). In October 2018, numerous independent news outlets reported on what Jonathan Sigrist, writing for Global Research, described as "one of the greatest Facebook account and page purges" in the platform's troubled history. In total, Sigrist reported, 559 pages and 251 personal accounts were "instantly removed" in the name of fighting "fake news" and "Russian propaganda." Many of the pages and accounts that Facebook took down, Sigrist wrote, were "political (often leftist), anti-war, independent journalists and media outlets" that had been targeted in 2016 by PropOrNot, the website endorsed by the *Washington Post* but subsequently discredited.[27]

In September 2018, FAIR's Alan MacLeod detailed how Facebook planned to join forces with "two propaganda organizations founded and funded by the US government: the National Democratic Institute (NDI) and the International Republican Institute (IRI)," allegedly in an effort to combat "fake news."

The NDI and the IRI were both established under an umbrella organization called the National Endowment for Democracy (NED), a nonprofit created by the US Congress in 1983 to influence politics and elections in developing countries. Facebook's collaboration with these organizations is especially concerning because, as MacLeod wrote, both organizations have "aggressively pursued regime change against leftist governments overseas." In the 1980s, the NDI worked to destabilize the Sandinista government in Nicaragua, and the IRI supported the attempted 2002 coup d'état against Venezuela's socialist president Hugo Chávez.

As MacLeod reported in September 2018, Facebook had also been "anxious to better curate what Brazilians saw on their feeds in the run-up to their presidential elections." Fifty-two percent of Brazilians get their news from Facebook, MacLeod noted. The company's new partnerships with the Atlantic Council and the two NED propaganda outfits gives the US government—which has a long history of meddling in Brazilian politics—yet another means of exerting influence over Brazil's democracy.

There has been very little corporate news coverage of Facebook's partnerships with US government propaganda organizations. As of January 31, 2019, one of the only articles on the topic in the establishment press was a Reuters report that MacLeod referenced in his piece.[28] That article briefly discussed the history of the IRI and the NDI but made no mention of either the blackouts of teleSUR English and Venezuelanalysis, or how Facebook's new algorithms have reduced traffic to leftist and progressive news sites. CNN, Fox News, and NBC News have provided offhand coverage, with only the most basic information, but none have framed Facebook's actions in terms of censorship. Reports by FAIR and independent news outlets, including Common Dreams, MintPress News, and Global Research, address the core issue: In partnership with Facebook, powerful organizations are working to control the flow of information to best reflect their interests, with little in the way of public scrutiny.

Facebook has also partnered with establishment news organizations in efforts to discredit independent news outlets and ban their social media pages. In February 2019, CNN published a report on Facebook's decision to ban the "In the Now" video channel and three of its offshoots, "Soapbox," "BackThen," and "Waste-Ed"— each of which is run by or associated with Maffick Media—because, according to CNN's report, "the pages pushing the videos do not disclose that they are backed by the Russian government."[29] CNN told a tale of videos intended to undermine American democracy, targeted to millennials on Facebook.

However, as Kevin Gosztola of Shadowproof and Alexander

Rubinstein of MintPress News subsequently disclosed, what CNN's article failed to report was that CNN misreported the facts, using its manufactured version of the story as a pretext for calling on Facebook to remove the pages used to share those videos. CNN's own report conceded that the banned pages "appear to have fallen into a gray area for Facebook." Although the pages sharing the videos "do not include information about their links to the Russian government," CNN reported, Facebook pages "were not previously required" to do so.

As Gosztola and Rubinstein reported, CNN sought to substantiate its story by enlisting the support of the Atlantic Council and the German Marshall Fund. The CNN story quoted Ben Nimmo of the Atlantic Council's Digital Forensic Research Lab. Nimmo—whose credibility has been called into question—told CNN that Russian-affiliated outlets claim to be editorially independent, but nonetheless routinely "boost Kremlin narratives, especially those which portray the West negatively." Maffick, Nimmo told CNN, "may technically be independent, but their tone certainly matches the broader Kremlin family."[30]

The German Marshall Fund had identified Maffick as a potential foreign news outlet, due to its connection with the Russian media organization RT (formerly Russia Today), and registered concerns about Maffick Media to CNN. In turn, CNN began to investigate by contacting Maffick employees, and were granted a lengthy interview with "In the Now" journalist Rania Khalek and Maffick Media's chief operating officer, J. Ray Sparks. Despite being provided with evidence of editorial independence and transparent funding sources, CNN contacted Facebook about Maffick Media; and despite finding no rule-breaking on Maffick's part, Facebook quickly removed the pages in question, in what MintPress News described as "indirect government censorship."

Facebook eventually reinstated the banned Maffick pages, Rubinstein reported. But Maffick employees believe that Facebook still needs to be more transparent, and they have called for the social media platform to establish consistent requirements that apply to all pages for disclosing funding sources.

3.

Indigenous Groups from Amazon Propose Creation of Largest Protected Area on Earth

Jessica Corbett, "Calling for 'Corridor of Life and Culture,' Indigenous Groups from Amazon Propose Creation of Largest Protected Area on Earth," Common Dreams, November 21, 2018, https://www.commondreams.org/news/2018/11/21/calling-corridor-life-and-culture-indige-nous-groups-amazon-propose-creation-largest.

Jonathan Watts, "Amazon Indigenous Groups Propose Mexico-Sized 'Corridor of Life,'" The Guardian, November 21, 2018, https://www.theguardian.com/environment/2018/nov/21/amazon-indigenous-groups-propose-mexico-sized-corridor-of-life.

Student Researcher: Robert Andreacchi (Sonoma State University)

Faculty Evaluator: Peter Phillips (Sonoma State University)

Sweeping development throughout the Amazon rainforest is an abiding concern for indigenous groups. The Amazon's extraordinary biodiversity is being destroyed for profits and political gain. In response, an alliance of some five hundred indigenous groups from nine countries, known as COICA—the Coordinator of the Indigenous Organizations of the Amazon River Basin—is planning to safeguard a "sacred corridor of life and culture" covering more than 700,000 square miles, an area about the size of Mexico. The alliance presented its Bogota Declaration, outlining "the principles and joint vision of the indigenous confederations to protect the Amazon rainforest by using a traditional and holistic perspective," at the 14th UN Biodiversity Conference, held in Egypt in November 2018.[31]

A report for Common Dreams quoted Tuntiak Katan, the alliance's vice president, who called the Amazon rainforest "the world's last great sanctuary for biodiversity" and said, "It is there because we are there. Other places have been destroyed."

The alliance aims to protect biodiversity in the "triple-A" corridor that spans the Andes mountains, the Amazon, and the Atlantic Ocean. This region faces challenges from agribusiness, mining, and the global climate crisis. But members of the alliance also aim to address territorial rights. As Common Dreams reported, they "don't recognize modern national borders created by colonial settlers." Katan, COICA's vice president, observed, "We know the governments will try to go over our heads." He said, "This is nothing new for us. We have faced challenges for hundreds of years."

New right-wing leaders in Brazil and Colombia threaten to undermine COICA's plans. In October 2018, Jair Bolsonaro, who is now

Brazil's president, indicated that he would only stay in the Paris climate agreement if Brazil was guaranteed sovereignty over indigenous land and the "triple-A" region. Juan Carlos Jintiach of COICA told *Common Dreams* that Bolsonaro's comments about environmental and indigenous issues are especially concerning because three-fourths of the environmental defenders assassinated in 2017 were indigenous leaders, and opposition to agroindustry is "the main cause for assassination of our leaders." Observing that indigenous peoples and communities "face costly and difficult processes to legalize their lands," while corporations "obtain licenses with ease," Jintiach called for Bolsonaro to obey all laws and ensure the rights and safety of the people of Brazil.

Although the corporate and independent press have covered right-wing president Jair Bolsonaro's intent to undermine indigenous rights in order to open Amazonian land for development, the coverage has almost entirely ignored COICA's proposal to create the world's largest protected area. For example, in January 2019 the *New York Times* covered Bolsonaro's order to transfer responsibility for certifying indigenous territories as protected lands to the business-friendly Ministry of Agriculture.[32] This otherwise detailed article made no mention of COICA's proposal for a sanctuary. In March 2019, the *Times* ran an article on efforts by indigenous groups to resist Bolsonaro's policies, but the *Times* positioned the article as an opinion piece rather than a news report.[33] The penultimate paragraph of that article included one sentence on the coalition of indigenous groups proposing an Amazon sanctuary, noting simply that Bolsonaro's election "calls into question the fate" of their proposal; this sentence linked to the *Guardian*'s November 2018 report.

4.

US Oil and Gas Industry Set to Unleash 120 Billion Tons of New Carbon Emissions

David Turnbull, "Report: U.S. Oil and Gas Expansion Threatens to Unleash Climate Pollution Equivalent to Nearly 1,000 Coal Plants," *Oil Change International*, January 16, 2019, http://priceofoil.org/2019/01/16/report-u-s-oil-and-gas-expansion-threatens-to-unleash-climate-pollution-equivalent-to-nearly-1000-coal-plants/.

Jake Johnson, "With US 'Drilling Towards Disaster,' Report Warns Anything Less Than Urgent Green New Deal will be 'Too Little, Too Late,'" *Common Dreams*, January 16, 2019, https://www.commondreams.org/news/2019/01/16/us-drilling-towards-disaster-report-warns-anything-less-urgent-green-new-deal-will.

Student Researcher: Tommy Hunt (City College of San Francisco)

Faculty Evaluator: Jennifer Levinson (City College of San Francisco)

The US oil and gas industry has the potential to "unleash the largest burst of new carbon emissions in the world" through 2050, according to a January 2019 report from Oil Change International, an organization that works to expose the true costs of fossil fuels and advocates for clean energy.

Oil Change International's coverage is based on a study, "Drilling Towards Disaster," produced in collaboration with 350.org, Amazon Watch, the Center for Biological Diversity, Food & Water Watch, Greenpeace USA, and a dozen other organizations.[34] According to the report, new US oil and gas development could enable 120 billion tons of new carbon pollution, the equivalent to "the lifetime CO_2 emissions of nearly 1,000 coal-fired power plants."

Between now and 2030, the United States is likely to account for 60 percent of the world's projected growth in oil and gas production. According to Kelly Trout, one of the report's coauthors, the findings present "an urgent and existential emergency for lawmakers in the United States at all levels of government."

The "Drilling Towards Disaster" report highlights a five-point agenda for what policymakers must do to check climate change, including, for example, banning new leases or permits for new fossil fuel exploration, production, and infrastructure; ending subsidies and other public finance for the fossil fuel industry; and championing a Green New Deal to promote transition to 100 percent renewable energy.

Asserting that there is "no more time to waste," another of the report's coauthors, Lorne Stockman, noted that, although the Trump administration and fossil fuel backers "portray climate change as a false choice between the economy and the environment," their actions "favor an irresponsible and outdated fossil fuel sector over a clean energy sector that has proven it can deliver on jobs, economic growth, and reliable cheap energy."

References to Oil Change International's "Drilling Towards Disaster" report have been limited to independent media outlets.[35] Corporate news outlets have not covered the report's release or its findings, including its prediction of 120 billion tons of new carbon

pollution or its five-point checklist to overhaul fossil fuel production in the United States. Instead, much of the corporate news media's coverage of carbon emissions has focused more narrowly on President Trump's proposal to amend existing emissions standards for passenger cars and light trucks and to establish new standards for future cars and trucks.[36] Although such coverage highlighted the stakes of Trump's proposal to weaken fuel-efficiency standards—the proposal "could be his most consequential climate-policy rollback yet," one *New York Times* report stated[37]—framing carbon emissions in terms of pollution from cars and trucks does not convey the extent of the problem. Instead, that frame effectively excludes from coverage the scope of new fossil fuel exploration, production, and extraction that led Oil Change International to characterize the potential for massive new carbon emissions as an "existential emergency" for US lawmakers.

5.

"Modern Slavery" in the United States and around the World

Edward Helmore, "Over 400,000 People Living in 'Modern Slavery' in US, Report Finds," *The Guardian*, July 19, 2018, https://www.theguardian.com/world/2018/jul/19/us-modern-slavery-report-global-slavery-index.

Student Researcher: Hogan Reed (University of Vermont)

Faculty Evaluator: Rob Williams (University of Vermont)

According to the 2018 Global Slavery Index, an estimated 403,000 people in the United States were living in conditions of "modern slavery" in 2016.[38] As the *Guardian* reported, the Global Slavery Index defines "modern slavery" broadly to include forced labor and forced marriage.

The Global Slavery Index (GSI) is produced by the Walk Free Foundation, an organization that combines research and direct engagement to influence governments and businesses to address modern slavery as a human rights issue. The GSI draws on national surveys, reports from other agencies, such as the United Nations's International Labour Organization, and databases of people who have been assisted in trafficking cases.

According to the 2018 Global Slavery Index, an estimated 40.3 million people were living in modern slavery in 2016, with females comprising the majority of the victims (71 percent). The index found the highest levels of modern slavery in North Korea, where an estimated 2.6 million people—or one-tenth of the population—are victims of modern slavery.

Andrew Forrest, one of Walk Free's cofounders, told the *Guardian* that the prevalence of modern slavery in the United States was "truly staggering" and "only possible through a tolerance of exploitation." The GSI noted that forced labor occurred "in many contexts" in the United States, including in agriculture, among traveling sales crews, and—as recent legal cases against GEO Group, Inc. have revealed— as the result of compulsory prison labor in privately owned and operated detention facilities contracted by the Department of Homeland Security.[39]

The report further noted that migrants—and especially migrant women and children—are "particularly vulnerable" to modern slavery in the United States due to a variety of factors, including immigration status, lack of familiarity with US employment protections, and the fact that migrants often work in jobs that are "hidden from the public view and unregulated by the government." In addition, the report noted, "Increasingly restrictive immigration policies have further increased the vulnerability of undocumented persons and migrants to modern slavery."[40]

As the *Guardian* reported, according to the GSI, the estimate of 403,000 people enslaved in the United States actually understates the country's role in contributing to global slavery, because the United States imports many products—including laptop computers, mobile phones, clothing, fish, cocoa, and timber—that are "at risk of being produced through forced labor."

The GSI made specific recommendations for how the US government could address modern slavery. These recommendations included stronger legislation to raise the minimum age for marriage to eighteen in all states, criminalizing forced marriage, and prohibiting criminalization of child victims of trafficking; improved support for victims, including training for officials who connect them with services; and standardizing data collection and developing a central repository to make national estimates of the prevalence of modern slavery "more feasible."[41]

The 2018 report showed a surprisingly high prevalence of modern slavery in developed nations, but a universal legal definition of "modern slavery" has yet to be established. As the *Guardian* reported, other anti-exploitation groups raised questions about the Walk Free Foundation's definition of slavery and its methodology for determining the numbers of affected people. For example, in a recent issue of *Anti-Trafficking Review*, an expert on international trafficking law, Anne Gallagher, argued that "universal, reliable calculation of the size of the problem, while an important goal to strive for, is not yet possible," due to a lack of shared definitions, standards, and measurement tools.[42]

Apart from the *Guardian* article, the 2018 Global Slavery Index received limited coverage in the *New York Times*, and by CNN and CBS News.[43] *The Times*'s coverage highlighted the case of a former North Korean slave who is now a student at Columbia University, leaving details about the prevalence of slavery in the United States to the article's later paragraphs. CNN noted that the report listed the United States as "a world leader" in addressing forced labor in supply chains, while CBS News reported that "the U.S. does better than most countries in tackling the issue." In March 2019 a *Forbes* article that reported on the United Nations's International Day of Remembrance of the Victims of Slavery and the Transatlantic Slave Trade drew on data from the Global Slavery Index, but also noted "limitations" to the data on modern slavery.[44]

6.

Survivors of Sexual Abuse and Sex Trafficking Criminalized for Self-Defense

Mariame Kaba, "Black Women Punished for Self-Defense Must be Freed from Their Cages," *The Guardian*, January 3, 2019, https://www.theguardian.com/commentisfree/2019/jan/03/cyntoia-brown-marissa-alexander-black-women-self-defense-prison.

Amy Goodman, "There are Thousands of Cyntoia Browns: Mariame Kaba on Criminalization of Sexual Violence Survivors," *Democracy Now!*, January 10, 2019, https://www.democracynow.org/2019/1/10/there_are_thousands_of_cyntoia_browns.

Kellie C. Murphy, "Beyond Cyntoia Brown: How Women End Up Incarcerated for Self Defense," *Rolling Stone*, January 28, 2019, https://www.rollingstone.com/culture/culture-features/cyntoia-brown-beyond-other-cases-775874/.

Olivia Exstrum, "Child Sex-Trafficking Victims Face Decades behind Bars for Killing Their Abusers. That Could End Soon," *Mother Jones*, May 9, 2019, https://www.motherjones.com/crime-justice/2019/05/cyntoia-brown-sara-kruzan-sex-trafficking-abuse-legislation/.

Student Researcher: Jaidene Samiec (North Central College)

Faculty Evaluator: Steve Macek (North Central College)

The case of Cyntoia Brown—who was sentenced in 2004, at age 16, to life in prison for killing a man who bought her for sex and raped her—garnered the support of A-list celebrities and received widespread news coverage. In January 2019, after Brown had served fifteen years in prison, Tennessee governor Bill Haslam granted her clemency, describing her case as "tragic and complex" and citing "the extraordinary steps Ms. Brown has taken to rebuild her life."[45]

In contrast to the spate of news coverage from establishment outlets, which focused on Brown's biography and the details of her case, independent news organizations—including the *Guardian*, *Democracy Now!*, *Rolling Stone*, and *Mother Jones*—stood out by reporting that cases like Brown's are all too common. Victims of sex trafficking and sexual violence are often prosecuted for acts of self-defense. In a January 2019 interview, Mariame Kaba, the cofounder of Survived and Punished, an organization supporting survivors of violence who have been criminalized for self-defense, told *Democracy Now!*, "There are thousands of Cyntoia Browns in prison."

In an article published by the *Guardian* in January 2019, Kaba wrote that multiple studies indicate "between 71% and 95% of incarcerated women have experienced physical violence from an intimate partner," and many have experienced "multiple forms of physical and sexual abuse" in childhood and as adults, a pattern that experts have described as the "abuse-to-prison" pipeline. On *Democracy Now!*, Kaba referred to activist Susan Burton, another incarcerated survivor, who has argued that the system essentially works to "incarcerate trauma" when sexually-abused victims are sentenced to prison for self-defense.

Tracing contemporary attitudes toward women of color defending themselves against sexual abuse back to myths that arose in the 19th century during slavery, Kaba noted in her *Guardian* article that black women "have always been vulnerable to violence" in the United States and "have long been judged as having 'no selves to defend.'" Today, she wrote, self-defense laws that are "interpreted generously" when applied to white men threatened by men of color are often interpreted "very narrowly" when women of color and gender nonconforming people invoke them in domestic violence and sexual assault cases.

While Cyntoia Brown's case eventually received national attention, the public remains unaware of many more stories like hers because establishment news outlets seldom treat them as newsworthy. For example, in 2012, Marissa Alexander was convicted in Florida of aggravated assault with a deadly weapon, when she used a gun (which she was licensed to own) to fire a single warning shot into the air to deter her abusive husband. In a pretrial hearing, the judge ruled that the state's "stand-your-ground" law did not apply to Alexander's defense because she did not "appear afraid." As Kaba reported in her *Guardian* article, a jury found Alexander guilty after just twelve minutes of deliberation. Alexander was sentenced to a mandatory minimum sentence of 20 years. In January 2017, after two years of house arrest and three years of incarceration, Alexander was freed through what Kaba described as "good lawyering and a national participatory legal defense organizing campaign."

Responding in part to publicity generated by Cyntoia Brown's case, lawmakers in Congress and three states have proposed legislation that would "overhaul how courts treat juvenile sex trafficking victims tried as adults for committing crimes against their abusers," *Mother Jones* reported in May 2019. Under existing state and federal laws, juvenile victims who commit serious crimes, such as murder, are often tried in adult courts—without considering that victims of sex trafficking may resort to violence in efforts to escape their situation. Historically, the trauma experienced by victims of sex trafficking "has not been well understood and hasn't been taken into account when deciding the cases of victims who commit crimes," Olivia Exstrum reported for *Mother Jones*.

Citing research on how the trauma of being sex trafficked can affect decision-making, especially by young people, the legislation in process in Congress and in Nevada, Arkansas, and Hawaii would have judges consider the effect of trauma on offenders' conduct and would give courts the authority to ignore mandatory minimum sentencing requirements in such cases. James Dold, the founder of the nonprofit Human Rights for Kids, which helped draft the model legislation, told *Mother Jones* that, to his knowledge, this is the first time that legislation at the federal or state level has sought to address defendants who have been victims of juvenile sex trafficking.

A 2019 United Nations report, issued by the United Nations Office on Drugs and Crime, found that human trafficking continues to rise.[46] According to the report, "Most of the victims detected globally are trafficked for sexual exploitation," and the "vast majority" of those victims are female.

Corporate news organizations provided considerable coverage of Cyntoia Brown's clemency. However, many of those reports treated Brown's case in isolation, emphasizing her biography or the advocacy on her behalf by celebrities such as Rihanna, Drake, LeBron James, and Kim Kardashian West.[47] On January 17, 2019, the *New York Times* published an article on how Brown's case had inspired "a push for juvenile criminal justice reform" in Tennessee, where she had been convicted and served her sentence.[48] Although this report noted that Brown was "a teenage trafficking victim," it focused on the sentencing of people who were minors when they committed crimes, rather than on sex trafficking or sexual violence as circumstances that lead some minors to engage in acts of self-defense that result in criminal prosecution. An NBC News report took a similar tack, emphasizing age ("young people tried in adult courts") and race ("one of many young black women and girls who land in the criminal justice system") without acknowledging either sex trafficking and sexual violence as factors that often lead to violent acts of self-defense, or racial inequalities in courts' interpretations of "stand-your-ground" laws when victims act to protect themselves.[49]

Reports that did link Cyntoia Brown's case to broader patterns of sexual violence and sex trafficking were often filed as opinion pieces, rather than news stories, by corporate news media, as was one exceptionally detailed piece, written by Andrea Powell and published by NBC News.[50] Powell, the founder and executive director of Karana Rising, a nonprofit that supports survivors of human trafficking, explained how credibility bias and racial stereotypes work against many survivors of sex trafficking when they are tried for "crimes they were forced to commit in self-defense or at the hands of their traffickers." Girls with histories of juvenile detention, sexual abuse, or running away from foster placements may be seen as less credible, she explained, while racial stereotypes underlie beliefs about girls of color being "less innocent and more sexually mature than their white peers."

Noting that the "history of child victims of sex trafficking being arrested as prostitutes or worse runs deep in the American criminal justice system," Powell wrote that, instead of arresting child victims, "we need to legally treat them as traumatized children in need of services." Powell pointed to New York State's "Safe Harbor" law, which protects and offers immunity to minors involved in any form of commercial sex, and HOPE Court of Washington, DC, which provides a special court program and direct services for youth survivors of commercial sex exploitation. Lastly, she noted that the best solution, "a controversial one," is to stop treating sex workers as criminals: "By treating all sex workers as criminals, we end up criminalizing sex trafficking victims."

7.

Flawed Investigations of Sexual Assaults in Children's Immigrant Shelters

Michael Grabell, Topher Sanders, and Silvina Sterin Pensel, "In Immigrant Children's Shelters, Sexual Assault Cases are Open and Shut," ProPublica, December 21, 2018, https://www.propublica.org/article/boystown-immigrant-childrens-shelter-sexual-assault.

Caitlin Owens, Stef W. Kight, and Harry Stevens, "Thousands of Migrant Youth Allegedly Suffered Sexual Abuse in U.S. Custody," Axios, February 26, 2019, updated February 27, 2019, https://www.axios.com/immigration-unaccompanied-minors-sexual-assault-3222e230-29e1-430f-a361-d959c88c5d8c.html.

Student Researchers: Austin Barcus, Maria Granados, Angel Palominos, and Carina Ramirez (Sonoma State University)

Faculty Evaluator: Susan Rahman (Sonoma State University)

Hundreds of police reports document allegations of sexual assaults in immigrant children's shelters since the surge of unaccompanied minors from Central America began in 2014, according to a December 2018 report by ProPublica. The report, based on six months of research that included reviewing internal documents obtained through public records requests, revealed "a largely hidden side of the shelters—one in which both staff and other residents sometimes acted as predators." ProPublica noted that these shelters have received $4.5 billion in government funding for housing and other services.

ProPublica's review of hundreds of police reports showed that, "again and again," police were "quickly—and with little investigation—closing the cases, often within days, or even hours." The number of cases of sexual assaults of immigrant children in shelters is likely greater than ProPublica could document, as records from shelters in Texas, "where the largest number of immigrant children are held," could not be obtained due to state laws in Texas that ban child abuse reports from being made public.

Noting "startling lapses" in how federal and state authorities investigated allegations of sexual assaults, ProPublica reported that, in many cases, responding officers filed brief information reports without investigating incidents as potential crimes. Because immigrant children in detention are frequently moved, a child could be moved out of the investigating agency's jurisdiction in just a few weeks, often without warning, even when an investigator wanted to pursue a case. When children are released, parents or relatives may

be reluctant to seek justice, avoiding contact with law enforcement because they are undocumented or living with someone who is.

A February 2019 article, based on Department of Health and Human Services documents given to Axios by Congressman Ted Deutch, appears to corroborate ProPublica's findings. As Axios reported, "From October 2014 to July 2018, the HHS' Office of Refugee Resettlement received 4,556 complaints, and the Department of Justice received 1,303 complaints" of sexual abuse against unaccompanied minors in US government custody. Of the cases reported to the Department of Justice (DOJ) in that time period, the Office of Refugee Resettlement (ORR) reported that other minors were perpetrators in 851 cases and adult staff accounted for 178 allegations of sexual abuse. The Axios article noted that the type of perpetrator was only known for cases that the ORR reported to the DOJ.

This topic has received some corporate news coverage, including reports by CBS News and the *New York Times*.[51] However, in contrast with ProPublica's coverage, those reports have not highlighted shortcomings in investigations of alleged sexual abuse or the lack of support for survivors following their abuse. The *New York Times* article, which provided substantial coverage, acknowledged that documents showing the number of sexual abuse complaints in government-funded detention facilities were "first reported by Axios." *USA Today* published an article by Michael Grabell and Topher Sanders, based on their ProPublica report.[52]

8.
US Women Face Prison Sentences for Miscarriages

Naomi Randolph, "What Losing Roe Would Mean for Women of Color," *Ms. Magazine*, January 22, 2019, https://msmagazine.com/blog/2019/01/22/losing-roe-mean-women-color/.

Student Researcher: Abby Ehrler (North Central College)

Faculty Evaluator: Steve Macek (North Central College)

Many people fear that the new Supreme Court will overturn *Roe v. Wade*, stripping women of their right to choose whether or not to procure an abortion. But there is more at stake, according to Naomi Randolph in a 2019 *Ms. Magazine* article: pregnant women could face a higher risk of criminal charges for miscarriages or stillbirths, due to lawmakers in numerous states enacting laws that recognize fetuses as people, separate from the women carrying them.

One example that Randolph provided is in Alabama, where voters recently passed a measure that "endows fetus' with 'personhood' rights for the first time, potentially making any action that impacts a fetus a criminal behavior with potential for prosecution." Collectively, laws like Alabama's have resulted in hundreds of American women facing prosecution for the outcome of their pregnancies.

In Arkansas, Anne Bynum was convicted of "concealing a birth" when she delivered a stillborn child at her home in 2015, per an Arkansas statute that leaves women vulnerable to conviction if they wait even a minute before contacting authorities.[53] In Mississippi, Rennie Gibbs faced murder and subsequently manslaughter charges at age sixteen after delivering a stillborn child.[54] Although experts advised that drugs were not the cause of the baby's death, the jury concluded she had "willfully, and feloniously" killed the child by using drugs.

The cases all vary in detail, but the commonality is women losing their rights if they are thought to be endangering a fetus. Commenting on efforts to charge women for any conduct that could conceivably endanger their pregnancies, in 2016 Lynn Paltrow, the director of the National Advocates for Pregnant Women, told the *Guardian*, "We have gone and created a unique, gender-based crime, where the action actually requires a pregnancy to be a crime."[55]

As Randolph detailed, this especially hurts women of color and low-income women, due to their lack of access to contraceptives, abortion, and treatment for mental health conditions or addiction. She added that they are also "most likely to lack the resources necessary to avoid incarceration, or to pay the fines and fees to get out of jail once they're locked up."

If *Roe v. Wade* is overturned, the criminalization of miscarriages could become an even bigger problem. The Trump administration has been combative to women's reproductive rights from day one. As Naomi Randolph explained, proposed policy changes to the Affordable Care Act would "allow employers to deny women no-cost birth control based on their religious and 'moral' beliefs." This followed proposals to change Title X, which could limit funding to family planning services like Planned Parenthood. The research shows that if access to birth control is diminished, the rates of unintended pregnancies will rise. Trump's conservative Supreme Court Justice appointee Brett Kavanaugh is believed likely to provide the fifth vote necessary to striking down *Roe v. Wade*. If that happens, women may not only face prosecution for seeking out abortions, but could also lose basic protections when they are pregnant and parenting.

The New York Times is the only corporate source that has discussed this topic. However, the *Times* has only touched on it in opinion pieces—including, notably, a feature from December 2018 titled "A Woman's Rights"[56]—rather than as a topic featured in headlines and news stories. This issue has mainly been covered by independent news sources such as *Ms. Magazine* and Rewire.News.

9.

Developing Countries' Medical Needs Unfulfilled by Big Pharma

Julia Kollewe, "Big Pharma 'Failing to Develop Urgent Drugs for Poorest Countries,'" *The Guardian*, November 20, 2018, https://www.theguardian.com/business/2018/nov/20/big-pharma-who-failing-to-develop-urgent-drugs-for-poorest-countries.

Student Researcher: Brandon Grayson (College of Marin)

Faculty Evaluator: Susan Rahman (College of Marin)

The world's biggest pharmaceutical companies have "failed to develop two-thirds of the 139 urgently needed treatments in developing countries," the *Guardian* reported in November 2018. *The Guardian*'s coverage was based on a report by the Access to Medicine Foundation (AMF),[57] a nonprofit organization that analyzes access to essential medicines such as infant vaccines for cholera and single-dose oral treatments for syphilis. An estimated two billion people globally lack access to urgently needed medicines.

The Access to Medicine Foundation's 2018 report monitored the availability of medications produced by 20 of the largest pharmaceutical companies to lower- and middle-income countries. Of the 139 drugs, vaccines, and diagnostic tests identified as urgently needed by the World Health Organization (WHO), 91 have not been developed by any of the pharmaceutical firms tracked by the report. Sixteen of WHO's prioritized diseases have "no projects at all," the *Guardian* reported.

The Access to Medicine Foundation's executive director, Jayasree K. Iyer, told the *Guardian*, "There have been massive improvements in global health in the past decades, with all major pharmaceutical companies taking action. To close the gaps that remain, a greater diversity of companies must get involved and stay engaged for the long haul."

The report highlighted the need for pharmaceutical companies to provide better access to existing cancer treatments, reflecting the rising impact of cancer in low- and middle-income countries. Noting that "[p]rogress in global health is not inevitable," the report found that in some countries mortality rates were stagnating or worsening. In 2017, for example, non-communicable diseases accounted for 73.4 percent of deaths, an increase of 22.7 percent since 2007.[58]

Only four companies—GSK, Johnson & Johnson, Sanofi, and

Merck—are carrying out nearly two-thirds of the most urgently needed research and development projects, a "fragile" situation, according to Iyer. She explained to the *Guardian* that a "retreat by even one of these players would have a significant impact."

The AMF's report also highlighted 45 best and innovative practices that could "help raise the level of standard practice" and "achieve greater access to medicine."[59]

In an effort to mobilize investors to pressure pharmaceutical companies to make more medicines available in developing countries, the foundation presented the findings of its report to 82 global investors at events in London, New York, and Tokyo.[60] As of April 2019, Access to Medicine reported that 90 major investors had pledged support for its research and signed its investor statement since the release of the 2018 Access to Medicine Index in November 2018.[61]

With the exception of a November 2018 article by Reuters, news of the Access to Medicine Index's findings appears to have gone unreported in the corporate press.[62]

10.

Pentagon Aims to Surveil Social Media to Predict Domestic Protests

Nafeez Ahmed, "Pentagon Wants to Predict Anti-Trump Protests Using Social Media Surveillance," Motherboard (Vice), October 30, 2018, https://motherboard.vice.com/en_us/article/7x3g4x/pentagon-wants-to-predict-anti-trump-protests-using-social-media-surveillance.

Student Researcher: Margaret Tabb (University of Vermont)

Faculty Evaluator: Rob Williams (University of Vermont)

The Pentagon aims to use social media surveillance "to preempt major anti-government protests in the US," Nafeez Ahmed reported for Motherboard in October 2018. While the Pentagon has been funding Big Data research to determine how social media surveillance can help predict the outbreak of conflict, terrorism, and civil unrest in the Middle East and North Africa, Ahmed reported that "the Pentagon isn't just interested in anticipating surprises abroad. The research also appears to be intended for use in the US homeland." Ahmed's Motherboard report is based on recently published research, official government documents, and patent filings.

A study titled "Social Network Structure as a Predictor of Social

Behavior: The Case of Protest in the 2016 US Presidential Election" examined the use of social media in anti-Trump protests after the 2016 presidential elections. Funded by the US Army Research Laboratory, the study concluded that post-elections protests could have been predicted by analyzing millions of American citizens' Twitter posts.[63] "Civil unrest is associated with information cascades or activity bursts in social media, and these phenomena may be used to predict protests," the study concluded. "Failure to predict an unexpected protest may result in injuries or damage." As Ahmed summarized, "This pivotal finding means that extensive real-time monitoring of American citizens' social media activity can be used to predict future protests." However, his report noted that, in its current form, the tracking software used is not entirely accurate.

Ahmed's report highlighted official government documents focused on domestic surveillance, including an updated doctrine on "homeland defense" issued by the US Joint Chiefs of Staff in April 2018.[64] The new doctrine, Ahmed reported, "underscores the extent to which the Trump administration wants to consolidate homeland defense and security under the ultimate purview of the Pentagon." According to the document, the Department of Defense must be active in, and central to, almost all homeland affairs. This is achieved, Ahmed reported, "by interlinking homeland security indelibly with 'homeland defense,'" where the latter is defined as a US military function, thus institutionalizing what Ahmed described as "seamless" Pentagon support for "homeland security" operations, including operations in the event of a domestic "insurrection." "This is the first time that an 'insurrection' has been described using the phrase 'homeland defense,' implying that the response would come under Pentagon jurisdiction," Ahmed wrote.

Ahmed's report also investigated the significance of two patents originally filed in 2013. One of the patents, approved in February 2018, is for a system to track and predict social events using "amplified signals extracted from social media." The second patent, partially approved in October 2017, is for technology that uses social network analysis to infer the locations of social media users. "Although these technologies were developed under the Obama administration," Ahmed wrote, "it appears their use is being accelerated by the Trump administration."

According to Ahmed's Motherboard report, "Taken in tandem with the US military's sudden interest in predicting anti-Trump protests after the 2016 elections, the Pentagon's upgraded homeland defense doctrine seems to be part of a wider effort by the Trump administration to prepare for domestic civil unrest in coming months and years."

As of May 2019, Project Censored's review of this story found no corporate news coverage of the Pentagon's program to preempt anti-government protests by surveilling social media content.

11.
Ukrainian Fascists Trained US White Supremacists

Max Blumenthal, "Blowback: An Inside Look at How US-Funded Fascists in Ukraine Mentor US White Supremacists," MintPress News, November 19, 2018, https://www.mintpressnews.com/us-backed-fascist-azov-battalion-in-ukraine-is-training-and-radicalizing-american-white-supremacists/251951/.

Whitney Webb, "FBI: Neo-Nazi Militia Trained by US Military in Ukraine Now Training US White Supremacists," MintPress News, November 9, 2018, https://www.mintpressnews.com/fbi-neo-nazi-militia-trained-by-us-military-in-ukraine-now-training-us-white-suprema-cists/251687/.

Rebecca Kheel, "Congress Bans Arms to Ukraine Militia Linked to Neo-Nazis," The Hill, March 27, 2018, https://thehill.com/policy/defense/380483-congress-bans-arms-to-controversial-ukrainian-militia-linked-to-neo-nazis.

Student Researcher: Tanner J. Swann (Indian River State College)

Faculty Evaluator: Elliot D. Cohen (Indian River State College)

While the Trump administration has fought to keep nationals of Iran, Libya, Somalia, Syria, and Yemen from traveling to the United States for fear that they are terrorists, domestic white supremacists who avow violence travel freely between the United States and the Ukraine, where they train with the neo-Nazi Azov Battalion militia, according to reports from MintPress News and The Hill.

A federal criminal rioting complaint, filed in Los Angeles in 2018, included an affidavit stating that four American white supremacists from the Rise Above Movement (RAM) trained with Ukraine's Azov Battalion.[65] The training took place after the white supremacist gang participated in violent riots in Huntington Beach and Berkeley, California, and in Charlottesville, Virginia, in 2017, Max Blumenthal reported for MintPress News.

According to Blumenthal, although RAM's "crude neo-Nazi ideology" has been on display at rallies and in well-publicized street battles, media coverage of RAM has "glossed over the group's attraction to a burgeoning trans-Atlantic conglomeration of white supremacists" centered in Ukraine and, specifically, the Azov Battalion.

Blumenthal quoted Ivan Katchanovski, a professor of political science at the University of Ottawa, who said that Azov's military experience and weapons give it "the ability to blackmail the government and defend themselves politically against any opposition." Noting that fascist organizations in Ukraine are stronger "than in any other country in the world," Katchanovski said that the Azov Battalion have threatened to overthrow the Ukrainian government if it "will not advance an ideology similar to theirs."

As Whitney Webb reported for MintPress News, the Azov Battalion's prominence is "the direct result of U.S. government policy toward Ukraine." In the name of combatting "Russian aggression," the United States has supported Ukraine's military with hundreds of millions of dollars' worth of security and programmatic and technical assistance—despite, as Webb reported, a "merging of Azov Battalion with the Ukrainian government." This aid "has repeatedly found its way to the Azov Battalion," she wrote.

In March 2018, Congress banned the arming of the Azov Battalion, as The Hill's Rebecca Kheel reported. Three previous House bills had included a ban on US aid to Ukraine funding the Azov Battalion, Kheel wrote, "but the provision was stripped out before final passage each year." In 2018, however, the $1.3 trillion omnibus spending bill that was signed into law stipulated that "none of the funds made available by this act may be used to provide arms, training or other assistance to the Azov Battalion." Affirming that white supremacy and neo-Nazism are "unacceptable and have no place in our world," Representative Rohit Khanna of California told The Hill he was "very pleased that the recently passed omnibus [bill] prevents the U.S. from providing arms and training assistance to the neo-Nazi Azov Battalion fighting in Ukraine."

According to The Hill's report, "It's unclear how much, if anything, from the United States has gone to Azov in the past." But Kheel pointed out that online posts from 2017 by the militia's news service showed Azov Battalion members testing US-made grenade launchers. Those posts were subsequently deleted, and the Ukrainian National Guard insisted that Azov does not possess the grenade launchers.

Although the omnibus spending bill ended direct US funding of the Azov Battalion, the United States still helps to arm the Ukrainian military. As Kheel reported, "The omnibus [bill] includes about $620.7 million in aid for Ukraine, including $420.7 million in State Department and foreign operations funds and $200 million in Pentagon funds." Webb's MintPress News article noted that, although US funds can no longer support the Azov Battalion, it "continues to receive arms from U.S. allies such as Israel."

In March 2018, ABC News reported on the US sale of anti-tank missiles to the Ukraine, but the article made no mention of the Azov Battalion's connections with Ukraine's military or government, or the role of white supremacists and neo-Nazis in those organizations.[66] In May 2019, MSNBC produced a three-minute video, "'Breaking Hate' Extreme Groups at Home and Abroad," that reported on the failed attempt by Andrew Oneschuk, a teen living at home with his parents, to join the Azov Battalion.[67] MSNBC's video provided scant detail about Azov and made no mention of prior reports on US white supremacists training with them.

12.
New 5G Network Spurs Health Concerns

Cindy L. Russell, "5 G Wireless Telecommunications Expansion: Public Health and Environmental Implications," *Environmental Research*, Vol. 165 (August 2018), 484–95, published online April 11, 2018, https://www.ncbi.nlm.nih.gov/pubmed/29655646.

Jody McCutcheon, "Frightening Frequencies: The Dangers of 5G," *Eluxe Magazine*, May 2018, https://eluxemagazine.com/magazine/dangers-of-5g.

Jason Plautz, "Grassroots Coalition Asks FCC to Slow 5G Expansion over Health Concerns," Smart Cities Dive, September 24, 2018, https://www.smartcitiesdive.com/news/grassroots-coalition-asks-fcc-to-slow-5g-expansion-over-health-concerns/532992.

Joel M. Moskowitz, "Scientists and Doctors Demand Moratorium on 5G," Electromagnetic Radiation Safety, April 26, 2018, https://www.saferemr.com/2017/09/5G-moratorium12.html.

Conan Milner, "Resistance to 5G: Roadblock to a High Tech Future or Warning of a Serious Health Risk?" *Epoch Times*, November 9, 2018, updated November 12, 2018, https://www.theepochtimes.com/resistance-to-5g-roadblock-to-a-high-tech-future-or-warning-of-a-serious-health-risk_2705116.html.

Nicole Karlis, "Why Public Health Experts are Worried about 5G, the Next Generation of Cell Network," Salon, December 4, 2018, https://www.salon.com/2018/12/03/why-public-health-experts-are-worried-about-5g-the-next-generation-of-cell-network.

Martin L. Pall, "Wi-Fi is an Important Threat to Human Health," *Environmental Research*, Vol. 164 (July 2018), 405–416, https://www.sciencedirect.com/science/article/pii/S0013935118300355.

Student Researcher: Jamie Wells (San Francisco State University)

Faculty Evaluator: Kenn Burrows (San Francisco State University)

The prevalence of wireless technologies has spawned a telecommunications revolution that increasingly exposes the public to broader and higher frequencies of the electromagnetic spectrum as we transmit data through a variety of devices. The telecom industry is promoting the replacement of the current cellular network, known as 4G, with a new generation of higher frequency 5G wavelengths to power the "Internet of Things," promising faster data processing, amazing new gadgets, and a lifestyle that mirrors science fiction. However, 5G will require a massive telecommunications network with many more wireless antennas, resulting in greater radiofrequency radiation (RFR) and increased health risks.

In an article published in *Environmental Research*, Cindy Russell wrote that, because this is the first human generation to experience "cradle-to-grave lifespan exposure" to high levels of human-made microwave radiofrequencies, the "true health consequences" of exposure will not be known for years or decades. Her article documented a range of questions regarding the safety of RFR in 2G, 3G, and 4G wireless technologies and it recommended precaution in the rollout of 5G technology.

RFR exposure has been classified as a potential 2B carcinogen, according to the World Health Organization's International Agency for Research on Cancer, and research has indicated that use of mobile phones could contribute to the formation of brain tumors. Other studies have concluded that RFR exposure is associated with DNA breaks (related to cancer), oxidative damage (which can lead to tissue deterioration and premature aging), disruption of cell metabolism, increased blood–brain barrier permeability, melatonin reduction (which can lead to insomnia), and many other illnesses and conditions.[68]

The effects of 5G technology on humans and the environment have been subject to fewer studies than the effects of 5G's predecessors, as Russell and other experts have noted. The addition of this 5G radiation to an already complex mix of lower frequencies will likely contribute to negative public health outcomes—both physically and mentally. The new 5G technology utilizes high-frequency millimeter waves (MMW), which give off the same dose of radiation as airport scanners. Continuous exposure to transmitters in close proximity to homes and workplaces may pose serious risks.

Yael Stein of Jerusalem's Hebrew University is a strong critic of the new 5G network. As Jody McCutcheon reported in an article for *Eluxe Magazine*, Stein has raised concerns about the adverse effects of MMW on human skin. In a July 2016 letter to the Federal Communications Commission, Stein advocated against 5G millimeter wave technology, noting that, with adoption of it, we should expect "more of the health effects currently seen with RF/microwave frequencies including many more cases of hypersensitivity (EHS), as well as many new complaints of physical pain and a yet unknown variety of neurologic disturbances."[69] The *Eluxe* article noted that the Department of Defense "already uses a crowd-dispersal method called the Active Denial System, in which MMWs are directed at crowds to make their skin feel like it's burning."

5G technology is not only bad for humans, it harms plant and animal life as well. *Eluxe* reported that one study found low-intensity MMW exposure causes stress responses in the cells of wheat shoots, which could have consequences for human food supplies. The 5G infrastructure would also pose a threat to our planet's atmosphere. The implementation of this massive telecom network will require the deployment of many short-lifespan satellites propelled by hydrocarbon rocket engines. Another study cited by *Eluxe* found that launching these rockets will give off enough carbon to pollute global atmospheric conditions.

There is little or no substantive corporate media coverage of 5G health concerns. A May 2018 CBS News report observed that US wireless companies anticipate installing 300,000 new antennas, "roughly equal to the total number of cell towers built over the past three decades," to support new 5G networks.[70] CBS reported that this has caused "outrage and alarm in some neighborhoods, as antennas go up around homes." Yet CBS's coverage made no mention of the coalition of 52 grassroots organizations, Americans for Responsible Technology, that has called on the Federal Communications Commission to delay deployment of 5G infrastructure due to "emerging science linking exposure to RF microwave radiation with serious biological harm," as Jason Plautz reported for Smart Cities Dive.

Instead, corporate news reports have focused on the proposed benefits of 5G—including, for example, faster data speeds, 3D imaging, and investment opportunities—while emphasizing lack of consensus among experts regarding any attendant health risks. This tendency can be seen in a November 2018 CNN article, "Federal Health Agencies Disagree over Link between Cell Phone Radiation and Cancer," which reported on "confusion and controversy" regarding science in a split between the National Institutes of Health and the Food and Drug Administration.[71]

Furthermore, corporate media often frame their stories in terms provided by the technology industry. For example, a February 2019 *Washington Post* article was based almost entirely on a report from the technology conglomerate Cisco, which indicated that the United States will only remain ahead of China and other nations in implementing 5G technology through "deregulation and policies favorable to the industry."[72] The only factors "complicating the picture," according to Cisco and the *Washington Post*, were "ongoing concerns about the security of networking equipment from companies such as China's Huawei." That article made no mention whatsoever of health or environmental risks associated with the corporate race for 5G supremacy.

13.

Corporate Food Brands Drive Massive Dead Zone in Gulf of Mexico

Reynard Loki, "Corporate Food Brands Drive the Massive Dead Zone in the Gulf of Mexico," Truthout, August 28, 2018, https://truthout.org/articles/corporate-food-brands-driving-the-massive-dead-zone-in-gulf-of-mexico/.
Oliver Milman, "'Dead Zone' in Gulf of Mexico Will Take Decades to Recover from Farm Pollution," *The Guardian*, March 22, 2018, https://www.theguardian.com/environment/2018/mar/22/dead-zone-gulf-of-mexico-decades-recover-study.

Student Researcher: Adriana Babicz (Sonoma State University)

Faculty Evaluator: Peter Phillips (Sonoma State University)

The dead zone in the Gulf of Mexico is the result of water polluted with manure and fertilizer runoff from major beef-producing states, including Texas, Oklahoma, Iowa, Kansas, and Nebraska. Dead zones are areas in a body of water that lack sufficient oxygen to support marine life. Covering approximately 8,000 square miles, the Gulf of Mexico's dead zone is about the size of New Jersey and ranks as the world's second-largest, surpassed only by the dead zone in the Gulf of Oman. As the *Guardian* and Truthout reported, the Gulf of Mexico's dead zone continues to grow because big food companies lack sustainability policies to prevent environmental pollution, including especially animal waste and fertilizer runoff from industrial farms.

As Reynard Loki wrote for Truthout, a study by Mighty Earth, an environmental action group, found that the largest fast food, grocery, and food service companies in the United States are "helping to drive one of the nation's worst human-made environmental disasters." In a survey of 23 major brands—including Target, McDonald's, Subway, Trader Joe's, and Whole Foods—Mighty Earth found that none have policies requiring "even minimal environmental protections from meat suppliers."[73] Mighty Earth's study, "Flunking the Planet," gave all but one of the companies a failing grade overall for environmental safeguards after considering the sources of animal feed, the processing of animals' manure, and overall greenhouse gas emissions. (Walmart earned a D-grade, based on its commitment to reducing supply chain emissions through its Project Gigaton initiative.)

"By not requiring environmental safeguards from its meat suppliers, the world's largest natural and organic foods supermarket—and most of its big-brand counterparts in the retail food industry, like McDonald's, Subway and Target—are sourcing and selling meat from some of the worst polluters in agribusiness, including Tyson Foods and Cargill," Truthout reported. Mighty Earth's study noted that the main source of water contamination is runoff from industrial farms that produce animal feed. The five largest meat companies "dominate" the supply chain, Mighty Earth reported, and bear "primary responsibility for driving the negative impacts as well as delivering solutions at scale."[74]

The runoff of nitrogen from chemical fertilizers poses nearly impossible challenges for the restoration of marine life in the Gulf. A study published in *Science* in April 2018 found that, even if all current nitrogen runoff was stopped, the Gulf would take "about 30 years to recover," according to the *Guardian*.[75] One of the *Science* study's coauthors, Nandita Basu, an associate professor of environmental sciences at the University of Waterloo, likened the challenge to going on a diet: "you can't expect results right away," she told the *Guardian*. A marine scientist at the Smithsonian Environmental Research Center,

Denise Breitburg, observed that the study "shows we need a scientific strategy and can't expect instant results, but we know what needs to be done to improve things."

As Mighty Earth reported in its study, big brand food retailers fail to use their influence to encourage more sustainable practices. According to Mighty Earth's report, companies like Walmart, Whole Foods, McDonald's, and Burger King "have the power to set and enforce standards requiring better farming practices from suppliers." Mighty Earth recommended that food companies require meat suppliers to implement sustainable feed sourcing, responsible manure management, and reductions in greenhouse gas emissions, and that these changes should be made with time-bound targets and should be verified by third-party audits, with progress reported to the public on a regular basis.[76]

Corporate news coverage has largely focused on the scale of the Gulf of Mexico's dead zone and its consequences—rather than on its causes, including industrial agriculture and corporate irresponsibility. In August 2017, CBS News discussed the size of the dead zone and interviewed fishermen who witnessed large decreases in fish populations at popular fishing spots.[77] In August 2017, the *Washington Post* published an article on dead zones around the world.[78] *National Geographic* published a substantive article on the topic the same month.[79] The findings and recommendations from Mighty Earth's "Flunking the Planet" study appear to have gone entirely unreported by the corporate press.

14.
FBI Surveilled Peaceful Climate Change Protesters

Adam Federman, "Revealed: FBI Kept Files on Peaceful Climate Change Protesters," *The Guardian*, December 13, 2018, https://www.theguardian.com/us-news/2018/dec/13/fbi-climate-change-protesters-iowa-files-monitoring-surveillance-.

Sarah Lazare and Simon Davis-Cohen, "Fossil Fuel Companies are Enlisting Police to Crack Down on Protesters," *In These Times*, April 16, 2019, http://inthesetimes.com/article/21821/fossil-fuel-companies-back-critical-infrastructure-bills-pipeline-protests.

Student Researcher: Melissa Reed (College of Marin)

Faculty Evaluator: Susan Rahman (College of Marin)

After three participants in a nonviolent protest at a BP oil refinery in Indiana were arrested in May 2016, the FBI opened a file on them, the *Guardian* reported in December 2018. The Indiana event was part of 350.org's Break Free from Fossil Fuels campaign, which engaged more than 30,000 people on six continents in what it described as the largest coordinated act of civil disobedience in the fight against climate change. Like Jonas Magram, Thom Krystofiak, and Inga Frick in Indiana, many of those nonviolent protestors were arrested for trespassing, or for blocking rail access to refineries.

As Adam Federman reported for the *Guardian*, "The FBI is prohibited from investigating groups or individuals solely for their political beliefs but has been criticized in the past for treating non-violent civil disobedience as a form of terrorism." The subject of the FBI file on Magram, Krystofiak, and Frick is categorized by the FBI as a "Sensitive Investigative Matter," a label, Federman explained, that often refers to cases involving political organizations which "therefore require a higher level of scrutiny." One of the FBI documents, catalogued by the agency as part of a related domestic terrorism case and obtained by the *Guardian* through a Freedom of Information Act lawsuit, stated that "350.org are referenced in multiple investigations and assessments for their planned protests and disruptions."

Federman wrote that in 2015 the *Guardian* revealed that the FBI had "violated its own rules" by failing to obtain the approval required to conduct its investigation into Texas activists campaigning against the Keystone XL pipeline.[80] That investigation, Federman summarized, continued for more than a year and "swept up numerous activists including one who later learned he was on a US government watchlist for domestic flights."

Mike German, a fellow with the Brennan Center for Justice and a former FBI agent, told the *Guardian* that FBI tracking of the three people arrested for civil disobedience in Indiana was "quite troubling." Absent information suggesting a planned act of violence, German said, there was little justification for creating such a file. The founder of 350.org, Bill McKibben, told the *Guardian*, "Trying to deal with the greatest crisis humans have stumbled into shouldn't require being subjected to government surveillance." However, McKibben observed, "when much of our government acts as a subsidiary of the fossil fuel industry, it may be par for the course."

An April 2019 report published by *In These Times* suggests the extent to which the oil industry seeks to enlist state government and to co-opt local law enforcement in order to protect itself from opposition. Sarah Lazare and Simon Davis-Cohen reported that in at least seven states "the oil industry has backed critical infrastructure bills that criminalize pipeline protests."

Drawing lessons from the protests at the Standing Rock Sioux Reservation against the Dakota Access Pipeline in 2016, fossil fuel industry associations began urging state lawmakers to support legislation that would define trespassing on energy plants and pipelines as felonies, Lazare and Davis-Cohen reported. The industry has publicly "supported, lobbied for, or testified on behalf of" critical infrastructure bills in Iowa, Illinois, Louisiana, Minnesota, North Dakota, Oklahoma, and Wyoming. Industry-based bills have passed in Iowa, Louisiana, North Dakota, and Oklahoma, and no fewer than eleven critical infrastructure bills have been introduced in 2019. Lazare and Davis-Cohen noted that fifteen people who protested the Bayou Bridge Pipeline were facing felony charges, punishable by as much as five years in prison and fines of $1,000, under Louisiana's new law. The model legislation for the critical infrastructure bills was developed by the American Legislative Exchange Council (ALEC).

In effect, Lazare and Davis-Cohen wrote, the oil industry is "working with the government to redefine criminality and then using that definition to lock up its opponents."

Lazare and Davis-Cohen also reported that the line between police and privately-hired security guards is "blurring." In 2013, for example, Kinder Morgan hired off-duty police officers from a Pennsylvania department to "deter protests" in order to avoid "costly delays" at a controversial gas pipeline construction site.[81] As the *Earth Island Journal* reported, "The company requested that the officers, though officially off-duty, be in uniform and marked cars."[82] More recently, Lazare and Davis-Cohen reported that some of the arrests in the Bayou Bridge Pipeline protests were made by off-duty police officers hired as guards by Energy Transfer Partners, the company responsible for building the pipeline.

Referencing the *Guardian*'s reporting on FBI surveillance of activists who protested the Keystone XL pipeline or participated in the 350.org Break Free from Fossil Fuels campaign, Lazare and Davis-Cohen noted antecedents in the bureau's COINTELPRO program, which targeted the Black Power and American Indian movements in the 1950s and 1960s because of their revolutionary potential. "Sectors of the growing climate movement, with their goal of upending one of the world's most powerful industries, likely stir similar fears—a sign of their effectiveness," Lazare and Davis-Cohen wrote.

As of May 2019, the corporate media have provided no coverage of the issues raised in Adam Federman's *Guardian* report or Sarah Lazare and Simon Davis-Cohen's article for *In These Times*.

15.
Trump Administration Threatens Endangered Species Act

Charles Pekow, "On Thin Ice: Will the Endangered Species Act Survive the Trump Administration?" *Earth Island Journal*, Spring 2019, http://www.earthisland.org/journal/index.php/magazine/entry/on-thin-ice-endangered-species-act-trump-administration.

Student Researcher: Madi Jones (College of Western Idaho)

Faculty Evaluator: Michelle Mahoney (College of Western Idaho)

The Endangered Species Act (ESA)—which currently protects more than 1,600 native plant and animal species in the United States and its territories—is "increasingly challenged by an administration that has little patience for laws and regulations that help protect our lands and wildlife," Charles Pekow wrote in an article published by *Earth Island Journal* in Spring 2019. In the two years since Donald Trump became president, Pekow reported, "at least 80 bills" seeking to undermine the ESA or remove species from the list have been introduced in Congress, and key federal agencies charged with implementing the ESA have proposed revisions to weaken vital elements of it.

For a little over a decade, according to the *Earth Island Journal*'s report, conservationists have fought to protect Pacific walruses under the Endangered Species Act. Protection for the walrus under the ESA was first proposed in 2008; in 2011, the US Fish and Wildlife Service (FWS) suggested that the Pacific walrus was threatened and endangered. But in October 2017, the Trump administration concluded that the Pacific walrus did not warrant listing. The FWS under Trump appointees explained that "impacts of the effects of climate change on the Pacific walrus population are based on speculation, rather than reliable prediction," Pekow reported. The Center for Biological Diversity (CBD) has sued the Trump administration over the decision, and that lawsuit is still pending.[83]

According to the CBD, since 1996 more than four hundred pieces of legislation have been proposed seeking to dismantle critical species protections. As Pekow reported, legislators often include these proposals as "riders to must-pass spending bills." Gray wolves in the Rocky Mountains lost protections this way after passage of a 2011 budget rider. However, as Pekow wrote, "The most critical blow to the Act has come from the federal agencies charged with implementing the ESA": the Fish and Wildlife Service, which manages plants, wildlife, and inland fisheries, and the National Marine Fisheries Service, which oversees ocean-going fish and marine mammals. In July 2018, the two agencies jointly proposed that species designated as "threatened" should no longer automatically receive the same protections as those designated as "endangered." In other words, Pekow summarized, "there would be no automatic prohibitions on the harming or killing of plants and animals designated 'threatened.'" The agencies also proposed overturning a provision of the ESA that restricts consideration of economic impacts when determining whether a species needed protection. The proposals would make it more difficult to add new species to the list and, Pekow noted, environmentalists fear that changes would also make it easier to delist species because their habitats are desirable to industry.

Beyond Pekow's detailed report for *Earth Island Journal*, the Trump administration's decision not to list the Pacific walrus has received limited coverage in other news outlets, including *USA Today* and the *Chicago Tribune*; *National Geographic* and *Popular Science* have also provided coverage.[84] *The Guardian* published a more in-depth piece on the topic in October 2017.[85]

The broader topic of the Trump administration's efforts to undermine the ESA has not been prominently reported, though in July 2018 the *Washington Post* published a reasonably detailed report on the joint proposal by the Fish and Wildlife Service and National Marine Fisheries Service to strip the ESA of key provisions.[86]

The following month, the *Post* also published an opinion piece by David Bernhardt, who was deputy secretary of the interior at the time.

In "The Greatest Good for Endangered Species," Bernhardt advocated a "modern vision of conservation" employing "federalism, public–private partnerships and market-based solutions to achieve sound stewardship."[87] Bernhardt wrote that the Trump administration "found room for improvement in the administration" of the ESA, which currently "places unnecessary regulatory burden on our citizens without additional benefit to the species." *The Post* failed to inform its readers of Bernhardt's background as a former lobbyist for the fossil fuel industry or of what one independent news outlet described as his "long track record of trying to weaken wildlife protections in favor of more extraction."[88]

16.
Underwater Avalanches Heighten Risks of Oil Catastrophes

Ian R. MacDonald, "Underwater Mudslides are the Biggest Threat to Offshore Drilling, and Energy Companies Aren't Ready for Them," The Conversation, March 11, 2019, https://theconversation.com/underwater-mudslides-are-the-biggest-threat-to-offshore-drilling-and-energy-companies-arent-ready-for-them-111904.

Ian MacDonald, "Are American Oil Platforms Prepared for Underwater Avalanches?" *Pacific Standard*, March 11, 2019, https://psmag.com/environment/are-oil-platforms-ready-for-underwater-avalanches.

Student Researcher: Thanh Nguyen (College of Western Idaho)

Faculty Evaluator: Michelle Mahoney (College of Western Idaho)

As bad as the 2010 BP Deepwater Horizon oil spill was, "the worst-case scenario" for an oil spill catastrophe is not losing control of a single well, as occurred in the BP disaster. Instead, "[m]uch more damage would be done if one or more of the thousand or so production platforms that now blanket the Gulf of Mexico were destroyed without warning by a deep-sea mudslide," Ian R. MacDonald reported for The Conversation in March 2019. Underwater mudslides could leave "a tangled mess of pipes buried under a giant mass of sediments," a scenario that oil company managers are not prepared to handle. In such a situation, the discharge could not be stopped with caps or plugs, and oil "might flow for decades."

As MacDonald reported, one instance of this type of catastrophe has already happened. A well located off the coast of Louisiana owned by Taylor Energy has been leaking oil since 2004. Government regulators and energy companies, MacDonald wrote, "should be doing much more to prevent such catastrophes at other sites."

Earthquakes are one trigger for deep-sea mudslides. The probability of mudslides in the Gulf of Mexico is high, due to regular seismic activity in the area. Studies to identify unstable slopes would improve our understanding of the seabed and potentially reduce the risks, MacDonald wrote.

Corporate media—including the *Washington Post*, CNN, and *Newsweek*—have covered the Taylor Energy disaster off the coast of Louisiana.[89] However, MacDonald's report for The Conversation, also reprinted in *Pacific Standard*, is distinctive for its detailed explanation of how underwater mudslides pose systemic threats for drilling operations throughout the Gulf of Mexico, and not only at the Taylor Energy site.

17.

More Than 25 Percent of Formerly Incarcerated People are Unemployed

Alfonso Serrano, "Out of Prison, Out of Jobs: Unemployment and the Formerly Incarcerated," ColorLines, July 10, 2018, https://www.colorlines.com/articles/out-prison-out-jobs-unemployment-and-formerly-incarcerated.

Prison Policy Initiative, "New Report Calculates the First Unemployment Rate for Formerly Incarcerated People: 27 Percent, Highest since Great Depression," *San Francisco Bay View*, September 29, 2018, https://sfbayview.com/2018/09/new-report-calculates-the-first-unemployment-rate-for-formerly-incarcerated-people-27-percent-highest-since-great-depression/.

Student Researcher: Briana Earls (Sonoma State University)

Faculty Evaluator: Mutombo M'Panya (Sonoma State University)

A 2018 report from the Prison Policy Initiative found that people released from prison are disproportionally discriminated against in the pursuit of work. The study—by Lucius Couloute, at the time a doctoral candidate in sociology at the University of Massachusetts, and Daniel Kopf, a reporter for Quartz—found that an average of 27 percent of formerly incarcerated people are unemployed.[90] That figure, Couloute and Kopf wrote, is greater than "the total U.S. unemployment rate during any historical period, including the Great Depression," when the unemployment rate reached nearly 25 percent.

Their study, "Out of Prison & Out of Work," drew on statistics from the 2008 Bureau of Justice Statistics's National Former Prisoner Survey data—the most recent available data—and showed that the unemployment rate for the five million formerly incarcerated people living in the United States was more than 27 percent, compared to 5.8 percent for the general population. ("Contemporary unemployment rates may differ," Couloute and Kopf wrote, "but we are confident that formerly incarcerated people are still substantially disadvantaged compared to the general public.")

Their report found that blacks, Hispanics, and women faced the most significant disadvantages in the search for work after leaving prison. From the 2008 data, 39 percent of Hispanic women, 27 percent of Hispanic men, 44 percent of black women, 35 percent of black men, 23 percent of white women, and 18 percent of white men faced unemployment after being released from prison. The numbers document what the study's authors described as a "prison penalty" that puts formerly incarcerated people—and especially blacks, Hispanics, and women—at disadvantages when it comes to finding work. (Couloute and Kopf acknowledged that "prison *alone*" does not account for high unemployment rates among formerly incarcerated people, but observed that "a wealth of data suggests that going to prison does negatively affect labor market outcomes.")

Couloute and Kopf also found that formerly incarcerated people were more likely to be actively looking for work than the general population. Their analysis showed 93 percent of formerly incarcerated people were either employed or actively looking for work, compared to 84 percent of the general population. Couloute and Kopf summarized, "Formerly incarcerated people want to work. Their high unemployment rate reflects public will, policy, and practice—not differences in aspirations."

The Prison Policy Initiative study also reported "promising policy choices available to lawmakers at each level of government" to help formerly incarcerated people gain employment, including implementation of a temporary basic income upon release, a short-term economic investment that would result in long-term cost savings; the expungement of criminal records, taking into account offense type and length of time since sentencing, so that prison sentences do not result in "perpetual punishment"; and banning of employer discrimination, potentially under Title VII of the Civil Rights Act of 1964, owing to racially disproportionate incarceration rates.

Despite the Prison Policy Initiative's study being what Couloute and Kopf described as "the first ever estimate" of unemployment among formerly incarcerated people in the United States, their findings appear to have received nearly no coverage in the establishment press. In July 2018, the editorial board of the Southern California News Group produced an editorial, "No One Benefits When Formerly Incarcerated People Can't Get a Job," that provided a reasonably detailed summary of the study, including its recommendations. A number of local newspapers belonging to the group, including the *Orange County Register*, *Inland Valley Daily Bulletin*, and *Pasadena Star-News*, published the editorial.[91] Otherwise, relatively limited coverage of what Couloute and Kopf termed the "prison penalty" has left out the study's findings and recommendations.

In August 2018, *USA Today* published an opinion piece on former inmates' experiences, which mentioned in passing that "[u]nemployment among former inmates is 27%" without citing the Prison Policy Initiative's study or discussing its recommendations.[92] A March 2018 CNN article reported that, in 2014, as many as 1.9 million formerly incarcerated people were out of work, according to a study by the Center for Economic and Policy Research.[93] Noting that many former inmates lack "relevant skills and work experience," the article also reported that employers are often reluctant to hire former inmates: "More than 60% of employers," CNN reported, "say they would 'probably not' or 'definitely not' be willing to hire an ex-offender."[94]

18.

Humanitarian Groups Promote Solutions to Extreme Violence in West Africa

Obi Anyadike, "Countering Militancy in the Sahel," New Humanitarian, February 26, 2019, https://www.thenewhumanitarian.org/in-depth/countering-militancy-sahel.

Student Researchers: Alyssa Lash, Caroline Lussier, and Erica Rindels (University of Massachusetts Amherst)

Faculty Evaluator: Allison Butler (University of Massachusetts Amherst)

In February 2019, the New Humanitarian published an overview of the "causes and humanitarian consequences of violent extremism in West Africa." The organization's report on extreme violence in northeast Nigeria, northern Cameroon, north and central Mali, and southern Niger was the result of a year of fieldwork in those areas, surveying not only the violence but also sustainable peace efforts based on the interconnected roles of economics, politics, and faith in sparking militancy and, potentially, creating peace. The detailed report covered root causes, recruitment, motivations, security forces, attempts to reduce the ranks of fighters, and the reintegration of former fighters.

Peer pressure, community identity, and the impact of trauma and humiliation from security forces play a huge role in recruitment. A United Nations Development Programme study found that the arrest or killing of family members was "the tipping point" in recruitment decisions for 70 percent of jihadists.[95] The power of faith provides a significant motivation for these groups as well, helping, for example, to frame conflict in ways that create a narrative and meaning for militants.

When it comes to identifying jihadists or potential recruits, security forces are not doing their best work, the study found. Arrests of suspected jihadists are often arbitrary and brutal, instead of the result of properly conducted police work. This causes people to be more fearful of the security services, instead of building trust in them. Amnesty and demobilization schemes provide better options, but they tend to be hampered by lack of funding and poor administration.

With extreme violence impacting many regions in West Africa, it is perhaps surprising that there are so few news articles on the topic in US establishment media. In April 2016, the Huffington Post published an article on why people join Nigeria's Boko Haram.[96] *The Washington Post* ran a similar article in April 2016.[97] West Africa's humanitarian crises receive more regular coverage from nonprofit organizations such as Oxfam International, which has released multiple articles on the "forgotten crisis" in West Africa.[98]

19.

Censorship of Al Jazeera Documentary Exposes Influence of Pro-Israel Lobby

Asa Winstanley and Ali Abunimah, "'National Security' Cited as Reason Al Jazeera Nixed Israel Lobby Film," Electronic Intifada, June 4, 2018, https://electronicintifada.net/content/national-security-cited-reason-al-jazeera-nixed-israel-lobby-film/24566.

Asa Winstanley, "Al Jazeera Denies Qatari Emir Censored Israel Lobby Film," Electronic Intifada, October 10, 2018, https://electronicintifada.net/blogs/asa-winstanley/al-jazeera-denies-qatari-emir-censored-israel-lobby-film.

"Watch the Film the Israel Lobby Didn't Want You to See," Electronic Intifada, November 2, 2018, https://electronicintifada.net/content/watch-film-israel-lobby-didnt-want-you-see/25876.

Amir Tibon, "Parts of Censored Al Jazeera Documentary on D.C. Israel Lobby Leaked," Haaretz, August 30, 2018, https://www.haaretz.com/israel-news/.premium-parts-of-censored-al-jazeera-documentary-on-pro-israeli-lobby-leaked-1.6432835.

Ben Norton, interview with Ali Abunimah and Max Blumenthal, "Leaked Clips from Censored Documentary on Israel Lobby Reveal Attacks on US Activists," Real News Network, September 10, 2018, https://therealnews.com/stories/leaked-clips-from-censored-documentary-on-israel-lobby-reveal-attacks-on-us-activists.

Max Blumenthal, "Censored Documentary Exposes Israel's Attack on Black Lives Matter," Mint-Press News, September 7, 2018, https://www.mintpressnews.com/black-lives-matter-israel-the-lobby/248917/.

Student Researcher: Gabrielle Kreidie (Drew University)

Faculty Evaluator: Lisa Lynch (Drew University)

A documentary film that aimed to expose Israel's covert influence campaign in the United States has been leaked to the media after the government of Qatar pulled it from Al Jazeera, a media outlet Qatar funds. In August 2018, excerpts of the censored documentary were leaked and later published by a number of online independent media outlets, including the Electronic Intifada, France's Orient XXI, and Lebanon's *Al-Akhbar*.

An undercover reporter for Al Jazeera became an intern at the Israel Project, a pro-Israeli organization in Washington, DC, in order to research and document what a November 2018 Electronic Intifada article summarized as "the efforts of Israel and its lobbyists to spy on, smear and intimidate US citizens who support Palestinian human rights, especially BDS," the boycott, divestment and sanctions movement.

One clip showed Julia Reifkind, then an employee of the Israeli embassy, discussing the Israeli government "giving our support" to front groups "in that behind-the-scenes way," and describing the use of fake Facebook profiles to infiltrate campus activist groups that support Palestine. In another segment, the executive director of the Israel on Campus Coalition, Jacob Baime, described how that group

coordinated with Israel's Ministry of Strategic Affairs, a semi-covert government agency that previous reports linked to a global campaign targeting the BDS movement.[99] Baime also described using anonymous websites to target activists, citing Canary Mission, an anonymous smear site targeting student activists, as "a good example." In another leaked excerpt, a group of students with fellowships from the right-wing Hoover Institution explained that their participation in a pro-Israeli demonstration was "astroturfing," a term used to describe the masked sponsorship of activism intended to give the appearance of grassroots advocacy.

The pro-Israel lobby successfully pressured the Qatari government not to release the Al Jazeera documentary. In June 2018, the Electronic Intifada reported, a Qatari government official stated that the film's release would be indefinitely delayed due to "national security" concerns.

As *Haaretz* reported in August 2018, the Qatari government censored the documentary as part of its effort "to win the support of major Jewish American organizations." Since 2017, when Saudi Arabia and the United Arab Emirates placed Qatar under partial blockade, Qatar has "intensified its lobbying efforts in the United States, in hopes of convincing the Trump administration to support it" in its dispute with the Saudis and the UAE, Amir Tibon reported. In that effort, Qatar has "invested millions of dollars" to court right-wing Jewish American organizations that support Israel's occupation of the West Bank. In exchange for censoring the Al Jazeera documentary, *Haaretz* reported, Qatar sought public messages of support by those groups.

In September 2018, Max Blumenthal reported that the censored Al Jazeera film also documented how Israeli operatives and US lobbyists coordinated efforts to recruit established black civil rights activists as pro-Israel proxies and to discredit the Movement for Black Lives after August 2016, when that activist coalition issued a platform that characterized Israel as an "apartheid state" and affirmed support for the BDS movement in response.

As of May 2019, the corporate news media appear to have entirely ignored Qatar's censorship of the Al Jazeera documentary and the evidence it provided of Israel's covert influence campaign in the United States.

20.
Scientists Accelerate Coral Reef Regrowth with Electricity

Alice Klein, "Divers are Attempting to Regrow Great Barrier Reef with Electricity," *New Scientist*, September 20, 2018, https://www.newscientist.com/article/2180369-divers-are-attempting-to-regrow-great-barrier-reef-with-electricity/.

Mike Wehner, "Letting Coral Reefs Die Will Actually Cost Us More Than Saving Them," BGR, June 14, 2018, https://bgr.com/2018/06/14/coral-reef-cost-recovery-effort/.

Student Researcher: Adam May (Sonoma State University)

Faculty Evaluator: Mackenzie Zippay (Sonoma State University)

The conservation group Reef Ecologic is using electrical currents to stimulate regrowth of damaged coral reefs, Alice Klein reported for *New Scientist* in September 2018. Coral reefs are crucial components of ocean ecosystems around the world, and damage to them from climate change and destructive fishing practices has been widely reported. Damaged coral regrows slowly, and rising ocean temperatures lead to bleaching that can cause entire reef systems to collapse permanently. As Klein reported, researchers have found that laying metal frames over damaged reefs and then running electric current through those frames draws in minerals that allow coral to grow up to four times faster than it otherwise would.

The technique is currently being used by conservationists with Reef Ecologic to restore sections of coral on Australia's Great Barrier Reef that were badly affected by mass bleaching events in 2016 and 2017. The same technique has previously proven successful on reefs in the Caribbean, the Indian Ocean, and Southeast Asia, Klein wrote.

A 2018 study published in the journal *Nature Communications* found that across the world's 71,000 kilometers (44,000 miles) of reef coastlines, coral reefs "reduce the annual expected damages from storms by more than $4 billion."[100] A research team at the University of California, Santa Cruz and the University of Cantabria in Spain estimated that coral reefs provide the United States, including the US territory of Puerto Rico, with $94 million in flood protection benefit each year. Reefs, the study's authors concluded, "provide a substantial first line of coastal defense and should be better managed for this benefit."

In June 2018, *USA Today* covered the study that determined the economic value of coral reef conservation,[101] but the corporate media have not done a good job of reporting the latest science on coral reef restoration. A December 2018 *New York Times* article focused on a study led by researchers at James Cook University in Australia, which found that the nation's 2016 heat wave killed many of the Great Barrier Reef's most heat-sensitive corals and "selected for the corals that could handle higher ocean temperatures."[102] The study, the *Times* concluded, "provides a measure of hope that coral reefs may be able to survive as oceans warm over the coming decades." A July 2018 report in the *New York Times*, "Beauty and Bleakness: The Efforts to Conserve Coral Reefs," featured lavish photographs, by Alexis Rosenfeld, of coral reefs and reef restoration efforts around the world. One of Rosenfeld's photographs published by the *Times* depicted restoration workers in diving gear, laying "metal foundations in the Maldives in the hopes that new coral will grow," but made no mention of Reef Ecologic's Great Barrier Reef project.[103] In 2015, the BBC reported on efforts in Indonesia to use electrically-charged metal frames to rejuvenate coral damaged by human activity;[104] and in 2016 the *Smithsonian* featured an extended article on the same Indonesian project.[105]

21.

Court Ruling Provides "Blueprint" to Reform Excessive, Discriminatory Policing in Schools

Mike Males, "California Decision Aims to End Aggressive Policing in Schools," *YES! Magazine*, February 14, 2019, https://www.yesmagazine.org/people-power/california-decision-aims-to-end-aggressive-policing-in-schools-20190214.

David Washburn, "Stockton Unified Settles State Complaint over Discriminatory Policing Practices," EdSource, January 22, 2019, https://edsource.org/2019/stockton-unified-settles-state-complaint-over-discriminatory-policing-practices/607559.

Student Researcher: Vinca Rivera-Perez (College of Marin)

Faculty Evaluator: Susan Rahman (College of Marin)

It is no wonder that school districts feel pressure to protect children. Between January 2015 and March 2019, there were 97 school shootings in 31 states that ended in the deaths of 94 people. Yet in January 2019, a state court in California ordered the Stockton Unified School District to rein in its use of "school resource officers" to protect students. The order was the result of a three-year investigation, conducted by the California Department of Justice, that revealed "widespread abuses" by police in Stockton schools, including "use of excessive force, unconstitutional and 'random and suspicionless' search and seizure procedures using dogs and pat-downs, and frequent arrests targeting even the youngest students," according to *YES! Magazine*. The procedures often resulted in students "being treated like criminals for misconduct typical of schoolchildren, especially those with disabilities," Mike Males reported. He characterized the final judgment, issued by Sacramento's Superior Court, as "unprecedented in strength and scope" and "a blueprint for reforming other districts that suffer from overpolicing."

The California Justice Department's investigation showed the district had turned thousands of minor student misbehaviors—commonplace in any school—into criminal offenses, disproportionately affecting black, Latino, and disabled students. School police overused handcuffs and restraints on students and conducted random and unannounced searches of students' belongings using police dogs, while school officials engaged in searches that violated students' rights to privacy under the Fourth Amendment. In many cases, overreactions by undertrained officers created escalations that led to student arrests.

A May 2015 analysis of state crime statistics by the Center on Juvenile and Criminal Justice revealed that in a district with around 40,000 students—94 percent of whom are people of color—Stockton's school officers had arrested more than 1,800 students on criminal charges in 2012.[106] That included 182 students who were age nine or younger, a rate 37 times higher than all other law enforcement agencies in California.

Analyzing incident reports, Justice Department investigators found that the district and its police systematically discriminated against black and Latino students when referring them to law enforcement and making arrests. As David Washburn reported for EdSource, investigators found that black students aged ten and over were 148 percent more likely to be arrested than other students, while Latino students aged ten and over were 124 percent more likely to be arrested than other students.

A January 1989 shooting at a Stockton elementary school left six people dead and led to the development of the district's use of armed school resource officers, *YES! Magazine* reported. But instead of protecting Stockton campuses from intruders, "these officers quickly turned to criminalizing the district's students." As fears that every school is at risk of a shooting drive demands to arm teachers, Males noted that "school resource officers painted as 'mentors' may seem a reasonable middle ground." However, in practice, school resource officers are often "bullies in blue," as the American Civil Liberties Union concluded in a multistate analysis.[107]

Noting that while the Stockton school district was under state investigation school arrests dropped by 75 percent, *YES! Magazine* described the court's decision as a "major milestone." The court's January 2019 ruling requires the district to establish clear policies and procedures for how and when administrators refer students to law enforcement, to reform use-of-force policies and practices, to ensure that searches or seizures conform with constitutional standards, and to hire a trained disability coordinator at the police department to ensure compliance with disability discrimination laws. It also requires Stockton schools to end officer arrests of students for disciplinary issues that do not constitute "a major threat to school safety."[108] The district will also be required to provide a list of arrested students so that their records can be expunged. The Justice Department will monitor the district for five years to ensure that it complies with the court's requirements.

The California decision to end aggressive policing in Stockton's schools received coverage in local news outlets, but little in the way of national attention.[109] Mike Males's report for *YES! Magazine* was distinctive in highlighting that the court's final 26-page judgment could provide a model for other school districts throughout the country to follow as a way of addressing excessive and often discriminatory policing in schools.

22.

Violence Rises after End of Mandated Monitoring in California's Juvenile Detention Centers

Samantha Michaels, "Use of Force in California State Juvenile Detention Facilities Has Jumped Threefold since Court Monitoring Ended," *Mother Jones*, February 21, 2019, https://www.motherjones.com/crime-justice/2019/02/use-of-force-in-california-state-juvenile-detention-facilities-has-jumped-threefold-since-court-monitoring-ended/.

Student Researchers: Citlali Mendoza, Kyle Slobodnik, Lauren Axberg, Molly Regin, and Nyia Roberts (Sonoma State University)

Faculty Evaluator: Susan Rahman (Sonoma State University)

What has changed in the three years since court-mandated monitoring of California's juvenile detention centers ended? As Samantha Michaels reported for *Mother Jones*, despite some good news—such as an overall decrease in the numbers of incarcerated youth—the situation is still "pretty grim," and violence in the state's juvenile detention centers has worsened significantly since court oversight ended. *Mother Jones*'s coverage was based on a February 2019 report, "Unmet Promises," by the Center on Juvenile and Criminal Justice.[110]

Until 2016, California's Division of Juvenile Justice was under court-mandated monitoring as part of a settlement in a lawsuit that charged the agency for abuse of detainees and failure to provide adequate medical care or rehabilitation. In early 2016, the agency was commended for groundbreaking improvements in its treatment and rehabilitation of juvenile offenders.

Since mandated reporting ended, however, the likelihood of a juvenile being assaulted has increased by 49 percent, according to the

Center on Juvenile and Criminal Justice's report. Similarly, reported use-of-force incidents involving staff that were out of compliance with the agency's policies rose by 45 percent; and staffers sometimes tried to cover up their alleged misbehavior. Furthermore, the number of attempted suicides has risen since mandated monitoring ended, from three between August 2015 and July 2016 to 28 since 2016. Lack of response by staff to detainees' medical needs decreases trust and worsens trauma for youth who, in many cases, already live with the effects of previous trauma.

The California Report, produced by KQED, an NPR-affiliate in San Francisco, also covered the Center on Juvenile and Criminal Justice's report on use of force in California's juvenile detention facilities.[III] Otherwise, establishment media outlets have failed to report this story.

23.

New Programs Make School Food Systems More Equitable

Korsha Wilson, "What School Lunches Have to Do with Fixing Wealth Inequality," *YES! Magazine*, November 13, 2018, https://www.yesmagazine.org/peace-justice/what-school-lunches-have-to-do-with-fixing-wealth-inequality-20181113.

"Nationwide Campaign Calls on Aramark, Compass Group, and Sodexo to Reform Unjust Business Practices, Invest in Real Food," Friends of the Earth, September 4, 2018, https://foe.org/news/nationwide-campaign-calls-aramark-compass-group-sodexo-reform-unjust-business-practices-invest-real-food/.

Lindsay Oberst, "Why School Lunches in America are Unhealthy and 10 Ways You Can Take Action to Improve Them," Food Revolution Network, August 29, 2018, https://foodrevolution.org/blog/school-lunch-in-america/.

Student Researcher: Diana Mayorga (City College of San Francisco)

Faculty Evaluator: Jennifer Levinson (City College of San Francisco)

School lunches are big business. As Korsha Wilson reported for *YES! Magazine* in November 2018, school districts nationwide spend a total of approximately three billion dollars annually on food contracts, most of which are with corporate food suppliers. As Beth Hopping, cofounder of the Food Insight Group, told *YES! Magazine*, "The wealth in the food system is concentrated in the hands of a few and has been extracted at the expense of the earth and people." Now, however, organizations such as the Farm to School Network and Wholesome Wave are working to make the food systems that supply schools more equitable.

New programs not only connect school children with local farms, they also create jobs in the community, and keep money in the community to support on-campus gardens and farm-fresh meals. A study in Georgia found that for every dollar the program spent, two dollars stayed in the state, instead of leaving to be invested in a large food company, *YES! Magazine* reported.

To succeed, however, organizations must adhere to local, state, and federal policies that often serve to benefit large, private food companies. "There's a lot of underground scaffolding that keeps our food systems the way that they are," Hopping told *YES! Magazine*. The goal is to rebuild that system "in a way that works for communities."

To address these challenges, some organizations have created regional farm-to-institution "hubs." These hubs employ trained personnel to clean and process local farm produce, meat, and dairy, which then go to schools, hospitals, and universities. These hubs also increase the community's number of skilled employees.

In 2018 Trump signed the US farm bill, legislation that sets policies for the agricultural industry. New provisions in the bill should make it easier for schools to work with local farms and buy their food locally. The hope is that these provisions will create equity for farms owned by women and people of color, and provide more nourishing food to underserved communities.

In September 2018, a grassroots alliance of ranchers, fishers, farmworkers, students, and environmental advocates, organized as the Community Coalition for Real Meals, called on the nation's three largest food service management companies—Aramark, Compass Group, and Sodexo—to shift from exclusive relationships with Big Food corporations to greater investments in real food that supports producers, communities, and the environment, Friends of the Earth reported. "Even though it flies below the radar screen, the cafeteria industry perpetuates major inequities in the world. But people are waking up," said Anim Steel, director of Real Food Challenge. "These big cafeteria corporations are going to have to make some fundamental changes if they want to satisfy this generation of students who are connecting the dots between their foodservice providers and problems in society."

As of May 2019, the corporate media appear to have entirely

ignored the story of how communities across the United States are working to make school food systems more equitable.

24.

Class Explains Millennials' "Stunted" Economic Lives

Victor Tan Chen, "Adulting While Poor," *Dissent*, Fall 2018, https://www.dissentmagazine.org/article/adulting-while-poor-millenial-homeownership.

Student Researcher: Jordan Watts (University of Vermont)

Faculty Evaluator: Rob Williams (University of Vermont)

While pundits and politicians explain downward mobility among millennials in terms of that generation's unrealistic expectations, indulgent spending, and antipathy toward adulthood, sociologist Victor Tan Chen explained that the Great Recession "stunted millennials' economic lives at a critical age" and that class inequalities—not "lousy values"—best explain many millennials' poor economic prospects. "Thanks in part to the country's widening income gap," Chen wrote, "the picture of 'how millennials are doing' is dramatically different depending on which segment of the population you happen to be looking at."

Defining *class* by income and education, with the working class making less than the median household and not possessing a four-year degree, Chen cited research showing that millennials who lack college degrees are more likely to be renting than those with degrees, and that working-class young adults are less likely to change residences than their better-educated peers.

Chen cited research that found four out of ten Americans in their early twenties get help from their parents to pay living expenses—evidence of what he described as a "private safety net." Young people increasingly depend on their parents' savings to transition into independent adulthood, but class inequalities mean that private safety nets benefit millennials from wealthier families more than millennials from families with lesser means. Pundits' calls for millennials to stop being lazy, dependent, and spineless, Chen wrote, are "tinged by class, whether they acknowledge it or not."

The solutions that Chen proposed focus on public policy. Specifically, Chen pointed to countries—such as Denmark and Sweden—

with social safety nets, including housing subsidies, education benefits, unemployment compensation, universal medical care, and job training programs and apprenticeships. "What distinguishes millennials," Chen concluded, "is how thoroughly their generation has been shaped by America's stark and growing class inequality."

By contrast, establishment news coverage of millennials' economic (mis)fortunes, in outlets such as CNBC and *USA Today*, has omitted class as an explanation for the decreased incomes millennials receive in comparison to their parents, opting instead to speculate about the apparently decreased desirability of home ownership.[112] In February 2017, the *New York Times* reported that "about 40 percent of 22-, 23- and 24-year-olds receive some financial assistance from their parents for living expenses," but the article did not frame millennials' lack of economic mobility in terms of class inequalities.[113]

25.

Google Screenwise: Consenting to Surveillance Capitalism

Sydney Li and Jason Kelley, "Google Screenwise: An Unwise Trade of All Your Privacy for Cash," Electronic Frontier Foundation, February 1, 2019, https://www.eff.org/deeplinks/2019/02/google-screenwise-unwise-trade-all-your-privacy-cash, republished by Common Dreams, February 4, 2019, https://www.commondreams.org/views/2019/02/04/google-screenwise-unwise-trade-all-your-privacy-cash.
Dami Lee, "Google Also Monitored iPhone Usage with a Private App," The Verge, January 30, 2019, https://www.theverge.com/2019/1/30/18204064/apple-google-monitoring-phone-usage-screenwise-meter.

Student Researcher: Fabrice Nozier (Drew University)

Faculty Evaluator: Lisa Lynch (Drew University)

Google has further blurred the lines between market research and corporate invasion of privacy with the introduction of Google Opinion Rewards, a survey app for Android and iOS users that allows them to earn "rewards." In exchange, Google gets access to the phone screens and web browser windows of the app's users. Rather than fooling regular users into acceding to secretive corporate "research" behind lengthy terms and conditions or hidden app permissions, Google disguises the overseeing function of Opinion Rewards as "metering"—a "funny word for surveillance," Sydney Li and Jason Kelley of the Electronic Frontier Foundation (EFF) reported.

The app's users earn from ten cents to $1.00 per survey, or an estimated $50–100 per year. Dozens of third-party blog posts and YouTube videos targeted at Opinion Rewards users share the best ways to earn quick money in large sums from the program. The questionable ethics behind Opinion Rewards, however, does not lie in the legitimacy of the program's payments, as users are "rewarded" through the trusted online company PayPal, but in the exchange that Google offers.

Opinion Rewards is segmented into two services, "Surveys App" and "Audience Measurement." The first is an app, available for download on both the Google Play Store and the App Store, that encourages users to complete surveys ranging "from opinion polls, to hotel reviews, to merchant satisfaction surveys."[114] The second, more dystopian option requires registered households to install the Screenwise mobile app and web extension which monitors internet usage. Google also encourages, but does not require, the installation of their "TV Meter," which monitors television usage through a built-in mic and an Opinion Rewards router and further tracks internet usage.

In January 2019, Google disabled the iOS version of the app because it violated Apple's distribution policies; but Google Opinion Rewards continues to be available to Android users, who have installed it more than ten million times as of July 2019, according to Google Play.[115]

Although it has been widely reported that corporate giants such as Google and Facebook seek to track our every move, listen to our conversations, access our smartphones' cameras, and even collect our Social Security numbers without our permission, Google's Opinion Rewards marks a change in corporate surveillance, with responsibility for opting-in shifted onto the surveilled users in exchange for 20-dollar gift cards and other "rewards."

In February 2019, the *New York Times* published an editorial that reported on Google and Facebook paying people to download apps that track their phone activity and usage habits, and called for the Federal Trade Commission to "become the privacy watchdog that this era so desperately needs" and urged new laws to "lay down basic guarantees of privacy that won't require you to wade through hundreds of thousands of words of legalese."[116] Apart from the *Times*'s editorial, the corporate media has neglected to cover how Google's push to "meter" the market contributes to mass surveillance.

Notes

1. Walter Lippmann, *Liberty and the News* (Princeton, New Jersey: Princeton University Press, 2008 [first published in 1920]), 7.
2. Ibid., 6, 2; see also 37.
3. Ibid., 6.
4. Ibid.
5. Ibid., 42–43.
6. Ibid., 59.
7. For more specific detail on the review process that Project Censored undertakes to reach this judgment, see the "Note on Research and Evaluation of *Censored* News Stories," below.
8. When those who control the news "arrogate to themselves the right to determine by their own consciences what shall be reported and for what purpose, democracy is unworkable," Lippmann wrote. "Public opinion is blockaded." Ibid., 6.
9. Ibid., 28.
10. Andy Lee Roth, comp. and ed., Introduction to "The Top *Censored* Stories and Media Analysis of 2016–17," in *Censored 2018: Press Freedoms in a "Post-Truth" World*, eds. Andy Lee Roth and Mickey Huff with Project Censored (New York: Seven Stories Press, 2017), 31–37, 33; and Andy Lee Roth, comp. and ed., Introduction to "The Top *Censored* Stories and Media Analysis of 2017–18," in *Censored 2019: Fighting the Fake News Invasion*, eds. Mickey Huff and Andy Lee Roth with Project Censored (New York: Seven Stories Press, 2018), 37–40, 39.

11. Lippmann, *Liberty and the News*, 34.

12. Reflecting on the effectiveness of US propaganda in promoting public support for the country's entry into World War I, Lippmann quoted with approval Frank I. Cobb, editor of the crusading New York *World*, who observed that millions of Americans "were willing to die for their country, but not willing to think for it." Cobb, quoted in Lippmann, *Liberty and the News*, 4.

13. Lippmann, *Liberty and the News*, 38.

14. Ibid., 53.

15. For information on how to nominate a story, see "How to Support Project Censored" at the back of this volume.

16. Validated Independent News stories are archived on the Project Censored website at https://www.projectcensored.org/category/validated-independent-news.

17. For a complete list of the Project's judges and their brief biographies, see the acknowledgments at the back of this volume.

18. "As Leak Investigations Surge, Our New Lawsuit Seeks the Trump Admin's Guidelines on Surveillance of Journalists," Freedom of the Press Foundation, November 29, 2017, https://freedom.press/news/lawsuit-seeks-government-guidelines-surveillance-journalists-leak-investigations-surge/.

19. Jack Stubbs and Ginger Gibson, "Russia's RT America Registers as 'Foreign Agent' in U.S.," Reuters, November 13, 2017, https://www.reuters.com/article/us-russia-usa-media-restrictions-rt/russias-rt-america-registers-as-foreign-agent-in-u-s-idUSKBN1DD25B.

20. On the use of national security letters, see Cora Currier, "Secret Rules Make It Pretty Easy for the FBI to Spy on Journalists," The Intercept, January 31, 2017, https://theintercept.com/2017/01/31/secret-rules-make-it-pretty-easy-for-the-fbi-to-spy-on-journalists-2/.

21. See, for example, John Fritze, "Trump Calls for Release of Classified Documents Tied to Russia Probe in Fox News Interview," *USA Today*, March 27, 2019, updated March 28, 2019, https://www.usatoday.com/story/news/politics/2019/03/27/donald-trump-release-classified-docs-tied-start-russia-probe/3295161002/; Liam Brennan, "The Truth about 'Spying' on the Trump Campaign," *New York Times*, May 3, 2019, https://www.nytimes.com/2019/05/03/opinion/trump-campaign-spying-fbi-russia-.html; and John Solomon, "Steele's Stunning Pre-FISA Confession: Informant Needed to Air Trump Dirt before Election," The Hill, May 7, 2019, https://thehill.com/opinion/white-house/442592-steeles-stunning-pre-fisa-confession-informant-needed-to-air-trump-dirt.

22. Matthew Rosenberg and Matt Apuzzo, "Court Approved Wiretap on Trump Campaign Aide over Russia Ties," *New York Times*, April 12, 2017, https://www.nytimes.com/2017/04/12/us/politics/carter-page-fisa-warrant-russia-trump.html. Subsequent coverage, by CNN, reported that Page "had been the subject of a secret intelligence surveillance warrant since 2014," according to unnamed US officials. See Evan Perez, Pamela Brown, and Shimon Prokupecz, "One Year into the FBI's Russia Investigation, Mueller is on the Trump Money Trail," CNN, August 4, 2017, https://www.cnn.com/2017/08/03/politics/mueller-investigation-russia-trump-one-year-financial-ties/index.html.

23. Quoted in Elliott Gabriel, "Facebook Partners with Hawkish Atlantic Council, a NATO Lobby Group, to 'Protect Democracy,'" MintPress News, May 22, 2018, https://www.mintpressnews.com/facebook-partners-hawkish-atlantic-council-nato-lobby-group-protect-democracy/242289/.

24. Quoted in Kevin Reed, "Facebook's Partnership with the Atlantic Council," World Socialist Web Site, September 8, 2018, https://www.wsws.org/en/articles/2018/09/08/atla-s08.html.

25. Eric Lipton, Brooke Williams, and Nicholas Confessore, "Foreign Powers Buy Influence at Think Tanks," *New York Times*, September 6, 2014, https://www.nytimes.com/2014/09/07/us/politics/foreign-powers-buy-influence-at-think-tanks.html.

26. For the impact of Facebook's policies on Slate, see Will Oremus, "The Great Facebook Crash," Slate, June 27, 2018, https://slate.com/technology/2018/06/facebooks-retreat-from-the-news-has-painful-for-publishers-including-slate.html; see also Monika Bauerlein and Clara Jeffery, "How Facebook Screwed Us All," *Mother Jones*, March/April 2019, https://www.motherjones.com/politics/2019/02/how-facebook-screwed-us-all/.

27. For a summary of criticism of PropOrNot, see Lloyd Grove, "Washington Post on the 'Fake News' Hot Seat," Daily Beast, December 9, 2016, updated April 13, 2017, https://www.thedailybeast.com/washington-post-on-the-fake-news-hot-seat; on the *Washington Post*'s subsequent efforts to distance itself from PropOrNot, see Andrew Beaujon, "Washington Post Appends Editor's Note to Russian Propaganda Story," *Washingtonian*, December 7, 2016, https://www.washingtonian.com/2016/12/07/washington-post-appends-editors-note-russian-propaganda-story/.

28. Joseph Menn, "Facebook Expands Fake Election News Fight, but Falsehoods Still Rampant," Reuters, September 19, 2018, https://www.reuters.com/article/us-facebook-elections/facebook-expands-fake-election-news-fight-but-falsehoods-still-rampant-idUSKCN1LZ2XY.

29. Donie O'Sullivan, Drew Griffin, Curt Devine, and Atika Shubert, "Russia is Backing a Viral Video Company Aimed at American Millennials," CNN, February 18, 2019, https://www.cnn.com/2019/02/15/tech/russia-facebook-viral-videos/index.html.

30. Ibid. On Nimmo's questionable record as a reliable source, see Jeb Sprague and Max Blumenthal, "Facebook Censorship of Alternative Media 'Just the Beginning,' Says Top Neocon Insider," MintPress News, October 24, 2018, https://www.mintpressnews.com/facebook-censorship-of-alternative-media-just-the-beginning-says-top-neocon-insider/250967/. Sprague and Blumenthal noted that Nimmo "embarked on an embarrassing witch hunt this year that saw him misidentify several living, breathing individuals as Russian bots or Kremlin 'influence accounts.' Nimmo's victims included Mariam Susli, a well-known Syrian-Australian social media personality, the famed Ukrainian concert pianist Valentina Lisitsa, and a British pensioner named Ian Shilling."

31. Coordinator of the Indigenous Organizations of the Amazon River Basin (COICA), "From Amazon Leaders to World Leaders: We Call for an Ambitious Post-2020 Agreement that Heals Our Mother Earth," Common Dreams, November 21, 2018, https://www.commondreams.org/newswire/2018/11/21/amazon-leaders-world-leaders-we-call-ambitious-post-2020-agreement-heals-our.

32. Ernesto Londoño, "Jair Bolsonaro, on Day 1, Undermines Indigenous Brazilians' Rights," *New York Times*, January 2, 2019, https://www.nytimes.com/2019/01/02/world/americas/brazil-bolsonaro-president-indigenous-lands.html.

33. Carol Giacomo, "Brazil's New President Threatens 'the Lungs of the Planet,'" *New York Times*, March 19, 2019, https://www.nytimes.com/2019/03/19/opinion/brazil-rain-forest.html.

34. Kelly Trout and Lorne Stockman, "Drilling Towards Disaster: Why U.S. Oil and Gas Expansion is Incompatible with Climate Limits," Oil Change International, January 2019, http://priceofoil.org/content/uploads/2019/01/Drilling-Towards-Disaster-Web-v3.pdf.

35. Mose Buchele, "Report Says Texas' Oil and Gas Boom Could Spell Climate 'Disaster,'" KUT (NPR, Austin, TX), January 17, 2019, https://www.kut.org/post/report-says-texas-oil-and-gas-boom-could-spell-climate-disaster; Justin Mikulka, "The Fracking Industry's Flaring Problem May be Worse Than We Thought," DeSmogBlog, January 29, 2019, https://www.desmogblog.com/2019/01/29/fracking-industry-gas-flaring-problem; and Andrea Germanos, "Climate Crisis be Damned, 'Shale Revolution' Poised to Make US Net Exporter of Oil in Three Years," Common Dreams, March 11, 2019, https://www.commondreams.org/news/2019/03/11/climate-crisis-be-damned-shale-revolution-poised-make-us-net-exporter-oil-three.

36. E.g., Brad Plumer, "How Big a Deal is Trump's Fuel Economy Rollback? For the Climate, Maybe the Biggest Yet," *New York Times*, August 3, 2018, https://www.nytimes.com/2018/08/03/climate/trump-climate-emissions-rollback.html; Tony Barboza, "Rolling Back Fuel Economy Standards Could Mean Bigger Cars—and Less Progress on Climate Change," *Los Angeles Times*, April 6, 2018, https://www.latimes.com/local/lanow/la-me-fuel-economy-impacts-20180406-story.html.

37. Plumer, "How Big a Deal is Trump's Fuel Economy Rollback?"

38. "The Global Slavery Index 2018," Walk Free Foundation, July 2018, 180, https://downloads.globalslaveryindex.org/ephemeral/GSI-2018_FNL_180907_Digital-small-p-1562169871.pdf.

39. "Country Studies: United States," Global Slavery Index 2018, July 2018, https://www.globalslaveryindex.org/2018/findings/country-studies/united-states/.

40. Ibid.

41. Ibid.

42. Anne T. Gallagher, "What's Wrong with the Global Slavery Index?" *Anti-Trafficking Review*, No. 8 (April 2017), 90–112, http://www.antitraffickingreview.org/index.php/atrjournal/article/view/228/216.

43. Satoshi Sugiyama, "Report Finds Surprisingly High Rate of Slavery in Developed Countries," *New York Times*, July 19, 2018, https://www.nytimes.com/2018/07/19/world/modern-slavery-report.html; Mark Tutton, "Modern Slavery in Developed Countries More Common Than Thought," CNN, July 19, 2018, https://www.cnn.com/2018/07/19/world/global-slavery-index-2018/index.html; and Kate Gibson, "'Modern Slavery' Ensnares Estimated 400,000 Americans," CBS News, August 3, 2018, https://www.cbsnews.com/news/modern-slavery-ensnares-an-estimated-400000-americans/.

44. Ewelina U. Ochab, "The Transatlantic Slave Trade and the Modern Day Slavery," *Forbes*, March 23, 2019, https://www.forbes.com/sites/ewelinaochab/2019/03/23/the-transatlantic-slave-trade-and-the-modern-day-slavery/#5144db912e55.

45. Mallory Gafas and Tina Burnside, "Cyntoia Brown is Granted Clemency after Serving 15 Years in Prison for Killing Man Who Bought Her for Sex," CNN, January 8, 2019, https://www.cnn.com/2019/01/07/us/tennessee-cyntoia-brown-granted-clemency/index.html.

46. "Human Trafficking Cases Hit a 13-Year Record High, New UN Report Shows," UN News, January 29, 2019, https://news.un.org/en/story/2019/01/1031552.

47. See, e.g., Christine Hauser, "Cyntoia Brown is Granted Clemency after 15 Years in Prison," *New York Times*, January 7, 2019, https://www.nytimes.com/2019/01/07/us/cyntoia-brown-clemency-granted.html; Gafas and Burnside, "Cyntoia Brown is Granted Clemency"; Lisa Respers France, "Celebs Celebrate Cyntoia Brown Clemency Decision," CNN, January 8, 2019, https://www.cnn.com/2019/01/08/entertainment/celebs-cyntoia-brown/index.html.

48. Christine Hauser, "Cyntoia Brown Inspires a Push for Juvenile Criminal Justice Reform in Tennessee," *New York Times*, January 17, 2019, https://www.nytimes.com/2019/01/17/us/cyntoia-brown-tennessee-criminal-justice.html.

49. Natelegé Whaley, "Cyntoia Brown Has Been Granted Clemency. But What's Next for Others Like Her?" NBC News, January 9, 2019, https://www.nbcnews.com/news/nbcblk/cyntoia-brown-has-been-granted-clemency-what-s-next-others-n956866.

50. Andrea Powell, "Cyntoia Brown's Clemency Must Begin a #MeToo Movement for Unacknowledged Sex Trafficking Survivors," THINK (NBC News), January 8, 2019, https://www.nbcnews.com/think/opinion/cyntoia-brown-s-clemency-must-begin-metoo-movement-unacknowledged-sex-ncna956101.

51. "Arizona Shelter Shut in Latest Case of Alleged Migrant Child Abuse," CBS News, October 10, 2018, https://www.cbsnews.com/news/arizona-shelter-shut-in-latest-case-of-alleged-migrant-child-abuse/; Matthew Haag, "Thousands of Immigrant Children Said They were Sexually Abused in U.S. Detention Centers, Report Says," *New York Times*, February 27, 2019, https://www.nytimes.com/2019/02/27/us/immigrant-children-sexual-abuse.html.

52. Michael Grabell and Topher Sanders, "Immigrant Youth Shelters: 'If You're a Predator, It's a Gold Mine,'" *USA Today*, July 27, 2018, https://www.usatoday.com/story/news/nation/2018/07/27/immigrant-children-detention-crime/853470002/.

53. The Editorial Board, "How My Stillbirth Became a Crime," Part 7 of "A Woman's Rights," *New York Times*, December 28, 2018, https://www.nytimes.com/interactive/2018/12/28/opinion/stillborn-murder-charge.html.

54. Jessica Mason Pieklo, "Murder Charges Dismissed in Mississippi Stillbirth Case," Rewire. News, April 4, 2014, https://rewire.news/article/2014/04/04/murder-charges-dismissed-mississippi-stillbirth-case/.

55. Molly Redden, "Jailed for Ending a Pregnancy: How Prosecutors Get Inventive on Abortion," *The Guardian*, November 22, 2016, https://www.theguardian.com/us-news/2016/nov/22/abortion-pregnancy-law-prosecute-trump.

56. The Editorial Board, "A Woman's Rights," *New York Times*, December 28, 2018, https://www.nytimes.com/interactive/2018/12/28/opinion/pregnancy-women-pro-life-abortion.html.

57. "2018 Access to Medicine Index," Access to Medicine Foundation, November 20, 2018, https://www.accesstomedicineindex.org/publications/2018-access-to-medicine-index.

58. Ibid., 10.

59. Ibid., 9.

60. "Goldman Sachs & UBS to Co-Host Investor Launches of 2018 Access to Medicine Index," Access to Medicine Foundation, November 5, 2018, https://accesstomedicinefoundation.org/news/goldman-sachs-ubs-to-co-host-investor-launches-of-2018-access-to-medicine-index.

61. "UBS Asset Management: 90th Investor to Endorse the Access to Medicine Index," Access to Medicine Foundation, April 19, 2019, https://accesstomedicinefoundation.org/news/ubs-asset-management-90th-investor-to-endorse-the-access-to-medicine-index.

62. Ben Hirschler, "Big Pharma Leaves Big Gaps: Drugmakers Urged to Do More for Poor," Reuters, November 20, 2018, https://www.reuters.com/article/us-health-pharmaceuticals-poor/big-pharma-leaves-big-gaps-drugmakers-urged-to-do-more-for-poor-idUSKCN1NP1FS.

63. Molly Renaud, Rostyslav Korolov, David Mendonça, and William Wallace, "Social Network Structure as a Predictor of Social Behavior: The Case of Protest in the 2016 US Presidential Election," *Recent Developments in Data Science and Intelligent Analysis of Information* (XVIII International Conference on Data Science and Intelligent Analysis of Information), August 5, 2018, 267–78, https://link.springer.com/chapter/10.1007/978-3-319-97885-7_27.

64. "Homeland Defense," Joint Publication 3-27, Joint Chiefs of Staff, April 10, 2018, https://fas.org/irp/doddir/dod/jp3_27.pdf.

65. *United States of America v. Robert Paul Rundo, Robert Boman, Tyler Laube, and Aaron Eason*, United States District Court, Central District of California, October 20, 2018, https://int.nyt.com/data/documenthelper/421-robert-rundo-complaint/0f1e76cdeef814133f24/optimized/full.pdf.

66. Conor Finnegan, "US Announces Sale of Anti-Tank Missiles to Ukraine over Russian Opposition," ABC News, March 1, 2018, https://abcnews.go.com/International/us-announces-sale-anti-tank-missiles-ukraine-russian/story?id=53450406.

67. Christian Picciolini, "'Breaking Hate' Extreme Groups at Home and Abroad," *Breaking Hate*, MSNBC, May 10, 2019, https://www.msnbc.com/msnbc-originals/watch/-breaking-hate-extreme-groups-at-home-and-abroad-59379781503.

68. For Project Censored's previous coverage of these findings, see John Michael Dulalas, Bethany Surface, Kamila Janik, Shannon Cowley, Kenn Burrows, and Rob Williams, "How Big Wireless Convinced Us Cell Phones and Wi-Fi are Safe," in *Censored 2019: Fighting the Fake News Invasion*, eds. Mickey Huff and Andy Lee Roth with Project Censored (New York: Seven Stories, 2018), 48–52, https://www.projectcensored.org/4-how-big-wireless-convinced-us-cell-phones-and-wi-fi-are-safe/; and Julian Klein, Casey Lewis, Kenn Burrows, and Peter Phillips, "Accumulating Evidence of Ongoing Wireless Technology Health Hazards," in *Censored 2015: Inspiring We the People*, eds. Andy Lee Roth and Mickey Huff with Project Censored (New York: Seven Stories Press, 2014), 62–64, https://www.projectcensored.org/14-accumulating-evidence-ongoing-wireless-technology-health-hazards/.

69. Yael Stein, "Letter to the FCC from Dr. Yael Stein MD in Opposition to 5G Spectrum Frontiers," Environmental Health Trust, July 9, 2016, https://ehtrust.org/letter-fcc-dr-yael-stein-md-opposition-5g-spectrum-frontiers/.

70. "5G Service is Coming—and so are Health Concerns over the Towers that Support It," CBS News, May 29, 2018, https://www.cbsnews.com/news/5g-network-cell-towers-raise-health-concerns-for-some-residents/.

71. Debra Goldschmidt and Jacqueline Howard, "Federal Health Agencies Disagree over Link between Cell Phone Radiation and Cancer," CNN, November 1, 2018, https://www.cnn.com/2018/11/01/health/cell-phone-radiation-cancer-nih-fda/index.html.

72. Brian Fung, "The Race to 5G Wireless Tech is On. A Report Finds Americans May Have an Early Lead," *Washington Post*, February 19, 2019, https://www.washingtonpost.com/technology/2019/02/19/race-g-wireless-tech-is-report-finds-americans-have-an-early-lead/.

73. Sarah Brickman, Ben Crair, and Lucia von Reusner, "Flunking the Planet: Scoring America's Food Companies on Sustainable Meat," Mighty Earth, August 2018, http://www.mightyearth.

org/wp-content/uploads/2018/08/Flunking-the-Planet-Americas-Leading-Food-Companies-Fail-on-Sustainable-Meat.pdf.

74. "Flunking the Planet: America's Leading Food Companies Fail on Sustainable Meat," Mighty Earth, undated [August 2018], http://www.mightyearth.org/meat-scorecard.

75. See K.J. Van Meter, P. Van Cappellen, and N.B. Basu, "Legacy Nitrogen May Prevent Achievement of Water Quality Goals in the Gulf of Mexico," *Science*, Vol. 360 No. 6387 (April 27, 2018), 427–30.

76. Brickman, Crair, and von Reusner, "Flunking the Planet," 4, 18.

77. "Gulf of Mexico Dead Zone is 'Largest' Ever Recorded in U.S.," CBS News, August 16, 2017, https://www.cbsnews.com/news/gulf-of-mexico-largest-dead-zone-ever-measured-fertilizer/.

78. Jenna Gallegos, "The Gulf of Mexico Dead Zone is Larger Than Ever. Here's What to Do about It," *Washington Post*, August 4, 2017, https://www.washingtonpost.com/news/energy-environment/wp/2017/08/04/gulf-of-mexico-dead-zone-is-larger-than-ever-heres-what-to-do-about-it/.

79. Casey Smith, "New Jersey-Size 'Dead Zone' is Largest Ever in Gulf of Mexico," *National Geographic*, August 2, 2017, https://news.nationalgeographic.com/2017/08/gulf-mexico-hypoxia-water-quality-dead-zone/.

80. Paul Lewis and Adam Federman, "Revealed: FBI Violated Its Own Rules while Spying on Keystone XL Opponents," *The Guardian*, May 12, 2015, https://www.theguardian.com/us-news/2015/may/12/revealed-fbi-spied-keystone-xl-opponents.

81. Adam Federman, "Kinder Morgan Paid Pennsylvania Police Department to 'Deter Protests,'" *Earth Island Journal*, May 21, 2015, http://www.earthisland.org/journal/index.php/articles/entry/kinder_morgan_paid_pennsylvania_police_department_to_deter_protests/.

82. Ibid.

83. See Ryan Shannon, "Lawsuit Targets Zinke's Secretive Program Undermining Wildlife Protection," Center for Biological Diversity, November 8, 2018, https://www.biologicaldiversity.org/news/press_releases/2018/endangered-species-11-08-2018.php.

84. Doyle Rice, "25 Species, Including Pacific Walrus, Denied Endangered Protection by Trump Administration," *USA Today*, October 4, 2017, updated October 5, 2017, https://www.usatoday.com/story/tech/science/2017/10/04/trump-administration-denies-endangered-species-protection-pacific-walrus-and-two-dozen-oth-25-specie/732704001/; Dan Joling, "As Sea Ice Melts, Some Say Walruses Need to be Protected as Threatened Species," *Chicago Tribune*, October 13, 2018, https://www.chicagotribune.com/news/nationworld/science/ct-sea-ice-melts-walrus-protection-20181013-story.html; Simon Worrall, "'Extreme Conservation' in the Most Hostile Places on Earth," *National Geographic*, September 28, 2018, https://www.nationalgeographic.com/environment/2018/09/arctic-conservation-species-climate-change-warming-book-talk/; Amelia Urry, "The Fate of Future Endangered Species Could Hinge on a Semantic Argument," *Popular Science*, July 30, 2018, https://www.popsci.com/endangered-species-act-future-walruses.

85. Oliver Milman, "Walruses Face 'Death Sentence' as Trump Administration Fails to List Them as Endangered," *The Guardian*, October 4, 2017, https://www.theguardian.com/us-news/2017/oct/04/walrus-endangered-species-trump-administration.

86. Darryl Fears, "Plan Strips Endangered Species Act of Key Provisions," *Washington Post*, July 20, 2018, A14; published online as "Endangered Species Act Stripped of Key Provisions in Trump Administration Proposal" on July 19, 2018, at https://www.washingtonpost.com/news/animalia/wp/2018/07/19/endangered-species-act-stripped-of-key-provisions-in-trump-administration-proposal/.

87. David Bernhardt, "The Greatest Good for Endangered Species," *Washington Post*, August 10, 2018, A17; published online as "At Interior, We're Ready to Bring the Endangered Species Act Up to Date" on August 9, 2018, at https://www.washingtonpost.com/opinions/at-interior-were-ready-to-bring-the-endangered-species-act-up-to-date/2018/08/09/2775cd8e-9a96-11e8-b55e-5002300ef004_story.html.

88. See Hannah Rider, "David Bernhardt's War on Wildlife," Westwise (Medium), March 29, 2019, https://medium.com/westwise/david-bernhardts-war-on-wildlife-10586ocfef2b.

89. Darryl Fears, "A 14-Year-Long Oil Spill in the Gulf of Mexico Verges on Becoming One of the Worst in U.S. History," *Washington Post*, October 21, 2018, https://www.washingtonpost.com/national/health-science/a-14-year-long-oil-spill-in-the-gulf-of-mexico-verges-on-becoming-one-of-the-worst-in-us-history/2018/10/20/f9a66fd0-9045-11e8-bcd5-9d911c784c38_story.html; A.J. Willingham, "An Oil Spill You've Never Heard of Could Become One of the Biggest Environmental Disasters in the US," CNN, October 24, 2018, https://www.cnn.com/2018/10/23/us/taylor-energy-oil-largest-spill-disaster-ivan-golf-of-mexico-environment-trnd/index.html; Daniel Moritz-Rabson, "14-Year-Long Oil Spill in Gulf Coast Likely to Become Worst in U.S. History," *Newsweek*, October 22, 2018, https://www.newsweek.com/14-year-oil-spill-become-worst-us-history-1181872.

90. Lucius Couloute and Daniel Kopf, "Out of Prison & Out of Work: Unemployment among Formerly Incarcerated People," Prison Policy Initiative, July 2018, https://www.prisonpolicy.org/reports/outofwork.html.

91. See, for example, The Editorial Board, "No One Benefits When Formerly Incarcerated People Can't Get a Job," *Orange County Register*, July 16, 2018, https://www.ocregister.com/2018/07/16/no-one-benefits-when-formerly-incarcerated-people-cant-get-a-job/.

92. Chandra Bozelko and Ryan Lo, "As Prison Strikes Heat Up, Former Inmates Talk about Horrible State of Labor and Incarceration," *USA Today*, August 25, 2018, https://www.usatoday.com/story/opinion/policing/spotlight/2018/08/25/nationwide-prison-strikes-labor-inmates-policing-usa/1085896002/.

93. Johnny Taylor, "How Businesses Can Help Reduce Recidivism," CNN, March 20, 2018, https://www.cnn.com/2018/03/20/opinions/businesses-can-reduce-recidivism-opinion-taylor/index.html.

94. Ibid. The CNN article attributed the 60 percent figure to a 2002 study sponsored by the Institute for Research on Poverty, based on survey data collected between 1992 and 1994.

95. "Journey to Extremism in Africa: Drivers, Incentives and the Tipping Point for Recruitment," United Nations Development Programme, 2017, http://journey-to-extremism.undp.org/en/reports.

96. Charlotte Alfred, "Why People Join Nigeria's Boko Haram," HuffPost, April 16, 2016, updated January 7, 2017, https://www.huffpost.com/entry/boko-haram-recruitment-tactics_n_571265afe4b06f35cb6fc595.

97. Hilary Matfess, "Here's Why So Many People Join Boko Haram, Despite Its Notorious Violence," *Washington Post*, April 26, 2016, http://www.washingtonpost.com/news/monkey-cage/wp/2016/04/26/heres-why-so-many-people-join-boko-haram-despite-its-notorious-violence/.

98. See, e.g., "West Africa: The Plights of a Forgotten Crisis," Oxfam International, undated, https://www.oxfam.org/en/west-africa-plights-forgotten-crisis [accessed May 2, 2019].

99. Asa Winstanley, "Meet the Spies Injecting Israeli Propaganda into Your News Feed," Electronic Intifada, January 24, 2018, https://electronicintifada.net/blogs/asa-winstanley/meet-spies-injecting-israeli-propaganda-your-news-feed.

100. Michael W. Beck, Iñigo J. Losada, Pelayo Menéndez, Borja G. Reguero, Pedro Díaz-Simal, and Felipe Fernández, "The Global Flood Protection Savings Provided by Coral Reefs," *Nature Communications*, Vol. 9, Article no. 2186 (2018), June 12, 2018, https://www.nature.com/articles/s41467-018-04568-z.

101. Doyle Rice, "Coral Reefs Save Billions of Dollars Worldwide by Preventing Floods," *USA Today*, June 12, 2018, https://www.usatoday.com/story/news/world/2018/06/12/coral-reefs-save-billions-dollars-worldwide-preventing-floods/695056002/.

102. Kendra Pierre-Louis, "Scientists Find Some Hope for Coral Reefs: The Strong May Survive," *New York Times*, December 10, 2018, https://www.nytimes.com/2018/12/10/climate/coral-reefs-natural-selection.html.

103. Ania Bartkowiak, "Beauty and Bleakness: The Efforts to Conserve Coral Reefs," *New York Times*, June 20, 2018, https://www.nytimes.com/2018/07/20/lens/beauty-and-bleakness-the-efforts-to-conserve-coral-reefs.html.

104. Katie Silver, "Could Electric Biorocks Save Coral Reefs?" BBC, May 7, 2015, http://www.bbc.com/future/story/20150506-why-we-should-electrify-the-ocean.

105. Steve Baragona, "This Coral Restoration Technique is 'Electrifying' a Balinese Village," *Smithsonian*, May 25, 2016, https://www.smithsonianmag.com/science-nature/coral-restoration-technique-electrifying-balinese-village-180959206/.

106. Michael Males, "Stockton, San Bernardino School District Officers Have Arrested over 90,000 Youths," Center on Juvenile and Criminal Justice, May 2015, http://www.cjcj.org/uploads/cjcj/documents/final_childcrime-stockton_supplement.pdf.

107. Megan French-Marcelin and Sarah Hinger, "Bullies in Blue: The Origins and Consequences of School Policing," American Civil Liberties Union, April 2017, https://www.aclu.org/report/bullies-blue-origins-and-consequences-school-policing.

108. [Proposed] Final Judgment, *The People of the State of California, ex. rel. Xavier Becerra, Attorney General of the State of California v. Stockton Unified School District*, Superior Court of the State of California, County of Sacramento, undated, marked received January 18, 2019, online at the Office of the Attorney General, State of California Department of Justice, at https://oag.ca.gov/system/files/attachments/press-docs/filed-proposed-final-judgment.pdf.

109. See, for example, Sawsan Morrar, "Stockton Schools Reach Settlement with State over Discrimination Allegations," *Sacramento Bee*, January 24, 2019, https://www.sacbee.com/news/local/education/article224973715.html.

110. Maureen Washburn and Renee Menart, "Unmet Promises: Continued Violence & Neglect in California's Division of Juvenile Justice," Center on Juvenile and Criminal Justice, February 2019, http://www.cjcj.org/uploads/cjcj/documents/unmet_promises_continued_violence_and_neglect_in_california_division_of_juvenile_justice.pdf.

111. Marisa Lagos, "State Juvenile Justice Facilities are Failing Kids, Report Finds," *The California Report*, KQED (San Francisco), February 19, 2019, https://www.kqed.org/news/11727255/state-juvenile-justice-facilities-are-failing-kids-report-finds.

112. "Millennials are Falling Behind Their Boomer Parents," CNBC, January 13, 2017, https://www.cnbc.com/2017/01/13/millennials-are-falling-behind-their-boomer-parents.html; "Millennials Earn 20% Less Than Boomers Did at Same Stage of Life," *USA Today*, January 13, 2017, https://www.usatoday.com/story/money/2017/01/13/millennials-falling-behind-boomer-parents/96530338/.

113. Quoctrung Bui, "A Secret of Many Urban 20-Somethings: Their Parents Help with the Rent," *New York Times*, February 9, 2017, https://www.nytimes.com/2017/02/09/upshot/a-secret-of-many-urban-20-somethings-their-parents-help-with-the-rent.html.

114. "Google Opinion Rewards," Google, undated, https://surveys.google.com/google-opinion-rewards/ [accessed June 29, 2019].

115. Dami Lee, "Google Disables App that Monitored iPhone Usage in Violation of Apple's Rules," The Verge, January 30, 2019, https://www.theverge.com/2019/1/30/18204350/google-screen-wise-app-ios-apple-violation; "Google Opinion Rewards," Google Play, July 8, 2019, https://play.google.com/store/apps/details?id=com.google.android.apps.paidtasks.

116. The Editorial Board, "How Silicon Valley Puts the 'Con' in Consent," *New York Times*, February 2, 2019, https://www.nytimes.com/2019/02/02/opinion/internet-facebook-google-consent.html.

CHAPTER 2

"Curiouser and Curiouser"
A Mad Hatter's Tea Party of
Junk Food News in 2018–2019[1]

Izzy Snow and Susan Rahman, with William Cohen,
James Giusti, Brandon Grayson, Grace Kyle, Shania
Martin, Juweria Mehtar, Mariya Mulla, Carla Naylor,
Melissa Reed, Vinca Rivera-Perez, Aria Schwartz,
Lakhvir Singh, and Haley Skinner

When logic and proportion have fallen sloppy dead
And the white knight is talking backwards
And the red queen's off with her head
Remember what the dormouse said
Feed your head, feed your head

—Grace Wing Slick[2]

Entertainment news is akin to the little white rabbit, whose eye-catching appearance intrigues consumers, guiding them to an escapist realm far from the conflict-focused headlines of corporate media. However, once we tumble down the rabbit hole of BuzzFeed's "Best Lewks from the Barr Testimony," or the E! channel's investigative reports on the latest Kardashian rancor, we find ourselves in a tizzy, jostled by empty-calorie nonsense. Project Censored founder Carl Jensen coined the term "Junk Food News" back in 1983 to describe the rise in trite sensationalist stories that consumed the major news media. These were news-less news stories that often crowded out the kind of investigative journalism required to maintain a healthy democracy. Thanks to Jensen, the news equivalent of late-night bingeing a bag of Oreo Minis finally had a name. Project

Censored has covered the Junk Food News phenomenon ever since and charted its unfortunately meteoric rise.

In recent years, Junk Food News has taken a darker turn down the rabbit hole, absent from the light of morality and further blundering into the unknown blackness of deceit, lies, and farcical reporters talking backwards. During the 2018–2019 news cycle, logic and proportion fell sloppy dead, torn apart by headlines that spread disinformation, propaganda, and utter nonsense. In this last year we as consumers have ended up in Wonderland, and who knows what we will find. Maybe that's the Cheshire Cat beaming down from the trees, or perhaps it is South Carolina Senator Lindsey Graham giggling at passersby. Perhaps we will run into Tweedledum and Tweedledee, or maybe we'll just discover House Speaker Nancy Pelosi and President Trump in matching striped T-shirts exchanging savage put-downs. The Red Queen may have added a splash of red paint to her roses, or perhaps it's her new accent piece—Arizona Representative Paul Gosar's "Liar, Liar, Pants on Fire" poster from the Michael Cohen testimony—that's attracting all of the White Knight's attention.[3]

At the Mad Hatter's tea party of the most popular Junk Food News stories from the 2018–2019 news cycle, Cardi B overshared birthing stories while eating marzipan bites, Meghan Markle and Prince Harry sipped on Darjeeling while nursing their newborn, representatives from the Kardashian clan (America's royalty) and Fashion Nova exchanged biting remarks over finger sandwiches, and leftover pound cake was used to dampen the Notre-Dame fire. While the focus on the foibles of both British and American royalty at first seemed delicious, these empty-calorie stories distracted from the relevant news that galvanizes civic action and engagement. The impending climate crisis is real, and we as humans have an opportunity to take measures to address and offset some of the damage we have done. If we spend our time consumed by the flashy Junk Food News headlines that read "eat me" and "drink me" at this Mad Hatter's tea party, we'll never be full or secure, but we're sure to get curiouser and curiouser.

THE BIBBED PRINCE AND THE GLOBAL PROBLEM CHILD

Since the day Meghan Markle and Prince Harry said their vows in St. George's Chapel, the world has been holding its collective breath for when they would spawn a rosy-cheeked, royal diaper-wearing, tabloid-bait baby. Then came October 2018, when every fan of the royal couple got the announcement they were waiting for: ROYAL BABY ON THE WAY! *The Sun* and *People* speculated on the pregnancy: Would the baby be American or British? Did Markle secretly have an in vitro fertilization (IVF) procedure done? How was she able to conceive so "late"? She's not in her birthing prime anymore, will she miscarry? How would Harry evolve from a "partier" to a responsible dad now? Establishment news websites were flooded with in-depth reports on every detail of the pregnancy, including extensive photo galleries that showcased Meghan's baby bump and think pieces on which designer dresses made her POP![4] During Harry and Meghan's Royal Tour stop in Australia, all attention was on the Australian governor general's gift to the unborn child.[5] In the eyes of the corporate media, the contents of the gift basket were decidedly more relevant than the increasing influence of a global activist movement, Extinction Rebellion.

Much of the discourse on diapers, crown-jeweled pacifiers, and royal bibs overshadowed crucial news about the global problem child, climate change. While corporate media obsessed over Markle's pregnancy, members of Extinction Rebellion protested government inaction on climate change in London. Extinction Rebellion protestors have used a variety of nonviolent techniques, ranging from gluing their hands to the gates of Buckingham Palace, to planting trees in Parliament Square, to digging a hole and placing a coffin in it to represent humanity's future if no further action is taken.[6] Extinction Rebellion began to act in response to the 2018 Intergovernmental Panel on Climate Change (IPCC) report that warned humans have only twelve years remaining to prevent the catastrophic effects of climate change. These effects include a massive loss of biodiversity, elevated sea levels, and the forced migration of millions of people.

Extinction Rebellion's primary goal is to create a "Citizens' Assembly" that would evaluate current research on climate change and map a strategic course for action to prevent its detrimental effects, for government and citizens alike.[7] Extinction Rebellion has successfully pressured the United Kingdom government to declare a global "climate emergency." While this is largely a symbolic gesture, it demonstrates the movement's effectiveness at raising awareness among politicians and the public. Still, Extinction Rebellion has made it clear that more action is necessary than simple symbolic declarations.[8] Their powerful activism is primarily supported by crowdfunding and grants from nongovernmental nonprofit organizations—not the glitz and glamour of royal money. Corporate media have largely avoided covering Extinction Rebellion, mainly because climate change isn't a feel-good celebrity story or a delicious inside scoop, but merely a daunting, unavoidable reality inconvenient to the powers that be. When the movement is covered, it is generally presented as radical and unnecessarily disruptive.

Inspired by Extinction Rebellion, a group of activists has taken to "birth-striking" in response to climate change. Birth-striking is a form of protest where people vow not to conceive children in response to the grim consequences of climate change. Many birth-strikers cite concerns about the ethics of bringing children into a world already burdened by overconsumption.[9] Rather than address the legitimate issues raised by birth-strikers, the corporate media had a field day with the whole concept of birth-strikes. It was as if the corporate media had found their Wonderland. After learning of the birth-strike movement, Tucker Carlson, one of the great sages of Fox News, told a birth-striker, "Have some kids, it'll make you happier."[10] Unfortunately, it seems Tucker missed the point of the movement. As it is, corporate media would prefer to share junk news on Markle's pregnancy over reporting on the birth-strike and the context of its cause. While the IPCC report warns that there may be only a dozen years left to prevent the consequences of climate change from becoming irreversible, at least corporate media has thoroughly enjoyed the minute-by-minute updates on the diaper-wearing prince. After all that hard-hitting news coverage, now he, and all the rest of us, have only eleven more years to go!

THE BALLAD OF THE BROKEN VAGINA

American rapper Cardi B publicly revealed her pregnancy in April 2018 while thousands of low-income immigrant women of color were ending theirs preterm. As Cardi spent the ensuing months dressing up her baby bump and taking pregnancy photoshoots amidst brightly colored floral arrangements, hundreds of low-income pregnant immigrant women wondered if they would be able to have a safe abortion or if they would have to self-induce it. Motherhood, like so much else through the looking-glass, is a vastly different experience depending upon one's privilege and socioeconomic status. For Cardi B, a celebrity worth millions of dollars, the corporate press voraciously reported whatever puff pieces about her pregnancy she would give them. Rumors of Cardi's pregnancy surfaced before she even officially announced it. Entertainment reporters followed the clues that her uncharacteristically boxy dresses were evidence of the musician's maternity.[11] At last, Cardi B gave birth to her daughter Kulture in July 2018, surrounded by friends, family, and her publicist. Her husband, rapper Offset of the famed music group Migos, filmed the birth, a move that was later criticized as using Cardi's pregnancy as a springboard for his own career and fame.[12]

Post-pregnancy, Cardi B shared details about her experiences as a mother. She revealed that she was offered millions of dollars to sell pictures of Kulture to a media outlet, but decided against it since she wasn't "ready yet."[13] Much to the delight of the establishment press, Cardi B finally shared a photo of her daughter's face in December 2018 for fans to obsess and ogle over. Cardi B also opened up about her struggles with childbirth and motherhood, lamenting on live television that Kulture "broke [her] vagina" and that she had to get stitches. On this subject, an article from Condé Nast's Self magazine argued that Cardi B used her fame to highlight the overlooked difficulties of childbirth: "postpartum complications . . . aren't talked about beforehand. . . . That's why it's so important for people like Cardi B to talk about what they experience publicly."[14]

Yet while Cardi B has the platform, the resources, and the media attention to speak out about her vaginal complications, an entire population of low-income immigrant Latina women must suffer through their pregnancies in silence. The fervent anti-immigrant, anti-Latinx sentiment from the current administration is a significant source of trauma and stress within the Latinx community in the United States. As a result, Latina mothers are more likely to experience health complications during pregnancy and childbirth. According to a study released in the *Journal of Epidemiology & Community Health*, the rate of preterm births for foreign-born Latina mothers increased from 7.3 percent prior to Donald Trump's presidential nomination to 8.4 percent following his inauguration. This is in stark contrast to the nearly unchanging preterm birth rates for women who were born in the United States.[15] It is difficult, after all, to feel safe in a country whose president has called your people rapists, criminals, and drug smugglers.

While *Roe v. Wade*, the historic 1973 Supreme Court case that legalized abortion, is at risk of being overturned, reproductive activists are raising awareness about drugs, such as Misoprostol, that allow women to terminate their pregnancies on their own at home. For immigrant women of color, however, obtaining such drugs at a clinic comes with risks. Navigating reproductive health clinics pres-

ents a series of threats, including potential harassment from protestors and being reported to Immigration and Customs Enforcement (ICE). In one study cited on Rewire.News, 39 percent of undocumented Latinas said that they felt reluctant to seek healthcare for fear of being deported; moreover, if they're caught obtaining pregnancy-terminating drugs illegally, they know that they'll likely face imprisonment. More and more immigrant women are consequently carrying unwanted pregnancies to term or self-inducing abortion solely because of the risks that accompany visiting a health clinic.[16]

Furthermore, the scarcity of Latinx-specific health services and support—especially for mothers and children—makes their struggles that much more severe, as they have a higher chance of mortality during childbirth than their white counterparts.[17] Such struggles don't just affect the current generation, but generations to follow. By the year 2035, one in four American women will identify as Latina. The issue thus clearly presents itself as a national crisis.[18]

Unlike Cardi, undocumented women of color rarely give birth in hospitals surrounded by an extensive support system, much less a publicist. They don't have access to the resources a pregnant US citizen might have, so they don't consider the same opportunities when making important decisions regarding their pregnancies. They are largely silenced by the Trump administration's anti-immigrant, anti-Latinx hate speech. While the corporate press retweets a GIF version of Cardi B's broken vagina comment, they compound the isolation of pregnant Latina immigrant women by neglecting to share their stories. This diverts attention from the issues that force a critical analysis of our country's actions and policies. The effective censorship of undocumented Latina immigrant stories makes the corporate media less of an independent fourth estate that maintains checks and balances on government, and more of an arm or adjunct of the Trump administration. Cardi's topical comment will quickly be replaced by a new, equally provocative remark from the rapper, who savors every morsel of her tabloid fodder. While these stories don't hold those in power accountable and continue to keep the issues facing Latina immigrant women in the dark, the corporate press is guaranteed to report on whatever Cardi B breaks next.

ASHES TO ASHES

The devastating Notre-Dame Cathedral fire that destroyed pieces of the famous Parisian Catholic monument in April 2019 drew international donations and messages of support. Even the land of the free and the home of the brave gave a fair share of contributions to the Cathedral's reconstruction fund. While American corporate media created supportive hashtags, slow-motion drone footage compilations, and even animated simulations of the fire, they failed to report on other fires that destroyed places of worship in the United States.

Millions across the globe expressed sympathy toward the French, who watched in anguish as their Gothic architectural wonder burned. Social media was flooded with prayers, tears, and stories about massively generous donations for Notre-Dame's reconstruction. Despite proof that the fire was set accidentally, corporate media speculated on hypothetical sinister motives by radical Islamists, stoking the fire of anti-Muslim rhetoric deeply embraced by so many in the US political establishment. Distracted by these Islamophobic delusions, the establishment press overlooked actual incidents of hate-based destruction in the United States.

Across the globe from the corporate media's main story, in southern Louisiana, three predominantly black churches were consumed by an arsonist's flames without a glimpse of corporate media coverage. The string of arsons began at St. Mary Baptist Church on March 26, then continued at the Greater Union Baptist Church on April 2, and ended at the Mount Pleasant Baptist Church on April 4. These churches, prominent community landmarks for their majority-black congregations, were all decimated by the arsonist over the course of one week. As closely linked hate crimes, these fires specifically targeted the southern Louisiana black community and reflect the general rise in hate crimes following President Donald Trump's election in 2016. Since Trump's presidential election, the FBI has recorded a 17 percent spike in hate crimes across America. In 2017 alone, there were 7,175 reported incidents of hate crimes, and these rates will only continue to rise while President Trump spews white supremacist rhetoric from the Rose Garden.[19]

Domestic hate crimes that remain a pervasive threat were given less attention than the flashy, dramatic story of Notre-Dame Cathedral's accidental fire. America's corporate media preferred to show a glamorous, apolitical cathedral turn to ashes in one of the wealthiest cities in the world than to address the racial injustices in their own backyard. America, they would have us believe, is too exhausted by its countless domestic hate crimes to acknowledge yet another one. It seems easier to turn a blind eye to such racially motivated attacks, as they carry political weight and a pressing need to further the conversation on race in America—important topics the establishment media would prefer not to face.

Where were the overwhelming messages of international support and charitable donations when three black churches in Louisiana were targeted and burned down by a white supremacist? While the coverage of the Notre-Dame disaster raked in donations and media attention, community organizers, in lieu of the support that global media attention could bring, created a GoFundMe page to raise money to rebuild the churches in Louisiana. After the drama of the Notre-Dame fire subsided, and after considerable petitioning, the corporate press, no doubt desperate for the next applicable use of the fire emoji in their social media profiles, finally turned to promote the churches' GoFundMe page and effectively helped raise $1 million in donations.[20] It is worth noting that the corporate media can influence positive change *when* they choose to do so.

These Baptist churches may not be "the symbol of beauty and history of Paris,"[21] but they are "[l]ongtime pillars of the African American community."[22] While precious artworks and relics were lost at Notre-Dame, in these church fires the United States lost decades' worth of artifacts, documents, and speeches from the Civil Rights movement.[23] To honestly face these attacks in Louisiana would require a long, hard look in the mirror, and a sober assessment of current racial politics in the United States. Can White America handle that?

What other fires were not being covered because of the sensationalism of Junk Food News? In the last few years there has been a shortage of news stories on two mosques that were targeted for arson in the United States. The first attack occurred in January 2017 in Victoria, Texas. A suspect was arrested and convicted of this hate crime in July 2018.[24] The other mosque arson was in San Diego, on March 29,

2019. Coverage for this second fire focused less on growing Islamophobic sentiment in the United States and more on the fire's possible connection to the Christchurch, New Zealand, shooting on March 15, 2019. The establishment press used the fire as an excuse to play *True Detective* with graffiti that was left in the mosque by the arsonists, as it referenced the Christchurch tragedy.[25] There was also scarcely any coverage of the Al-Aqsa Mosque in Jerusalem, which caught fire on the same day as the Notre-Dame Cathedral.[26] Recent coverage of arson attempts on Jewish synagogues, apart from one mention of an arson attack that destroyed the largest yeshiva in Russia on April 19, 2019, have mainly focused on either Jewish contributions to the rebuilding of Notre-Dame, or a baseless conspiracy theory that Jews and Muslims burnt down the Cathedral.[27]

The disparity between the search results for the Notre-Dame fire and hate crimes within the United States reveals deliberate neglect on the part of the corporate press to address domestic social issues in favor of splashy, politically uncontentious drama. The media should act as the moderators for a healthy debate on race relations in the United States, but instead they circumvent the conversation altogether. This maintains racial tension and allows corporate media sponsors to continue to profit from sensationalist stories that focus on racial conflict. Countering that trend, social uproar attracted media attention to the social justice issue of the Mount Pleasant Baptist Church, Greater Union Baptist Church, and St. Mary Baptist Church fires. This effective community engagement demonstrates that the corporate press can be held accountable when more people speak their minds, resulting in more voices being heard. If more people work to keep the news media accountable, perhaps corporate media will have no choice but to present more equitable and just representation in their reporting efforts.

STYLE OVER SUBSTANCE

In early 2019, corporate media was inundated with updates on the Kardashian vs. Fashion Nova saga, a flame war to end all flame wars. It all started when America's favorite Kardashian, Kim, stepped out in a revealing vintage 1998 Thierry Mugler cut-out gown for the Hollywood Beauty Awards. Hours after the Hollywood Beauty Awards, a knock-off vintage Thierry Mugler gown appeared on the Fashion Nova website. This was met with accusations that Kim Kardashian has been leaking her designer looks to fast fashion sites like Fashion Nova before she even wears them in public. However, the allegation was apparently false, as it sparked a feud with the online retail site. Kim denied having any involvement with Fashion Nova and slammed Fashion Nova for ripping off her designer looks on Twitter. Fashion Nova also released a statement claiming they have "not worked directly" with Kim.[28]

This tasty, zero-calorie Junk Food News story is one instance of a long-scale, continuous public relations narrative that the Kardashians are the routine victims of fashion plagiarism. Within hours of the stars sporting designers' couture and vintage pieces, online retailers market knock-off products online. Kim later addressed the situation, claiming, "It's devastating to see these fashion companies rip off designs that have taken the blood, sweat, and tears of true designers who have put their all into their own original ideas. I've watched these companies profit off my husband's work for years and now that it's also affecting designers who have been so generous to give me access to their beautiful works, I can no longer sit silent."[29] Thus started a full-fledged feud between the fashion company and the Kardashian clan.

While a bright-neon yellow vest is decidedly not as high-end as a vintage Thierry Mugler gown, it symbolizes a movement with more considerable societal significance than the Kardashian vs. Fashion Nova debate. While talk of Kim Kardashian's fashion draws international attention, corporate media in the United States have been conspicuously silent about the Yellow Vest movement in France. Since October 2018, outraged French citizens have taken to the streets to protest wealth inequality perpetuated by the French government. It began in response to president Emmanuel Macron raising gas prices while cutting taxes for the rich. The protesters wear highly visible yellow safety vests—necessary items kept in every car in case of emergency, now made to symbolize resistance against the continued favoritism of the power elite. The protesters utilize anonymity and strength in numbers, taking to the streets in demonstrations and shutting down traffic to raise awareness for their cause. The Yellow Vest movement is a genuine populist uprising and an example of a continuously sustained protest against economic inequality. It is a revolt of the working and middle class against the power elite.[30]

But while corporate media focus on Kim Kardashian's asinine proclamations and assets, they seem content to ignore what economist and professor Richard D. Wolff calls the most critical movement of the 21st century thus far.[31] Although corporate media do make an occasional reference to the changes sweeping France, their coverage deliberately discredits the Yellow Vest movement. They do this through sensationalizing and ridiculing the movement's activist efforts in news stories. One such example includes a February 2019 *New York Times* report, "Anti-Semitic Taunts by Yellow Vests Prompt French Soul-Searching." The article refers to a recent protest as "another episode of anguished national soul-searching over the problem of persistent anti-Semitism in France, and the evolution of the Yellow Vest movement from gas-tax protest to violent street revolt with hints of menace and hooliganism."[32] This rhetoric incorrectly paints the Yellow Vest movement as a racist, alt-right, quasi-fascist movement instead of a legitimate protest by the people against their government. And while it is essential to call attention to problematic associations amongst protesters, this type of coverage trivializes their cause.

The corporate media perhaps tiptoe around France's Yellow Vest movement to avoid discussing similarly egregious wealth disparity—and protest against it—in the United States. Corporate media do not profit by making their sponsors nervous, and the prospect of an anonymous mass revolt against obscene wealth does not bode well at anybody's board meeting. Celebrity endorsements constitute much safer clickbait for ad revenues than a leaderless revolutionary current, so it's a no-brainer that the corporate press would rather add fuel to the Kardashian vs. Fashion Nova fire than address the wealth disparity in this country. It may prove dire for democracy, but at least the Kardashians will be on hand to pick up the scraps of the fallen US flag and turn them into their latest fashion statement—that is, until Fashion Nova creates its own Betsy Ross–style knock-off.

MOONWALKING THROUGH MOLESTATION

The infamous Michael Jackson exposé documentary *Leaving Never-land* premiered at the 2019 Sundance Film Festival on January 25, 2019, and was broadcast on HBO in two parts less than two months later, in early March.[33] Directed by Dan Reed, *Leaving Neverland* told the stories of Wade Robson and James Safechuck, who allege that, while they were children, Jackson sexually abused them at his home, Neverland Ranch, and elsewhere over a period of several years. As the documentary aired in the United States and the United Kingdom, sexual abuse allegations against Catholic priests surfaced in the cor-porate news cycle but were afforded significantly less coverage than the Jackson controversy. The more than 2,600 new allegations of abuse by priests and church employees in the United States reported between August 2018 and February 2019 were just the latest addi-tions to the quagmire that is sexual abuse in the Catholic Church.[34]

For centuries, allegations of the sexual abuse of minors have been made against Catholic priests. According to BishopAccountability.org, a site that keeps a tally of cases of Catholic sexual abuse, the Catholic Church has paid more than $3 billion to settle sexual abuse claims as of 2012. As of 2019, the site found that more than 6,800 priests in the United States have been credibly accused of sexual abuse, with more than 19,000 confirmed victims.[35] In February 2019, the pope spoke publicly on the matter, saying that "in people's justified anger, the Church sees the reflection of the wrath of God, betrayed and insulted by these deceitful consecrated persons," and that "it is our duty to pay close heed to this silent, choked cry." While this impassioned state-ment may seem like an indication of change for the Church, it was accompanied by no new policies dedicated to preventing abuses and supporting victims.[36]

The corporate press focused on the scandal of sexual abuse alle-gations against Catholic priests instead of on the critical facts of the crimes. The stories typically highlighted and sensationalized the experiences of the victims. This diverted attention from the fact that the Church actually has made efforts to cover up abuses and con-tinues to employ offenders. For example, most articles that covered the February 2019 meeting in Vatican City which addressed the issue of child sexual abuse didn't critique the Church's responses to those allegations. It was clear that the meeting was designed to serve up fast Junk Food News stories, and the press gleefully chomped down on the empty-calorie performance. The coverage addressed the significance of the meeting and the waning popularity of the Church. Some sources, such as the *New York Times*, mentioned that the Church's efforts to curb sexual abuse exacerbated the problem and revealed long-standing structural and institutional issues. Although the Catholic Church released a list of names of pedophiles within the clergy, they published no actual information about their work history or current employment. As indicated by the *New York Times*, such selective information conceals how the Catholic institution shuffles around known sex offenders so that they can continue to work in the Church.[37]

Though the corporate coverage of the Vatican meeting was positive, discussion forums and other online communities were quick to point out the irony of the pope's statements. His subtle framing advanced the narrative that the Catholic Church's image was tainted by a few bad apples, rather than calling it out as the fundamentally dysfunctional institution that it is. The Catholic Church has betrayed communities and its own moral values by suppressing allegations and allowing abusers to continue to work for the Church. While accusations in recent years have been given the Hollywood treatment, with films such as *Spotlight* and docu-series on *CBS This Morning*, these victims' stories are sensationalized when not outright ignored.

Meanwhile, establishment and corporate news sources that covered the Michael Jackson abuse allegations rarely focused on the victims' stories at all, and instead were largely concerned with casting doubt on the victims. Since the documentary was released, prominent celebrities, including Madonna and Boy George, have defended the deceased Jackson. Boy George noted that the word "alleged" is missing from the documentary, and he described how, with the accusations in *Leaving Neverland*, it is "just taken almost for granted that this is what happened and therefore we all should accept it."[38] The goal of the documentary was to get the victims to talk about their abuse as an act of resistance against a system and a man that had silenced them for so long. The documentary may be the closest the victims can get to vindication, as the Michael Jackson estate is suing HBO for airing the documentary and speaking against his legacy. In the wake of the #MeToo and Time's Up movements, this documentary opens up a dialogue on how our society and Hollywood view and address victims of sexual assault, especially children. However, that dialogue is not reflected in conversations about the sexual abuse scandal within the Catholic Church, where victims are not being listened to, but treated merely as PR problems.[39]

There's a lot of differences between the Catholic Church and Michael Jackson, but they're both some smooth criminals. They have both, with the cooperation of the corporate media, silenced their victims, and, in the Church's case, effectively concealed vital information about the abusers from the public. Both scandals drew massive public attention, yet the perpetrators found ways to slide through the cracks and get away with their crimes. In both the coverage of Michael Jackson's scandal and the cases of sexual abuse in the Catholic Church, we see more attention being paid to the violators than to the victims. While Wade Robson and James Safechuck are relentlessly interrogated by the corporate media, that same media describe the Catholic sexual abuse scandal as a series of isolated incidents by corrupt priests, leaving unaddressed the systemic corruption within the larger institution of the Catholic Church. Substantive news is spun into a web of Junk Food News infotainment, further blurring the lines between Junk Food News and accurate investigative reporting—and as a result, we the public, much like Alice, descend further into Wonderland, undoubtedly to encounter the next moonwalking smooth criminal.

CONCLUSION

Our extended stay at the Hatter's tea party of Junk Food News has created a global madness. News consumers are getting curiouser and curiouser, as our hunger for investigative reporting is only fed with Junk Food News, infotainment that says "eat me" in swirly fondant but does little to feed our heads. While we sang "Que Será, Será" to the Catholic Church and wished both US and British royal babies a very merry unbirthday, we neglected the rising influence of activist movements that may spur substantive change beyond the ubiquitous attention-grabbing GIFs, blogs, and headlines. This chapter is but a small sampling of the cornucopia of absurd events the establishment press found worthy of our time. This is time that we will never get back, and spending it on junk instead of substantial stories, investigations, and activism can make for a very unmerry unbirthday for us all. As we travel further into the Wonderland of the corporate media news cycle, the real world we recognize grows more and more distant, and only time will tell what bite-sized "drink me" and "eat me" infotainment awaits.

IZZY SNOW attended College of Marin in Kentfield, California, for two years and will transfer to Barnard College at Columbia University in the fall of 2019. Izzy has loved working with Susan Rahman and the team at Project Censored for the *Censored 2019* and *Censored 2020* publications, and as a guest on the *Project Censored Radio Show*.

SUSAN RAHMAN is a professor of sociology at a number of northern California institutions. She is vice president of the Media Freedom Foundation. Susan loves collaborating with students on Project Censored content. She is a mother and activist and lives in northern California with her family.

Notes

1. Lewis Carroll, *The Annotated Alice:* Alice's Adventures in Wonderland & Through the Looking-Glass *by Lewis Carroll; with Illustrations by John Tenniel*, Definitive Edition, ed. Martin Gardner (New York: W.W. Norton, 2000 [Carroll's *Alice's Adventures in Wonderland* was first published in London by Macmillan and Co. in 1865]), 69–78.
2. Jefferson Airplane, "White Rabbit," *Surrealistic Pillow* (RCA Victor LSP-3766, 1967). The song, written by Grace Slick, was recorded on November 3, 1966, and released February 1, 1967.
3. Anne Flaherty, with Benjamin Siegel and Quinn Owen, "'Liar, Liar, Pants on Fire!' GOP Focus on Discrediting Cohen, Don't Ask about Trump," ABC7 News (San Francisco), March 1, 2019, https://abc7news.com/liar-liar-pants-on-fire-gop-focus-on-discrediting-cohen-dont-ask-about-trump/5159574/.
4. Ainhoa Barcelona, "Meghan Markle's Pregnancy Evolution—Month by Month in Pictures," *HELLO!*, March 19, 2019, https://www.hellomagazine.com/healthandbeauty/mother-and-baby/gallery/2019031971042/meghan-markle-baby-bump-month-by-month-evolution-last-engagement/1/.
5. Staff writers, "Meghan, Harry Got 236 Gifts on Australasian Trip," News.com.au, April 6, 2019, https://www.news.com.au/entertainment/celebrity-life/royals/meghan-harry-got-236-gifts-on-australasian-trip/news-story/9fe78290c2b23ff8b1d489c3719100fd.
6. Mattha Busby, "Extinction Rebellion Activists Stage Die-In Protests across Globe," *The Guardian*, April 27, 2019, https://www.theguardian.com/environment/2019/apr/27/extinction-rebellion-activists-stage-die-in-protests-across-globe.

7. Mattha Busby, "Extinction Rebellion and Momentum Join Forces on Climate Crisis," *The Guardian*, April 29, 2019, https://www.theguardian.com/environment/2019/apr/29/extinction-rebellion-and-momentum-join-forces-on-climate-crisis.

8. Mark Tutton, "UK Parliament Declares 'Climate Emergency,'" CNN, May 1, 2019, https://www.cnn.com/2019/05/01/europe/uk-climate-emergency-scn-intl/index.html.

9. Elle Hunt, "BirthStrikers: Meet the Women Who Refuse to Have Children until Climate Change Ends," *The Guardian*, March 12, 2019, https://www.theguardian.com/lifeandstyle/2019/mar/12/birthstrikers-meet-the-women-who-refuse-to-have-children-until-climate-change-ends.

10. Tim Hains, "Tucker Carlson to 'Birth Strike' Activist: Have Some Kids, It'll Make You Happier," RealClearPolitics, March 13, 2019, https://www.realclearpolitics.com/video/2019/03/13/tucker_carlson_to_birth_strike_activist_have_some_kids_itll_make_you_happier.html.

11. Nicola Dall'Asen, "Cardi B Shared a Stunning Maternity Shoot and All Her Makeup is under $18," Revelist, July 13, 2018, http://www.revelist.com/beauty-news-/cardi-b-maternity-shoot/13007/naturally-flawless-liquid-foundation-10-bh-cosmetics/8.

12. Nicole Saunders, "Offset Shares a Video of Cardi B Giving Birth to Baby Kulture," *Harper's Bazaar*, February 11, 2019, https://www.harpersbazaar.com/celebrity/latest/a26289750/cardi-b-gives-birth-kulture-video/.

13. Alyssa Bailey, "Cardi B Finally Shared the First Full Photo of Her Baby, Kulture," *Elle*, December 6, 2018, https://www.elle.com/culture/celebrities/a25418039/cardi-b-baby-kulture-first-face-photo/.

14. Zoe Weiner, "Cardi B Reveals More Details about Giving Birth—and Says It 'Broke My Vagina,'" Self (Condé Nast), October 19, 2018, https://www.self.com/story/cardi-b-giving-birth-broke-my-vagina.

15. Carolina Moreno, "Our Anti-Immigrant Atmosphere May be Contributing to Dangerous Birth Complications for Latinas," HuffPost, October 23, 2018, https://www.huffpost.com/entry/latinas-preterm-labor-immigrant-hate_n_5bce3130e4b0a8f17eef6d71.

16. Tina Vasquez, "Self-Induced Abortion's Risks Could Leave Immigrant Women Choiceless," Rewire.News, January 17, 2019, https://www.rewire.news/article/2019/01/17/self-induced-abortion-risks-could-leave-immigrant-women-choiceless/.

17. Moreno, "Our Anti-Immigrant Atmosphere."

18. Diana N. Derige, "Latina Health Under Attack, As Anti-Immigrant Sentiment Worsens," Women's eNews, October 9, 2018, https://womensenews.org/2018/10/latina-health-under-attack-as-anti-immigrant-sentiment-worsens/.

19. Yanqi Xu, "Explaining the Numbers behind the Rise in Reported Hate Crimes," PolitiFact, April 3, 2019, https://www.politifact.com/truth-o-meter/article/2019/apr/03/hate-crimes-are-increasingly-reported-us/.

20. Kayla Epstein, "After Notre Dame Fire, a GoFundMe Ensured Black Churches Burned in Louisiana Got $1 Million, Too," *Washington Post*, April 17, 2019, https://www.washingtonpost.com/nation/2019/04/17/after-notre-dame-fire-gofundme-ensured-black-churches-burned-louisiana-got-million-too/.

21. Adam Nossiter and Aurelien Breeden, "Fire Mauls Beloved Notre-Dame Cathedral in Paris," *New York Times*, April 15, 2019, https://www.nytimes.com/2019/04/15/world/europe/notre-dame-fire.html.

22. Epstein, "After Notre Dame Fire."

23. Jamiles Lartey, "Louisiana: Advocates Concerned after Three Black Churches Burned in a Week," *The Guardian*, April 9, 2019, https://www.theguardian.com/us-news/2019/apr/09/louisiana-church-fires-black-congregations-targeted.

24. Madison Park, "Man Found Guilty of Hate Crime in Burning of Texas Mosque," CNN, July 17, 2018, https://www.cnn.com/2018/07/17/us/texas-mosque-fire-hate-crime/index.html.

25. Joel Shannon, "California Mosque Arson Suspect Left Graffiti about New Zealand Attack, Police Say," *USA Today*, March 26, 2019, https://www.usatoday.com/story/news/nation/2019/03/26/california-mosque-arson-suspect-new-zealand-graffiti-police/3281949002/.

26. Tom O'Connor, "Jerusalem's Al-Aqsa Mosque Fire Burns at the Same Time as Flames Engulf Notre Dame Cathedral in Paris," *Newsweek*, April 15, 2019, https://www.newsweek.com/notre-dame-fire-aqsa-mosque-1397259.

27. Cnaan Liphshiz, "2 Jewish Philanthropists Pledge $134 Million toward Restoring Notre Dame," The Times of Israel, April 18, 2019, https://www.timesofisrael.com/2-jewish-philanthropists-pledge-122-million-toward-restoring-notre-dame/; "Arson Reported at Russia's Largest Yeshiva during Passover," AP News (Associated Press), April 19, 2019, https://www.apnews.com/c6bfb1d05d1d4592bace577a2c68b399.

28. Lauren Alexis Fisher, "Is Kim Kardashian Helping Fast Fashion Sites Knock Off Her Designer Looks?" *Harper's Bazaar*, February 20, 2019, https://www.harpersbazaar.com/fashion/designers/a26428007/kim-kardashian-leaking-fashion-nova-knockoffs/.

29. Chavie Lieber, "Kim Kardashian's Love-Hate Relationship with Fast Fashion, Explained," Vox, February 26, 2019, https://www.vox.com/the-goods/2019/2/26/18241625/kim-kardashian-fast-fashion-fashion-nova-missguided.

30. Jake Cigainero, "Who are France's Yellow Vest Protesters, and What Do They Want?" NPR, December 3, 2018, https://www.npr.org/2018/12/03/672862353/who-are-frances-yellow-vest-protesters-and-what-do-they-want.

31. Richard D. Wolff, "Richard D. Wolff Lecture on Worker Coops: Theory and Practice of 21st Century Socialism," a talk at Levy Economics Institute of Bard College on April 22, 2016, posted to YouTube by Levy Economics Institute on April 25, 2016, https://www.youtube.com/watch?v=a1WUKahMm1s.

32. Adam Nossiter, "Anti-Semitic Taunts by Yellow Vests Prompt French Soul-Searching," *New York Times*, February 18, 2019, https://www.nytimes.com/2019/02/18/world/europe/france-antisemitism-yellow-vests-alain-finkielkraut.html.

33. Lavanya Ramanathan and Elahe Izadi, "How 'Leaving Neverland' Puts Michael Jackson's Cultural Legacy and $2 Billion Empire in Jeopardy," *Washington Post*, March 4, 2019, https://www.washingtonpost.com/lifestyle/style/how-leaving-neverland-puts-michael-jacksons-cultural-legacy-and-2-billion-empire-in-jeopardy/2019/03/04/310e6124-3ea3-11e9-9361-301ffb5bd5e6_story.html.

34. Alex Sundby, reported by Matthew Sheridan, Elizabeth Gravier, and Alexandra Myers, "In Six Months, Abuse Allegations against over 2,600 Priests and Church Workers Have been Revealed," CBS News, February 21, 2019, https://www.cbsnews.com/news/catholic-priests-accused-list-priests-church-workers-revealed-accused-of-abuse-today-2019-02-21-live-stream-updates/.

35. "Collated USCCB Data: On the Number of U.S. Priests Accused of Sexually Abusing Children and the Numbers of Persons Alleging Abuse," BishopAccountability.org, June 30, 2017, updated June 1, 2018, http://www.bishop-accountability.org/AtAGlance/USCCB_Yearly_Data_on_Accused_Priests.htm.

36. Pope Francis, "Meeting on 'The Protection of Minors in the Church,' (21–24 February, 2019)," The Protection of Minors in the Church (Vatican), February 24, 2019, https://www.pbc2019.org/home.

37. Jason Horowitz and Elizabeth Dias, "Pope Francis Ends Landmark Sex Abuse Meeting with Strong Words, but Few Actions," *New York Times*, February 24, 2019, https://www.nytimes.com/2019/02/24/world/europe/pope-vatican-sexual-abuse.html.

38. Boy George, "Boy George on the Michael Jackson Documentary | WWHL," an interview with Andy Cohen on the television show *Watch What Happens Live with Andy Cohen*, broadcast on Bravo on April 30, 2019; posted to YouTube by Watch What Happens Live with Andy Cohen on April 30, 2019, https://www.youtube.com/watch?v=zGRcXRTktyM.

39. Ramanathan and Izadi, "How 'Leaving Neverland' Puts Michael Jackson's Cultural Legacy."

CHAPTER 3

Comforting the Powerful, Ignoring the Afflicted

News Abuse in 2018–2019

John Collins, Nicole Eigbrett, Jana Morgan,
and Steve Peraza

Facts do not at all speak for themselves, but require a socially acceptable narrative to absorb, sustain and circulate them.

—Edward Said[1]

INTRODUCTION

When we reviewed the patterns of News Abuse in US establishment media a year ago, we used the metaphor of a magician's trick to describe how News Abuse works: by diverting the public's attention away from key elements of important, widely reported stories, establishment media minimize the stories' deeper importance, distort what is happening, or otherwise encourage the public to interpret the stories in ways that fall into line with the interests of the power elite.[2] Sadly, this past year demonstrated that these patterns have not abated. Despite the chaotic winds swirling around the Trump administration, major establishment outlets continue to perform their traditional ideological role by policing the borders of "acceptable" public discourse. Even when providing detailed coverage of major stories, these outlets too often frame issues in a way that leaves questions of structural power in the background or renders them nearly invisible. This type of framing also functions as a form of censorship, and it's what former Project Censored director Peter Phillips labeled "News Abuse" back in 2002.

Bringing our experience as independent journalists with Weave News (www.weavenews.org) to bear on these questions, we focused our analysis on four News Abuse stories from 2018 to 2019: the death of Senator John McCain, the debate surrounding Brett Kavanaugh's nomination to the Supreme Court, the migrant "caravan" from Central America's "Northern Triangle" to North America, and the election of a group of women of color dubbed "the Squad" to the US Congress. What we found was a heavy reliance on tropes, frames, and narratives that served to shield elite groups and the US empire itself from critical scrutiny while marginalizing or casting doubt on the voices of the relatively powerless.

While these constitute by now quite familiar tactics from the corporate media playbook, it remains disheartening, if not altogether surprising, that the major outlets continue to employ the tools of News Abuse so brazenly while the public's demand for critical, constructive journalism grows ever more emphatic. Independent reporters and media watchdogs may have their work cut out for them most at times of social and political struggle and crisis, as it's only by exposing news media complicity in abuses of power that the powerful can be held accountable for their predations upon the oppressed.

JOHN MCCAIN: MEDIA MYTHOLOGIES OF AN IMPERIALIST "MAVERICK"

In his influential 1989 book *Discourse and the Construction of Society*, Bruce Lincoln highlights the role of what he calls "sentiment evocation"—appeals to emotion—in helping alternative discourses and frameworks gain a hearing and, by extension, helping to create the conditions for social change.[3] Dominant discourses, though, also make heavy use of sentiment evocation, often in an effort to reinforce existing social hierarchies and relations. In the hands of establishment media outlets, sentiment evocation can play a key role in coverage that falls under the category of News Abuse. Establishment media coverage of the death of Senator John McCain reveals some of the complexities of the process. Amidst ongoing liberal concern over "norm erosion" during the first two years of the Trump administration,[4] establishment outlets responded to McCain's death by providing the public with a steady diet of emotional appeals to American patriotism, exceptionalism, and innocence. In the process, they helped normalize the worst excesses of the country's imperial militarism while also keeping Trump himself at the center of the news cycle.

The days following McCain's death on August 25, 2018, saw a heavy outpouring of establishment media coverage, including breaking news stories, lengthy obituaries, a variety of opinion pieces and editorials, and significant attention devoted to the debate over Donald Trump's slow and tepid reaction to the news. All eight news outlets surveyed here—the *New York Times*, *Washington Post*, *Wall Street Journal*, *USA Today*, NPR, CNN, Fox News, and MSNBC—provided sustained, detailed reporting on the story. This analysis focuses on substantial articles published during the first week following McCain's death (August 25 – September 1), when key narratives about the former presidential candidate crystallized.

News Abuse always involves a combination of what is present and what is absent. In the case of the McCain story, the coverage featured the strategic use and repetition of a number of key words and tropes that were quite consistent with how McCain had been covered for much of his political career. Through sentiment evocation, those characterizations play on the emotional need of centrist audiences to believe in a certain image of American politics and American empire.[5] At the same time, the coverage was also clearly marked by what analyst Norman Solomon called "obit omit—obituaries that are flagrantly in conflict with the real historical record."[6] Consequently, we need to pay special attention to those aspects of the historical record that were either left out or left in the background of the story.

The first trope about McCain centers on the word "maverick," which originated as a term for unbranded cattle and has come to be used to describe particular individuals who take independent positions. As Branko Marcetic argued in an insightful piece for *Jacobin*, the idea of McCain as a political "maverick" was a carefully constructed image decades in the making.[7] McCain's support for campaign finance reform in particular played a key role in forming a narrative that eventually became a virtual truism despite McCain's overall record as a solid GOP loyalist. By 2018, the trope was so entrenched that it would have been shocking not to see the word peppered all across front-page headlines. In this, the establishment media did not disappoint: initial coverage of McCain's death on August 25 included news and op-ed headlines such as "John McCain, 'Maverick' of the Senate and Former POW, Dies at 81," "John McCain, a Maverick We Can Learn From," "Six Memorable Moments when John McCain Earned a Reputation as a 'Maverick,'" and "From a POW Prison, John McCain Emerged a 'Maverick.'"[8] The use of scare quotes often signaled a backhanded recognition of the term's constructed nature, yet without the necessary critical distance to acknowledge the beltway media's own central role in propagating it in the first place.

McCain the "maverick" was the perfect alibi for a political and media system that excludes systemic critiques while providing an endless spectacle of 24-hour "debate" between, and sometimes within, the two establishment parties. The alibi, in this case, works through a particular kind of sentiment evocation: the nostalgic appeal to a distinctly American, white, male notion of "rugged individualism" associated with the colonial frontier and the so-called "Wild West." Much as fascism, in the words of Walter Benjamin, offers the masses "a chance to express themselves" in the absence of any real opportunity for economic justice, the trope of McCain the "maverick" offers a periodic dose of highly circumscribed and choreographed "rebellion" as a substitute for a political system that would truly address the needs of ordinary Americans.[9]

A second, equally ubiquitous trope concerns McCain's military service, and here the country's tradition of "support the troops" rhetoric obviously looms large when it comes to sentiment evocation. Typical of this trope was Fox News's decision to begin its initial obituary by describing McCain as "a war hero who survived five years as a prisoner of war in Vietnam."[10] While Fox managed to avoid mentioning the senator's vocal opposition to the US use of torture, other outlets heavily emphasized the importance of that stance, writing of the "lessons" that the country could learn from McCain's principled position.

Meanwhile, the insertion into the conversation of Donald Trump, who famously avoided military service through a series of deferments during the Vietnam era, offered an opportunity to reinforce the narrative of McCain's heroism. Trump had stated of McCain during the 2015 campaign, "He's a war hero because he was captured. I like people that weren't captured."[11] The Trump–McCain feud would continue until, and even after, the senator's death, with the contrast between now-President Trump's insensitive comments and McCain's military bona fides providing endless fodder for cable news shows and sober newspaper articles alike. Going well beyond a recognition of McCain's service in Vietnam, for example, the *Wall Street Journal* was quick to point out that he "came from a family that had fought in every American war since the revolution."[12]

And what of those wars? Perhaps most importantly, what of the many post-Vietnam invasions, proxy wars, "interventions," and other military adventures that McCain could always be counted on to support? Many outlets were quick to recount the feel-good stories about how some of McCain's former antagonists in Vietnam later came to admire him as a "good friend" for his role in promoting strong US–Vietnam ties after the war.[13] The sentiment evocation in such coverage contributes directly to the reproduction of a narrative that cuts the brutality of imperialism with a heavy dose of wishful American innocence. In other cases, such as Roger Cohen's *New York Times* column on August 31, 2018, the warmongering is papered over with phrases such as "man of conviction," "American global commitment," and "self-sacrifice."[14]

By contrast, few establishment outlets were willing to ask the obvious question: How do the family members of the millions killed and displaced in US and US-supported wars in Iraq, Afghanistan, Yemen, Central America, and elsewhere feel about the man who never hesitated to back the use of military force in the service of US empire? While socialist critics such as Ashley Smith and anti-imperialist reporters such as Mehdi Hasan pointed out that support for US wars inevitably means participation in war crimes,[15] NPR stayed safely within the accepted framework of McCain the heroic (if occasionally flawed) "idealist." Speaking on *Morning Edition*, NPR's Pentagon correspondent Tom Bowman emphasized McCain's belief in "American power as a moral force" and his steadfast desire to "promote democracy around the world."[16] Aside from a single reference to *Chinese* imperialism, the word "imperialism" does not appear a single time in any of the nearly 200 reports on McCain published by the eight selected outlets during the week following his death. It was similarly difficult to locate any acknowledgment that the tactics of the US military might raise as many ethical red flags as the torture McCain so famously condemned on the basis of his own experience.

Given his outsized role in the nation's history of militarism, McCain's death could have provided an opportunity to engage with the implications of that history. In this light, his antagonistic connection with antiwar activists such as Medea Benjamin, the founder of Code Pink, is instructive. Interviewed on *Democracy Now!*, Benjamin observed, "I just spent the last weekend with Veterans for Peace, people who are atoning for their sins in Vietnam by trying to stop new wars. John McCain hasn't done that."[17] And indeed he hadn't—but he had clashed with Code Pink protesters in 2015 as they interrupted a Senate hearing to demand the arrest of former secretary of state Henry Kissinger for war crimes. "[Y]ou're going to have to shut up, or I'm going to have you arrested," replied McCain, the Senate Armed Services Committee Chair. "If we can't get the Capitol Hill police in here immediately—get out of here, you low-life scum."[18] This interaction, also not referenced in any of the establishment coverage reviewed here, adds a critical layer to a third trope regarding McCain: his supposed sense of "decency" and "honor."

Finally, it is worth noting how much of the coverage following McCain's death referenced his popularity among members of the Washington press corps, who typically attributed this close relationship to the senator's personal efforts or magnetism. *The Washington Post*, for example, cited his legendary "knack with the media"[19] and his ability to "make journalists love him," as if reporters were purely passive objects of his irresistible charm. A more plausible explanation is that McCain benefited from the unwillingness of the press to ask basic questions about the global impact of the policies he championed. As John McCain's record of enthusiastic support for imperialism passed largely uncriticized, the establishment media ensured that the spin he proudly stood for would continue long after his death.

CAN'T HUMANIZE A CARAVAN: CENTRAL AMERICAN REFUGEES AND THE PROBLEM OF METANARRATIVE

In 2018, national media outlets like the *New York Times, Washington Post,* Fox News, and *USA Today* reported extensively on the "immigrant caravan," a massive procession of more than 5,000 Latinx migrants who walked from the "Northern Triangle" states in Central America (Honduras, Guatemala, and El Salvador) to Mexico and the United States in search of a better life. The selection of the term "caravan" to describe this migrant population created a problematic metanarrative in the establishment media. The dominant interpretation of the "immigrant caravan" is that it was a ragtag group of Latinx migrants trying to resettle in North America, illegally if need be. Only secondarily do the conditions that fueled this Central American diaspora get sustained analysis in the media. As a result, the "immigrant caravan" has come to represent a threat to national security in the United States, further fueling an incipient 21st-century nativism among citizens who view Latinx as unwanted visitors.

The term "immigrant caravan" fails to describe accurately the mass migration of Central American migrants to North America in 2018. According to the *Oxford English Dictionary,* British English speakers use the term "caravan" to denote a mobile home, a vehicle in which passengers might live.[20] Others use the term to describe itinerant traders and priests from the ancient world who traversed the Eurasian steppes or the Sahara Desert to circulate ideas, people, and goods. American English speakers, on the other hand, define a caravan as a "company of travelers journeying together. . . . A single file of vehicles. . . ." The latter definition explains why the US national press labeled the migrants an "immigrant caravan," publishing photographs of thousands of Central Americans walking together as one.[21] The problem is that the term connotes itinerancy without acknowledging the chaotic conditions that pushed migrants out of the Northern Triangle in the first place.

National correspondents worked diligently to document how Central American migrants perceived their decision to walk to North America, but the men and women journalists interviewed represented themselves more like refugees than the traders or priests that the term "caravan" might imply. They identified record levels of violence and few opportunities to earn a living as the main factors pushing them out the Northern Triangle. For example, Edwin Enrique Jimenez Flores, a truck driver who left Tela, Honduras, in the summer, cited gang violence as the main reason to migrate. Jimenez Flores called city police to arrest gang members who violently assaulted his brother. As retribution, the gang members threatened his life. "I spent four months hidden. I couldn't even go into the street. I can't go back," he said.[22] Daisy Guardado had a similar story. She fled Honduras because gang members killed her brother and attacked her daughter. Traumatized and forced into hiding, Guardado chose to leave her homeland: "I [was] so scared," she explained, "I didn't know what to do."[23]

In addition to gang violence, Central American migrants abandoned states because of their stagnant economies. According to the Washington Office on Latin America, 64.3 percent of all households in Honduras in 2017 lived in poverty. The Northern Triangle as a region has a rural poverty rate of 60 percent.[24] It should not come as a surprise, therefore, that some migrants moved north to find living-wage work. Bayron Cardona Castillo, for example, decided to leave Honduras for better social and economic opportunities. As he told reporters, "The truth is, what we're looking for is a way to live in peace, in tranquillity, with employment. . . . In my case, all I ask is an opportunity, a chance to work and help my family."[25]

To call these Central American migrants an "immigrant caravan" elides the chaotic conditions that caused them to head north. The term "caravan" connotes itinerancy with a purpose; caravans come to town to sell goods or to spread ideas. The Central American migrants who walked to the United States were not traveling to serve their interests; they were traveling because the economic and law enforcement sectors in their countries had all but collapsed, creating uninhabitable conditions in their communities. A far more accurate term for these migrants would have been "refugees," people forced to leave their countries because of exigent circumstances like war, persecution, and natural disaster. There is a moral obligation to help refugees, however; this obligation simply does not exist when a population is labeled a "caravan."

President Donald Trump and pundits for Fox News, a conservative-leaning media outlet, intended for the term "immigrant caravan" to rattle conservative Republican constituents. Trump popularized the term to raise fear about "illegal immigrants" and generate support for his immigration policy, which seeks not only to restrict immigration further but also to erect a wall along the entire US border with Mexico. In April 2018, Trump tweeted that US Border Patrol agents should have more discretionary power to jail "illegal immigrants." They needed new powers, he urged, because "'Caravans' [of illegal aliens are] coming."[26] Inside these caravans, Trump intimated, were rogues, rapists, criminals, and terrorists, sneaking into the United States to harm citizens, leech off social safety net programs, and steal economic opportunities from working-class [white] Americans. Trump's deployment of nativist rhetoric should come as no surprise, since he began publicly vilifying Latinx immigrants as soon as he announced his presidential campaign in June 2015, when he claimed that Mexico was sending rapists and criminals to the United States and he promised to protect citizens by building a "great wall" to stem illegal immigration from Central and South America.[27] Indeed, stereotyping and discriminating against Latinx migrants featured prominently in his rise to the presidency.

Fox News correspondents and conservative pundits joined Trump in fearmongering over the "immigrant caravan," partly to advance Trump's immigration agenda, and partly to gain readers and viewers by creating controversy. Pundits on the Right wrote salacious tales to support Trump and galvanize the base around the issue of immigration. Nativist sentiments, in one instance, enflamed a debate between Fox News anchor Tucker Carlson and immigrant rights activist Enrique Morones. Carlson verbally accosted Morones after the activist expressed empathy for the migrants. For Morones, the migrants were refugees, and the United States should help them, especially because US intervention in the Northern Triangle has caused some of the political and economic instability in the region. "You hate America," Carlson barked at Morones. From Carlson's perspective, Morones unfairly blamed America for the immigration problem. While the US may have a "sinful" past in the Northern Triangle, he suggested, this history was not a justification for illegal immigration. To suggest that the "immigrant caravan" had a just cause, Carlson exhorted, was anti-American.[28]

If fighting illegal immigration was a patriotic duty, protecting citizens from Latinx rogues and criminals was a presidential duty, according to FrontPage Mag writer Lloyd Billingsley. He praised Trump for taking a tough stance against the "immigrant caravan," because the migrants were unwanted and potentially dangerous: "The United States did not request the arrival of any person in the caravan, and none has any right to enter the United States. The unvetted caravaners might be gang members, criminals or terrorists. So the president was right to say the border is getting 'more dangerous.'"[29] If allusions to patriotism and law and order were not enough to mobilize the base, conservatives had no qualms about circulating "immigrant caravan" conspiracy theories. Former Immigration and Customs Enforcement (ICE) officer David Ward even claimed that the "immigrant caravan" was a socialist conspiracy to test citizens' political values. "This was an organized plan and deliberate attack on the sovereignty of the United States by a special interest group," said Ward. "They rallied a bunch of foreign nationals to come north into the United States to test our resolve."[30]

While conservative pundits' support for President Trump and his outlook on immigration was not surprising, the inability of establishment news outlets with a more liberal orientation to control the narrative was odd, to say the least. The problem was that liberal pundits focused coverage on migrants' experiences before and after the walk and offered commentary on conservatives' campaign of misinformation without countering the terms of the "caravan" story.[31] In most circumstances, such a strategy would be successful, because migrants can explain the unlivable conditions that would push them north and liberal commentators can expose the inaccuracies in some conservatives' reports. In this case, however, even liberal pundits' efforts to document facts and rehumanize the migrants could not overcome the metanarrative framing the entire controversy. Migrants and refugees can be humanized in the national press. Caravans, on the other hand, are groups of travelers, trinkets, and beasts of burden. As liberals learned, it is hard to humanize a "caravan" of people.

One *New York Times* columnist came close to unveiling the root cause of the "immigrant caravan" controversy in the national press. In his essay "Trying to Fight, Not Spread, Fear and Lies," Nicholas Kristof argued that the establishment media played a pernicious role in the story. In his view, the national media facilitated the controversy to sell papers and recruit new cable viewers. "The news business model," Kristof explained, "is in part about attracting eyeballs, and cable television in particular sees that as long as the topic is President Trump, revenues follow. So when Trump makes false statements about America being invaded by Central American refugees, he not only gets coverage, but also manages to control the media agenda."[32] Kristof advanced two important criticisms here: First, he condemned Trump's use of misinformation and fearmongering to malign the "immigrant caravan"; and second, he chided establishment news outlets for running stories with sham information just to sell their news. Kristof missed the bigger picture, however. Yes, the national press *should* check facts before running stories, and they should *not* publish inaccuracies even if the people quoted are famous and can sell newspapers and TV shows. But making these changes would not have stopped the spread of fear and lies, because the people being vilified were not given a label that connoted peoplehood. Ironically, Kristof called the migrants "Central American refugees," a term that unmistakably humanizes the travelers and carries with it a moral and political obligation to help them. Herein was the best strategy to challenge the "immigrant caravan" controversy—stop calling the population a "caravan."

The stories that the US media tell shape national conversations and consciousness. As important as telling the story, but not nearly as well understood, is the impact of *how* one tells the story—the setting, characters, tropes, and selected words that writers use. In his classic postmodern monograph *Metahistory*, historian Hayden White argued that the structure of stories—the way that certain tropes presuppose how plots unfold—can sometimes determine how historians interpret their research data. The emplotment of certain types of stories can prefigure what an historian will write about their research, even before they have completed the analysis.[33] As Hayden White theorized, labels like "immigrant caravan" work to skew the results of any reporting, even ostensibly positive and sympathetic journalism. The term muted the Central American crises pushing people out of the Northern Triangle and, rather subtly, dehumanized the refugees.

"THE SQUAD": VISIBLE SAVIORS, INVISIBLE MOVEMENTS

The US midterm elections of 2018 were a rallying point for liberal Democrats determined to take Congress back from Republicans. After more than a year of nightmarish policies under the Trump administration, new candidates emerged at every level of government, and voters elected a record-breaking number of women into Congress, with 35 winning seats in the US House of Representatives and five winning seats in the Senate—bringing the total number of women serving in the House to 102 (plus four nonvoting members representing Washington, DC, and US territories), the total number women serving in the Senate to 25, and the total number of women who can vote in Congress to 127.[34] Many of the newly elected members of Congress were hailed for being "firsts" in their districts and in the legislative branch of government: female, immigrant and refugee, millennial, black, Somali, Native American, Asian American, Palestinian, Muslim, and openly LGBTQ. The newly elected members were also overwhelmingly left of center; of the 42 women elected to the House and Senate for the first time, 38 ran as Democrats.[35]

Unfortunately, establishment media coverage of this important development in 2018 met the criteria for News Abuse by fixating on female Democratic congressional candidates in two specific ways: by relying on a neoliberal savior trope of newly elected progressive, Democratic women, and by simultaneously erasing the sustained grassroots organizing that is fundamental for radical change to occur. This coverage limited the possibilities for informed civic participation aimed at systemic change and further reinforced the hegemonic, corporate capitalist, two-party political system of governance.

Examining the broader circumstances of the 2018 midterms, we find that establishment media eagerly filled the role of reporting on Donald Trump's every tweet and tantrum as well as the resultant ridicule and admonishment from his high-profile critics on the Left. Many of the female congressional candidates were fit into the oversimplified narrative of ideological conflict between Trump and vehemently anti-Trump Democrats. Headlines run immediately before and after the elections from November 5 to 7, 2018, included

- ▶ "Trump vs. Democratic Women: Headline Fight of the 2018 Campaign" (*Wall Street Journal*)[36]
- ▶ "Women Lead Parade of Victories to Help Democrats Win House" (*New York Times*)[37]
- ▶ "A Record Number of Women Will Serve in Congress (with Potentially More to Come)" (National Public Radio)[38]
- ▶ "New 'Year of the Woman'? Over 100 Female Candidates Set to Win Seats in Congress, Make History" (*USA Today*)[39]

Although increased gender representation in elections and public office may be a net gain for US democracy, it would be foolish to assume that the work of achieving that representation is complete, as the United States's elected offices still have a long way to go before reaching gender parity. Data from the Rutgers Center for American Women and Politics shows that, despite comprising more than half the population and the voters, women still accounted for less than a third of all 2018 candidates for Congress, the governors' offices, and other statewide executive seats.[40]

Leaving that data out of the story, establishment media became hooked on judging the latest batch of congresswomen by their opinions of President Trump. Four women running for seats in the House gained particular attention due to their politics, identities, and history-making races: Alexandria Ocasio-Cortez of New York, Ilhan Omar of Minnesota, Ayanna Pressley of Massachusetts, and Rashida Tlaib of Michigan. The candidates, all women of color running for Congress for the first time, fondly referred to one another as "sisters in service" and soon became known as "the Squad."[41] They pledged to use all their resources if elected to shut down the Trump administration, but they also ran on unabashedly progressive platforms and proudly challenged the "old guard" of establishment Democrats.

By presenting the Squad as the new progressive champions of the Democratic Party and Congress, the media framed a narrative that these women's bold leadership would pull the United States out the

Trump quagmire. Tlaib was featured in an interview with Boston NPR affiliate WBUR with the headline, "Rep.-Elect Rashida Tlaib Says She Will Work to Get Trump 'to Follow the Law.'"[42] *U.S. News & World Report* called the four women "The Freshman Congressional Renegades."[43] Alongside Democratic women candidates in general, *USA Today* linked their motivations to resisting Trump a few times in the same article:

> Women will represent two-thirds of the districts that Democrats flipped, building on momentum from the "Resist" movement that followed President Donald Trump's election in 2016. . . . Women were poised to make significant electoral gains in this "Year of the Woman" election. Their historic involvement follows the massive Women's March to resist Trump's presidency and the #MeToo movements' protest against sexual misconduct in the workplace.[44]

The overwhelming attention on these women, ranging from fascination and adoration to shock and disgust, catapulted them to celebrity-like status—and particularly, in the case of Ocasio-Cortez, to extraordinary popularity on social media. She gave Instagram followers unparalleled access to the legislative process by recording live videos during and after each day of congressional orientation, leading to the growth of her already massive follower count.[45] Ocasio-Cortez's age and leftist values made her a particular target for Fox News critique, and the *Washington Post* even went so far as to report on her trolling of the conservative news channel in Spanish after commentators poked fun at her.[46]

This fixation on the Squad's identities and history-making ethnic, religious, gender, and age representation actually diminished critical conversation around and in-depth analysis of progressive and leftist policies. Following Pressley's primary win in September, NPR published a piece titled "Ayanna Pressley's Upset Victory Shows Power of Women of Color in Democratic Politics"; according to that report,

> The Democratic Party has referred to African-American women as the backbone of the party, but in recent years,

some black organizers have expressed frustration that the party has not invested in recruiting black candidates. Pressley's victory is a sign that organizers and activists are no longer willing to wait for the party's blessing. It's also a sign that issues of representation rather than ideology are motivating voters in Democratic primaries.[47]

News consumers were led to believe that a handful of progressive Democratic congresswomen would transform the United States through a mosaic of singular actions targeted against the Trump administration. Though many voters and news consumers held, and still hold, this optimistic perspective, it overemphasized the role of individual politicians whose leftist values are still in the significant minority in Congress. It also placed significant pressure on members of the Squad to amplify leftist policies that would be a radical departure from most federal legislating, and are unfortunately not likely to be brought forward and approved on the House floor anytime soon.

Establishment media's individualistic focus on the congresswomen also led to them ignoring the broader systems and institutions that participated in and influenced the Squad's effectiveness in multiple spheres. Establishment outlets, for instance, pushed the narrative of growing tensions between new progressives and incumbent Democrats in Congress, many of whom are part of the party establishment and/or are assuredly centrist. On Pressley, CNN wrote, "Rising Democratic star Ayanna Pressley is testing whether her party is willing to cast aside its experienced and reliable veterans in favor of a new generation of leaders who argue they are more suited for politics in the Donald Trump era."[48] A week after the November election, the members-elect went to Washington, DC, for congressional orientation, where Ocasio-Cortez made headlines for joining a climate change protest outside then–House Minority Leader Nancy Pelosi's office.[49] Ocasio-Cortez's commitment to her activist roots began serving as a litmus test for other Democrats and especially party leadership.

The recurring question of which direction the Democratic Party is being "pushed in" ultimately served to reinforce the system of two corporate-capitalist parties who dictate the rules of elections and governing. Members of the Squad, however, proved that they were not elected into Congress to simply fall into party lines. In fact, Ocasio-Cortez and Tlaib were endorsed by the Democratic Socialists of America. All four women were also endorsed by Justice Democrats and Brand New Congress, two PACs that aim to overturn existing power structures within Congress. Since the same corporate class backing the major political parties also owns and controls establishment media, painting the Squad as an emerging threat to status quo democracy became imperative.

Moreover, establishment media's neoliberal lens caused the Squad to be watered down into sound bites and images, not remembered for the grassroots movements that elected them into office. Tlaib and Omar were touted for being the first Muslim women in Congress.[50] Pressley was hailed as one of hundreds of black women running for office in 2018, and the first black woman to join the Massachusetts congressional delegation.[51] After Ocasio-Cortez's primary win in June against Representative Joseph Crowley, a nineteen-year incumbent from Queens who had not faced a primary challenger in fourteen years, the *New York Times* labeled her "A 28-Year-Old Democratic Giant Slayer."[52]

Who were the people behind the Squad who organized, mobilized, and voted for their progressive values? These four candidates won campaigns by foregrounding leftist policies that separated them from establishment Democrats: Ocasio-Cortez rallied on Medicare for All and urgent measures to slow climate change; Pressley declared that she would abolish Immigration and Customs Enforcement (ICE); and Tlaib and Omar took anti-imperialist foreign policy stances and openly supported Palestine. To create the transformational systems change that the Squad is advocating, there needs to be a mass movement of people ready to make it happen. Those people are out there— but establishment media had zero interest in giving them a platform.

Most of the national establishment outlets ignored the Squad's congressional races until the final days leading up to the elections. The horse race–style coverage of any political race is abusive to the public, barraging news consumers with minute updates, gains, losses, and polling numbers that do not always accurately represent voter turnout, as demonstrated in Ocasio-Cortez's and Pressley's winning primary races. Some local media outlets did do the candidates more justice by reporting on their races from day one, but others fed into establishment narratives that lacked nuance and frequently missed the mark.

Finally, it is necessary to address the underlying cynicism any left-leaning voter may hold, even after a history-making election cycle: Is diversity in politics going to lead us any closer to liberation when the same political system remains in place? The concept of diversity has been co-opted by the neoliberal capitalism that serves white supremacy, as each intersectional identity becomes a commodifiable check mark symbolizing progress. It is meaningful to see faces and stories of people other than white, cis-heterosexual males securing high-profile positions of power, but this does not necessarily translate into material change. The US corporate, partisan political system does not provide room for nuance nor truly progressive policy proposals. So while our "firebrand progressives" are finally giving the mic to leftist values, the overall hegemonic discourse within Congress and government is neoliberal at best, centrist and conservative in swaths, and far from socialist or guided by radical thought by any measure. The question remains: can politicians with oppressed and marginalized identities remain subversive within an institution that is inherently white supremacist, heteropatriarchal, sexist, and classist? If Omar, Tlaib, Pressley, and Ocasio-Cortez are truly committed to building the grassroots movements that sent them to Congress into a political revolution, then the answer must be yes.

THE WALL STREET JOURNAL, BRETT KAVANAUGH, AND THE PARTISAN DEFENSE OF PATRIARCHY

In late 2018, the United States was captivated and divided by the controversy surrounding Brett Kavanaugh's nomination to the Supreme Court. What began as a standard vetting process swiftly turned into a new chapter of the culture wars when Kavanaugh was accused of sexually assaulting Christine Blasey Ford in high school. Coming in the midst of the #MeToo movement, the accusation sparked an avalanche of media coverage, including investigative articles, opinion pieces, and editorials. A close look at editorials from two key establishment media outlets, the *New York Times* and the *Wall Street Journal*, reveals that the latter traded repeatedly in News Abuse as it sought to protect patriarchal elites from legitimate analysis of their structural power.

An examination of those editorials shows that both the *Times* and the *Journal* took an avid interest in the topic. In September and October 2018, the *Times* published thirteen editorials on Kavanaugh, eleven of which were published after Ford's accusations emerged. Similarly, the *Journal*'s editorial board published ten pieces, nine of which came after the accusations. Notably, the *Journal* also published an op-ed by Kavanaugh himself after his bombastic testimony in response to the Senate's questioning over Ford's allegations.[53] Furthermore, from September 9 to October 13, 2018, the *Times* published approximately 200 articles and opinion pieces that included the words "Kavanaugh" and "Ford," and the *Journal* published approximately 150.[54]

While these numbers demonstrate that the outlets shared nearly equal interest in the Kavanaugh–Ford story, further analysis shows clear divergences in the types of coverage. *The Times* provided appropriate reporting on the accusations while also offering ample space to connect the controversy to the broader cultural conversation about sexual assault, power, and gender.[55] *The Journal*, by contrast, tended to divert its readers' attention away from any discussion that might shed light on the structural privileges enjoyed by the white, male, upper-class elites who make up its traditional audience.

A keyword search for the terms "Kavanaugh" and "patriarchy," "sexist/sexism," "culture war," "misogyny," "rape culture," or "toxic masculinity" illustrated these patterns. Out of the roughly 200 pieces surveyed in the *Times*, those terms appeared approximately 75 times, but out of the roughly 150 *Journal* articles, there were only six instances.[56] While the two papers dedicated nearly the same amount of editorial space to the topic, the *Journal* failed to connect the dots in a way that could have provoked meaningful conversation and critical reflection on dominant social structures. While the term "MeToo" appeared in nearly every *Times* article, it appeared in less than a third of the articles published in the *Journal*.

The difference in coverage becomes even clearer as one digs into the work of the respective editorial boards. Editorials are considered the institutional opinion of the newspaper and are written to be catchy and thought-provoking. The fact that they are not news articles does not absolve the authors of their responsibility to the facts.

The *Times* editorials generally (although not always) tried to strike a neutral tone by presenting evidence from both sides of the Kavanaugh–Ford debate. They allowed for the possibility of Kavanaugh's innocence, called for an impartial FBI investigation, and, most importantly, connected the story to the broader issue of sexual assault and the difficulties women face in coming forward with accusations. While still offering a limited perspective, the *Times* at least had *something* to say about this important societal issue.

On the other hand, by offering a sustained defense of Kavanaugh, the *Journal*'s editorial team went out of its way to undermine and even ridicule the structural analysis offered by the #MeToo movement and by critics of rape culture. With each additional editorial focused on Ford's accusations, the language became increasingly aggressive. One editorial in particular, "The #MeToo Kavanaugh Ambush," prefigured the rage and enmity shown by Kavanaugh in his response to the accusations before the Senate.[57]

Both editorial boards made reference to Senate "norms" and called for an end to partisan bickering and politicking. In "The Supreme Court Confirmation Charade," the *Times* criticized both parties for politicizing such an important process and emphasized that, for the good of the country, the Supreme Court needs to maintain its credibility.[58] The *Journal*'s critiques, however, were wholly one-sided, sometimes to the point of conveniently forgetting recent history. In "The #MeToo Kavanaugh Ambush," they argued that Ford's allegations amounted to "character assassination" and that Senator Dianne Feinstein's delay in bringing the accusations forward amounted to a last-minute "political stunt" designed to hold up the nomination.[59]

In "The Never Conservatives" and "Who's Attacking Political Norms Now?," the *Journal* accused Democrats of violating "democratic norms" in their handling and the timing of Ford's accusations.[60] The GOP's destruction of the filibuster, however, was never raised. Unlike in the *Times* editorials, the only mention of Merrick Garland's stolen Supreme Court seat came when the *Journal* petulantly asserted that Democrats would have done the same as Republicans had they been in the position to do so. For the *Journal*, owned by Rupert Murdoch's News Corp, it seems that party criticism only goes one way.

As for the Kavanaugh accusations themselves, the editorials again revealed important differences. *The Times* acknowledged the credibility of Ford's testimony, properly cited evidence and investigative efforts by providing quotes and links to source material, and consistently called for an impartial investigation by the FBI. *The Journal,* however, at no point acknowledged the possibility that Ford could be telling the truth, cherry-picked and at times misled readers with their evidentiary references, and rarely provided links or direct quotes. The editorial board even cynically referred to the accusations as a part of the "Anita Hill playbook," alluding to the accusations of sexual harassment faced by Clarence Thomas in 1991 prior to his confirmation to the Supreme Court. Hill, a former subordinate to Thomas at the Department of Education and Equal Employment Opportunity Commission, testified before the Senate Judiciary Committee on Thomas's behavior and was widely vilified and disbelieved at the time for coming forward with her accusations.

Rather than seeking the truth no matter where it leads, the *Jour-*

nal's editorial board, only a quarter of whom are women, relied on a number of arguments that have long been used by those seeking to cast doubt on accusations of sexual assault. For example, before Ford had even had the opportunity to testify, the *Journal* called the accusations "too distant, too disputed and too late in the day" to be worth investigating.[61] The implication was that if survivors wait "too long" to report, their accusations do not count. They called into question Ford's memories, her motivations for coming forward, and her desire to remain anonymous. *The Journal* did not acknowledge, as the *Times* did, that the difficulty of coming forward leads many women to wait years before doing so. They further attempted to cast doubt on Ford's accusations by noting that there were no other accusers, stating that "every #MeToo miscreant is a repeat offender."[62] Yet, when another woman did come forward, that logic was quickly forgotten: Deborah Ramirez was categorized as part of a smear campaign "abetted if not orchestrated by Democrats."[63]

The Journal's failure to provide even a semblance of objectivity became still clearer in its evaluation of Kavanaugh and Ford's testimonies. *The Times* pointed out inconsistencies in both stories but highlighted the fact that Kavanaugh's testimony was often misleading and that he sometimes lied about seemingly innocuous things to try to maintain his image as a "choir boy" in high school. Yet the *Times* consistently maintained that there must be a presumption of innocence and that the hearings were a job interview, not a court of law. Conversely, the *Journal*'s editorial board all but exonerated Kavanaugh before he had even testified and never once allowed for the possibility that Kavanaugh may have assaulted any of his accusers.

Indeed, Kavanaugh's rage and disrespectful behavior during his testimony only solidified the *Journal*'s support. The editorial board called his testimony "as powerful and emotional as the moment demanded," asserting that his anger was self-righteous and that all of us would have done the same.[64] Despite the numerous college and high school associates who commented on Kavanaugh's drinking and belligerent behavior, and despite the components of his yearbook that seemed to contradict his characterization of himself as a model teenager, the editors claimed there was no evidence he had ever behaved badly toward women. *The Times* acknowledged that Kavanaugh is owed the presumption of innocence, but also insisted that his testimony demonstrated that he lacked the temperament and was too divisive to be a Supreme Court justice.

While the *Journal* knew better in the current political climate than to directly call Ford a liar, its characterization of her spoke volumes. They conceded that she was a sympathetic witness, but also used coded, sexist language in stating that she seemed "emotionally fragile."[65] They also patronizingly claimed to believe that Ford was sincere, but that her memories were just mixed up.[66] In sum, the *Journal*'s editorial treatment of Ford's accusations read like propaganda for the Republican Party, failing to serve the broader public.

Beyond the specific accusations, the fight over Kavanaugh's nomination to the Supreme Court did not happen in a vacuum. There were numerous cultural conversations happening concurrently with the nomination process, such as the #MeToo movement, as well as broader conversations about power, who has it, and who can be held accountable. Any honest assessment of the events would naturally need to incorporate those factors. Once again, the *Times* met that obligation far better than the *Journal*.

The *Times* pointed out the hypocrisy of Republican senators claiming they would take the accusations seriously and listen to Ford's testimony, when Senate Majority Leader Mitch McConnell was simultaneously telling supporters they intended to "plow right through" to confirm Kavanaugh.[67] The *Times* also pointed out the resurgence of the "boys will be boys" excuse so often used in response to allegations of sexual misconduct. Equally important, the *Times* devoted two of its editorials to reporting on the impact of the Kavanaugh hearings on women.[68] One of the editorials, "Women are Watching," came the day after Ford's testimony, and noted how the Republican Party's treatment of Ford connected with the experiences of many women who are afraid to come forward and report their abuse.[69] The piece also noted that Ford's testimony galvanized thousands of supporters to march in the streets, confront senators on Capitol Hill, and take to Twitter to tell their stories. At a time when Republicans cling to a message of "male victimhood" and worry that "good men" will be driven away from public service for fear of facing false accusations, the *Times* characterized the Kavanaugh hearings as just one component of the antipathy the Trump administration has shown toward women, noting efforts to undermine women's access to birth control and abortion and weaken protections for victims of sexual assault.

Rather than acknowledging the importance and legitimacy of the #MeToo movement, the *Journal* tried to paint it as a political cudgel being used by the Democrats to save a Supreme Court seat and take back the Senate.[70] The editors didn't bother to remind the public that Democrats had actually turned on one of their own, Senator Al Franken, when allegations of sexual assault were raised against him, ultimately leading to his resignation from the Senate. Almost none of the *Journal*'s editorials discussed the difficulties women (and men) face in reporting sexual assaults, especially those perpetrated by powerful men.

Corporate media outlets often focus on the political game between Democrats and Republicans, an approach that tends to leave little room for a deeper examination of societal factors such as misogyny, toxic masculinity, and prejudice against sexual assault survivors. Arguably, both outlets' editorial boards could have made a greater effort to delve more deeply into those issues. However, analysis clearly shows that in this instance the *Journal* entirely failed to meet its obligation to the public, putting partisan agendas ahead of the need to help readers understand the broader significance of the Kavanaugh case. For a society that desperately needs to confront structures of entrenched patriarchal power, that failure represents a damaging case of News Abuse.

CONCLUSION

As the quote from Edward Said at the start of the chapter indicates, news coverage is never as simple as presenting "facts" that automatically "speak for themselves." Instead, Said calls our attention to how the use of narratives, tropes, and other framing devices can profoundly shape the circulation, perception, and impact of information about the world. There is nothing inherently objectionable in the use of such devices; indeed, part of Said's point is that whenever information is shared socially, some form of narrativization is almost inevitable. As our analysis indicates, however, establishment media's narrativization of events too often crosses the line into News Abuse. One reason for this problem lies in the nature of establishment media themselves and their role as gatekeepers of what is "socially acceptable" (to use Said's phrase). Even as they seek to uncover new information, they can find themselves imprisoned by "established" narrative structures and ideological assumptions. These include the overly narrow structure of the two-party system as well as unspoken assumptions about US militarism and imperialism; the supposed "threats" facing the nation; the primacy of electoral politics over other forms of politics; and the relative value of some lives over others. Challenging the abusive nature of such coverage remains one of the most crucial tasks in the struggle for media freedom and the larger struggle for democracy itself.

JOHN COLLINS is Professor of Global Studies at St. Lawrence University. He is also a founder of Weave News (www.weavenews.org), which emerged out of his seminar on global news analysis, and he currently serves as the organization's editorial director. He has written extensively on the Palestinian liberation struggle and its global ramifications, most recently in *Global Palestine* (Hurst/Oxford University Press, 2011).

NICOLE EIGBRETT is a citizen journalist and former director of communications for Weave News. She is a Chinese transnational and transracial adoptee and an organizer within the adoptee and broader Asian American and Pacific Islander community. Hailing from the Finger Lakes region of New York, Nicole now works in Boston at the intersections of public service, progressive policy, and critical media literacy. She graduated from St. Lawrence University in 2014 with a BA in global studies and languages.

JANA MORGAN is a founder of Weave News. She also serves as the director of advocacy and campaigns for the International Corporate Accountability Roundtable (ICAR), a coalition that fights to ensure that corporations respect human rights. Jana holds an MA in international relations from the Maxwell School of Syracuse University and resides in Washington, DC.

STEVE PERAZA is an assistant professor in the Department of History and Social Studies Education at SUNY College at Buffalo. He earned his PhD in US history, specializing in law and slavery. For Weave News, Steve contributes to "The Poverty Report," which examines the multidimensional problem of poverty in the United States.

Notes

1. Edward Said, "Permission to Narrate," *Journal of Palestine Studies*, Vol. 13 No. 3 (Spring 1984), 27–48, 34.

2. John Collins, Nicole Eigbrett, Jana Morgan, and Steve Peraza, "The Magic Trick of Establishment Media: News Abuse in 2017–2018," *Censored 2019: Fighting the Fake News Invasion*, eds. Mickey Huff and Andy Lee Roth with Project Censored (New York: Seven Stories Press, 2018), 119–39.

3. Bruce Lincoln, *Discourse and the Construction of Society: Comparative Studies of Myth, Ritual, and Classification* (New York/Oxford: Oxford University Press, 1989), 8–11.

4. Jared Bernstein, "Key Dangles and Norm Erosions in the Age of Trump," *Washington Post*, July 31, 2017, https://www.washingtonpost.com/news/posteverything/wp/2017/07/31/key-dangles-and-norm-erosions-in-the-age-of-trump/.

5. In the context of the US political spectrum, the term "centrists" is used here to refer to so-called "moderate" Democrats and traditional conservatives whose positions define the limits of "establishment" views.

6. Amy Goodman, interview with Norman Solomon, Mehdi Hasan, and Medea Benjamin, "Obit Omit: What the Media Leaves Out of John McCain's Record of Militarism and Misogyny," *Democracy Now!*, August 27, 2018, https://www.democracynow.org/2018/8/27/obit_omit_what_the_media_leaves.

7. Branko Marcetic, "John McCain Wasn't a Hero," *Jacobin*, August 27, 2018, https://www.jacobinmag.com/2018/08/john-mccain-was-not-hero-obituary-war-racism-sexism.

8. Karen Tumulty, "John McCain, 'Maverick' of the Senate and Former POW, Dies at 81," *Washington Post*, August 25, 2018, https://www.washingtonpost.com/local/obituaries/john-mccain-maverick-of-the-senate-and-former-pow-dies-at-81/2018/08/25/d9219b7e-a7b8-11e8-97ce-cc9042272f07_story.html; Nicholas Kristof, "John McCain, a Maverick We Can Learn From," *New York Times*, August 25, 2018, https://www.nytimes.com/2018/08/25/opinion/john-mccain-death.html; N'dea Yancey-Bragg, "Six Memorable Moments when John McCain Earned a Reputation as a 'Maverick,'" *USA Today*, August 26, 2018, https://www.usatoday.com/story/news/politics/2018/08/26/six-times-sen-john-mccain-earned-title-maverick/1104737002/; Don Gonyea and Brakkton Booker, "From a POW Prison, John McCain Emerged a 'Maverick,'" *All Things Considered*, NPR, August 25, 2018, https://www.npr.org/2018/08/25/574516674/from-a-pow-prison-john-mccain-emerged-a-maverick.

9. Walter Benjamin, "The Work of Art in the Age of Mechanical Reproduction," in *Illuminations*, ed. Hannah Arendt, tr. Harry Zohn (New York: Schocken Books, 1968 [the essay was written in German in 1935–1936, and first published in French translation in the *Zeitschrift für Sozialforschung*, Vol. 5 No. 1 (1936), 40–68]), 217–51, 241.

10. Alex Pappas, "John McCain Dead at 81," Fox News, August 25, 2018, https://www.foxnews.com/politics/john-mccain-dead-at-81.

11. Erik Ortiz, "'He's Not a War Hero': Donald Trump Mocks John McCain's Service," NBC News, July 18, 2015, https://www.nbcnews.com/politics/2016-election/hes-not-war-hero-donald-trump-mocks-john-mccains-service-n394391.

12. Siobhan Hughes, "Sen. John McCain, a War Hero Who Became a Political Heavyweight, Dies at 81," *Wall Street Journal*, August 28, 2018, https://www.wsj.com/articles/sen-john-mccain-former-presidential-candidate-once-a-prisoner-of-war-dies-1535243058.

13. Ivan Watson, Jo Shelley, and Mark Phillips, "John McCain Remembered in Vietnam as a Friend, Not an Enemy," CNN, August 30, 2018, https://www.cnn.com/2018/08/29/asia/john-mccain-remembered-in-vietnam-intl/index.html.

14. Roger Cohen, "McCain and a Requiem for the American Century," *New York Times*, August 31, 2018, https://www.nytimes.com/2018/08/31/opinion/mccain-death-american-legacy.html.

15. See Mehdi Hasan, "Despite What the Press Says, 'Maverick' McCain Has a Long and Distinguished Record of Horribleness," The Intercept, July 27, 2017, https://theintercept.com/2017/07/27/john-mccain-fake-maverick-horrible-record/; and Ashley Smith, "A Hero for Their Class, Not for Ours," *Socialist Worker*, September 4, 2018, https://socialistworker.org/2018/09/04/a-hero-for-their-class-not-for-ours.

16. Tom Bowman, "Sen. John McCain's Enduring Impact on the U.S. Military," *Morning Edition*, NPR, August 27, 2018, https://www.npr.org/2018/08/27/642160104/sen-john-mccain-s-enduring-impact-on-the-u-s-military.

17. Goodman, interview with Solomon, Hasan, and Benjamin, "Obit Omit."
18. Ibid.
19. Callum Borchers, "A Near-Constant in John McCain's Career: His Knack with the Media," *Washington Post*, August 26, 2018, https://www.washingtonpost.com/politics/2018/08/26/constant-john-mccains-career-his-knack-with-media/.
20. "caravan," s.v., def. 4, *Oxford English Dictionary*, 2nd ed. (Oxford, UK: Clarendon Press, 1989), 879.
21. "caravan," s.v., defs. 1 and 2, *The American Heritage Dictionary of the English Language*, 4th ed. (New York: Houghton Mifflin Company, 2006), 278.
22. Josh Hafner and William Cummings, "'I Don't Care If I Die': Migrants Speak Out on the Caravan, and What They Left Behind," *USA Today*, October 23, 2018, https://www.usatoday.com/story/news/nation-now/2018/10/23/migrants-caravan-speak-out-why-they-left-everything-us/1738913002/.
23. Kirk Semple, "After Arduous Journey, Migrants See Stubborn Obstacle: Trump," *New York Times*, April 26, 2018, https://www.nytimes.com/2018/04/26/world/americas/migrant-caravan-trump-mexico.html.
24. "Why Central American Families are Fleeing Their Homes," Washington Office on Latin America, undated, https://www.wola.org/wp-content/uploads/2018/01/Families-Fleeing-Factsheet.pdf [accessed May 20, 2019].
25. Kirk Semple, "Inside an Immigrant Caravan: Women and Children, Fleeing Violence," *New York Times*, April 4, 2018, https://www.nytimes.com/2018/04/04/world/americas/mexico-trump-caravan.html.
26. Donald Trump (@realDonaldTrump), Twitter post, April 1, 2018, 6:56 a.m., https://twitter.com/realDonaldTrump/status/980443810529533952.
27. Alexander Burns, "Donald Trump, Pushing Someone Rich, Offers Himself," *New York Times*, June 16, 2015, https://www.nytimes.com/2015/06/17/us/politics/donald-trump-runs-for-president-this-time-for-real-he-says.html.
28. Tucker Carlson, interview with Enrique Morones, "'You Hate America': Tucker Battles Illegal Immigration Advocate over Honduran 'Caravan' to US," *Tucker Carlson Tonight*, Fox News, April 2, 2018, https://insider.foxnews.com/2018/04/02/tucker-carlson-illegal-immigration-debate-enrique-morones-border-angels-honduras-caravan.
29. Lloyd Billingsley, "DACA Declared Dead as Border Anarchy Intensifies," FrontPage Mag, April 3, 2018, https://www.frontpagemag.com/fpm/269778/daca-declared-dead-border-anarchy-intensifies-lloyd-billingsley.
30. Jeremy W. Peters, "'You Hate America!': How the 'Caravan' Story Exploded on the Right," *New York Times*, April 4, 2018, https://www.nytimes.com/2018/04/04/us/politics/caravan-conservative-media-immigration.html.
31. See, for example, Semple, "Inside an Immigrant Caravan"; and Kevin Sieff and Joshua Partlow, "Faced with Months-Long Wait in Mexico, Some Caravan Migrants Decide to Go Home," *Washington Post*, November 28, 2018, https://www.washingtonpost.com/world/the_americas/faced-with-months-long-wait-in-mexico-some-caravan-migrants-decide-to-go-home/2018/11/28/a62828e8-f32e-11e8-99c2-cfca6fcf610c_story.html.
32. Nicholas Kristof, "Trying to Fight, Not Spread, Fear and Lies," *New York Times*, November 23, 2018, https://www.nytimes.com/2018/11/23/opinion/sunday/media-midterms-trump.html.
33. Hayden White, *Metahistory: The Historical Imagination in Nineteenth-Century Europe* (Baltimore, Maryland: John Hopkins University Press, 1973).
34. Drew Desilver, "A Record Number of Women will be Serving in the New Congress," Pew Research Center, December 18, 2018, https://www.pewresearch.org/fact-tank/2018/12/18/record-number-women-in-congress/.
35. Catie Edmondson and Jasmine C. Lee, "Meet the New Freshmen in Congress," *New York Times*, January 3, 2019, https://www.nytimes.com/interactive/2018/11/28/us/politics/congress-freshman-class.html.

36. Gerald F. Seib, "Trump vs. Democratic Women: Headline Fight of the 2018 Campaign," *Wall Street Journal*, November 5, 2018, https://www.wsj.com/articles/trump-vs-democratic-women-headline-fight-of-the-2018-campaign-1541429076.

37. Susan Chira and Kate Zernike, "Women Lead Parade of Victories to Help Democrats Win House," *New York Times*, November 6, 2018, https://www.nytimes.com/2018/11/06/us/politics/women-midterms-historic.html.

38. Danielle Kurtzleben, "A Record Number of Women Will Serve in Congress (with Potentially More to Come)," *All Things Considered*, NPR, November 7, 2018, https://www.npr.org/2018/11/07/665019211/a-record-number-of-women-will-serve-in-congress-with-potentially-more-to-come.

39. Nicole Gaudiano, "New 'Year of the Woman'? Over 100 Female Candidates Set to Win Seats in Congress, Make History," *USA Today*, November 6, 2018, updated November 7, 2018, https://www.usatoday.com/story/news/politics/elections/2018/11/06/women-candidates-midterms/1845639002/.

40. Edmondson and Lee, "Meet the New Freshmen in Congress."

41. Antonia Blumberg, "Rashida Tlaib, Alexandria Ocasio-Cortez Post 'Squad' Pics of Diverse New Members of Congress," HuffPost, November 12, 2018, https://www.huffpost.com/entry/rashida-tlaib-alexandria-ocasio-cortez-post-squad-pics-of-diverse-new-members-of-congress_n_5bea1284e4b044bbb1a798a1.

42. Jeremy Hobson, "Rep.-Elect Rashida Tlaib Says She Will Work to Get Trump 'to Follow the Law,'" *Here & Now*, 90.9 WBUR-FM (Boston), November 27, 2018, https://www.wbur.org/hereandnow/2018/11/27/rashida-tlaib-congress-ice-trump.

43. David Catanese, "The Freshman Congressional Renegades," *U.S. News & World Report*, December 27, 2018, https://www.usnews.com/news/politics/articles/2018-12-27/the-new-renegades-coming-to-congress.

44. Gaudiano, "New 'Year of the Woman'?"

45. Talya Minsberg, "How Alexandria Ocasio-Cortez is Bringing Her Instagram Followers into the Political Process," *New York Times*, November 16, 2018, https://www.nytimes.com/2018/11/16/us/politics/ocasio-cortez-instagram-congress.html.

46. Keith McMillan, "Alexandria Ocasio-Cortez Trolls Fox News in Spanish," *Washington Post*, November 24, 2018, https://www.washingtonpost.com/arts-entertainment/2018/11/24/alexandria-ocasio-cortez-trolls-fox-news-spanish/.

47. Asma Khalid, "Ayanna Pressley's Upset Victory Shows Power of Women of Color in Democratic Politics," *Morning Edition*, NPR, September 4, 2018, https://www.npr.org/2018/09/04/644700516/ayanna-pressleys-surprise-upset-shows-women-of-color-s-power-in-democratic-polit.

48. Eric Bradner, "Democrats Measure Their Desire for Change in JFK's Old District," CNN, September 1, 2018, https://www.cnn.com/2018/08/31/politics/massachusetts-house-primary-ayanna-pressley-mike-capuano/index.html.

49. Nicole Gaudiano, "On Her First Day of Orientation on Capitol Hill, Alexandria Ocasio-Cortez Protests in Pelosi's Office," *USA Today*, November 13, 2018, https://www.usatoday.com/story/news/politics/2018/11/13/alexandria-ocasio-cortez-nancy-pelosi/1987514002/.

50. Eli Watkins, "First Muslim Women in Congress: Rashida Tlaib and Ilhan Omar," CNN, November 6, 2018, https://www.cnn.com/2018/11/06/politics/first-muslim-women-congress/index.html.

51. Audie Cornish, interview with Ayanna Pressley, "Hundreds of Black Women are Running in Federal, State and Local Elections This Year," *All Things Considered*, NPR, October 31, 2018, https://www.npr.org/2018/10/31/662696787/hundreds-of-black-women-are-running-in-federal-state-and-local-elections-this-ye.

52. Vivian Wang, "Alexandria Ocasio-Cortez: A 28-Year-Old Democratic Giant Slayer," *New York Times*, June 27, 2018, https://www.nytimes.com/2018/06/27/nyregion/alexandria-ocasio-cortez.html.

53. Brett M. Kavanaugh, "I am an Independent, Impartial Judge," *Wall Street Journal*, October 4, 2018, https://www.wsj.com/articles/i-am-an-independent-impartial-judge-1538695822.

54. This timeline covers the period from the days leading up to the announcement of the first accusations to the week following Kavanaugh's confirmation.

55. It is worth noting that both the *Washington Post* and the *New Yorker* broke significant parts of the overall story surrounding this controversy.

56. *The Washington Post*'s results were similar to those of the *New York Times*.

57. The Editorial Board, "The #MeToo Kavanaugh Ambush," *Wall Street Journal*, September 17, 2018, https://www.wsj.com/articles/the-metoo-kavanaugh-ambush-1537197395.

58. The Editorial Board, "The Supreme Court Confirmation Charade," *New York Times*, September 1, 2018, https://www.nytimes.com/2018/09/01/opinion/kavanaugh-supreme-court-confirmation.html.

59. The Editorial Board (*Wall Street Journal*), "The #MeToo Kavanaugh Ambush."

60. The Editorial Board, "The Never Conservatives," *Wall Street Journal*, October 3, 2018, https://www.wsj.com/articles/the-never-conservatives-1538608630; The Editorial Board, "Who's Attacking Political Norms Now?" *Wall Street Journal*, October 14, 2018, https://www.wsj.com/articles/whos-attacking-political-norms-now-1539552494.

61. The Editorial Board, "The Dirt and Delay Playbook," *Wall Street Journal*, September 14, 2018, https://www.wsj.com/articles/the-dirt-and-delay-playbook-1536966589.

62. The Editorial Board (*Wall Street Journal*), "The #MeToo Kavanaugh Ambush."

63. The Editorial Board, "The Politics of Destruction," *Wall Street Journal*, September 24, 2018, https://www.wsj.com/articles/the-politics-of-destruction-1537831889.

64. The Editorial Board, "Confirm Brett Kavanaugh," *Wall Street Journal*, September 27, 2018, https://www.wsj.com/articles/confirm-brett-kavanaugh-1538089143.

65. Ibid.

66. The Editorial Board, "Kavanaugh and the Senate's Honor," *Wall Street Journal*, October 4, 2018, https://www.wsj.com/articles/kavanaugh-and-the-senates-honor-1538695662.

67. The Editorial Board, "G.O.P. Leaders Can't Even Fake Respect for Christine Blasey Ford," *New York Times*, September 21, 2018, https://www.nytimes.com/2018/09/21/opinion/republicans-christine-blasey-ford-brett-kavanaugh.html.

68. The Editorial Board, "Women are Watching," *New York Times*, September 28, 2018, https://www.nytimes.com/2018/09/28/opinion/brett-kavanaugh-jeff-flake-gop-women.html; The Editorial Board, "Supreme Battle Lines," *New York Times*, October 3, 2018, https://www.nytimes.com/2018/10/03/opinion/brett-kavanaugh-supreme-court-protests.html.

69. The Editorial Board (*New York Times*), "Women are Watching."

70. The Editorial Board (*Wall Street Journal*), "The Politics of Destruction."

CHAPTER 4

Media Democracy in Action

Contributions by Kathryn Foxhall (Society of
Professional Journalists), Russ Kick (AltGov2),
Matthew Crain and Anthony Nadler (Data &
Society), Brendan DeMelle and Ashley Braun
(DeSmogBlog), Alexandra Bradbury (Labor Notes),
and Aaron Delwiche and Mary Margaret Herring
(Propaganda Critic); edited and introduced
by Steve Macek

For more than four decades Project Censored has been documenting
how the news that the public receives is shaped, filtered, and slanted
by government agencies, the military, affluent media owners, advertisers, Republican and Democratic politicians, business-funded think
tanks, lobbyists, PR flacks, and other elite interests. Every year, the
annual *Censored* volume enumerates important stories that were
either completely ignored by the establishment press or given only
minimal, cursory coverage. Every year, the book contains analyses
of the propaganda, disinformation, and outright acts of censorship that have distorted public perceptions and constrained policy
debates about topics such as military spending, immigration, poverty,
workers' rights, and global climate change, among many others.

It would be easy to conclude from our annual compendium of sup-
pressed stories and media malpractice that Project Censored believes
positive change—in our media, our politics, and our communities—
is simply impossible. Nothing could be further from the truth.

Project Censored is committed to the idea that grassroots media
activism, independent journalism, critical media literacy education,
and diligent monitoring and analysis of the commercial media's
blind spots can counteract the influence of propaganda and illumi-
nate the pressing social, political, and economic problems that plague

our world. Indeed, we think media reform activism and critical media literacy offer the best possible chance not just of changing our corporate-controlled media system but of revitalizing and renewing our corrupt, money-dominated democracy.

Since 2004, Project Censored's yearbook has included a chapter highlighting the efforts of activists, teachers, journalists, and media-producers whose work is defined by media activism, education, and analysis in the service of democracy and freedom of expression.

This year's chapter features contributions from a collection of groups and individuals who each in their own way strive to shine a critical light on issues and problems that rarely receive the attention they deserve from outlets like ABC, CNN, and the *New York Times*.

The first two entries examine the largely covert steps that the US government and other public institutions have taken in recent years to restrict journalists and citizens' access to vital information. Kathryn Foxhall of the Society of Professional Journalists (SPJ) explains the threat posed to quality journalism by the recent upsurge in policies at every level of government and at many businesses aimed at controlling reporters' access to employees. Investigative journalist Russ Kick tells the remarkable story of how he discovered that various US government agencies were requesting permission to destroy their records and how he fought to bring transparency and accountability to the process by which such agencies gain permission to purge their files.

Over the past two years, the media has given wall-to-wall coverage to allegations that the Russian government sought to influence the outcome of the 2016 US presidential election via shady social media profiles and online ads. However, as Matthew Crain and Anthony Nadler argue in their piece, the general potential for political manipulation built into the "digital influence machine" created by Silicon Valley tech companies like Facebook and Google deserves greater scrutiny than it has received, and the digital infrastructure on which it depends requires much greater democratic accountability.

While reporting on climate change by establishment news outlets like the *New York Times* and the *Washington Post* has improved slightly in recent years, these outlets have not been as conscientious in exposing systematic attempts by climate change deniers to cast doubt on the reality and science of global warming. In their contribution, Brendan DeMelle and Ashley Braun of DeSmogBlog provide an overview of how their blog counters fossil fuel industry lies about global warming and investigates the front groups and PR operatives responsible for producing them.

As Christopher R. Martin shows in his incisive new book *No Longer Newsworthy: How Mainstream Media Abandoned the Working Class*, most big commercial news organizations in the United States today no longer have even a single labor or workplace reporter on staff and increasingly cater their content to affluent, upscale audiences.[1] Alexandra Bradbury's contribution to this chapter explains how Labor Notes—which is both a magazine and an umbrella organization for rank-and-file labor activists—covers news about labor struggles and stories about grassroots union activism too often passed over by a corporate press that has increasingly written off workers as "not newsworthy."

Finally, Aaron Delwiche and Mary Margaret Herring discuss how the long-established website they help to run, Propaganda Critic, equips citizens with the tools of propaganda analysis and criticism needed to defend against media manipulation, and they describe how the site has been updated to teach users about new and nefarious forms of digital disinformation.

The groups and initiatives explored in this chapter are a perfect antidote to the despair that can often arise from dwelling on the censorship, spin, "Junk Food News," and misinformation documented elsewhere in this yearbook. They are living proof that the struggle for an independent media, an informed citizenry, and a real democracy continues . . . and continues to be as vibrant as ever.

CENSORSHIP THROUGH PUBLIC INFORMATION OFFICERS

Kathryn Foxhall

In 2014 the Centers for Disease Control and Prevention admitted that its staff had developed a pattern of mishandling dangerous pathogens.[2] It's the agency most responsible for infectious diseases and they were not being careful.

Around the same time, the Food and Drug Administration found it had vials of the monster virus smallpox in storage that apparently had not been inventoried for decades.[3]

Smallpox! Estimated to have killed 300 million people in the 20th century alone. When it was declared eradicated in humans in 1979, the agreement was that there would be only two stockpiles of the virus kept in secure labs, one in Russia and one in the United States.

The FDA promised to clean up its store rooms.[4] A review of the CDC situation found that staff had been scared to report the situation internally.[5]

But the bigger scandal was that the staff in those situations had been forbidden to ever speak to the press, or at least forbidden to speak without the bosses' guards tagging along.[6]

Everyone in those agencies is thus silenced today. So if there are areas the FDA still didn't clean up or if CDC staff are still playing games with anthrax, we likely won't find out.

History

Something astounding has happened over the past 20 to 30 years.

Agencies and organizations throughout the country have instituted a surge of policies that block reporters from communicating with staff unless they are monitored by authorities, often known as "public information officers" (PIOs).

The Society of Professional Journalists has warned that these restrictions constitute censorship and pose a grave risk to public welfare.[7] The society has created a web feature to address and document the issue.[8]

But such press controls are now a cultural norm. They are being implemented in state and local government, schools, hospitals, businesses, police departments, and even universities.

At the federal level, reporters used to be able to walk agencies' halls and call employees at will. It was practical and often yielded enlightening results. And now it's been largely prohibited.

How could we let these restrictions happen? How are they different from restrictions in authoritarian regimes?

Aspects of These Controls

There are at least two crucial aspects to these controls, both with severe consequences: reporters are blocked from speaking to staff at an organization without the PIO authorities' oversight; then, when reporters do seek clearance from the PIOs, they are often not allowed to speak to whom they want. Masses of other obstructions are built upon that same choke point: the authorities demand questions in writing, give non-answers, oversee conversations, and direct staff members as to what may or may not be said.

The limitations seem to get steadily worse. I estimate contact between reporters and staff inside many federal agencies is down by at least 90 percent.

But life goes on, some might counter. Reporters keep getting stories—so what's the problem?

A key *New York Times* reporter covering energy and environment policy, Coral Davenport, said in 2017 that in the previous decade she had had almost zero contact with Environmental Protection Agency (EPA) career staff.[9] Those ten years included the months in which some EPA staff knew about little kids in Flint continuing to drink lead in water.[10]

In 2018 *Washington Post* reporters did an extensive piece on the off-label use of medications.[11] One of the reporters said they repeatedly asked the FDA for access to experts to provide comments for the story, to no avail.

We, the press, just weren't there. By turning a blind eye to those closed doors and gagged people, we turn a blind eye to horrific situations.

Some reporting is excellent, at least as far as we, the outsiders, can tell. Reporters still have some people talking to them and they show great prowess in fishing stories from behind thick bureaucratic walls. Ironically, that is a big part of the problem. Journalistic skill camouflages the fact that, for example, the more than 17,000 employees in the FDA are under harsh prohibitions to essentially never communicate with a reporter.[12] The great majority remain silent, even when news outlets publish amazingly unenlightened stories.

News outlets often publish stories based on agencies' press

releases or briefings without warning that they have no idea what all the silenced staff of those agencies might say. The same reporters who manage to produce good work despite the restrictions placed on them would be amazed if they could walk an agency's halls or talk to staff at will. Just imagine what stories they could uncover with direct access to unadulterated facts.

Seven SPJ-sponsored surveys by Carolyn S. Carlson, Paymon Kashani, Megan Roy, Roberta Jackson, David Cuillier, and Lindsey Tulkoff from 2012 to 2016 show that throughout the country political and general assignment reporters, science reporters, education reporters, and police reporters all indicate there are major problems with the controls they are subjected to.[13]

Most chilling perhaps were the survey results from police reporters, 56 percent of whom said they rarely or never get to interview police officers without the involvement of a PIO.[14]

Asked why they monitor interviews, some police PIOs said things like "to ensure that the interviews stay within the parameters that we want."[15]

Taken together, all the surveys indicate that millions of people are being effectively silenced.

Perhaps news outlets don't talk about this because of misplaced pride in a work ethic that says a "good" reporter gets the story regardless of any restrictions. Perhaps reporters are scared to hurt their own credibility by admitting that they can't gain access to major institutions.

Kids drinking lead in water, gymnasts abused for decades, and a fentanyl epidemic brewing for years: these were all hidden stories until they were practically dropped on reporters' heads. The public depends on journalists to be there and give voice to all the people and stories that have been silenced, but journalists can only do their jobs properly when they're afforded the opportunity to access the facts. Given the overwhelming case against press controls, perhaps it's time to fight for the right to routinely speak to people without censors.

KATHRYN FOXHALL has reported on federal agencies for more than 40 years, witnessing firsthand the increasing controls on reporting, often through public information officers. Alarmed at the threat posed by these restrictions on important information, she has worked for more than ten years on the issue with the SPJ and other groups. Her blog is at http://profficecensorship.blogspot.com.

PRESSURING THE NATIONAL ARCHIVES TO BE MORE TRANSPARENT ABOUT THE DESTRUCTION OF GOVERNMENT DOCUMENTS

Russ Kick

From the standpoint of transparency, the process of deciding when federal agencies can pulp their documents is fundamental, yet it receives little public oversight or attention. Until recently the process was kept obscure, but that changed in spring 2019 due to pressure I applied.

The National Archives and Records Administration (NARA) is responsible for retaining the documents produced by most of the federal government. Almost every federal agency must abide by NARA's rules regarding records.

NARA tells these agencies how long they must keep their documents. Only 1–3 percent of federal documents are designated as "permanent," meaning that they must never be destroyed. The other 97–99 percent of documents are eventually shredded, wiped from hard drives, or otherwise destroyed. The time frame for keeping documents varies wildly—some documents can be destroyed as soon as they're no longer needed, while others must be kept for at least 70 years.

There are two ways that documents get scheduled for destruction or, very rarely, permanent retention: Typically, NARA issues government-wide records-retention schedules for broad types of documents, such as meeting minutes. But when an agency has certain types of documents specific to that agency, it sends a proposal, called a "request," to NARA. This proposal describes the category of documents—which could be FBI surveillance recordings, passenger complaints to the Transportation Security Administration, Superfund cost documentation at the EPA, etc.—and what the agency would like to do with them. Agencies usually ask to destroy entire categories of documents within years, though at other times they may ask to destroy them within months or decades.

A staff member at NARA's Records Management Services division then appraises each request. Usually, the appraiser approves the agency's proposal.

But that initial approval is tentative, because the process is then opened up for public comment. Nevertheless, NARA almost always grants final approval following the public comment period, no doubt due, in no small part, to the difficulty the public has had in even learning about the agencies' requests.

Here's why the process has been so obscure:

Two or three times per month in the Federal Register, NARA announces the proposals it has received from agencies. The way it worked from 1985 to early 2019 was that you—an interested member of the public—had to write to NARA and ask to be sent the proposals and appraisals you wanted. NARA didn't post these crucial documents, even though it easily could have begun doing so in 1994, when its website launched.

But making these requests was kind of tricky. You had to request a proposal from NARA within 30 days of its announcement in the Federal Register. Once you received it, you had no more than 30 days to comment. To make matters worse, after public comments were filed, there was no easy way to check on the status of a proposal. As a result, agencies were often given approval to destroy government documents with little or no oversight from the public.

Spotlight on an Obscure Process

In 2017 I started paying close attention to this process. When I saw that an agency was proposing to destroy documents that sounded especially important, I would request the full proposal and accompanying appraisal.

That is how I discovered that Immigration and Customs Enforcement (ICE) wanted to destroy all documents about the deaths and rapes of people detained in its facilities after a retention period of 20 years, and that NARA had given preliminary approval to that awful request. I posted the proposal and appraisal on my website and let some reporters know. The American Civil Liberties Union (ACLU) quickly picked up on the story, and it went viral.[16] NARA subsequently announced that it would be requiring ICE to make unspecified changes to its proposal.

In the first half of 2018 I discovered that the National Security Agency (NSA) proposed to destroy all complaints and inquiries it receives about civil liberties after a retention period of only one year.[17]

In the summer of 2018 I started requesting *every* documents-destruction proposal that NARA received, as well as every appraisal by NARA of those proposals. I posted them all on a dedicated page on my website.

Still, nothing much happened—not until I got a gigantic request that the Interior Department had sent to NARA proposing to destroy massive amounts of documents about oil and gas leases, mining, dams, wells, timber sales, fishing, endangered species, critical habitats, land acquisition, and lots more.

I decided to highlight that mega-proposal on a separate webpage[18] and informed reporters, open government proponents, and environmental activists.

The interest was explosive. Scientists, environmentalists, animal rights activists, and transparency advocates were furious. NARA was flooded with public comments on the proposal. NARA eventually received more than 12,000 comments, thousands more than the agency receives on most proposals.

Further Reforms Needed

In March 2019, NARA made a major announcement: It would immediately begin posting online all schedules for records-destruction proposals, create an online system to allow public comment on those proposals, and extend the public comment period from 30 to 45 days. NARA directly credited this sea change to the "clear, widespread interest from the public" in the previously obscure, arcane process[19]—interest that was triggered by the proposal from the Interior Department.

So, mission accomplished, right? Well, not exactly.

There needs to be an online clearinghouse on the NARA website devoted to the entire process, where all proposals and appraisals are posted. That way, at any given moment, you could see every records-destruction request currently in the public comment stage, as well as the ones that have moved to further stages in the process.

Moreover, there's still no way to check on a proposal's status at any given moment. And what if NARA asks an agency to make a change to its proposal, but the agency refuses? Parts of this process are still taking place inside a black box.

NARA's attitude toward government documents and their value is also a problem. The National Archives still believes that only 1–3 percent of federal records are worth keeping permanently. All others can eventually be thrown down the memory hole.

Back in the pre-digital era, when all records were on paper, the need to be highly selective about what was preserved forever was understandable. There are at NARA only so many miles—yes, miles—of shelf space available to house physical documents. But in an age when most government documents are born digital, there's no excuse for not keeping the vast majority of records permanently. Sure, it'll take petabytes (and exabytes and zettabytes) of storage space, but that's easily doable compared to storing millions of tons of paper.

The process has to be widened to include other stakeholders. Transparency organizations need a seat at this table. And so do subject-matter experts. When the Internal Revenue Service proposes to destroy documents, tax experts need to be consulted. NARA should formally ask immigration groups about ICE proposals, historians about State Department proposals, military experts about Army proposals, librarians about Library of Congress proposals, and so on.

It was possible to pressure NARA into greatly, though imperfectly, increasing transparency. I believe it's possible to pressure them to implement these other crucial reforms, and we need to keep trying.

RUSS KICK is a writer, anthologist, transparency activist, and Freedom of Information Act nerd. He's written five published books and created thirteen anthologies, including the *New York Times*–bestselling *Graphic Canon* series. He's created several websites devoted to forcing institutional transparency, with the two active ones being AltGov2 (https://altgov2.org) and Animal Info Sanctuary (https://animalinfosanctuary.org).

BEYOND "BAD ACTORS": DIGITAL ADVERTISING AND POLITICAL MANIPULATION

Matthew Crain and Anthony Nadler

For years it seemed that Silicon Valley technology companies enjoyed an endless supply of public good will. Their platforms were useful, engaging, and often free. Some were even described as inherently democratic. Today, big tech's honeymoon phase appears to be ending. Nowhere is this clearer than at Facebook, where cascading scandals involving invasive data collection, security breaches, discriminatory practices, and inflaming violence have invigorated public debate over the social media giant's impact on democracy.

Stoking this "techlash" were revelations that foreign operatives used Facebook in attempts to spread disinformation, exacerbate political divisions, and influence electoral outcomes in the 2016 US elections. Under mounting public pressure, Facebook and other companies have primarily framed such problems as a matter of "bad actors" hijacking their platforms for electoral disruption.[20] Their mitigation efforts have largely entailed more rigid gatekeeping to keep illegitimate ads and accounts at bay and increased measures of detection to remove those that slip through the cracks.

The "bad actors" narrative has been propelled by concerns around foreign political interference, but it is rooted in a deeper refusal to acknowledge that data-driven influence peddling is the core business model of Facebook and its ilk. Leveraging surveillance data to strategically target audiences is not some rogue use of social media; it is a fundamental feature. As Dipayan Ghosh and Ben Scott put it in their summary of the 2016 US presidential election, political manipulation campaigns are "digital marketing 101."[21]

Our research, in partnership with the Media Manipulation Initiative (MMI) at the Data & Society Research Institute, suggests that the "bad actors" strategy for addressing the problems of political manipulation is at best a partial solution.[22] The MMI looks at the design and capacities of media infrastructures that are vulnerable to manipulation and examines how technical systems might be recalibrated to prioritize accountability and fairness.

Tech companies have built an enormous digital influence machine—a set of overlapping technologies for surveillance and targeting designed to make commercial and political advertising more efficient. To win consent to build such a supercharged surveillance system, tech companies have historically promised users and regulators that targeted advertising is mutually beneficial to consumers and advertisers.[23] In this bargain, users are supposed to receive "more relevant" ads. According to Facebook, "When we ask people about our ads, one of the top things they tell us is that they want to see ads that relate to things they care about."[24]

However, political operatives and others have quickly figured out that the capacities of digital ad systems allow for much more. On top of making advertisements *more relevant* to users' pre-existing interests, data-driven techniques can also be used to make users *more pliable* for advertisers. Political operatives can use targeted advertising to identify vulnerabilities to influence a population.[25]

With targeted advertising, political operatives can experiment with messages designed to make different groups feel an opponent represents an emotionally-charged threat to their identity. For instance, in 2016 Russia-linked operatives ran hundreds of ads targeted to specific audiences suggesting that Hillary Clinton had insulted their group's dignity and/or threatened their safety in a variety of ways. Some ads alleged that Clinton espoused disrespect for specific occupations, like coal mining, or racial groups, like African Americans. Others alleged she would confiscate guns.

Such strategies are not unique to online advertising, but digital ad systems offer significant advantages over traditional ads. First, social media platforms allow advertisers to empirically test numerous messages across different audience segments. They can receive instantaneous feedback to see which versions of ads elicit sharing, liking, or other types of engagement among various audiences. This is known as "split testing" or "A/B testing," and it helps political operatives refine tactics as they probe for just the right images, words, and targeting parameters to optimize impact.

Second, data-driven targeting allows advertisers to profile users and reach only those suspected to be most sensitive to particular identity threats. This is more cost-effective and may also reduce the well-known backlash effect of inflammatory political advertising over mass media channels, which always risks mobilizing opposition. One way political operatives have used such targeted threats is to try to stir in-fighting among coalitions of their opponents.[26] Dark money political advertisers may take the greatest advantage of such manipulative strategies because users cannot learn the identities or motives of the ad sponsors.

Given that platforms like Facebook and Google bring in billions of dollars of ad revenue per year, it is not surprising that they have been reluctant to make significant changes to their advertising systems. Yet a meaningful approach to political manipulation requires going beyond the "bad actor" framework. We must address the advertising-driven communications infrastructures that facilitate political manipulation.

This requires shifting the design and governance of digital media architectures away from private control calibrated for profit maximization. Instead, democratic publics must have a strong voice in deciding how digital platforms operate. A top priority should be public policies that reform the structures of digital advertising systems. Regulations must make these systems less capable of using data to manipulate people through finely targeted messages.

Another proposal that would have widespread popular resonance is a ban on data-driven advertising by dark money political groups. Groups that refuse to reveal their funders should not be allowed to leverage intimate knowledge about users in attempts to influence them. Passing a law to such an effect will clearly not solve all the problems with digital manipulation, but we see a demand for such a ban as a starting point for mobilizing a broad coalition of activists and citizens. It could set a precedent to build momentum for further democratic accountability in digital infrastructure.

To read our report on the Digital Influence Machine and learn more about Data & Society's Media Manipulation Initiative, visit https://data-society.net/output/weaponizing-the-digital-influence-machine/.

MATTHEW CRAIN is an assistant professor of media, journalism, and film at Miami University. His research is centered on the historical development and democratic implications of digital advertising and consumer surveillance.

ANTHONY NADLER is an associate professor of media and communication studies at Ursinus College and currently a fellow at the Tow Center for Digital Journalism at Columbia University. His research focuses on civic communication, online politics, digital advertising, and propaganda.

DESMOG: CLEARING THE PR POLLUTION THAT CLOUDS CLIMATE AND ENERGY SOLUTIONS

Brendan DeMelle and Ashley Braun

Since launching in 2006, DeSmogBlog has pulled no punches in calling the fossil fuel industry to account for its well-funded campaigns to cast doubt on climate science, to block or hamstring clean energy technologies, and to seed misinformation intended to distract or discourage the public and policymakers from long-overdue action to avert climate chaos.

In addition to DeSmog's daily news articles and in-depth investigative series by a global team of journalists and researchers spanning three continents, the blog's research database profiles more than 650 individuals and organizations, providing a one-stop resource to learn about the merchants of doubt responsible for spreading disinformation, with detailed funding data, quotes, and deeds updated on a rolling basis.

When *Time* magazine named DeSmog one of its "Best Blogs of 2011," calling us "the antidote" and "a necessary corrective" to global warming misinformation, we were honored, of course.[27] They also criticized our "jihad against gas fracking"—an apparent slight that we still consider a compliment. We had released our "Fracking the Future" report in 2010, presciently pointing out major potential risks to the environment, public health, and democracy from hydraulic fracturing (fracking), which was then just taking off in the United States. Look where we are now.

In recent years, DeSmog has launched deep investigations into the expansion of oil and gas infrastructure (pipelines, fossil fuel terminals, and petrochemical plants) in the United States, Europe, and Australia. That expansion has been the result of increasing global reliance on polluting fossil fuel energy and feedstocks.

In our "Finances of Fracking" series, DeSmog reporters Justin

Mikulka and Sharon Kelly chronicle the rickety financials that the fracking boom is based on—now amounting to piles of debt that can only be repaid via the continued growth of fossil fuel demand at the exact moment that society needs to hastily phase out such polluting energy sources.

Between 2007 and 2017, the oil and gas industry lost $280 billion betting on the shale boom, which was fueled by prolific Wall Street financing—reminiscent of the mid-2000s housing bubble.[28] Even as the industry continues to borrow heavily just to recoup costs, much less to generate profits, Mikulka and Kelly have found that the great promise of the shale revolution is also threatened by another specter: declining production at every well.

At the same time, fracking has unearthed a massive oversupply of hydrocarbons that aren't profitable to transport to market—chiefly, vast amounts of methane and what the industry calls "natural gas liquids." The methane is flared or vented into the atmosphere, contributing air pollution and high global warming potential, while, in typical fashion, the fossil fuel industry came up with a lucrative "solution" to their other waste problems: plastics and petrochemicals.

Our "Fracking for Plastics" series follows the industry's "Hail Mary" attempt to turn more and more fracked hydrocarbons into plastics that will choke our oceans and pollute our bodies. Sharon Kelly is exploring industry's quest for billions of dollars' worth of subsidies to create a new fracking-fueled "Plastics Belt" across Ohio, Pennsylvania, and West Virginia, and expanding a heavily polluted corridor along the Gulf Coast known as "Cancer Alley."

If the more than $200 billion in projected petrochemical investments are completed, analysts predict that the United States would flip from one of the world's highest-cost producers of plastics and chemicals to one of the cheapest. The expansion would lock in decades more oil and gas drilling—independent from the ongoing transition to renewable energy—with profound consequences for a planet already imperiled by climate change and pollution crises.

DeSmog also seeks to shine a supportive spotlight on the growing grassroots resistance and Keep It in the Ground movements, which face increasingly militarized responses from a desperate industry and its beholden political forces.

In September 2016, when a pipeline security company used pepper spray and attack dogs on Standing Rock Sioux Tribe members and their swelling numbers of supporters protesting construction of the Dakota Access Pipeline, national and international media suddenly focused attention on the escalating conflict centered in North Dakota. By that time, however, DeSmog had been covering the dynamics of Energy Transfer Partners's multi-billion-dollar fracked oil pipeline for more than a year and a half.

In Louisiana's Atchafalaya Basin, a designated National Heritage Area with towering cypress trees older than the Louisiana Purchase, the same company that built Dakota Access rammed through another oil pipeline, the Bayou Bridge, at the tail end of a pipeline network that begins in North Dakota. Multimedia reporter Julie Dermansky's reporting for DeSmog repeatedly took her over the scene in a small plane, out on the water, and onto contested land along the pipeline's route.

Often, Dermansky was the only reporter left holding a camera when people stood in the way of pipeline construction, making her a powerful witness to the growing US resistance to fossil fuel pipelines. Working in Louisiana, a conservative state where the oil and gas industry is used to government rubber-stamping, she has ensured this fight is covered at every step, from the initial permit hearings to the courtroom battles of landowners fighting against a private corporation's use of eminent domain to install an oil pipeline for the purported "public good."

Dermansky keeps a "go bag" packed by the front door for whenever the inevitable next incident occurs, whether it's a protest, spill, or natural disaster.

Other important DeSmog projects include www.kochvsclean.com, which tracks Koch brothers–funded attacks on electric vehicles and clean energy; and our resident "bomb train" expert Justin Mikulka's ongoing look at risky oil-by-rail transport. Wherever industry plays dirty, DeSmog strives to be the antidote.

Find DeSmogBlog online at www.desmogblog.com.

BRENDAN DEMELLE is executive director of DeSmogBlog. He is also a freelance writer and researcher whose work has appeared in *Vanity Fair*, Huffington Post, *Corporate Knights*, and other outlets.

ASHLEY BRAUN is managing editor of DeSmogBlog. She is also a freelance science journalist whose work has appeared in publications such as *The Atlantic*, Slate, *Scientific American*, and *Discover Magazine*.

LABOR NOTES: PUTTING THE MOVEMENT BACK IN THE LABOR MOVEMENT

Alexandra Bradbury

Every daily newspaper has a business section, but almost none has even a single labor reporter anymore. You might see establishment news coverage when there's a strike or lockout—often getting the details wrong and parroting the employer's talking points. But where can you read nuanced reporting on, say, a grassroots movement by rank-and-file Teamsters to reject contract concessions pushed jointly by their employer and their union leaders?

You'll find it in *Labor Notes* magazine, at https://labornotes.org.

In 2018 we devoted extensive coverage to the "vote no" campaign at UPS, in the nation's largest private sector contract, interviewing dozens of Teamsters about why members opposed a deal that would pay new drivers less, and how they were organizing against it. While 54 percent of UPS workers ultimately voted in favor of rejecting the deal, top union leaders nonetheless exploited a loophole to force the deal through, adding fuel to a growing opposition movement inside the union.[29] In all, our coverage of the vote and its aftermath garnered more than 150,000 pageviews—mainly, we believe, from rank-and-file drivers and warehouse workers. No other news outlet followed the story in such depth.

Labor Notes was formed in 1979 to bring together rank-and-file movements for greater democracy and militancy in the unions of auto workers, mine workers, Teamsters, and steelworkers. These activists were fighting similar battles but mostly didn't know each other. Labor Notes aimed to help them cohere into one big movement.

Fast-forward 40 years, and Labor Notes has grown into an unusual hybrid of magazine, training center, and organizing network—the hub of what we affectionately call "the troublemaking wing of the labor movement." Activists build solidarity and skills at our one-day local Troublemakers Schools and our renowned biennial conference, which, in 2018, drew 3,000 people from 47 states and 26 countries.[30]

We're still indisputably the place to go to learn how to change your union from below, and to link up with others who share the same vision. We've also become a respected resource for training and information; many unions send members to our conferences and bulk-order *A Troublemaker's Handbook 2*, *How to Jump-Start Your Union*, and *Secrets of a Successful Organizer*, books we distilled mainly from our reporting.

Labor Notes staff do the lion's share of reporting, but we also publish many firsthand accounts by workers, who are encouraged to write up their own campaigns so others can learn from their successes and missteps.

A hospital X-ray tech in Buffalo explained how he and his coworkers shamed their employer out of cutting one worker's pay by organizing a tongue-in-cheek fundraising drive featuring jars of pennies.[31] Two Macy's department store workers in Seattle coauthored an account of creative contract tactics—feather boas included—that got hundreds of new members involved.[32] A shop steward at a West Virginia grocery store told how she led an impromptu "march on the boss" that cowed a manager into tearing up an unfair disciplinary measure on the spot.[33]

For a long time Labor Notes was keeping a flame alive in the wilderness. While many unions were accepting employers' demands for concessions, we taught how to resist them. While many unions turned their focus to legislative politics or public relations, we insisted that the cornerstone of power is workplace action and the readiness to strike. While many unions consolidated decision-making into a select few hands, we argued that a union must be run democratically to truly build power. While many unions narrowed their focus onto bread-and-butter issues, we encouraged members to set their sights higher and think about demands that would benefit whole communities and transform society.

The mainstream strategies did not work out well for labor. Under the pressure of an employer onslaught of union-busting and off-shoring, for decades the number of union members in the United States has been shrinking and real wages have been plummeting. Employer-backed anti-union groups mounted a series of legislative and judicial attacks that instituted "right to work" laws in a majority of states—creating a short-term financial incentive for workers to opt out of union membership. In 2018 the Supreme Court's decision in *Janus v. AFSCME* established "right to work" as standard policy across the entire public sector.

It's a measure of how alienated many unions had become from the workers they represented that they assumed this ruling would open them up to big membership losses. Our survival guide *Rebuilding Power in Open-Shop America* described how certain unions operating in open-shop states or sectors still manage to win campaigns and maintain high rates of membership. So far we've distributed 18,000 copies.

We've seen a surge of interest in bottom-up strategies. There's an uptick in strikes, especially but not only among K–12 teachers. Labor Notes has helped to build and sustain the teacher strike wave, including the 2018 red-state uprising that swept from West Virginia to Kentucky, Oklahoma, and Arizona, and mobilizations that followed in California, Colorado, North Carolina, Oregon, South Carolina, Washington, and Wisconsin.

The groundswell can be traced back to Chicago teachers, whose landmark 2012 strike for "the schools Chicago's students deserve" sparked the imagination of teachers throughout the country. Labor Notes collaborated with Chicago teachers on a book about how they transformed their union and built up to that strike, *How to Jump-Start Your Union: Lessons from the Chicago Teachers*. We helped form the United Caucuses of Rank-and-File Educators, a social justice union network that became a hub for cross-union collaboration across dozens of teacher locals and caucuses. The leaders of the red-state strikes were quickly attracted to the resources and support this network offers; it helped some of them turn what could have been flash-in-the-pan eruptions into sustained organization.

Meanwhile, the political landscape in this country has shifted too. Working people are setting their sights higher, influenced by high-profile strikes, the Fight for $15, and the popular demands for Medicare for all, universal access to higher education, and a Green New Deal. The possible demise of organized labor looms, but so does an opposite and equally real possibility—a new upsurge that could dramatically expand unions' numbers, power, and fighting spirit in a short period, as occurred during the 1930s in the private sector and during the 1960–1970s in the public sector.

Today, Labor Notes is one of the labor movement's main sources of energy, excitement, and hope. Scratch any recent inspiring strike or struggle and you're likely to find that Labor Notes activists and resources helped make it possible. If the upsurge comes, we will be at the center among those helping to build it.

ALEXANDRA BRADBURY is editor and co-director of *Labor Notes*.

PROPAGANDA CRITIC: A TOOL FOR ANALYZING PROPAGANDA IN THE 21ST CENTURY

Aaron Delwiche and Mary Margaret Herring

Why Do We Need Propaganda Critic?

In the wake of the 2016 elections, journalists, educators, and political activists expressed alarm about the destructive influence of fake news, bots, sockpuppets, and trolls. Unfortunately, many argue that responsibility for fixing these problems rests on the shoulders of public officials and social media platforms.

Some say that Facebook, Twitter, and YouTube should terminate the accounts of individuals and organizations that distribute harmful or offensive propaganda. Others call for the implementation of algorithms that would identify, flag, and delete problematic online content. There are even some who suggest that the only way to solve these problems is to pass legislation that would make it impossible to speak anonymously online.

Censorship is a bad idea, whether it is carried out by human beings or implemented via computer code. The right to speak anonymously is an essential human liberty. Politicians and technocrats cannot save us. Censorship and government regulation will not cure the problems that plague democracy at a national and global level.

Propaganda Critic is premised on the belief that all of us—regardless of party affiliation—are capable of stepping up and renewing our commitment to civic engagement and authentic democratic dialogue. By studying the ways that other people seek to persuade us, and by reflecting on the logical fallacies and emotional underpinnings of our own political statements, we can help to revitalize the lost art of political conversation.

What is Propaganda Critic?

Established almost 25 years ago when the web was in its infancy, the site Propaganda Critic (https://propagandacritic.com) is dedicated to promoting techniques of propaganda analysis among critically-minded individuals.

The site is inspired by the pioneering work of the Institute for Propaganda Analysis (IPA). From 1937 to 1942, journalists, social scientists, and educators affiliated with the IPA published a series of books and pamphlets that offered accessible explanations of common propaganda techniques.

The IPA was most well-known for identifying seven basic propaganda devices: name-calling, glittering generalities, the transfer technique, testimonials, the "plain folks" appeal, card stacking, and the bandwagon technique. According to political communication researchers James E. Combs and Dan Nimmo, "[T]hese seven devices have been repeated so frequently in lectures, articles, and textbooks ever since that they have become virtually synonymous with the practice and analysis of propaganda in all of its aspects."[34]

Although the seven devices identified by the IPA are still useful, they do not sufficiently account for the contemporary crises that threaten democracies around the world. In recent years, sophisticated propagandists have used artificially intelligent agents (bots) and fake user accounts (sockpuppets) to flood online spaces with disinformation. These developments have upended traditional assumptions about the nature of propaganda, highlighting the urgent need for new critical tools that global citizens can use to seek the truth.

For this reason, with support from Trinity University and the Mellon Initiative for Undergraduate Research in the Arts and Humanities, we recently overhauled Propaganda Critic to better fit our new communication landscape. In addition to updating all of the original content, we added nearly two dozen new articles and commissioned artwork from the comic artist Carol Lay to teach users about new forms of propaganda.

What Will You Find on the Site?

The website's *Core Concepts* section draws attention to recent developments in propaganda. Articles in that section discuss the ubiquity of propaganda, the use of bots to propagate disinformation, the rise of phony user accounts known as sockpuppets, the role of opaque algorithms in influencing social media updates, the collection of user behavior by social media platforms, and the rise of "the fake audience."

The section *Everybody is Biased* explains that we are all inhibited by cognitive biases or "faulty ways of thinking" hardwired into the human brain. Articles in that section discuss anchoring (our tendency to believe the first information we hear about any new topic), the sleeper effect (the well-documented tendency to remember and be influenced by claims while forgetting the source of those claims), the way repetition can be used to establish the "truth" of a claim, reactance (our propensity to condemn perceived infringements on our freedoms), and declinism (the widespread inclination to remember the past nostalgically while fearing the future).

The section *Decoding Propaganda* is focused primarily on the seven original IPA devices for analyzing propaganda messages, but also includes a few additional considerations for contemporary discourse. Articles in that section discuss name-calling (using negatively loaded words to discredit ideas), glittering generalities (using positive words to elevate ideas), euphemisms (using neutral words to sanitize unpleasant realities), the transfer technique (linking an idea to something that is widely held in high regard), the testimonial technique (using celebrities to promote an idea), the "plain folks" appeal (presenting an idea as being "of the people"), faulty logic and unwarranted extrapolations, and the fear appeal (promoting an idea by terrifying the audience).

The *Case Studies* section provides a more detailed look at how these persuasive techniques and technologies have been used in real-world situations. Articles in that section talk about the fabricated terrorist attack on a Columbian Chemicals plant in 2014, a US military sock-puppet operation termed Operation Earnest Voice, a massive Chinese sockpuppet operation called the 50 Cent Army, the ways that white nationalists in the United States deployed phony accounts in a (failed) attempt to influence the outcome of the 2017 election in France, and how ISIS uses networks of bots to disseminate recruiting propaganda and beheading videos.

The *Examples* section invites visitors to apply their critical thinking skills by scrutinizing examples of political propaganda collected from across the political spectrum. That section includes a manifesto from the America First Party, agitation propaganda from Antifa, examples of anti-American propaganda from Afghanistan, a press release from Enron, a flyer from the International Workers Association, conspiracy theories from the John Birch Society, an analysis of professional basketball from the Maoist International Movement, and excerpts from Newt Gingrich's classic treatise *Language: A Key Mechanism of Control*.

The *Tools for Fighting Back* section explains how to spot fake news, suggests strategies for detecting media bias, highlights telltale characteristics of bots and sockpuppets, and profiles resources that can be used to debunk rumors and to fact-check claims.

To learn more, visit our website at https://propagandacritic.com.

AARON DELWICHE is a professor in the Department of Communication at Trinity University in San Antonio, Texas. He coedited *The Participatory Cultures Handbook* (Routledge, 2012), and his recent work includes a chapter about the history of computer bulletin board systems in *The SAGE Handbook of Social Media* as well as an article about the rise of the "fake audience" for *The SAGE Handbook of Propaganda*. Aaron earned a PhD in communications from the University of Washington. He can be contacted at adelwich@trinity.edu.

MARY MARGARET HERRING is a philosophy and communication major at Trinity University, and she expects to graduate in May 2020. Fascinated with dystopian visions and extremist politics, she values the role of authentic deliberation in sustaining the public sphere. In 2018, Mary Margaret earned a summer research grant from the Mellon Initiative.

STEVE MACEK, who edited and introduced this chapter, is professor of communication and chair of the Department of Communication and Media Studies at North Central College in Naperville, Illinois. He is the author of *Urban Nightmares: The Media, the Right, and the Moral Panic over the City* (University of Minnesota Press, 2006), and his op-eds and essays about the media, politics, and free speech issues have been published in a wide range of magazines and newspapers, including *Z Magazine, St. Louis Journalism Review, Atlanta Journal-Constitution, Columbus Dispatch*, and *News & Observer* (Raleigh, North Carolina).

Notes

1. Christopher R. Martin, *No Longer Newsworthy: How the Mainstream Media Abandoned the Working Class* (Ithaca, NY: Cornell University Press, 2019).
2. Lena H. Sun, "CDC Chief Admits Pattern of Safety Lapses after Mishandling Anthrax, Other Pathogens," *Washington Post*, July 16, 2014, https://www.washingtonpost.com/national/health-science/cdc-chief-admits-pattern-of-safety-lapses-after-mishandling-anthrax-other-pathogens/2014/07/16/af778ce2-0cfe-11e4-8c9a-923eccoc7d23_story.html.
3. Segaran Pillai, "FDA Review of the 2014 Discovery of Vials Labeled '*Variola*' and Other Vials Discovered in an FDA-Occupied Building on the NIH Campus," Food and Drug Administration, December 13, 2016, https://www.fda.gov/media/101811/download.
4. Ibid.
5. "Recommendations of the Advisory Committee to the Director Concerning Laboratory Safety at CDC," Centers for Disease Control and Prevention, January 13, 2015, currently online at https://timedotcom.files.wordpress.com/2015/03/acd-lab-safety-recommendations-2015-01-16.pdf. [accessed June 28, 2019]. In the text, "ELSW" refers to the External Laboratory Safety Workgroup assigned to review the situation following the mishaps.
6. See, for instance, Charles Seife, "How the FDA Manipulates the Media," *Scientific American*, October 1, 2016, https://www.scientificamerican.com/article/how-the-fda-manipulates-the-media/; and Peter Sullivan, "CDC Tells Employees Not to Talk to the Press: Report," The Hill, September 12, 2017, https://thehill.com/business-a-lobbying/350224-cdc-tells-employees-not-to-talk-to-the-press-report.
7. "Resolution No. 2: Calling on Journalists to Oppose the Mandate Clearance Culture," Society of Professional Journalists, September 9, 2017, submitted to the Excellence in Journalism Conference in Anaheim, California, www.spj.org/res2017.asp#2.
8. "Public Information Officers," Society of Professional Journalists, undated, www.spj.org/pios.asp [accessed June 13, 2019].
9. Ibid.
10. Josh Sanburn, "Why the EPA is Partly to Blame for the Flint Water Crisis," *Time*, January 22, 2016, https://time.com/4190643/flint-water-crisis-susan-hedman-epa/.
11. Amy Ellis Nutt and Dan Keating, "One of America's Most Popular Drugs—First Aimed at Schizophrenia—Reveals the Issues of 'Off-Label' Use," *Washington Post*, March 30, 2018, https://www.washingtonpost.com/national/health-science/one-of-americas-most-popular-drugs--first-aimed-at-schizophrenia--reveals-the-issues-of-off-label-use/2018/03/28/78a538ca-1e27-11e8-b2d9-08e748f892c0_story.html.
12. The estimated number of FDA employees is based on "Detail of Full-Time Equivalent Employment," Food and Drug Administration, August 7, 2018, https://www.fda.gov/media/106372/download.
13. See "Public Information Officers: SPJ Surveys," Society of Professional Journalists, undated, https://www.spj.org/pios.asp#surveys [accessed June 13, 2019].
14. Carolyn S. Carlson and Paymon Kashani, "Mediated Access: Crime Reporters' Perceptions of Public Information Officers' Media Control Efforts, Use of Social Media, Handling of Body Camera Footage and Public Records," Society of Professional Journalists, March 2016, https://www.spj.org/pdf/sunshineweek/crime-reporters-survey-report.pdf, 11.

15. Carolyn S. Carlson and Paymon Kashani, "Mediated Access: Police Public Information Officers' Media Management Efforts, Use of Social Media, Handling of Body Camera Footage and Public Records," Society of Professional Journalists, March 2016, https://spj.org/pdf/sunshineweek/police-pios-survey-report.pdf, 3.

16. "Request for Records Disposition Authority," National Archives and Records Administration, June 20, 2017, posted on https://altgov2.org/wp-content/uploads/DAA-0567-2015-0013_Record_Schedule.pdf; Victoria López, "ICE Plans to Start Destroying Records of Immigrant Abuse, Including Sexual Assault and Deaths in Custody," American Civil Liberties Union, August 28, 2017, https://www.aclu.org/blog/immigrants-rights/ice-and-border-patrol-abuses/ice-plans-start-destroying-records-immigrant. Project Censored covered this story, including Victoria López's report, as one of the most important but overlooked news stories of 2017–18; see Ellisha Huntoon, Katherine Epps, Kelly Van Boekhout, and Mickey Huff, "ICE Intends to Destroy Records of Inhumane Treatment of Immigrants," in *Censored 2019: Fighting the Fake News Invasion*, eds. Mickey Huff and Andy Lee Roth with Project Censored (New York: Seven Stories Press, 2018), 67–68, https://www.projectcensored.org/12-ice-intends-to-destroy-records-of-inhumane-treatment-of-immigrants/.

17. Russ Kick, "The NSA Wants to Destroy Records of Complaints & Allegations," AltGov2, September 6, 2018, https://altgov2.org/nsa-complaints.

18. Russ Kick, "Dept of the Interior: Records Destruction Request," AltGov2, October 16, 2018, updated October 25, 2018, https://altgov2.org/doi-records-destruction/.

19. Laurence Brewer, "Memorandum to Federal Agency Contacts: Change to the Public Comment Process for Records Schedules," NARA Bulletin AC 12.2019, Federal Records Management (National Archives and Records Administration), March 4, 2019, https://www.archives.gov/records-mgmt/memos/ac12-2019.

20. Jon Swartz, "Facebook's Sandberg: 'There will Always be Bad Actors,'" *Barron's*, March 22, 2018, https://www.barrons.com/articles/facebooks-sandberg-there-will-always-be-bad-actors-1521751804.

21. Dipayan Ghosh and Ben Scott, "Russia's Election Interference is Digital Marketing 101," *The Atlantic*, February 19, 2018, https://www.theatlantic.com/international/archive/2018/02/russia-trump-election-facebook-twitter-advertising/553676/.

22. Anthony Nadler, Matthew Crain, and Joan Donovan, "Weaponizing the Digital Influence Machine: The Political Perils of Online Ad Tech," Data & Society, October 17, 2018, https://datasociety.net/output/weaponizing-the-digital-influence-machine/.

23. See, for example, Pablo Chavez, "Our Senate Testimony on Online Advertising and Google-DoubleClick," Public Policy Blog (Google), September 27, 2007, https://publicpolicy.googleblog.com/2007/09/our-senate-testimony-on-online.html.

24. "Making Ads Better and Giving You More Control," Help Center, Facebook, undated, https://m.facebook.com/help/585318558251813 [accessed June 13, 2019].

25. Michael Reilly, "Is Facebook Targeting Ads at Sad Teens?" *MIT Technology Review*, May 1, 2017, https://www.technologyreview.com/s/604307/is-facebook-targeting-ads-at-sad-teens/.

26. Young Mie Kim, "Beware: Disguised as Your Community, Suspicious Groups May Target You Right Now for Election Interference Later," Project DATA (Digital Ad Tracking & Analysis), University of Wisconsin–Madison, August 8, 2018, https://journalism.wisc.edu/wp-content/blogs.dir/41/files/2018/08/nonwhite-recruitment-and-suppression.Russia.Kim_.v.3.080818.pdf.

27. Bryan Walsh, "Best Blogs of 2011: DeSmogBlog," *Time*, June 6, 2011, http://content.time.com/time/specials/packages/article/0,28804,2075431_2075447_2075499,00.html.

28. Bradley Olson and Lynn Cook, "Wall Street Tells Frackers to Stop Counting Barrels, Start Making Profits," *Wall Street Journal*, December 13, 2017, https://www.wsj.com/articles/wall-streets-fracking-frenzy-runs-dry-as-profits-fail-to-materialize-1512577420.

29. Alexandra Bradbury, "Update: Teamster Brass Overrule Member 'No' Vote at UPS," Labor Notes, October 18, 2018, https://labornotes.org/2018/10/updated-teamster-brass-overrule-member-no-vote-ups.

30. The 2020 Labor Notes Conference is scheduled for April 17–19, 2020, in Chicago. See "Save the Date: 2020 Labor Notes Conference," Labor Notes, undated, https://labornotes.org/2020 [accessed June 13, 2019].

31. Patrick Weisansal II, "Steward's Corner: Pennies for Evelyn," Labor Notes, June 6, 2019, https://labornotes.org/2019/06/stewards-corner-pennies-evelyn.

32. Nichole Booker and Curtisy Bryant, "Macy's Workers Win Sick Days by Fighting Back Fashionably," Labor Notes, March 28, 2019, https://labornotes.org/2019/03/macys-workers-win-sick-days-fighting-back-fashionably.

33. Auriana Fabricatore, "How We Marched on Our Boss," Labor Notes, June 7, 2018, https://labornotes.org/2018/06/how-we-marched-our-boss.

34. James E. Combs and Dan Nimmo, *The New Propaganda: The Dictatorship of Palaver in Contemporary Politics* (New York: Longman, 1993), 193.

CHAPTER 5

WHAT'S BURNING?

Written by
Adam Bessie

Illustrated by
Marc Parenteau

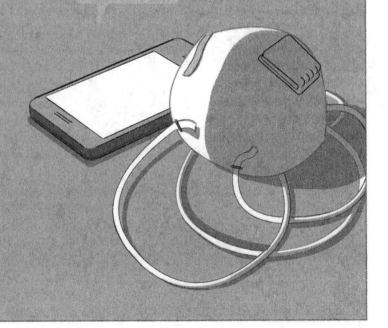

The town of Paradise was lost on a Thursday. I got the alert almost immediately.

Scrolling through the realtime torrent of apocalyptic images...

...I was torn about what to make of a tragedy filtered through the tiny screen.

I mean, how should I respond? By hitting "like"?*

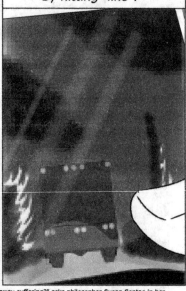

*"What to do with such knowledge as photographs bring of faraway suffering?" asks philosopher Susan Sontag in her last published work, *Regarding the Pain of Others*. Her thoughts frame what has become a more pressing question with the global expansion of social media.

That first night, the cellphone screen filtered the conflagration.

But the next day, the ash cloud descended on the Bay Area. So, we had to put on our own filters.*

What does it do?

There's a lot of tiny bad things in the air today...

...the mask'll stop those bad guys from getting in your lungs.

Outside, it looked like the aftermath of an asteroid strike.

* This essay owes an enormous debt to media scholar Neil Postman, whose works *Amusing Ourselves to Death: Public Discourse in the Age of Show Business* and *Technopoly: The Surrender of Culture to Technology* helped refine our thoughts on the state of both the natural and media ecosystems.

Like a lot of kids, my son has had serious asthma fits. Because California burns every year, we keep N95* masks in the house.

Are they gonna close school?

But that doesn't mean I feel all that confident that he'll be protected wearing one.

I doubt it.

AQI's only 125 right now.

AQI or Air Quality Index, measures the density of harmful particulates. Yes, there's an app for that. I find myself using it a lot in recent years.

Basically, if AQI hits 150, you don't want to be exposed to any unfiltered air at all. Even with a mask, it can feel like smoking a pack of Marlboros.

:cough:

:cough:

*N for *not* oil resistant, and *95* meaning it's rated to block 95% of particulates larger than 0.3 microns in diameter. (A mask of this type is the minimum protection needed to reduce the harm these tiny particles can cause.)

CENSORED 2020

Some kids miss school for Snow Days. My son is growing up with Smoke Days. The 2017 Tubbs Fire was his first.

Dad?

Yeah?

The AQI was well over 150. His kindergarten was closed for most of the week.

Can we go to Chuck E. Cheese?

What? *I'm* not cheesy enough for you?

BoOp
BoOp
zAp

One afternoon we spent playing—of all things—a firefighter video game.*

diNG
BoOdleOOp
zAp
zAp

* As we played that game, cartoonist Brian Fies's home was consumed by the Tubbs Fire. His arresting graphic memoir *A Fire Story* is highly recommended.

The month before Paradise burned, I was teaching E.M. Forster's 1909 dystopian sci-fi classic, The Machine Stops.

"One dies immediately in the outer air..."

In Forster's post-apocalyptic future, the environment is destroyed by industrialization.

"...the surface of the earth is only dust and mud..."

A real stretch, I know.*

"...no life remains on it..."

* "Science fiction is not predictive; it is descriptive," writes Ursula K. Le Guin in the introduction to her classic *The Left Hand of Darkness*. We couldn't agree more. Predictions are a fool's errand. Giving us an advanced sense of the not-yet-literally-describable contours of the present is where sci-fi has always excelled.

I teach dystopias all the time, but I wish they weren't so damned relevant.

After reading The Machine Stops, many students have told me they could relate to the idea of a society driven underground by disaster...

"Imagine, if you can, a small room..."

"..hexagonal in shape, like the cell of a bee."

clic

...each person living in their own private bubble...

...protectively quarantined.*

boop

* "American public life has become increasingly ideologically segregated as newspapers have given way to screens," according to a 2018 MIT study which visually mapped the social distances between our "filter bubbles".

During the Camp Fire, my son's school was open but had its windows firmly shut. The best quarantine they could manage.

As I left, I stopped to take a selfie in my filter mask. Ok, five selfies...

... I had to get the lighting right.

Ostensibly, I took the photos to remember what it looks like when the sky is an ash heap. But the technology I use to do it makes a difference.

The tool I use to remember also packages me as content for a vast hive of machines. #yesfilter.*

clic

tap

* In a certain regard, selfies are what historian and media critic Daniel Boorstin would call "pseudo-events". That is, they are happenings whose form is shaped by—and whose primary purpose is to be ingested by—a technological media, rather than actions that are focused on affecting those physically present during their occurrence.

You could say the filter mask selfie is an apt icon of our situation in industrialized countries like the U.S.

The mask is itself a form of personal quarantine, meant to shield us from an environmental situation out of control.*

It's easy to be deluded about what problems we solve by our personal actions.

After all, wearing a mask doesn't have any effect on even the local weather, let alone global climate.

Still it seems, we can't help snapping a pic.

But in packaging crisis as content, do we not commodify disaster? Brand and sell it like a cup of coffee?

* Andrew Szasz calls this type of thing a form of "inverted quarantine". Rather than respond collectively to threats, our atomized society favors "solutions" that involve individually consuming new products. For more, see his work *Shopping Our Way to Safety: How We Changed from Protecting the Environment to Protecting Ourselves.*

We want to be seen, but the platforms we use don't see us as individuals.

Our likes, our shares, whatever their intent, all are refined into fuel for the machine.

789 k Views   124k Likes
#filtermask, #airpocalypse, #mask, #maskedup, #AQI

Once uploaded, our thoughts are no different than cat videos or ads for razor blades. Be they posts about our anxieties, or aestheticized images of disaster...

2.4 M Views   853k Likes
#smog, #airpocalypse, #SF, #smoke, #filter, #filtermask, #SanFrancisco

...for the machines that keep us watching, the only value is in how much of our attention is harnessed, how often, and for how long.*

* A large number of social media platforms utilize the attention controlling, random-reward design principles pioneered by the makers of slot machines. For more, see Natasha Dow Schüll's book *Addiction by Design: Machine Gambling in Las Vegas*.

Our attention gets chopped finer and finer until it combusts at the slightest spark. It can be very difficult to put out that fire.

Daddy!

What is it?

Check it out! I made the Titanic!

We can all use a little help.*

Adam, put the phone down.

You ready to go?

*Whatever the result, it bears some scrutiny to ask yourself whether or not social media actually facilitates genuine connection, or whether it mostly functions to punctuate your time on earth by fragmenting your attention. For some useful prompts on this, read Jaron Lanier's book *Ten Arguments for Deleting Your Social Media Accounts Right Now.*

On Nov. 25, 2018, the Camp Fire was 100% contained. In the weeks after, filter mask selfies stopped trending...

...but we still have a load of N95s in the cupboard.

After all, fire season is year-round now.

ADAM BESSIE writes comics. Some of the national outlets that have published his work include *The New Yorker, The Boston Globe, The Atlantic,* Truthout, and the Project Censored book series. Adam is a community college English professor in the Bay Area. He teaches courses on graphic novels and science fiction. His comics can be found at https://adambessie.com.

MARC PARENTEAU is a California-based cartoonist and editor. He is the visual editor for the ethnoGRAPHIC series at the University of Toronto Press. His work has been featured by *The Atlantic,* Vox, and Splinter Media, among other outlets. More at www.mparenteau.com.

Works Cited

Daniel J. Boorstin, *The Image: A Guide to Pseudo-Events in America* (New York: Atheneum Publishers, 1962).

Brian Fies, *A Fire Story* (New York: Abrams ComicArts, 2019).

John Kelly and Camille François, "This is What Filter Bubbles Actually Look Like," *MIT Technology Review,* August 22, 2018, https://www.technologyreview.com/s/611807/this-is-what-filter-bubbles-actually-look-like/.

Jaron Lanier, *Ten Arguments for Deleting Your Social Media Accounts Right Now* (New York: Henry Holt and Co., 2018).

Ursula K. Le Guin, "Introduction," *The Left Hand of Darkness* (New York: Ace Books, 1976 [first published by Ace Books, without the introduction, in 1969]).

Neil Postman, *Amusing Ourselves to Death: Public Discourse in the Age of Show Business* (New York: Penguin Books, 1985).

Neil Postman, *Technopoly: The Surrender of Culture to Technology* (New York: Knopf, 1992).

Natasha Dow Schüll, *Addiction by Design: Machine Gambling in Las Vegas* (Princeton, NJ: Princeton University Press, 2012).

Susan Sontag, *Regarding the Pain of Others* (New York: Farrar, Straus and Giroux, 2003).

Andrew Szasz, *Shopping Our Way to Safety: How We Changed from Protecting the Environment to Protecting Ourselves* (Minneapolis, MN: University of Minnesota Press, 2009).

CHAPTER 6

Kashmir Uncensored
Tortured by the World's Largest Democracy

Ifat Gazia and Tara Dorabji

In February 2019, a Kashmiri suicide bomber killed more than forty Indian military personnel, spurring air strikes between India and Pakistan and bringing the nuclear rivals toward the brink of war.[1] Kashmir made global headlines, yet the media establishment reported on the conflict as if it were merely a border dispute, as if there were no people involved, without asking what could have caused a young man to take such a desperate action. Most of the articles failed to mention the routine and blatant human rights violations occurring in Kashmir, or the decades-long independence movements. In June 2018, the United Nations (UN) released its first report on human rights violations in Kashmir, finding that Indian authorities have used excessive force to supress the movement for self-determination, including unlawful killings, torture, disappearances, and rapes.[2]

Control of Kashmir is split between three nuclear nations—China, India, and Pakistan—with the largest portion administered by India. The militarization is extreme. There are 700,000 armed forces in Indian-administered Kashmir, making it the most militarized zone in the world.[3]

Militarization and censorship reinforce each other in Kashmir, with the government closely monitoring journalists. "Every journalist is on their radar," said Kashmiri journalist Irfan Mehraj.[4] While local journalists are closely scrutinized, foreign journalists and human rights groups are routinely denied visas to the valley. According to Reporters Sans Frontières, it is "nearly impossible" for international journalists to obtain media visas to Indian-administered Kashmir.[5] In 2017, French filmmaker Paul Comiti was arrested and detained for filming an event with pellet gun victims.[6]

What is the world's largest democracy so afraid to share with the world?

TORTURE IN KASHMIR

"They picked me up and took me to the Army Center, where I was tortured. In Qalamabad Handwara Camp, they used a roller for torture," explained Nazir Ahmad Sheikh, who was taken in 1994 by the 14th Dogra Regiment, an infantry regiment of the Indian Army headed by Major Multani. Heavy stone rollers are often used as a method of torture, and army personnel throw their weight on top of the rollers. Sheikh lost both legs and four of his fingers as a result of the torture. Despite having a case filed against them in court, the perpetrators have not faced any prosecution.[7] Since 1990, there has not been a single prosecution of Indian armed forces for human rights violations in Kashmir.[8]

According to the Jammu Kashmir Coalition of Civil Society (JKCCS)'s 2017 report on human rights in Jammu and Kashmir, torture continues to be the most ignored and underreported subject in the region.[9] By keeping both international journalists and human rights activists out of the region, the Indian government creates conditions that allow it to continue to act with impunity.[10]

"They hit me like corn cobs are shelled to obtain maize. This threshing was so harsh that many wooden canes got broken in the process," explained 20-year-old Masood, who was arrested in August 2002 along with his entire cricket team under charges that the team was "anti-India and pro-Pakistan." Masood was blindfolded, chained, hung upside down, and left unconscious before being released. For the next fifteen years, Masood and his teammates continued to be intermittently arrested and tortured. In 2017, the charges were dropped, but Masood endures lifelong scars from the torture committed against him on false charges.[11]

In May 2019, human rights groups released the first comprehensive report on torture in the region. Based on 432 case studies, the report, "Torture: Indian State's Instrument of Control in Indian Administered Jammu and Kashmir," determined that 70 percent of the torture victims were civilians. Doctors, paramedics, and journalists in particular have been regularly targeted and assaulted since the early 1990s.[12]

In 1990, the sixteen-year-old son of a schoolteacher was killed by the Central Reserve Police Force in Cheeni Chowk, Anantnag. Devastated, the schoolteacher left his job to join the freedom movement. As an activist, he was continuously arrested and tortured. Fed up with the violence perpetrated against him, he joined the insurgency and was arrested as a militant in 1996. During detention, his flesh was burnt around his hands and stomach; his heel was chopped off so that he could not run again. His case succinctly illustrates how torture inflicted by the State can fuel militancy.[13]

Only a small percentage of people who have been tortured go to hospitals for treatment, even when medical attention is needed, due to fear of state reprisal and social stigma.[14] Retaliation for speaking about torture or even receiving medical treatment for it can be severe, and security forces have raided hospitals to arrest injured patients, destroyed or damaged medical equipment, and threatened, beaten, detained, and even killed doctors and other medical staff.[15]

A social and political activist, who requested to remain anonymous, explained some of the torture methods that were used on him: "There were different techniques and methods. All of those techniques—be it electric currents, rollers on legs, be it stretching, or beating with canes—all that kicking and boxing is basically called third degree [torture]." He was arrested for the first time in 1996, when he was a social and political activist who had decided to use nonviolent means to organize and resist after witnessing countless atrocities, including his brother's murder in custody. "I saw the crackdowns and cordons, how those people were tortured, beaten, and sometimes killed," he said. He was arrested multiple times in the course of his years as an activist. During one arrest, security forces bathed and cleaned him up and he thought he was going home. Instead, they took him into a beautiful garden filled with reporters, who had been informed that the army had caught a hardcore militant. He recounted, "So they gave me a piece of paper and threatened me that I should read it in front of the media, saying that I attacked army vehicles and other things. I didn't read it. After that, I was transferred to many torture centers."[16]

Documented forms of torture perpetrated by the Indian State

include beating; stripping people naked; hanging them upside down; electrocuting genitals; rubbing feces, petrol, and/or chili pepper in wounds, eyes, and genitals; and cutting flesh from the body.[17]

Between 2008 and 2017, thousands of people were arrested and tortured in Kashmir.[18] Throughout the region, torture is a contemporary state practice used to exercise control, inflict physical pain, and curb dissent. Victims are not only physically and mentally brutalized, but are even killed in Indian custody.[19] In 2019, a 28-year-old was killed in Cargo, a notorious torture center in Srinagar, as a result of torture inflicted by government forces.[20] The machine of torture was created not only to overpower a victim but also to break the victim's individual will and the collective will of the people. As George Orwell warned in his book *1984*, torture is not actually a means to something else, but an end in itself.[21] Dehumanizing victims during torture is the essence of this inhumane practice.[22]

Torture is also a widely used instrument to terrorize large populations, intimidate them, interrogate them, coerce confessions, or simply punish those who are thought to be sympathizers or relatives of pro-Pakistan and pro-independence militias, referred to as "militants."[23] One out of every five Kashmiris report experiencing some form of torture, ranging from verbal abuse, kicking, and slapping to waterboarding, extraction of nails, and electrocution of genitals. Sexual violence continues to be perpetrated by government forces. In 2016, a sixteen-year-old girl was molested by an army officer and then coerced into recording a video statement absolving him of responsibility.[24] In February 2018, 143 cases of documented sexual violence were submitted to the Jammu & Kashmir State Human Rights Commission for investigation.[25] Despite a petition calling for inquiries into these cases, "no progress" has been made on any of them, according to the International Federation for Human Rights and its partner organizations.[26]

Many innocent civilians are tortured while detained under the Jammu and Kashmir Public Safety Act (PSA), which allows for anyone to be held for up to two years without charges or trial.[27] Between March 2016 and August 2017, more than a thousand people were detained under the Public Safety Act.[28] In 2016, human rights activist Khurram Parvez was arrested and detained under the PSA to prevent him from attending a session of the United Nations Human Rights Council in Geneva.[29]

Children are also tortured and held under the Public Safety Act.[30] In 2012, the PSA was amended to prohibit the detention of children under the age of eighteen.[31] Nevertheless, in 2016 and 2017, human rights groups found evidence that the Indian armed forces continued to detain children under the PSA.[32] Children as young as thirteen years old have been victims of severe torture by military and police personnel. From 2003 to 2017, 144 children were killed while Indian armed forces carried out operations.[33] In 2018, at least 31 children were killed as a result of violent incidents perpetrated by the State.[34] Since the early 1990s, boys as young as age ten have been swept up in identification checks, which have often led to killings, tortures, or disappearances.[35] Many of these children suffer from Post-Traumatic Stress Disorder (PTSD) and struggle to continue their education. In 2016 in the Batamaloo area of Kashmir, a seventeen-year-old boy who was arrested on charges of throwing stones at military personnel was released after months of detention. In addition to torturing the boy in detention, government forces provided no information about the boy to his family. Firsthand accounts attest to the fact that many juveniles are arrested in the absence of their guardians and the legally-required First Information Reports (FIRs) are not filed.[36]

"My only crime was that I expressed my outrage about [the] killing of some innocent Kashmiri brothers," another young man from Kashmir who requested anonymity recounted. "I did that by pelting [a] few stones. I was arrested late in the night during Ramadan when I was coming out of the mosque after praying Taraweeh [late night special prayers during the Muslim month of fasting]. Even though I was a juvenile, they arrested me—rather, dragged me for almost a mile—and then put me in the police jeep. No legal guardian was present there, and for days to come our family members were not allowed to meet us. In [the] middle of the night some drunk policemen would come and beat us ruthlessly."[37] According to a government report in Kashmir, the majority of the people detained under the PSA are accused of being stone-pelters.[38]

Another seventeen-year-old Kashmiri boy was charged under Section 307 of the Indian Penal Code (that is, "attempt to murder") because he pelted stones during a protest after Friday prayers in the Batamaloo area of Kashmir. When asked what Section 307 meant, he said he had no idea.[39] Yet government forces think nothing of denying such a minor contact with family, legal counsel, and medical support.

EVOLVING RESISTANCE MOVEMENTS

The history of the resistance movement in Kashmir goes back hundreds of years. As various rulers have come and gone, Kashmiris have continued to resist the atrocities perpetrated against them.[40] When India and Pakistan were formed as independent nations in 1947, the postcolonial partition by the British led to the greatest mass migration in human history and sparked communal violence, which continues to fuel the conflict today—but the partition was only one of many causes of struggle for the Kashmiri resistance movement, and was neither the first nor the last.[41] Be it the shawl weavers' protest in 1865, labor unrest in 1924, the mass mobilizations against Maharaja Hari Singh's rule in 1931, peaceful protests post-1947, decades-long demands for a plebiscite,[42] or the recent bloody mass protests against the Indian occupation in the valley, Kashmiris continue to fight for their self-determination.

Following the United Nations intervention in the region in 1948, Kashmir was effectively divided in two, with two-thirds of the area controlled by India and one-third controlled by Pakistan. A de facto border, called the "Cease-fire Line," was created, and ultimately redesignated the "Line of Control" in 1972. The United Nations directed both countries to withdraw their armies and hold a plebiscite to allow for Kashmiris to determine their own future. But the armies never withdrew, and there has never been a vote on who should rule Kashmir.

Since 1947, more than 100,000 Kashmiris have lost their lives in the conflict over the region.[43] Since 1990, more than 8,000 people have disappeared.[44] Thousands of mass graves have been found, but comprehensive forensic and DNA tests have not been done.[45] Between 2008 and 2018, extrajudicial killings claimed the lives of 1,081 civilians.[46]

For now, India, the world's largest democracy, attempts to use media to control the narrative, military to control the ground, and torture to control the psyche of the Kashmiri people, all in hopes of smashing the independence movement. Yet the independence movement continues to evolve and take on new forms.

By 2008, social media was widely adopted, making it easier for Kashmiris to participate in freedom movements by telling and sharing their own stories. Facebook and Twitter helped fuel the massive uprisings in 2008, 2010, 2014, and 2016.[47]

The year 2016 was one of the most violent in the history of the conflict in Kashmir. The killing of the militant commander Burhan Wani by Indian forces in July 2016 propelled a new wave in the resistance movement.[48] Burhan Wani was a successful student and cricket player who leveraged social media, developing a huge following on Facebook.[49] "He had revived the face of militancy in Jammu and Kashmir, he had given it a totally human face," said Irfan Mehraj, who grew up during the 1990s, when militancy had a very different face.[50] "He would also record short videos and release [them] on YouTube. His way of communicating political ideology and politics was very unique and appealed to people who use social media." Two hundred thousand people attended Wani's funeral.[51] Protests continued for months after his death, as did network blackouts. Burhan Wani's use of social media helped reignite the fire of community activism for freedom in Kashmir.[52]

INTERNET BANS: SILENCING DISSENT

The media establishment often fails to report what is really happening on the ground in Kashmir—Indian media present a narrative of Pakistani militants attacking innocent soldiers, while international journalists are denied entry. In 2016 alone, 145 civilians were killed by army forces.[53] "What you saw in the newspaper, in news channels, is not even thirty percent of what is happening. A lot is not being covered," said journalist Irfan Mehraj.[54] In Kashmir, news media are often banned. *The Kashmir Reader*, a local Kashmiri paper, was banned by the Indian government for three months during the 2016 uprising, in which more than 12,000 civilians were injured.[55] Earlier, on July 15, 2016, Jammu and Kashmir police raided the offices of three local papers: *Greater Kashmir, Kashmir Times,* and *Rising Kashmir.* Newspaper issues were seized and staff were detained. All three newspapers were forbidden from publishing for three days.[56]

Internet access is also routinely blocked in Kashmir. In 2016, the government closed down internet facilities for more than five months, disrupting internet access for approximately seven million people.[57] In August 2016, the government attempted a complete communications blackout in Kashmir, cutting all broadband and mobile services for several days.[58] According to a study by Jan Ryzdak, a research fellow at Stanford University's Global Digital Policy Incubator, 47 percent of India's internet shutdowns take place in Indian-occupied Jammu and Kashmir. The study also suggests that internet blackouts are "a logical extension of curfews." Following the killing of Burhan Wani in 2016, network shutdowns lasted for 203 days.[59] According to an internet freedoms group, internet services were suspended 32 times in 2017, compared to ten times in 2016.[60] By March 2019, internet services had already been suspended 23 times, just a quarter of the way into the year.[61]

The Indian government is not the only source of telecommunications restrictions for Kashmiris. In 2016, Facebook deactivated pages for filmmakers and researchers, including those of Kashmiris living abroad. California-based academic Huma Dar had her Facebook page suspended after posting images of Burhan Wani's funeral. In addition, a Delhi-based documentary filmmaker, Sanjay Kak, had his page suspended. Dibyesh Anand, an academic at the University of Westminster, found his posts were removed and his account was twice suspended for 24 hours. Facebook apologized to Anand both times after he contacted them.[62]

The 2018 UN report on Kashmir recommended that the Indian authorities "fully respect the right of self-determination of the people of Kashmir as protected under international law."[63] Yet on the same day that the UN report was issued, the founding editor of *Rising Kashmir* was assassinated in the Press Colony in Srinagar, Kashmir. One of his last messages was a retweet of an article from *Rising Kashmir* titled "India Rejects UN Report on India."[64]

Nevertheless, even in the face of torture, repression, and murder, Kashmiris continue to fight for self-determination. In the words of

Kashmiri journalist Irfan Mehraj, "The endurance is such that when people think about the amount of torture people have faced, you can only rise from it." Mehraj explains, "We have shown that resistance works. Resistance works in the way that we are here still."[65]

IFAT GAZIA is a human rights researcher, filmmaker, and journalist from Kashmir. She has a postgraduate degree in media in development from the School of Oriental and African Studies (SOAS), University of London. She is currently a PhD student at the University of Massachusetts Amherst, where she is studying communications.

TARA DORABJI is a mother, radio journalist at KPFA, filmmaker, strategist at the Center for Cultural Power, and a writer published in Al Jazeera, *TAYO Literary Magazine*, *Huizache*, the Center for Asian American Media, Mutha, the *Chicago Quarterly Review*, and in the books *Good Girls Marry Doctors* (Aunt Lute Press) and *All the Women in My Family Sing* (Nothing but the Truth Publishing). Follow her at https://dorabji.com.

Notes

1. Rifat Fareed, "At Ground Zero of Kashmir Unrest, Residents See No Ends to Deaths," Al Jazeera, February 21, 2019, https://www.aljazeera.com/news/2019/02/ground-kashmir-unrest-residents-deaths-190211132496615.html.
2. "Report on the Situation of Human Rights in Kashmir: Developments in the Indian State of Jammu and Kashmir from June 2016 to April 2018, and General Human Rights Concerns in Azad Jammu and Kashmir and Gilgit-Baltistan," Office of the United Nations High Commissioner for Human Rights, June 14, 2018, https://www.ohchr.org/Documents/Countries/IN/DevelopmentsInKashmirJune2016ToApril2018.pdf, 17.
3. Ajaz Ashraf, "'Do You Need 700,000 Soldiers to Fight 150 Militants?': Kashmiri Rights Activist Khurram Parvez," Scroll, July 21, 2016, https://scroll.in/article/812010/do-you-need-700000-soldiers-to-fight-150-militants-kashmiri-rights-activist-khurram-parvez.
4. Irfan Mehraj, journalist, interviewed by Tara Dorabji, Srinagar, May 2018.
5. "Report on the Situation of Human Rights in Kashmir," 33.
6. Ibid.
7. Nazir Ahmad Sheikh, interviewed by Tara Dorabji, Srinagar, May 2018.
8. "Key Human Rights Issues of Concern in Indian-Administered Jammu & Kashmir," International Federation for Human Rights, Association of Parents of Disappeared Persons, and Jammu Kashmir Coalition of Civil Society, March 2019, http://jkccs.net/wp-content/uploads/2019/03/Briefing-Note_FIDH.pdf, 6.
9. "Annual Human Rights Review 2017," Jammu Kashmir Coalition of Civil Society, December 31, 2017, https://jkccs.files.wordpress.com/2017/12/jkccs-annual-human-rights-review-2017.pdf, 17.
10. "Report on the Situation of Human Rights in Kashmir," 32.
11. Masood (name changed to protect his identity), interviewed by Ifat Gazia, Poonch, October 2018.
12. "Torture: Indian State's Instrument of Control in Indian Administered Jammu and Kashmir," Association of Parents of Disappeared Persons and Jammu Kashmir Coalition of Civil Society, February 2019, http://jkccs.net/wp-content/uploads/2019/05/TORTURE-Indian-

State%E2%80%99s-Instrument-of-Control-in-Indian-administered-Jammu-and-Kashmir. pdf, 14.

13. Abdullah (name changed to protect his identity), interviewed by Ifat Gazia, Anantnag, September 2017.

14. Asia Watch and Physicians for Human Rights, "The Human Rights Crisis in Kashmir: A Pattern of Impunity," Human Rights Watch, June 1993, https://www.hrw.org/sites/default/files/reports/INDIA937.PDF.

15. Ibid.

16. Social and political activist (anonymous), interviewed by Tara Dorabji, Srinagar, May 2018.

17. "Torture: Indian State's Instrument of Control," 13.

18. Association of Parents of Disappeared Persons and Jammu Kashmir Coalition of Civil Society, "Annual Human Rights Review 2018: A Review of Human Rights in Jammu and Kashmir," Jammu Kashmir Coalition of Civil Society, December 28, 2018, https://jkccs.net/wp-content/uploads/2018/12/Annual-Report-2018.pdf.

19. Fayaz Bukhari, "Death of Man in Custody in Indian Kashmir Sparks Protests," Reuters, March 19, 2019, https://www.reuters.com/article/us-india-kashmir-protests/death-of-man-in-custody-in-indian-kashmir-sparks-protests-idUSKCN1R01BH.

20. "Quarterly HR Review: 162 Killings, 89 CASO's, 23 Internet Blockades," Jammu Kashmir Coalition for Civil Society, April 2019, http://jkccs.net/quarterly-hr-review-jan-mar-2019/.

21. "The object of persecution is persecution. The object of torture is torture. The object of power is power." George Orwell, *1984* (New York: Harcourt, 1977 [first published in London by Secker & Warburg in 1949]), 252.

22. Robert de Neufville, "The Object of Torture," Big Think, March 3, 2010, https://bigthink.com/politeia/the-object-of-torture.

23. Jean Drèze, "A Never-Ending Nightmare in Kashmir," The Wire, January 10, 2018, https://thewire.in/politics/torture-testimonies-detained-youth-kashmir.

24. "Key Human Rights Issues of Concern," 13.

25. Ibid.

26. Ibid.

27. "Report on the Situation of Human Rights in Kashmir," 16.

28. Ibid., 25.

29. Ibid., 32.

30. Rabia Noor, "Public Safety Act Being Misused against Juveniles in Kashmir," The Quint, May 1, 2018, https://www.thequint.com/voices/opinion/public-safety-act-being-misused-against-juveniles-in-jammu-and-kashmir.

31. "Report on the Situation of Human Rights in Kashmir," 16.

32. Ibid., 25.

33. "Key Human Rights Issues of Concern," 13.

34. Ibid.

35. Tim McGirk, "Kashmiri Student Tells of Torture," *The Independent*, May 25, 1993, https://www.independent.co.uk/news/world/kashmiri-student-tells-of-torture-tim-mcgirk-in-srinagar-reports-on-the-increasing-evidence-of-2325054.html.

36. Anonymous 1, interviewed by Ifat Gazia, Srinagar, August 2017.

37. Anonymous 2, interviewed by Ifat Gazia, Srinagar, August 2017.

38. Azaan Javaid, "As Kashmiri Politicians Debate PSA, Data Show North Kashmir Worst Affected," The Wire, February 5, 2019, https://thewire.in/rights/as-kashmir-politicians-debate-psa-data-show-north-kashmir-worst-affected.

39. Anonymous 2, interviewed by Ifat Gazia, Srinagar, August 2017.

40. Kabir Deb, "The Legacy of Azaadi: The History of Kashmir Revolution," Countercurrents, January 16, 2019, https://countercurrents.org/2019/01/16/the-legazy-of-azaadi-the-history-of-kashmir-revolution/.

41. Crispin Bates, "The Hidden Story of Partition and Its Legacies," BBC, March 3, 2011, http://www.bbc.co.uk/history/british/modern/partition1947_01.shtml.

42. Kritika Goel, "Kashmir Plebiscite Explained, But Is the Debate Still Relevant?" The Quint, February 26, 2019, https://www.thequint.com/explainers/kashmir-plebiscite-india-pakistan-explained.

43. Zaib un Nisa Aziz, "The Pursuit of Kashmir," *The Herald*, February 2, 2019, https://herald.dawn.com/news/1153341.

44. "Key Human Rights Issues of Concern," 1.

45. Ibid., 6.

46. Ibid., 3.

47. Jon Boone, "Kashmir Death Toll Reaches 23 in Protests at Killing of Rebel Leader," *The Guardian*, July 11, 2016, https://www.theguardian.com/world/2016/jul/11/kashmir-death-toll-23-protests-shooting-burhan-wani-independence-violence.

48. Adfer Shah, "The Poster Boy of Militancy in Kashmir," *South Asia Journal*, July 21, 2016, http://southasiajournal.net/the-poster-boy-of-militancy-in-kashmir/.

49. Jason Burke, "Kashmir Conflict Ebbs as New Wave of Militant Emerges," *The Guardian*, August 11, 2013, https://www.theguardian.com/world/2013/aug/11/kashmir-conflict-new-wave-militants.

50. Irfan Mehraj, journalist, interviewed by Tara Dorabji, Srinagar, May 2018.

51. Mehrunnisa Wani, "Why Kashmir Has a Right to Self-Determination," *Forbes*, March 20, 2019, https://www.forbes.com/sites/mwani/2019/03/20/why-the-focus-needs-to-be-kash-miris-right-of-self-determination/#1f88a7fb2ae8.

52. Piyasree Dasgupta, "Who Was Burhan Wani and Why is Kashmir Mourning Him?" Huffington Post, November 7, 2016, updated June 2, 2017, https://www.huffingtonpost.in/burhan-wani/who-was-burhan-wani-and-why-is-kashmir-mourning-him_a_21429499/.

53. Sameer Yasir, "Kashmir Unrest: What was the Real Death Toll in the State in 2016?" Firstpost, January 2, 2017, https://www.firstpost.com/india/kashmir-unrest-what-was-the-real-death-toll-in-the-state-in-2016-3183290.html.

54. Irfan Mehraj, journalist, interviewed by Tara Dorabji, Srinagar, May 2018.

55. Gaurav Vivek Bhatnagar, "'Kashmir Reader' Hits Stands Again After Three-Month Ban," The Wire, December 28, 2016, https://thewire.in/rights/kashmir-reader-ban-mehbooba; Al Jazeera editors and Rifat Fareed, "Kashmir Newspaper Banned for 'Inciting Violence,'" Al Jazeera, October 3, 2016, https://www.aljazeera.com/news/2016/10/kashmir-newspaper-banned-inciting-violence-161003061348246.html.

56. "Report on the Situation of Human Rights in Kashmir," 31.

57. Ibid., 30.

58. Ibid., 31.

59. Jan Rydzak, "Of Blackouts and Bandhs: The Strategy and Structure of Disconnected Protest in India," SSRN (Social Science Research Network), February 7, 2019, https://papers.ssrn.com/sol3/papers.cfm?abstract_id=3330413.

60. "Report on the Situation of Human Rights in Kashmir," 32.

61. "Quarterly HR Review."

62. Vidhi Doshi, "Facebook Under Fire for 'Censoring' Kashmir-Related Posts and Accounts," *The Guardian*, July 19, 2016, https://www.theguardian.com/technology/2016/jul/19/facebook-under-fire-censoring-kashmir-posts-accounts.

63. "Report on the Situation of Human Rights in Kashmir," 49.

64. Shujaat Bukhari (@bukharishujaat), tweet on Twitter, June 14, 2018, https://twitter.com/bukharishujaat?lang=en.

65. Irfan Mehraj, journalist, interviewed by Tara Dorabji, Srinagar, May 2018.

CHAPTER 7

Stonewalled

Establishment Media's Silence on the Trump Administration's Crusade against LGBTQ People

April Anderson and Andy Lee Roth

INTRODUCTION: THE ROLLBACK

In July 2016, at the Republican National Convention, Donald Trump reminded his audience of the recent mass shooting at a gay night-club in Orlando, Florida, and he boasted, "As your president, I will do everything in my power to protect our L.G.B.T.Q. citizens."[1] Make no mistake, Donald Trump and his administration are no allies of the lesbian, gay, bisexual, transgender, queer community.

At the convention, the GOP advanced what the president of the Log Cabin Republicans called "the most anti-LGBT Platform in the Party's 162-year history"[2]—including a commitment to overturning marriage equality, with endorsements of conversion therapy and the First Amendment Defense Act—and they made Trump their party's nominee. Days before the convention, Trump had selected Mike Pence as his running mate. As governor of Indiana, Pence had responded to the state's legalization of same-sex marriage by signing into law a "religious freedom" bill that many interpreted as sanctioning discrimination against LGBTQ people, just one example of Pence's consistent record of anti-LGBTQ positions.[3]

As president, Donald Trump has acted to undo protections, policies, and progress that LGBTQ Americans, their allies, and the Obama administration had fought to establish or strengthen. By naming staunch anti-LGBTQ advocates to key cabinet positions, appointing a pair of conservative anti-LGBTQ Supreme Court justices, stacking circuit courts with judges who consistently rule against LGBTQ rights, creating a secretive Religious Liberty Task Force, reinterpreting Title VII's definition of sex discrimination, and weakening the Affordable Care Act, which provided healthcare coverage to many LGBTQ individuals and their families for the first time, the Trump administration has been dismantling LGBTQ Americans' legal protections and social safety nets, potentially relegating members of the LGBTQ community to the status of second-class citizens.[4]

At the same time, the National Coalition of Anti-Violence Programs documented 52 anti-LGBTQ homicides in 2017, which they noted is "the highest number of anti-LGBTQ homicides in our 20-year history of tracking this information," and "an 86% increase in single incident reports from 2016."[5] As hate crimes rise, the Department of Justice has taken steps to remove questions from the National Crime Victimization Survey—which provides crucial data on criminal victimization of LGBTQ people—as part of a larger effort to erase LGBTQ people from federal statistics.[6] In addition, many critics have noted that Trump's silence on state-sponsored homophobia and transphobia in other nations—including Brazil, Brunei, and Russia, where the situation in Chechnya is especially atrocious—puts LGBTQ people around the world "at grave risk."[7] The Trump administration's February 2019 announcement that it intended to develop a global campaign to decriminalize homosexuality in dozens of nations around the world has been met with skepticism from the LGBTQ community in the United States.[8]

While the establishment press has focused on sensational stories—such as the allegedly staged attack against actor and singer Jussie Smollett—news coverage has tended to mute, marginalize, or censor the Trump administration's steady rollback of LGBTQ protections and rights.

Our interest in examining news coverage of LGBTQ issues during the Trump era originated with the feeling that the nation's most prominent news organizations were failing to report the full scope of the Trump administration's negative impacts on members of the LGBTQ community. So we began to conduct a detailed content analysis of four major establishment newspapers and a variety of independent news publications, to answer three fundamental questions about contemporary news coverage of LGBTQ issues:

1. Whom do journalists treat as authorized sources of newsworthy information and opinion?
2. What arguments are made in support of, or opposition to, LGBTQ inclusion and equality?
3. What topics receive prominent coverage, and which ones remain marginal or excluded?

The first question addresses what sociologist William Gamson has analyzed as *media standing*.[9] For Gamson, media standing refers to the status of individuals and organizations whom journalists quote directly as authorized sources of newsworthy information and opinion. Media standing, he elaborates, is "not the same as being covered or mentioned in the news"; instead, it involves being treated as an agent, rather than as an object discussed by others, and is therefore "a measure of achieved cultural power."[10] Which groups of people achieve media standing for news coverage of LGBTQ issues?

Our second question—about the arguments made for and against LGBTQ rights—links to the extensive research literature on news *framing*. News stories do not simply focus public attention on specific events or issues (which scholars have described as *agenda setting*); they also provide interpretive frameworks that influence how people make sense of those events and issues. News frames define problems, identify causes, convey moral judgments, and promote remedies.[11] In this chapter, we examine how advocates of LGBTQ rights and their opponents deploy competing frames for making sense of a variety of issues, including, for example, state and municipal nondiscrimination laws and ordinances.

Examining which issues receive prominent coverage, and which remain marginal or excluded, connects our findings to research on news *filters*. As Edward S. Herman and Noam Chomsky described in *Manufacturing Consent*, news reported by corporate outlets is subject to filters that "fix the premises of discourse and interpretation, and the definition of what is newsworthy in the first place."[12] Stories, topics, and perspectives that do not serve corporate interests face bias and, potentially, censorship. In addition to analyzing the stories and topics covered in our data set, we also seek to assess which, if any, relevant issues the news outlets in our study excluded from coverage.

To provide context for our data and findings, we first consider prior research on LGBTQ news coverage.

LGBTQ NEWS COVERAGE

News coverage of LGBTQ people and issues has progressed dramatically in the past 90 years. Before World War II, gays and lesbians were "unmentionable" in US newspapers and magazines, according to Edward Alwood's history, *Straight News*.[13] During the war, military psychiatrists defined homosexuality as a mental disorder; as a result, Alwood wrote, news accounts of homosexuals during the war years typically framed them as "unfit for military service."[14] In the 1940s and 1950s, news coverage was infused with homophobia, "invariably" concluding that homosexuality was "a growing social problem."[15] Into the 1960s, newspapers seldom mentioned homosexuals in any other context than bar raids and arrests.[16] *The New York Times*'s first coverage of the June 1969 Stonewall riots consisted of six paragraphs, run on page 33, with no byline.[17] A second article, "buried on page twenty-two" of a subsequent issue, concluded the *Times*'s coverage of Stonewall.[18]

Even as LGBTQ people and issues became more prominent in the 1970s and 1980s, homophobia remained entrenched at the nation's most prominent newspapers. In 1974, the *Los Angeles Times* used the term *fag* in a front-page headline, while well into the 1980s the *New York Times*'s executive editor, A.M. "Abe" Rosenthal, was known for his "personal and professional antagonism toward homosexuals."[19]

Although Alwood's history of gays, lesbians, and the news media concluded that, by 1996, "gays and lesbians appear in the news almost routinely," he also noted that "the widespread antigay attitude in news coverage has been rooted in structural bias of the media," including especially news professionals' tendencies to "favor the established power base and defend the status quo."[20]

That status quo had shifted considerably by September 2002, when the *New York Times* began to publish reports of same-sex commitment ceremonies in its Sunday Styles section.[21] Sociologist James Joseph Dean wrote that this change by the nation's most prestigious newspaper contributed to "a post-closeted culture of open lesbian and gay couples" and the "social integration and cultural normalization of gay couples as equal to their straight counterparts."[22] More generally, as Sarah Kate Ellis wrote in her introduction to the 2016 edition of the *GLAAD Media Reference Guide*, "Media coverage of LGBTQ people has become increasingly multi-dimensional, reflecting both the diversity of the community and the growing visibility of LGBTQ people's families and relationships."[23]

Surprisingly few recent studies have researched the important role that news plays in presenting and shaping public representations of LGBTQ people and issues. Before 2015, when the Supreme Court ruled in *Obergefell v. Hodges* that the Fourteenth Amendment guarantees same-sex couples the right to marry, most contemporary research into LGBTQ news coverage focused on marriage equality.[24] Although other scholars have critically examined how a focus on "mainstream" LGBTQ issues—such as same-sex marriage and military service—has "silenced queer voices,"[25] or how news coverage represents transgender identities,[26] research on how news frames LGBTQ issues has often been narrow in focus and has largely failed to distinguish between sexual orientation and gender identity.[27]

DATA AND METHODS

We analyzed coverage of LGBTQ issues in four major establishment newspapers—the *New York Times*, *Washington Post*, *Los Angeles Times*, and *Wall Street Journal*—as well as stories from the *Advocate*, the oldest and largest LGBTQ publication in the United States, and coverage published by independent newsweeklies, such as the *Eugene Weekly* and the *Colorado Springs Independent*.[28] Using two ProQuest databases—US Newsstream and Alt-Press Watch—we collected every relevant news article from January 2016 through November 2018. This 35-month period spanned the run-up to the 2016 presidential elections through the 2018 midterm elections.

Our search string included the terms *Trump*, *LGBT*, *LGBTQ*, *gay*, *lesbian*, *homosexual*, *bisexual*, and *transgender*, as well as variants on these terms (e.g., *LGBTQI*, *gays*, *homosexuality*).[29] Our data collection focused on news articles. We excluded editorials, opinion pieces, and letters to the editor. Thus defined, our search produced a data set of 152 relevant news articles.[30]

The unit of analysis for exploration of *media standing* (that is, who is quoted as a newsworthy source) was the individual direct quotation. Our data set included 1,056 direct quotations. For each direct quotation, we coded news outlet, date of publication, location of the quote in the article, how the quoted source was identified, and the quote's position on LGBTQ rights.

Our coding for sources' identities included their occupation or official status, gender, and sexual orientation.[31] We coded sources' gender and sexual orientation as they were identified in the news articles themselves. We address the significance of this point in more detail in our findings. In the case of direct quotations that took a clear position either in support of LGBTQ rights or in opposition to them, we coded their position. Not every quotation in our data set involved a source taking a position on LGBTQ rights, much less a clear position. For this reason, the figures we report on position, below, are smaller than those reported for our other coding categories.

To ensure that our coding was reliable, we undertook three preliminary rounds of coding in which each of us coded the same sets of articles. After each round we compared coding decisions, discussing instances where our interpretations differed and determining increasingly specific criteria for how to accurately code challenging cases. Ultimately we achieved an intercoder reliability rate of 93.0 percent, which is especially strong given the challenges of coding for position.

MEDIA STANDING

Whom do journalists treat as authorized sources of newsworthy information and opinion on LGBTQ issues? As summarized in Table 1, government officials are by far the most frequently quoted category of sources, accounting for 46.8 percent of the direct quotations in our data, followed by representatives of civil liberties organizations (19.7 percent), and sources from legal (6.8 percent) and educational (6.5 percent) fields.

TABLE 1. DISTRIBUTION OF QUOTATIONS BY SOURCE TYPE

Source Type Quotations	Total	(%)
Government	494	(46.8)
Civil Liberties	208	(19.7)
Legal	72	(6.8)
Education	69	(6.5)
Religious	56	(5.3)
Activist (unaffiliated)	28	(2.7)
Family/Parent	25	(2.4)
Business	17	(1.6)
Other*	87	(8.2)
TOTAL	1,056	(100)

*The *Other* category includes a frequently-quoted RAND study, medical professionals, ordinary citizens, and quotations attributed to other news organizations.

Within the *government* category, the president was quoted 101 times (9.6 percent of the total number of quotations on LGBTQ issues in our data)—more often, that is, than any other group except for representatives of civil liberties organizations.[32] Federal government officials—including the attorney general and representatives from the departments of Justice, Education, and Housing and Urban Development—were quoted 100 times (9.5 percent), nearly as often as the president. State government officials, including legislators, were quoted more often (8.4 percent, n=89) than members of Congress (5.2 percent, n=55). Military officials, including, for example, the Secretary of Defense and Department of Defense spokespeople, accounted for 6.2 percent (n=65) of the quotations in our data.

Representatives of civil liberties organizations frequently achieved media standing, accounting for nearly 20 percent of the quoted sources in our data. The majority of those quotations (14.9 percent, n=157) originated with groups focused specifically on LGBTQ rights, including, for example, Human Rights Campaign, Lambda Legal, and the National Center for Transgender Equality. A smaller number of these quotations (4.8 percent, n=51) represented civil liberties organizations whose mission includes but is not specifically focused on LGBTQ issues, such as the American Civil Liberties Union (ACLU), the Southern Poverty Law Center, and the Leadership Conference on Civil and Human Rights. As prior research has shown, in establishment news coverage, civil liberties organizations such as the ACLU often constitute the primary alternative to official governmental perspectives.[33]

The *legal* category (6.8 percent) counted quotations attributed to judges (including Supreme Court justices), attorneys, and the texts of court decisions. Sources categorized as *education* (6.5 percent) included teachers, university faculty and administrators, students, school board members, and the texts of school policies. Religious leaders and organizations—including, for example, the Family Research Council, the Alliance Defending Freedom, and the Ethics & Religious Liberty Commission of the Southern Baptist Convention—accounted for 5.3 percent of the quotations. Tony Perkins, the president of the Family Research Council, was quoted at least thirteen times in our data.

Much less frequently, news stories in our data directly quoted activists unaffiliated with any specific organization (2.7 percent), parents and family members of LGBTQ people (2.4 percent), and representatives of businesses (1.6 percent). The sources we coded as *other*, a residual category, include a frequently-quoted RAND study, medical professionals, ordinary citizens, and quotations attributed to other news organizations.

Our findings on the distribution of sources—and especially the prevalence of government officials as favored sources—are consistent with prior research in two ways. First, an extensive and growing body of research has established that journalists favor sources with official accreditation or status.[34] Second, as Herbert J. Gans observed in a pioneering study of news production, when determining story importance, journalists and editors orient to rank in governmental and other hierarchies, with the president at those hierarchies' pinnacle.[35] Our findings corroborate these well-established patterns.

Notably, however, we find the journalistic preference for government officials is considerably stronger among corporate news outlets than among independent news outlets. Whereas the *New York Times, Washington Post, Los Angeles Times,* and *Wall Street Journal* quoted government officials 49.8 percent of the time (n=458), the *Advocate* and independent newsweeklies in our data quoted them just 26.3 percent of the time (n=36). Though establishment and independent media quoted civil liberties groups with comparable frequency (19.2 percent and 22.6 percent, respectively), establishment news outlets were much less likely than independent news organizations to grant media standing to unaffiliated activists (1.6 percent for establishment outlets versus 9.5 percent for independent outlets). Similarly, establishment outlets were also far less likely than their independent counterparts to treat the views of family members of LGBTQ people—including spouses, parents, and children—as newsworthy (1.4 percent for establishment outlets versus 8.8 percent for independent outlets). In summary, although the corporate news outlets in our data adhere firmly to the well-established pattern of favoring official, and especially governmental, sources, the independent news outlets we studied were much more likely to give authoritative voice to unofficial sources, including family members of LGBTQ people and activists who were not affiliated with any specific organization.

Sources' Reported Sexual Orientations

Given our news stories' focus on LGBTQ issues, we wanted to know how often journalists quoted LGBTQ people as newsworthy sources, but the news stories in our data set rarely identified quoted sources in terms of their sexual orientation. Table 2 summarizes our findings.

TABLE 2. DISTRIBUTION OF QUOTES BY SOURCES' REPORTED SEXUAL ORIENTATION

Source Type Quotations	Total	(%)
Not Specified	867	(91.9)
Gay	49	(5.2)
Lesbian	17	(1.8)
Bisexual	5	(0.5)
Heterosexual/Straight	5	(0.5)
TOTAL	943*	(99.9)**

*Total number of quotations is less than in Table 1 due to exclusion of official documents and reports, for which sexual orientation does not apply.

**Rounding error accounts for the 99.9 percent total.

In our data, at least 7.5 percent of the quoted sources identified as gay, lesbian, or bisexual.[36] Although the actual numbers of gay, lesbian, and bisexual people in the United States are difficult to determine, these figures are higher than recent estimates of the nation's adult population indicate.[37] This finding could be interpreted as evidence that journalists are making good faith efforts to represent "the diversity of opinion and experience within the LGBTQ community," as the *GLAAD Media Reference Guide* has recommended.[38] Bisexual sources count as a noteworthy exception, however. Whereas the University of California, Los Angeles (UCLA)'s Williams Institute found that 1.8 percent of adults in the United States identify as bisexual, members of this group are barely included as quoted sources in our news data.[39]

When we distinguish between corporate and independent news outlets, though, the data on sexual orientation tell a slightly different story. While establishment outlets are more likely to quote sources identified as gay (5.6 percent for corporate, 2.5 percent for independent), independent news outlets are considerably more likely to quote sources identified as lesbian (5.0 percent for independent versus 1.3 percent for corporate) or as bisexual (2.5 percent for independent versus 0.6 percent for corporate).

Sources' Reported Gender Identities

In addition to tracking whether and how often news articles identified quoted sources' sexual orientations, we wanted to identify the frequency with which news articles identified these sources in terms of their gender identities. As summarized in Table 3, a significant majority of the sources quoted in our data were identified as men (65.1 percent). Sources identified as women account for slightly more than one quarter of the sources quoted (26.4 percent). Nearly 6 percent of the direct quotations in our data were attributed to sources identified as either transgender women (4.0 percent) or transgender men (1.9 percent).

TABLE 3. DISTRIBUTION OF QUOTES BY SOURCES' REPORTED GENDER

Source Type Quotations	Total	(%)
Cisgender Men	614	(65.1)
Cisgender Women	249	(26.4)
Transgender Women	38	(4.0)
Transgender Men	18	(1.9)
Cannot Determine*	24	(2.5)
TOTAL	943**	(99.9)***

*Cannot Determine includes sources for whom neither their name nor any description of them, including pronouns, clearly conveyed their gender identity.

**Total number of quotations is less than in Table 1 due to exclusion of official documents and reports, for which gender does not apply.

***Rounding error accounts for the 99.9 percent total.

The representation of women's voices, though low, is still significantly higher than the results reported in prior research on media standing. For example, in their 1994 study of television news programs, *By Invitation Only*, David Croteau and William Hoynes found that women accounted for just 10.3 percent of the guests on ABC's *Nightline* and 13.1 percent of the guests on PBS's *NewsHour*.[40]

Though Croteau and Hoynes found little difference between ABC's and PBS's gender representations in their study, we find more significant differences between the establishment news outlets and independent news outlets in our data. Notably, women are more likely to be treated as newsworthy sources by independent news outlets (34.5 percent) than by corporate outlets (25.2 percent).

No prior studies that we could find have assessed how frequently transgender people achieve media standing as quoted sources. This is an important topic for future research on news coverage of LGBTQ issues. The frequency of transgender voices in our data (5.9 percent) is nearly ten times greater than a 2016 estimate, by UCLA's Williams Institute, of the percentage of transgender adults in the United States (0.6 percent).[41] However, we also find that independent news outlets are far more likely than their corporate counterparts to grant media standing to transgender men and women. Transgender women accounted for 10.1 percent of the quoted sources in independent news articles, and 3.2 percent of the quoted sources in corporate news articles; similarly, transgender men accounted for 7.6 percent of the quoted sources in independent news articles, and 1.1 percent of the quoted sources in corporate news articles.

To summarize, our findings of whom journalists treat as newsworthy in news coverage of LGBTQ issues reflects both news professionals' long-standing preference for sources with official status—including, especially, government officials—and enduring imbalances in the representation of male and female voices. That noted, insofar as they held official positions of one kind or another, members of the lesbian, gay, and transgender communities were directly quoted with sufficient frequency to be understood, in Gamson's terms, as "serious players" and "individuals or groups who have enough political power to make a potential difference in what happens."[42] This may seem like a modest outcome, given that the news stories we examined focus specifically on LGBTQ issues, but, as Gamson indicates, achieving media standing is a "measure of achieved cultural power," and, as the *GLAAD Media Reference Guide* states, "inclusive news media coverage" plays "an important role in expanding public awareness and understanding of LGBTQ people."[43]

With a detailed understanding of whom journalists currently treat as newsworthy, we turn next to consider the positions articulated by those sources.

ARGUMENTS FOR AND AGAINST LGBTQ RIGHTS

The majority of quoted sources that took a clear position articulated support for LGBTQ rights, inclusion, and equality (62.1 percent). This pattern holds for both corporate news outlets (61.1 percent) and independent news outlets (68.9 percent), as summarized in Table 4:

TABLE 4. POSITION ON LGBTQ RIGHTS

	Total QUOTES (%)	Corporate News QUOTES (%)	Independent News QUOTES (%)
PRO	372 (62.1)	321 (61.1)	51 (68.9)
CON	227 (37.9)	204 (38.9)	23 (31.1)
TOTAL*	599 (100)	525 (100)	74 (100)

*Table 4 does not include every quotation in the data because a number of quotes did not address LGBTQ rights at all and other quotes articulated neutral positions on LGBTQ rights.

A closer examination of the *pro* and *con* positions articulated by quoted sources reveals additional patterns within each category. The examples that we present below represent some of the major themes found in the data we examined.

Pro Arguments

Pro arguments, advocating for LGBTQ rights and inclusion, typically invoked the principle of *equality*, as can be seen in (1) and (2):

(1) *Washington Post*, February 12, 2017 [On the Trump administration's proposal to challenge a policy, enacted by President Obama, authorizing students to use bathrooms that match their gender identities.]

> "This is a callous attack on hundreds of thousands of students who simply want to be their true selves and be treated with dignity while they work to get an education, just like every other student," Mara Keisling, executive director of the National Center for Transgender Equality, said in a statement. "Transgender students thrive when treated equally, but too often, they are not."[44]

(2) *Los Angeles Times*, February 19, 2018

> "We're seeing proposals around the country that would make it harder for trans people to go to work, go to school,

participate in public life, or even do things as simple as go to the store or go to a restaurant with their family," said Jay Wu, communications manager at the National Center for Transgender Equality. "If laws like this pass, they can send a message to transgender people and their families that they are not as worthy as their peers and that they don't deserve to have the same rights as everyone else."[45]

In (1), Mara Keisling asserts that "[t]ransgender students thrive when treated equally." Equal treatment affords these students "dignity" and allows them to be their "true selves." In contrast, the Trump administration's proposal is "a callous attack." Similarly, in (2), Jay Wu emphasizes how proposals—including, for example, the law passed by North Carolina in early 2016 that barred transgender people from using restrooms that aligned with their gender identity—not only make it more difficult for transgender people to "participate in public life," but also diminish transgender peoples' worth and rights.

In the following example, the quoted source, ACLU lawyer Joshua Block, explicitly invokes "civil rights protections" to express opposition to the Trump administration's proposal to define gender as a biological fact determined at birth. That government proposal is characterized in the same *Washington Post* article as a "fresh and direct aim at transgender rights."

(3) *Washington Post*, October 24, 2018

> "What this would do is exclude transgender people from all the civil rights protections that everyone else takes for granted," said Joshua Block, a senior staff attorney with the ACLU's LGBT project. Eventually, he said, the matter is likely to be resolved by the Supreme Court.[46]

Block characterizes the proposal to define gender in terms of biology, as determined at birth, as discriminatory ("What this would do is exclude transgender people from . . .") at a fundamental level (". . . all the civil rights protections . . .") and, therefore, unthinkable (". . . that everyone else takes for granted").

A number of *pro* arguments extend the principle of equality, exemplified in (1–3), by linking LGBTQ inclusion to the history of civil rights in the United States, as in (4) and (5).

(4) *New York Times*, **August 30, 2017** [From a letter to President Trump, signed by 140 House Democrats, opposing his proposed ban of transgender people from military service.]

> In 1948, when President Truman moved to racially integrate the military, voices were raised in protest. They were raised again in 2010, when Congress at last repealed "Don't Ask, Don't Tell." At every turn, those voices have been proven wrong.[47]

(5) *Los Angeles Times*, **February 19, 2018**

> "I would say what we're seeing with transgender people is history repeating itself," said Seth Galanter, senior director at the National Center for Youth Law. "We saw the same thing 60 years ago with integrating black and white kids together. We saw it 40 years ago integrating kids with disabilities into public schools, and now we're seeing it with transgender people," he said.[48]

In (4), opposition to transgender people serving in the military is linked with previous opposition to the inclusion of people of color ("In 1948 . . .") and of gays, lesbians, and bisexuals (". . . when Congress at last repealed 'Don't Ask, Don't Tell.'") in the military. "At every turn," the congressional representatives assert, "those voices have been proven wrong." In (5), Seth Galanter proposes that integration of transgender people in public schools is "history repeating itself." In (5), the quoted source invokes past civil rights history as a frame that legitimizes the inclusion of transgender people; in (4), by contrast, the source invokes more recent decisions (the repeal of "Don't Ask, Don't Tell") to discredit the exclusion of transgender people.

Another type of *pro*-LGBTQ argument—seen frequently in coverage about the proposed ban of transgender people from military service—frames LGBTQ Americans in terms of *citizenship* and, specifically, loyalty, as evident in (6) and (7).

(6) *New York Times*, **August 24, 2017**

> "As transgender service members, we are and have always been soldiers, sailors, airmen, Marines, and Coast Guardsmen first," said Blake Dremann, the president of Sparta, an L.G.B.T. military group with 500 active-duty members. "We serve our country honorably, in good faith."[49]

Transgender members of the military "serve our country honorably, in good faith," Dremann asserts. They have done so, he contends, by putting their military service "first," before their sexual orientation or gender identity.

In (7), the quoted source, Aaron Belkin, comments on Donald Trump's proposed ban on transgender military recruits as a reflection of the president's "ideological goals."

(7) *Wall Street Journal*, **March 24, 2018**

> "There is no evidence to support a policy that bars from military service patriotic Americans who are medically fit and able to deploy," [Belkin] said. "Our troops and our nation deserve better."[50]

In this example, Belkin characterizes transgender service members as "patriotic Americans," and he invokes the principle of equality: The criteria of medical fitness and readiness to deploy should apply equally to all recruits and service members.

In (7), the quoted source also contests the grounds for a policy that would exclude transgender people ("There is no evidence to support a policy that bars . . ."). In the data we examined, *pro* arguments frequently framed efforts to diminish the rights of LGBTQ people as based on ideology rather than evidence. For example, after President Trump received widespread criticism for his proposed ban of transgender people from military service, he announced in March 2018 that he might allow transgender troops currently in the military to remain, though they would be required to serve according to their gender at birth. *The New York Times* quoted Joshua Block, an ACLU staff lawyer, as saying, "What the White House has released tonight is transphobia masquerading as policy."[51] Similarly, in October 2017, the *Wall Street Journal* quoted Jennifer Levi, a lawyer who had represented plaintiffs in a case challenging Trump's proposed transgender military ban, on the court's decision to temporarily block that ban, which Levi described as "hugely important." Levi said, "The court seemed to see completely through the smokescreen the government tried to create and determined that there's no military justification for excluding transgender people from serving."[52] In both instances, quoted sources characterize the Trump administration's proposed policies as disingenuous (a "smokescreen") and prejudicial ("transphobia masquerading as policy").

Con Arguments

We also found recurrent themes in the positions articulated by sources opposed to LGBTQ equality. These *con* arguments often invoked economics, government overreach and coercion, or religious freedom.

In announcing his proposed ban on transgender people serving in the military, Donald Trump mobilized an economic argument to justify his position, as displayed in (8).

(8) *Los Angeles Times*, July 27, 2017

> "Our military must be focused on decisive and overwhelming victory and cannot be burdened with the tremendous medical costs and disruption that transgender in the military would entail."[53]

In addition to "disruption," Trump's widely quoted tweet also identified "tremendous medical costs" as a reason to exclude transgender people from military service. Notably, in their coverage of Trump's announcement, the *Los Angeles Times*, *New York Times*, and *Wall Street Journal* all cited cost estimates from a 2016 study, commissioned by the

Pentagon and conducted by the RAND Corporation, which found, in the words of the *Los Angeles Times* report, that medical costs associated with transgender troops were "negligible—between $2.4 million and $8.4 million a year, or about 0.1% of Pentagon healthcare spending."[54] Each time these newspapers cited Trump's economic argument, they also countered it with the findings from the RAND study.

More often, *con* arguments invoked *government overreach* and coercion, as can be seen in the following examples. Both (9) and (10) are drawn from an article about reactions to President Obama's directive on the use of school bathrooms and locker rooms by transgender students.

(9) *New York Times*, **May 14, 2016**

> Despite the federal directive and a civil rights complaint by the American Civil Liberties Union, the school district in Marion County, Fla., said it would not change its bathroom policy. "It's just an overreaching federal government that didn't follow the rules," said Nancy Stacy, a board member. "They're just bullying everybody."[55]

(10) *New York Times*, **May 14, 2016**

> The policy drew a swift backlash from conservative politicians, groups and parents. In Texas, Lt. Gov. Dan Patrick appealed to local school boards and superintendents not to abide by the directive, noting that there were just a few weeks left in the school year and time over the summer to fight the policy with legislation or legal action. "We will not be blackmailed," he said.[56]

The school board member quoted in (9) portrays the Obama administration's directive as "overreaching," against "the rules," and "bullying." In (10), the Texas lieutenant governor characterizes it as blackmail. These arguments invoke longstanding disputes in US political history over the balance of states' rights and federal political powers by invoking federal "overreach," "bullying," and "blackmail."

The theme of rights is also asserted on behalf of religious beliefs in a number of *con* arguments, as can be seen in (11), from an article on efforts by conservative legal groups to shift debate over marriage equality to speech rights. As the *Wall Street Journal* reported, Christian small-business owners, including bakers, florists, and videographers who provide services for weddings, argued that laws protecting sexual minorities from discrimination violated their free exercise of religion by forcing them to serve same-sex weddings.

(11) *Wall Street Journal*, June 17, 2017

> "We're telling marriage stories, not merely documenting the ceremonies," Mr. Larsen, co-owner of Telescope Media Group, said. "We want to tell stories about marriage that are consistent with the Bible, which shaped our beliefs. Currently, we can't do that in the state of Minnesota."[57]

The quoted source, Carl Larsen, co-owner of a Minnesota film production company, describes the state's nondiscrimination laws—violation of which can be punished by up to 90 days in jail—as at odds with a Christian conception of marriage, and thus a violation of his religious freedom.

Notably, the most frequently quoted source with an official religious affiliation, the president of the Family Research Council, Tony Perkins, seldom speaks in overtly religious terms.[58] Instead, Perkins employs secular language—for example, to describe a "victory" on behalf of the rights of parents and their children—as displayed in the following pair of examples:

(12) *Wall Street Journal*, February 23, 2017

> Socially conservative groups, who had rallied against the Obama administration's interpretation, praised the [Trump administration's] change. "The Trump administration's reversal of this mandate on schools is a victory for parents, children, and privacy," said Tony Perkins, president of the Family Research Council.[59]

(13) *New York Times*, February 23, 2017

"The federal government has absolutely no right to strip parents and local schools of their rights to provide a safe learning environment for children," said Tony Perkins, president of the Family Research Council.[60]

In (12), Perkins's description of the Trump directive as "a victory for parents, children, and privacy" implicitly erases transgender school children and their parents. Similarly, in (13), Perkins's statement effectively nullifies transgender students and their parents, even as it invokes widely cherished ideals (parents' and schools' rights to provide a "safe learning environment"). In instances such as these, the Family Resource Council's stated vision of "a prevailing culture in which all human life is valued, families flourish, and religious liberty thrives"[61] appears to privilege a concealed evangelical Christian conception of selective liberty over "all human life" and flourishing families.

Other *con* arguments are less subtle. For example, an April 2017 *New York Times* article reported on Trump's nomination of Mark E. Green, a Tennessee state senator and former Army flight surgeon, to serve as secretary of the Army. The article noted that previously, as a Tennessee state legislator, Green "made a number of controversial assertions about L.G.B.T. rights," including at a 2016 appearance before a Tea Party audience in Chattanooga.

(14) *New York Times*, April 8, 2017

During that same appearance, Mr. Green was asked what military rank and file thought about "the social revolutions being imposed upon them by this government." He responded that "if you poll the psychiatrists, they're going to tell you that transgender is a disease."[62]

Green overtly calls transgender identity a "disease," and he makes a spurious appeal to authority by attributing the position to "the psychiatrists." After the full extent of Green's prejudicial statements against gay, bisexual, and transgender individuals became more widely known, he withdrew his nomination in May 2017.[63]

For the most part, the establishment newspapers in our study refrained from quoting virulently homophobic or transphobic statements. By contrast, the *Advocate*, an LGBTQ magazine, consistently published direct quotations articulating homophobic or transphobic positions in candid, vitriolic language. For example, in its August/September 2016 issue, the *Advocate* quoted Roy Moore, then–chief justice of the Alabama Supreme Court and future Senate candidate:

(15) *The Advocate*, August/September 2016

Moore happily used his position to subvert marriage equality, illegally ordering state judges to continue denying marriage licenses to same-sex couples. (Moore had previously described homosexual intimacy as "a crime against nature, an inherent evil, and an act so heinous that it defies one's abilities to describe it.")[64]

The *Advocate* noted that Moore had been suspended from the court for his refusal to comply with federal law on marriage equality. But it also noted that, in a March 2016 ruling, Moore had written that the Supreme Court's "redefinition" of marriage in *Obergefell v. Hodges* created "an unnatural form of marriage." According to Moore's 94-page opinion, "the ultimate goal" of "the homosexual movement" is "to drive the nation into a wasteland of sexual anarchy that consumes all moral values."[65]

The *Advocate*'s 50th anniversary issue, published in 2017, included a feature, "The Biggest Homophobes," that documented "some of the most odious homophobes from *Advocate* history," including the "anti-LGBT media mogul" James Dobson of Focus on the Family, the Family Research Council's Tony Perkins, and then–attorney general Jeff Sessions.[66] Coverage of this sort helps to explain one of our more surprising findings: *The Advocate* published a balance of *pro* and *con* quotations. In fact, unlike the corporate news outlets included in our study, the *Advocate* published slightly more *con* quotations (55.9 percent) than *pro* quotations (44.1 percent). It may be that the *Advocate* most powerfully fulfills its duty as a voice for LGBTQ people, and its role as an alternative to the establishment press, not only by giving voice to members of the LGBTQ community but also by documenting some of the more virulent statements made by public figures opposed to equal rights and inclusion for LGBTQ people. We return to consider this point in more detail in the chapter's conclusion.

NEWS THEMES

What was Covered

We also analyzed the story topics that the establishment and independent press covered as newsworthy. Figure 1 shows that, of the articles that featured quotes on LGBTQ issues, corporate coverage focused on the transgender military ban (27.8 percent of their total reporting on LGBTQ issues), nondiscrimination laws and ordinances frequently characterized as "bathroom bills" (14.8 percent), and LGB rights in general (14.8 percent). Combined, these themes comprised more than 57 percent of the LGBTQ topics covered by establishment media articles in our data set.

In comparison, the independent media covered a much broader scope of topics related to LGB rights in general (21.9 percent), religious freedoms (9.4 percent), and the election (15.6 percent). Independent news outlets also picked up on topics that the establishment media entirely failed to report—for example, LGBTQ healthcare issues (9.4 percent).

The most striking difference in coverage between the establishment and independent media was the number of articles published related to the transgender military ban and "bathroom bills." When combined, the establishment media's reporting on the transgender military ban and "bathroom bills" accounted for 42.6 percent of their coverage of LGBTQ issues. In comparison, the independent media reported substantially less on those two issues, which, combined, comprised less than 10 percent of their news coverage of LGBTQ issues.

At a time when the media landscape is in momentous flux, epitomized by budget cuts and layoffs for news reporting and a host of

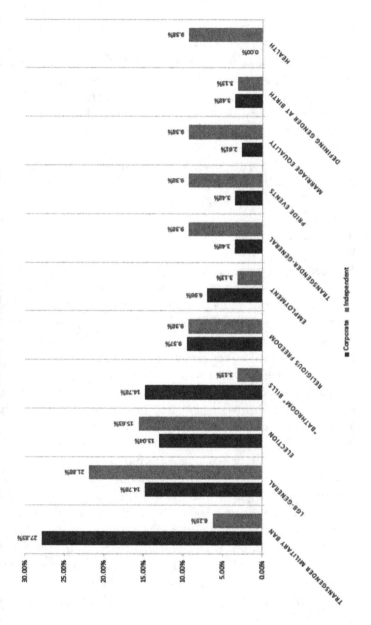

FIGURE 1. THEMES IN CORPORATE AND INDEPENDENT NEWS COVERAGE, JANUARY 2016—NOVEMBER 2018

■ Corporate ■ Independent

	Corporate	Independent
HEALTH	9.38%	0.00%
DEFINING GENDER AT BIRTH	3.13%	3.48%
MARRIAGE EQUALITY	9.38%	2.61%
PRIDE EVENTS	9.38%	3.48%
TRANSGENDER-GENERAL	9.38%	3.48%
EMPLOYMENT	3.13%	6.96%
RELIGIOUS FREEDOM	9.38%	9.57%
"BATHROOM" BILLS	3.13%	14.78%
ELECTION	15.63%	13.04%
LGB-GENERAL	21.88%	14.78%
TRANSGENDER MILITARY BAN	6.25%	27.83%

online developments, LGBTQ media are particularly vulnerable.[67] As major outlets such as the Huffington Post and BuzzFeed continue to reduce their funding for reporting on LGBTQ issues, it is imperative that establishment newspapers with the widest scope of influence provide the public with accurate and comprehensive coverage.

The spotlight that establishment newspapers focused on the transgender military ban and so-called "bathroom bills" left a host of other noteworthy news stories in the dark. This type of reporting provides the public with a narrow understanding of the much-wider range of issues on which Trump administration policies directly or indirectly impact the lives of LGBTQ people and their communities.

What was *Not* Covered

On January 29, 2019, the actor and singer Jussie Smollett reported to Chicago police that he was the victim of a hate crime. Smollett, who is black and identifies as gay, alleged that he was brutally assaulted in downtown Chicago by two individuals who yelled racist and homophobic slurs at him, beat him, doused him with chemicals, and left him with a rope wrapped around his neck. Initially, local police acknowledged they were treating the incident as a "possible hate crime," but in a strange turn of events, the perpetrators agreed to cooperate with investigators and implicated Smollett, saying he orchestrated what they described as a faked incident.[68]

The Smollett story saturated headlines, in the United States and abroad. This coverage was often sensational in tone, spurring some critics to voice concerns that the case might diminish the public's understanding of how frequently hate crimes target the LGBTQ community and the extent to which such crimes are typically underreported, and that hoaxes might lead to fewer people reporting actual hate crimes.[69] As the *New York Times* reported in February 2019, according to the Center for the Study of Hate and Extremism at California State University, San Bernardino, between 2016 and 2018 fewer than 50 of an estimated 21,000 hate crime cases were found to be false.[70]

While the establishment press provided nonstop coverage of Smollett's original allegations and subsequent arrest, other crucial stories with connections to the LGBTQ community went almost entirely unreported. To document this disparity in coverage, we used ProQuest's US Newsstream database to search for news coverage of the following topics:

▸ the creation of the Religious Liberty Task Force—established on July 30, 2018 by then–attorney general Jeff Sessions—which aims to establish religious faith as a justification for the implementation of broad legal exemptions that would allow discrimination against the LGBTQ community;[71]

▸ the Department of Health and Human Services (HHS)'s announcement of the formation of a new Conscience and Religious Freedom Division, which would permit healthcare providers to decline to provide care for patients, based on religious and/or philosophical reasons;[72]

▸ the removal of LGBTQ protections from the trilateral United States–Mexico–Canada Agreement (the USMCA);[73] and

▸ efforts to pass the federal Equality Act, which would provide broad non-discrimination protections for LGBTQ people, ensuring equal access to employment, housing, credit, education, public spaces and services, federally funded programs, and jury service.[74]

Using ProQuest's US Newsstream database, we identified, in the period between January 29, 2019 and April 15, 2019, seven news articles in the print editions of the *New York Times*, *Washington Post*, *Wall Street Journal*, and *Los Angeles Times* that covered the Equality Act; and no articles at all on the Religious Liberty Task Force, the removal of LGBTQ protections from the USMCA, or HHS's new Division of Conscience and Religious Freedom. In contrast, during the same time period, at least 90 stories in the print editions of those four newspapers covered Smollett's alleged attack.

While the press reported extensively on the sensational story of Smollett's assault, the subsequent revelations that he had faked the attack, and debate over the meaning of all this for actual hate crimes motivated by racism or homophobia, news coverage that was at best sporadic diminished the significance of policies and legislation—

such as efforts to pass the federal Equality Act and the removal of LGBTQ protections from the trilateral United States–Mexico–Canada Agreement—with the potential for much broader impacts on the LGBTQ community.

CONCLUSIONS

Writing in 1996, Edward Alwood, in his study *Straight News*, observed that "news media rarely focus on the leaders of the gay and lesbian rights organizations."[75] In 2019, we find that news coverage has changed in important ways. Today, journalists from both corporate and independent news outlets consistently treat spokespersons for the leading LGBTQ organizations as newsworthy sources of information and opinion. People who identify as lesbian, gay, or bisexual account for more than 7 percent of the quoted sources in our data; and transgender women and men represent nearly 6 percent of the sources deemed sufficiently newsworthy to be directly quoted. Compared with Alwood's assessment, our findings indicate progress in the inclusivity of LGBTQ news coverage. This reflects positively on contemporary journalists and news organizations.

Not all of our findings are equally encouraging. Although news coverage may have become more inclusive, journalists continue to strive for objectivity by providing spuriously "balanced" coverage.[76] A commitment to "balance" entails special risks in coverage of LGBTQ issues: As Alwood noted in *Straight News*, reporters "write about the rights and dignities of gays as controversial topics that require 'balance,' giving antigay fanatics a platform from which to propound their bigotry under the guise of providing 'the other side.'"[77] The news coverage we examined suggests a continuation of this tendency, but we note a shift in coverage that makes the bigotry Alwood identified in the 1990s more subtle now. As we have noted, with the exception of the *Advocate*, the news outlets we examined seldom publish virulently homophobic or transphobic statements. On the surface, this appears to counter Alwood's conclusion, and to fulfill GLAAD's recommendation that journalists take care to "distinguish between opposing viewpoints on LGBTQ issues and the defamatory rhetoric that fuels prejudice and discrimination."[78]

Based on our data, we find that news representations of opposing viewpoints can avoid defamatory rhetoric but nonetheless indirectly promote prejudice and discrimination. Consider, for example, one of the most frequently quoted sources in our data, Tony Perkins, the president of the Family Research Council. Establishment newspapers, including the *New York Times, Washington Post, Los Angeles Times*, and *Wall Street Journal*, regularly treat Perkins as an authorized source of information and opinion on LGBTQ issues. In the news coverage we analyzed, journalists quoting Perkins failed to note that, in 2010, the Southern Poverty Law Center listed his organization as an anti-gay hate group;[79] or that GLAAD identifies Perkins prominently in its Commentator Accountability Project, which tracks "the commentators who are most often asked to opine on issues like marriage equality or non-discrimination protections" even though their views "represent nothing but extreme animus towards the entire LGBTQ community."[80]

Instead, the articles that quoted Perkins portrayed him as a fair partisan, engaged in legitimate debate. This representation is possible because journalists quoted Perkins's relatively mild statements (as depicted in examples (12) and (13), above) without making public his more virulent claims, which have been thoroughly documented by GLAAD's Commentator Accountability Project.[81] News stories that omit expressions of extreme prejudice serve to normalize opposition to LGBTQ protections and equality, and thus to aid the agendas of prejudiced individuals and organizations such as Tony Perkins and the Family Research Council.

What, then, should responsible journalists do? On the one hand, they do not want to promote prejudice or discrimination by providing bully pulpits for homophobic or transphobic voices. On the other hand, defamatory comments and virulent opinions may sometimes be newsworthy—not as "balance," but rather as accurate representations of the animus that underlies many of the more "reasonable" positions expressed in opposition to equal rights and protections for LGBTQ people.

There is no simple answer to this dilemma, but the question of how to cover extreme homophobic and transphobic viewpoints is one that every journalist, editor, and publisher ought to be confronting. As stakeholders with an interest in the content and quality of the news, members of the public should also be more aware of how reporters' professional judgments regarding who and what to quote shape the content of the news available to us and, consequently, frame public debate on those issues.

Nowhere is the question of news judgment clearer than in reporters and editors' choices of which events to pursue as news. In this study, we identify significant shortcomings at two levels of analysis in the scope of news coverage of LGBTQ issues.

First, in our comparison of corporate and independent news coverage, we found significant differences in focus. During the time frame we examined, corporate news recurrently highlighted two controversial topics, the nondiscrimination laws and ordinances frequently characterized as "bathroom bills" and Trump's proposed transgender military ban. In our data, coverage of these two topics accounted for more than 40 percent of the LGBTQ news stories published by the *New York Times, Washington Post, Los Angeles Times,* and *Wall Street Journal.* By contrast, the *Advocate* and independent newsweeklies provided more frequent coverage of a broader range of topics that affect the LGBTQ community—including, for example, concerted efforts by the Trump administration and Republicans in Congress to repeal or undermine the 2010 Affordable Care Act, which had dramatically increased the number of insured LGB people.[82] Just as independent news organizations authorize a more diverse and inclusive range of people as newsworthy, they also cover a broader spectrum of topics. Members of the public seeking fair, accurate, and inclusive coverage of issues affecting LGBTQ communities are better served by independent news organizations than by those organizations' corporate counterparts.

A second shortcoming in the scope of LGBTQ news coverage is the tendency among both corporate and independent news organizations to render important issues all but invisible. A motivated news consumer can undoubtedly find informative reporting about the establishment of the Religious Liberty Task Force, the removal of LGBTQ protections from the trilateral United States–Mexico–Canada Agreement, or the potential of the Equality Act to provide LGBTQ people with protections from discrimination in employment, housing, education, and other key services and spaces. Nonetheless, even relatively well-informed members of the public are unlikely to come across news stories on these topics unless they actively search for them. Insofar as news coverage sets an agenda for what the public considers important, these blind spots in news coverage are consequential.

Skeptics might counter that this is merely the same problem facing all kinds of important stories in this era of digital news inflation. However, as multiple studies document increased prejudice—and violence—against LGBTQ people in the United States, and as global human rights organizations expose and oppose barbaric state-sanctioned policies and practices affecting LGBTQ people in numerous countries, including Brazil, Brunei, and Russia, the stakes could not be higher: News coverage that marginalizes crucial LGBTQ issues, in combination with the Trump administration's discriminatory policies, poses grave dangers for members of LGBTQ communities, in the United States and abroad.

ACKNOWLEDGMENTS: Thanks to James Joseph Dean and Nick Wolfinger for helpful comments on earlier versions of this chapter.

APRIL ANDERSON is a member and advocate of the LGBTQI+ community and works as a Research and Instruction Librarian at Macalester College in Saint Paul, Minnesota. They earned their master's degree in library and information science from the School of Information at San José State University, where they were first introduced to Project Censored while taking a course on information secrecy.

ANDY LEE ROTH, PHD, is a sociologist and serves as Project Censored's associate director. His articles and research have appeared in *YES! Magazine*, scholarly journals including *Media, Culture & Society* and the *International Journal of Press/Politics*, and previous volumes of the *Censored* yearbook.

Notes

1. "Transcript: Donald Trump at the G.O.P. Convention," *New York Times*, July 22, 2016, https://www.nytimes.com/2016/07/22/us/politics/trump-transcript-rnc-address.html.

2. Gregory T. Angelo, president of the Log Cabin Republicans, which represents LGBT conservatives, as quoted in Eugene Scott, "Log Cabin Republican President: GOP Passed Most Anti-LGBT Platform in Party History," CNN, July 14, 2016, https://www.cnn.com/2016/07/14/politics/log-cabin-republicans-platform-gop-convention/index.html.

3. Amanda Holpuch, "Before He was Trump's Running Mate, Mike Pence Led the Anti-LGBT Backlash," *The Guardian*, October 4, 2016, https://www.theguardian.com/us-news/2016/

oct/04/mike-pence-led-anti-lgbt-backlash-trump. See also GLAAD's entry for Mike Pence in its "Trump Accountability Project," undated, https://www.glaad.org/tap/mike-pence [accessed April 19, 2019].

4. See, for example, Sean Cahill, Sophia Geffen, and Tim Wang, "One Year In, Trump Administration Amasses Striking Anti-LGBT Record," Fenway Institute, January 18, 2018, https://fenwayhealth.org/wp-content/uploads/The-Fenway-Institute-Trump-Pence-Administration-One-Year-Report.pdf; Sean Cahill, Tim Wang, and Bishar Jenkins, "Trump Administration Continued to Advance Discriminatory Policies and Practices against LGBT People and People Living with HIV in 2018," Fenway Institute, January 16, 2019, https://fenwayhealth.org/wp-content/uploads/Trump-Administration-Impact-on-LGBTs-Year-Two-Brief_Web.pdf; on the Affordable Care Act, also see Kellan Baker, "LGBT Protections in Affordable Care Act Section 1557," *Health Affairs* blog, June 6, 2016, https://www.healthaffairs.org/do/10.1377/hblog20160606.055155/full/.

5. Emily Waters, Larissa Pham, Chelsea Convery, and Sue Yacka-Bible, "A Crisis of Hate: A Report on Lesbian, Gay, Bisexual, Transgender and Queer Hate Violence Homicides in 2017," National Coalition of Anti-Violence Programs (New York City Anti-Violence Project), 2018, http://avp.org/wp-content/uploads/2018/01/a-crisis-of-hate-january-release.pdf, 5, 6.

6. Rachel Dowd, "DOJ Proposes Roll Back of Data Collection on Crime Victimization of LGBT Youth," Williams Institute (UCLA School of Law), April 11, 2018, https://williamsinstitute.law.ucla.edu/press/press-releases/doj-proposes-roll-back-of-data-collection-on-crime-victimization-of-lgbt-youth/; see also Cahill, Wang, and Jenkins, "Trump Administration Continued to Advance Discriminatory Policies," 6–7.

7. Chad Griffin, "The Trump Administration's Silence on LGBTQ Rights is Unconscionable," *Washington Post*, April 10, 2019, https://www.washingtonpost.com/opinions/2019/04/10/trump-administrations-silence-lgbtq-rights-is-unconscionable/. Griffin is president of the Human Rights Campaign.

8. On the announcement of the campaign by US Ambassador to Germany Richard Grenell, the highest-profile openly gay person in the Trump administration, see, for example, Josh Lederman, "Trump Administration Launches Global Effort to End Criminalization of Homosexuality," NBC News, February 19, 2019, https://www.nbcnews.com/politics/national-security/trump-administration-launches-global-effort-end-criminalization-homo-sexuality-n973081; on skepticism, see, e.g., Heather Cassell, "Trump Administration's Gay Decriminalization Strategy Draws Skepticism," *Bay Area Reporter*, February 27, 2019, https://www.ebar.com/news/news//272935. Cassell wrote that Trump "appeared not to be aware of Grenell's strategy when a reporter asked him about it in the Oval Office February 20."

9. William Gamson, "Media and Social Movements," in *International Encyclopedia of the Social & Behavioral Sciences*, Neil J. Smelser and Paul B. Baltes (Amsterdam: Elsevier Science, 2001), 9468–72.

10. Gamson, "Media and Social Movements," 9471.

11. See, e.g., Robert M. Entman, *Projections of Power: Framing News, Public Opinion, and U.S. Foreign Policy* (Chicago: University of Chicago Press, 2004).

12. Edward S. Herman and Noam Chomsky, *Manufacturing Consent: The Political Economy of the Mass Media* (New York: Pantheon Books, 1988), 2.

13. Edward Alwood, *Straight News: Gays, Lesbians, and the News Media* (New York: Columbia University Press, 1996), 19.

14. Ibid., 20.

15. Ibid., 56.

16. Ibid., 62.

17. Ibid., 84. Alwood summarized the report: "In sterile language it described the clash in terms of problems faced by the police. It mentioned nothing about the recent rash of arrests at gay bars or the history of police harassment."

18. Ibid., 86; see also p. 314.

19. Ibid., 316, 166. Rosenthal's homophobia affected news reporters and story coverage at the *Times* until Max Frankel took over as the *Times's* executive editor in 1986.

20. Ibid., 315, 7.
21. *The Times*'s executive editor, Howell Raines, explained, "In making this change, we acknowledge the newsworthiness of a growing and visible trend in society toward public celebrations of commitment by gay and lesbian couples—celebrations important to many of our readers, their families and their friends." "Times Will Begin Reporting Gay Couples' Ceremonies," *New York Times*, August 18, 2002, https://www.nytimes.com/2002/08/18/us/times-will-begin-reporting-gay-couples-ceremonies.html.
22. James Joseph Dean, *Straights: Heterosexuality in Post-Closeted Culture* (New York: New York University Press, 2014), 24.
23. *GLAAD Media Reference Guide*, 10th ed. (GLAAD, October 2016), https://www.glaad.org/reference, 4. "Unfortunately," Ellis noted, "anti-LGBTQ individuals and organizations continue to see their incendiary rhetoric and inaccurate, sensationalistic distortions of LGBTQ people's lives legitimized through news stories, features, and profiles. Such inclusion, despite the best efforts of reporters striving for fair and accurate coverage, devalues the quality of journalism and misinforms audiences."
24. See, for example, Deirdre M. Warrant and Katrina R. Bloch, "Framing Same-Sex Marriage: Media Constructions of California's Proposition 8," *Social Science Journal*, Vol. 51 No. 4 (December 2014), 503–513; Andrea M. Hackl, C. Reyn Boyer, and M. Paz Galupo, "From 'Gay Marriage Controversy' (2004) to 'Endorsement of Same-Sex Marriage' (2012): Framing Bisexuality in the Marriage Equality Discourse," *Sexuality & Culture*, Vol. 17 No. 3 (September 2013), https://www.researchgate.net/publication/257771352_From_Gay_Marriage_Controversy_2004_to_Endorsement_of_Same-Sex_Marriage_2012_Framing_Bisexuality_in_the_Marriage_Equality_Discourse; and Po-Lin Pan, Juan Meng, and Shuhua Zhou, "Morality or Equality? Ideological Framing in News Coverage of Gay Marriage Legitimization," *Social Science Journal*, Vol. 47 No. 3 (September 2010), 630–45.
25. Mary C. Burke and Mary Bernstein, "How the Right Usurped the Queer Agenda: Frame Co-optation in Political Discourse," *Sociological Forum*, Vol. 29 No. 4 (December 2014), 830–50, https://onlinelibrary.wiley.com/doi/abs/10.1111/socf.12122.
26. For example, Andrea M. Hackl, Amy B. Becker, and Maureen E. Todd, "'I am Chelsea Manning': Comparison of Gendered Representation of Private Manning in U.S. and International News Media," *Journal of Homosexuality*, Vol. 63 No. 4 (2016), 467–86.
27. On distinctions between sexual orientation and gender identity, see, e.g., Rosalind P. Petchesky, "The Language of 'Sexual Minorities' and the Politics of Identity: A Position Paper," *Reproductive Health Matters*, Vol. 17 (Issue 33) (2009), 105–110, https://www.tandfonline.com/doi/full/10.1016/S0968-8080%2809%2933431-X.
28. In addition to the *Eugene Weekly* and the *Colorado Springs Independent*, the independent newsweeklies included in our study were *Creative Loafing Charlotte* (Charlotte, North Carolina), *Isthmus* (Madison, Wisconsin), *Mountain Xpress* (Asheville, North Carolina), *Salt Lake City Weekly* (Salt Lake City, Utah), and *Gambit* (New Orleans, Louisiana).
29. To capture as many relevant articles as possible, we included the term *homosexual* in our search string, even though the *New York Times*, *Washington Post*, and Associated Press restrict usage of the term, and the *GLAAD Media Reference Guide* identifies it as an "outdated term considered derogatory and offensive to many lesbian and gay people." See *GLAAD Media Reference Guide*, 6, 7.
30. Our data set includes 56 articles from the *New York Times*, 28 from the *Washington Post*, 21 from the *Wall Street Journal*, 20 articles from assorted independent newsweeklies, 14 from the *Advocate*, and 13 from the *Los Angeles Times*.
31. We would have liked to code for race/ethnicity also; however, the news articles we examined very rarely referenced the race/ethnicity of quoted sources. For a pioneering study of media standing that takes a critical look at the lack of racial/ethnic diversity in featured news sources, see David Croteau and William Hoynes, *By Invitation Only: How the Media Limit Political Debate* (Monroe, ME: Common Courage, 1994).
32. The most repeated quotations in our data set came from the president's declaration—via Twitter on July 26, 2017—that he intended to ban transgender people from military service. News

outlets not only reported Trump's three tweets directly after he sent them, they also repeatedly quoted these tweets in subsequent news coverage. For critical discussion of the president's use of Twitter, see Matt Thompson, "How to Spark Panic and Confusion in Three Tweets," *The Atlantic*, January 13, 2019, https://www.theatlantic.com/politics/archive/2019/01/donald-trump-tweets-transgender-military-service-ban/579655/; and Nolan Higdon and Mickey Huff, *United States of Distraction: Media Manipulation in Post-Truth America (and what we can do about it)* (San Francisco: City Lights Publishers, 2019), 84–86.

33. Andy Lee Roth, "Framing Al-Awlaki: How Government Officials and Corporate Media Legitimized a Targeted Killing," in *Censored 2013: Dispatches from the Media Revolution*, eds. Mickey Huff and Andy Lee Roth with Project Censored (New York: Seven Stories, 2012) 345–73, 354–55, https://www.projectcensored.org/framing-al-awlaki-how-government-officials-and-corporate-media-%e2%80%a8legitimized-a-targeted-killing/.

34. See, e.g., Leon V. Sigal, *Reporters and Officials: The Organization and Politics of Newsmaking* (Lexington, MA: D.C. Heath and Company, 1973); Gaye Tuchman, *Making News: A Study in the Construction of Reality* (New York: The Free Press, 1978); Mark Fishman, *Manufacturing the News* (Austin: University of Texas Press, 1980); Croteau and Hoynes, *By Invitation Only*; and Andrew L. Roth and Emilie L. Vander Haar, "Media Standing of Urban Parkland Movements: The Case of Los Angeles' Taylor Yard, 1985–2001," *City & Community*, Vol. 5 No. 2 (June 2006), 129–51, https://onlinelibrary.wiley.com/doi/abs/10.1111/j.1540-6040.2006.00166.x.

35. Herbert J. Gans, *Deciding What's News: A Study of CBS Evening News, NBC Nightly News, Newsweek, and Time, 25th Anniversary Edition* (Evanston, IL: Northwestern University Press, 2004 [New York: Random House, 1979]), 147–48. In addition to governmental rank, Gans noted other hierarchies based on "power, wealth, or prestige"; see also Croteau and Hoynes, *By Invitation Only*, 177–79.

36. To avoid misunderstanding, the figures reported here demonstrate how often journalists proactively described or identified quoted sources in terms of their sexual orientation. Because we were interested in how *news reports* identified quoted sources, we did not rely on any external sources when determining how to code this category. For this reason, the number of sources who identify as gay, lesbian, or bisexual is likely greater than reported in Table 2.

37. A 2011 report from UCLA's Williams Institute estimated that 3.5 percent of adults in the United States identify as lesbian, gay, or bisexual. See Gary J. Gates, "How Many People are Lesbian, Gay, Bisexual, and Transgender?" Williams Institute (University of California, Los Angeles School of Law), April 2011, https://williamsinstitute.law.ucla.edu/wp-content/uploads/Gates-How-Many-People-LGBT-Apr-2011.pdf. A more recent survey, published by Gallup in 2018, estimated that in 2017 4.5 percent of American adults identified as lesbian, gay, bisexual, or transgender. Unfortunately, this report does not distinguish sexual orientation from gender identity. See Frank Newport, "In U.S., Estimate of LGBT Population Rises to 4.5%," Gallup, May 22, 2018, https://news.gallup.com/poll/234863/estimate-lgbt-population-rises.aspx.

38. *GLAAD Media Reference Guide*, 4.

39. Gates, "How Many People are Lesbian, Gay, and Transgender?" On the marginalization of bisexual perspectives in coverage of LGBTQ issues, see *GLAAD Media Reference Guide*, 20.

40. Croteau and Hoynes, *By Invitation Only*, 75-9, 111–13. Our study focuses on print news and theirs focused on TV news; and their study was conducted in 1994. On gender diversity in news, see also Gans, *Deciding What's News*, 175.

41. Andrew R. Flores, Jody L. Herman, Gary J. Gates, and Taylor N.T. Brown, "How Many Adults Identify as Transgender in the United States?" Williams Institute (University of California, Los Angeles School of Law), June 2016, http://williamsinstitute.law.ucla.edu/wp-content/uploads/How-Many-Adults-Identify-as-Transgender-in-the-United-States.pdf. In 2011, the Williams Institute estimated that the figure was 0.3 percent; see Gates, "How Many People are Lesbian, Gay, Bisexual, and Transgender?"

42. Recall that Gamson defines media standing as a more active and thus more powerful status than merely being "covered or mentioned" in the news. Gamson, "Media and Social Movements," 9471.

43. Gamson, "Media and Social Movements," 9471; *GLAAD Media Reference Guide*, 4.

44. Sandhya Somashekhar and Moriah Balingit, "DOJ Brief Signals a Policy Shift for Transgender Students," *Washington Post*, February 12, 2017, A8.

45. Jaclyn Cosgrove, "As Gays Make Gains, Trans People Face More Obstacles; The Conservative Right, with Trump's Aid, Targets a New Community," *Los Angeles Times*, February 19, 2018, A2; published online as "Even as Gay Rights Battles are Won, Transgender People Continue to Face Obstacles," at https://www.latimes.com/nation/la-na-transgender-rights-20180219-story.html.

46. Laura Meckler, Samantha Schmidt, and Lena H. Sun, "Trump Administration Considering 'Different Concepts' Regarding Transgender Rights, with Some Pushing Back Internally," *Washington Post*, October 24, 2018, https://www.washingtonpost.com/national/trump-admin-istration-considering-different-concepts-regarding-transgender-rights-with-some-pushing-back-internally/2018/10/22/0668f4da-d624-11e8-83a2-d1c3da28d6b6_story.html.

47. Helene Cooper, "Directive on Transgender Troops is Delayed for Study," *New York Times*, August 30, 2017, A19; published online as "Mattis Says Panel Will Study Trump's Transgender Military Ban," at https://www.nytimes.com/2017/08/29/us/politics/mattis-trump-trans-gender-ban.html.

48. Cosgrove, "As Gays Make Gains."

49. Julie Hirschfeld Davis, "Trump Planning to Authorize Pentagon to Enact Ban on Transgender Troops," *New York Times*, August 24, 2017, A15; published online as "Military Transgender Ban to Begin Within 6 Months, Memo Says" on August 23, 2017, at https://www.nytimes.com/2017/08/23/us/politics/trump-military-transgender-ban.html.

50. Gordon Lubold, "Trump Allows Current Transgender Troops but Bans Future Recruits," *Wall Street Journal*, March 24, 2018, A3, https://www.wsj.com/articles/trump-allows-current-trans-gender-troops-but-bans-future-recruits-1521855712.

51. Helene Cooper and Thomas Gibbons-Neff, "New Policy Lets Transgender Troops Stay in Service, but with Restrictions," *New York Times*, March 24, 2018, A13; published online as "Trump Approves New Limits on Transgender Troops in the Military," at https://www.nytimes.com/2018/03/24/us/politics/trump-transgender-military.html.

52. Brent Kendall and Gordon Lubold, "Judge Blocks Trump's Transgender Military Ban for Now," *Wall Street Journal*, October 30, 2017, https://www.wsj.com/articles/judge-blocks-trumps-transgender-military-ban-for-now-1509390314.

53. W. J. Hennigan, "Trump Moves to Bar Transgender Service Members; The President's Abrupt Announcement on Twitter Could Affect Thousands of Military Personnel," *Los Angeles Times*, July 27, 2017, A1, A12. The same day, Trump's Twitter announcement also made front-page headlines in the *New York Times* and the *Washington Post*; the *Wall Street Journal*'s report appeared on that paper's third page. All four newspapers quoted Trump's tweet directly.

54. Hennigan, "Trump Moves to Bar." As quoted in newspaper coverage, the RAND study also projected "little or no impact on unit cohesion, operational effectiveness or readiness."

55. Jack Healy and Richard Pérez-Peña, "Solace and Fury as Schools React to Gender Policy," *New York Times*, May 14, 2016, A1; published online on May 13, 2016, as "Solace and Fury as Schools React to Transgender Policy," at https://www.nytimes.com/2016/05/14/us/trans-gender-bathrooms.html.

56. Ibid.

57. Ian Lovett, "Conservatives Aim to Shift Debate over Gay Weddings to Speech Rights," *Wall Street Journal*, June 17, 2017, https://www.wsj.com/articles/conservatives-aim-to-shift-debate-over-gay-weddings-to-speech-rights-1497700802.

58. According to the Family Research Council, its mission is "to advance faith, family, and freedom in public policy and the culture from a biblical worldview." "Vision and Mission Statements," Family Research Council, undated, https://www.frc.org/mission-statement [accessed April 10, 2019].

59. Louise Radnofsky and Rebecca Ballhaus, "Transgender Bathroom Guidance Dropped," *Wall Street Journal*, February 23, 2017, A3; published online on February 22, 2017, as "Trump Administration Rescinds Obama Rules on Transgender Bathroom Use," at https://www.

wsj.com/articles/trump-administration-set-to-rescind-obama-rules-on-transgender-bathroom-use-1487790631.

60. Jeremy W. Peters, Jo Becker, and Julie Hirschfeld Davis, "Trump Rescinds Obama Directive on Bathroom Use," *New York Times*, February 23, 2017, A1; published online on February 22, 2017, as "Trump Rescinds Rules on Bathrooms for Transgender Students," at https://www.nytimes.com/2017/02/22/us/politics/devos-sessions-transgender-students-rights.html.

61. "Vision and Mission Statements," Family Research Council.

62. Helene Cooper and Maggie Haberman, "Rights Record of Nominee for Army Job is Criticized," *New York Times*, April 8, 2017, A17; published online on April 7, 2017, as "L.G.B.T. Advocates Criticize Nominee for Army Secretary," at https://www.nytimes.com/2017/04/07/us/politics/mark-green-army-secretary-nominee-lgbt-criticism.html.

63. Helene Cooper, "Trump's 2nd Nominee for Army Secretary Withdraws," *New York Times*, May 5, 2017, https://www.nytimes.com/2017/05/05/us/politics/mark-green-army-secretary-nominee-withdraws.html.

64. Mark Joseph Stern, "God vs. the Constitution," *The Advocate*, August/September 2016, 14; published online on July 1, 2016, at https://www.advocate.com/politics/2016/7/01/god-vs-constitution.

65. Ibid.

66. "The Biggest Homophobes," *The Advocate*, June/July 2017, 102–103.

67. Trish Bendix, "Does LGBT Media Have a Future?" BuzzFeed, January 25, 2019, https://www.buzzfeednews.com/article/trishbendix/future-of-lgbt-media-out-advocate-autostraddle-into-grindr.

68. Chris Francescani, "What Happened? Timeline of Investigation into Jussie Smollett's Attack Claim," ABC News, June 24, 2019, https://abcnews.go.com/US/timeline-alleged-jussie-smollett-attack/story?id=61124090.

69. See, for example, Annalisa Merelli, "The Jussie Smollett Case Shows Exactly Why We Need to Take Hate Crimes More Seriously," Quartz, February 20, 2019, https://qz.com/1551186/jussie-smollett-proves-why-we-should-take-hate-crimes-more-seriously/.

70. Audra D.S. Burch, "Hate Crime Hoaxes are Rare, but Can be 'Devastating,'" *New York Times*, February 22, 2019, https://www.nytimes.com/2019/02/22/us/fake-hate-crimes.html.

71. On impacts of the Trump administration's efforts to promote "conscience rights" and "free exercise of religion," see, for example, "Trump Administration Finalizes Rule that Will Make It Harder for LGBT People to Access Health Care," Fenway Health, May 2, 2019, https://fenwayhealth.org/trump-administration-finalizes-rule-that-will-make-it-harder-for-lgbt-people-to-access-health-care/; and Rachel Bergman, "HHS Office for Civil Rights Overhauled Its Mission and Vision Statements on Its Website," Sunlight Foundation, May 1, 2019, https://sunlightfoundation.com/2019/05/01/hhs-office-for-civil-rights-overhauled-its-mission-and-vision-statements-on-its-website/.

72. "HHS Announces New Conscience and Religious Freedom Division," U.S. Department of Health & Human Services, Office for Civil Rights, January 18, 2018, https://www.hhs.gov/about/news/2018/01/18/hhs-ocr-announces-new-conscience-and-religious-freedom-division.html; Dan Diamond and Jennifer Haberkorn, "Trump to Overhaul HHS Office, Shield Health Workers with Moral Objections," *Politico*, January 16, 2018, updated January 17, 2018, https://www.politico.com/story/2018/01/16/conscience-abortion-transgender-patients-health-care-289542.

73. Nick Duffy, "Trump Strips LGBT Rights from USMCA Trade Deal with Mexico and Canada," Pink News, December 3, 2018, https://www.pinknews.co.uk/2018/12/03/trump-usmca-mexico-canada/.

74. In May 2019, a senior official in the Trump administration announced its opposition to the Equality Act. Chris Johnson, "Exclusive: Trump Comes Out against Equality Act," *Washington Blade*, May 13, 2019, https://www.washingtonblade.com/2019/05/13/exclusive-trump-comes-out-against-equality-act/.

75. Alwood, *Straight News*, 326.

76. On the pitfalls of "balanced" news coverage, see Robert M. Entman, *Democracy Without Citizens: Media and the Decay of American Politics* (New York: Oxford University Press, 1989).

77. Alwood, *Straight News*, 323.

78. *GLAAD Media Reference Guide*, 4.

79. Sean Lengell, "Family Research Council Labeled a 'Hate Group,'" Washington Times, November 24, 2010, https://www.washingtontimes.com/news/2010/nov/24/frc-labeled-a-hate-group/.

80. Commentator Accountability Project, GLAAD, undated, https://www.glaad.org/cap [accessed April 17, 2019].

81. See the entry for Tony Perkins, Commentator Accountability Project (GLAAD), undated, https://www.glaad.org/cap/tony-perkins [accessed April 17, 2019].

82. Between 2013 and 2015 the percentage of LGB adults without health insurance decreased from 22 percent to 11 percent. See Cahill, Geffen, and Wang, "One Year In," 18.

CHAPTER 8

"Fake News"

The Trojan Horse for Silencing Alternative News and Reestablishing Corporate News Dominance

Emil Marmol and Lee Mager

> . . . the people can always be brought to the bidding of
> the leaders. That is easy. All you have to do is tell them
> they are being attacked and denounce the pacifists for
> lack of patriotism and exposing the country to danger. It
> works the same way in any country.
>
> —Hermann Göring[1]

Throughout living memory, the US public has been kept in a constant state of panic and fear by politicians and the corporate media who serve as their stenographers. For much of the second half of the 20th century the bogeyman of choice was the Cold War–era Soviet Union. Under the cover of having to keep the communists at bay, the United States perpetrated dozens of atrocities, including colonial and imperial wars of aggression, the assassination of political leaders, violent coups, acts of sabotage, and the suffocation of leftist movements both domestically and abroad. Then, once the Soviet threat had lost most of its fear value, we were instructed to fear and loathe the omnipresence of Islamic terrorism. Once again, the US government was free to commit any atrocity it desired, including the assassination of its own citizens, under the pretext of protecting the "homeland"[2] from this external, existential threat.

Compared to how long Soviet Russia was purported to represent an existential menace, the diminishing returns of Islamic terrorism as a threat became clear relatively quickly. Before we knew it, America needed a new enemy. A new, preferably already familiar enemy that would suit the current imperial ambitions and geopolitical strategy of the ruling elites. Enter, stage right, the Russians, with their former Cold War KGB man, President Vladimir Putin. The incessant contemporary corporate news drumbeat of anti-Russian hysteria is matched only by the merciless repetition of the assorted variants of the words "communism" and "terrorism" that preceded it. The Russians, the corporate media would have one believe, are hidden under every rock and within every crevice, ready to inflict malicious harm upon the world's body politic. On US-focused online political discussion forums, particularly Reddit, levels of paranoia and hysteria may even have exceeded those of the Cold War, with countless accusations against out-of-favor account-holders of being secret "Russian bots" programmed to subvert discourse and sow discord. The unevidenced postulation of a small number of secret "Russian bots" subverting democracy in the world's most powerful state has been repeated uncritically in corporate news media as well.[3]

In the United States for the past several years the Russians and Putin have been the focus of intense criticism and unyielding rebuke. The alleged crimes—by which we mean unproven rumors at best and gross distortions of reality at worst—that the Russian government has been accused of include imperialist aspirations, annexing Crimea by force,[4] downing Malaysia Airlines Flight MH17,[5] poisoning the Skripals in the United Kingdom,[6] poisoning Hillary Clinton,[7] planting spy Maria Butina in the United States,[8] militarily aiding despotic governments,[9] promoting Brexit,[10] hacking voting systems in 21 US states,[11] and hacking the electrical grids of the state of Vermont and Ontario, Canada.[12] They have even been accused of training whales that have been "harassing" the fishermen of a North Atlantic Treaty Organization (NATO) ally, Norway.[13]

The most scandalous and unforgivable crime the Russians are alleged to have committed, however, involves colluding with Donald Trump to subvert the 2016 US presidential election in Trump's favor—the conspiracy theory known as "Russiagate." Almost immediately after the 2016 election, rumors, innuendo, and accusations about Russian hacking and collusion proliferated to explain the Democrats' loss.[14] Thus began the narrative the corporate media has been trumpeting incessantly ever since, which they continuously rehash to instill distress and abhorrence in the public mind about our relentless foes, the Russians. The US government, for its part, has brought the heads of social media before congressional committees, publicly excoriating them for permitting this political non-event to happen.[15]

As of this writing, Russiagate has hit a brick wall, with Robert Mueller's investigation revealing that there was no collusion between the Trump campaign and the Russians to subvert the election.[16] This collusion claim therefore certainly qualifies as an unwarranted conspiracy theory: "a proposed explanation of some historical event (or events) in terms of the significant causal agency of a relatively small group of persons—the conspirators—acting in secret."[17] Yet it is rarely described as such by corporate media, since its main purveyors have been that very same corporate media. Despite Mueller's findings, much of the public remains largely convinced that the Russians, via a purportedly Kremlin-backed troll farm called the Internet Research Agency (IRA) located in St. Petersburg, tilted the election to Trump's advantage. In the name of aggressively eliminating a non-existent Russiagate fake news threat, the social media giants, major tech firms, corporate news media outlets, and the US government through its affiliated organizations have collaborated to aggressively eliminate legitimate and trustworthy, alternative, and independent news media online.[18] The public is naturally being fed the line that this targeted harassment and persecution is undertaken for the sole purpose of safeguarding freedom and democracy against those who wish to cause us harm. As history has demonstrated, maleficent behavior by those holding power is most easily committed under the guise of protecting the nation against supposed evildoers.

Before delving into the actors and methods behind this recent campaign to censor the alternative and independent press in the United States, it would be beneficial to first dispel the belief that the IRA had any discernable effect on the outcome of the US election. The IRA bought $100,000 worth of Facebook ads. Of that, $46,000 was spent before the election, while the remainder was spent after the election.[19] According to Facebook, 25 percent of the ads "were never shown to anyone."[20] And just because they were displayed does not mean they were ever viewed, as Facebook users only read about 10 percent of the content in their newsfeeds.[21] Russian ads amounted to .0004 percent of total content on Facebook and represented only one of 23,000 Facebook newsfeed posts.[22] Over a two-year period, between 2015 and 2017, Facebook logged 33 trillion posts; the IRA generated 80,000 of them.[23] Facebook's total content for those two years was "413 million times more than the 80,000 posts" from the IRA.[24] Russian-linked tweets amounted to .74 percent of Twitter's election-related traffic.[25] Twitter has confirmed that 200 accounts were linked with "Russian interference" out of their 328 million accounts.[26] Russian Twitter accounts made up at most .02 percent of tweets related to the election.[27] Google has reported a total of $4,700 from "Russian-linked ad spending."[28] To put the amount of money spent by the IRA into perspective, consider the fact that the Trump and Clinton campaigns spent $81 million on Facebook ads alone.[29] The IRA spent .05 percent as much.[30] In total, $6.5 billion was spent on the 2016 elections,[31] with $2.4 billion on the presidential election alone.[32] Facebook's total revenue for 2016 was more than $27 billion.[33]

Furthermore, the overwhelming majority of Russian ads had nothing to do with the election and many did not favor one candidate over another.[34] A Senate-commissioned study of the ads reported that, of the total content published on social media by the IRA, only 11 percent was election-related, and an even smaller proportion, 7 percent of their Facebook posts and 6 percent of their tweets, mentioned either of the two presidential candidates by name.[35] Regarding the IRA's content, Facebook vice president of ads Rob Goldman stated that "swaying the election was *NOT* the main goal."[36] The ads were amateurish, inept, and oftentimes absurd in nature.[37] Award-winning author, Russian dissident, and longtime critic of Vladimir Putin, Masha Gessen, commented that the posts were "not sophisticated," were written in "sub-literate English," and were "truly absurd . . . caricatures of American political propaganda."[38] Many experts and researchers concur that the IRA's efforts as well as fake news media overall had little impact on those exposed to it and likely had no effect on the outcome of the election.

It is also important to note that no proof has been provided of Russian government involvement in any fake news electioneering. Even the strongest statements in corporate media merely claim without evidence that the owner of the "troll farm" responsible for most of the Facebook ads is an "ally" of Putin; for instance, the *New York Times* reported that the "Internet Research Agency [is] owned by a businessman, Yevgeny V. Prigozhin, who is a close ally of President Vladimir V. Putin of Russia."[39] One would hope that if the Russian government had indeed been involved, they would have been able to conduct a more sophisticated and professional operation, given the implicit respect bestowed upon their intelligence agencies by the US government.

Considering that the Russian-based fake news and disinformation campaign has been roundly debunked insofar as having any notable or measurable effect on the US election, we argue that the fake news hysteria created by those in government and echoed by the corporate news media is being harnessed and used as a pretext for the suppression of dissent and counterhegemonic viewpoints while re-establishing the corporate press's preeminence as the sole purveyor and manufacturer of public opinion.[40]

The following section will examine the actors involved in these attacks on free speech, as well as their methods of maligning, suppressing, and censoring alternative news online. Next, we will focus on the ways that government-funded organizations, the corporate press, social media giants, and tech firms are working hand in hand to reinvigorate and rebuild public fealty to sources of establishment news and information. To conclude the chapter, we will examine why this effort is being undertaken and who stands to gain and lose by it.

THE CENSORS

[There is] a rapidly growing landscape of censorship of news critical of American corporate and political leaders who are trying to defend themselves from an increasingly angry population. It's a story as old as civilization: a wealthy and powerful elite fending off popular unrest by trying to contain knowledge of how the insiders gain at the others' expense, at home and abroad.

—Joe Lauria[41]

One of the first salvos fired against the alternative press was a concerted effort by the *Washington Post* and the website PropOrNot, in the form of an article authored by Craig Timberg, titled "Russian Propaganda Effort Helped Spread 'Fake News' during Election, Experts Say."[42] The primary "experts" cited in the article are associated with PropOrNot. However, those purported experts spoke on condition of anonymity and did not provide a methodology for arriving at any of their claims, including the spectacular assertion that Russian disinformation on Facebook was viewed more than 213 million times by an unsuspecting public. *The Washington Post* published and stood by the article despite the glaring shortcomings of PropOrNot's credibility. PropOrNot had only come into existence a few months prior to the article's publication, and had demonstrated an amateurish and unprofessional, taunting style of messaging via social media. The most problematic aspect of the article was the promotion of PropOrNot's McCarthyite blacklist of web-based news outlets that they claim are "routine peddlers of Russian propaganda," either knowingly spreading Russian propaganda or serving as "useful idiots."[43] Included among the news sources blacklisted by PropOrNot are such well-regarded and award-winning alternative news websites as Black Agenda Report, Consortium News, *CounterPunch*, Naked Capitalism, Truthdig, Truthout, and WikiLeaks. Not satisfied with merely creating a blacklist that was widely disseminated and endorsed by the corporate media, PropOrNot has called upon the government to investigate these alternative news websites for espionage, and developed a web browser plugin that flags these websites as Russian propaganda.

PropOrNot provided no substantiating evidence as rationale for including any particular websites on their blacklist, yet this libelous behavior was apparently acceptable to the editors at the *Washington Post*, including the executive editor Marty Baron, who tweeted in support of Timberg's article, while later stating he did not endorse PropOrNot as an organization.[44] PropOrNot recommends establishment mouthpieces such as the BBC, the *New York Times*, NPR, and the *Wall Street Journal*, but blacklists Russian government–funded news sources RT and Sputnik as sources of Russian propaganda. Say what one will of RT, there are clearly no grounds to consider them less credible than any state-funded news organization, including the

British government–funded BBC. Indeed, the BBC's long record of serving as a peddler of biased news in the interests of Western economic and political elites makes them an unlikely candidate for commendation in the fight against spreading propaganda.[45]

Given PropOrNot's unsubtle alignment with the interests of NATO, it would seem their guiding principle in defaming the alternative press is to silence those who question US foreign policy and Western hegemony more generally. Toward that end, it should come as no surprise that one of the other "experts" cited in the *Washington Post* article is Clint Watts. Watts is a former FBI special agent on the Joint Terrorism Task Force and has been heavily involved in US intelligence and the security apparatus.[46] He provided key "expert" witness testimony to a Senate Intelligence Committee on Russian interference in the 2016 US elections.[47] He is currently a fellow at the hawkish, conservative think tank Foreign Policy Research Institute,[48] and has written prolifically to help promote the false Russiagate narrative.[49]

In October 2018, after Facebook conducted a massive purge of pages on its platform, some of which were listed on PropOrNot's blacklist, PropOrNot ominously tweeted, "All of these are cross

platform & have websites, but one thing at a time."[50] While not as unsubtle as PropOrNot, tech giant Google has created a blacklist of its own, though theirs is algorithmic. In April 2017, as part of an initiative called Project Owl, Google changed its search algorithm in an effort to fight fake news and "surface more authoritative content."[51] This was justified on a blogpost by Ben Gomes, now head of search at Google, where he argued that the changes were in response to the problem of fake news, "where content on the web has contributed to the spread of blatantly misleading, low quality, offensive or downright false information."[52] He claims that Google intends to "provide people with access to relevant information from the most reliable sources available."[53] To help with this effort, Google has contracted more than 10,000 "search quality" raters whose job it is to flag content that, in Gomes's words, includes "misleading information, unexpected offensive results, hoaxes and unsupported conspiracy theories."[54] The work done by these search quality raters is then used, in turn, to improve the Google search algorithm's ability to more efficiently and automatically demote "such low-quality content and help us to make additional improvements over time."[55]

Google accounts for 90 percent of searches conducted on the internet. Any changes they make to their algorithm will have drastic consequences regarding information to which the public is privy. The effects of Google's algorithmic changes make it clear that the sources it considers unauthoritative, unreliable, and misleading are frequently also critical of, and challenge, the status quo. Since their changes were implemented in April 2017, there has been a precipitous decline in traffic for many of the internet's most respected, popular, and trusted sources of independent and alternative news sources, including Common Dreams, Consortium News, *Counter-Punch, Democracy Now!*, Global Research, Media Matters for America, MintPress News, Truthout, WikiLeaks, and the World Socialist Web Site.[56] It is also worth noting that Microsoft's web browser, Bing, has implemented similar changes to its algorithms.[57]

In May 2019 a number of right-wing alternative news pundits were outright banned from Facebook, under the rationale of controlling "hate speech," and many on the Left applauded such measures, given the frequently offensive statements coming from the now-banned pundits.[58] However, such censorship can prove to be a dangerous, slippery slope, and should be resisted by the Left; the giant tech firms' sudden commitment to selectively persecuting offensive content might simply be an excuse to test the waters for further censorship, beginning by erasing content that most of the public disagrees with in the first place. Those applauding such Orwellian disappearance measures may very well find themselves on the receiving end of them in the future, once regulations are embedded and accepted as the norm.

An internal Google document leaked to the public, titled "The Good Censor," makes unequivocally clear the tech industry's new stance on the control of information.[59] The document acknowledges that Google, Facebook, and Twitter "now control the majority of our online conversations" and that they are all moving "away from unmediated free speech and towards censorship and moderation."[60] There are a litany of excuses given for this unacceptable move toward censorship, which include the threat of fake news disseminated by "Russian-based entities" and "Russian involvement" during the 2016 election campaign; tech users' bad behavior, as Google claims that "human beings en masse don't behave very well"; and the need to "monetize content through its organization," "increase revenues," and "protect advertisers from controversial content."[61] Google frames free speech as a "utopian" ideal, arguing that it is better for us to be presented with content from authoritative sources, because "rational debate is damaged when authoritative voices and 'have a go' commentators receive equal weighting."[62] Google tells us that, in response to the spread of misinformation and fake news, the public is "turning to [corporate] mainstream media outlets for trustworthy information." In Google's implicitly stated estimation, those trustworthy outlets are *"The New Yorker, New York Times, Washington Post,* the *Wall Street Journal* and the *Guardian."*[63] In the leaked document, Google places itself as the unsolicited and unelected guardian of the public's best interests, arguing in essence that the rabble must be protected from its own irrationality and from treacherous foreign actors.

Social media giants Facebook and Twitter have likewise taken drastic measures to combat the supposed Russian scourge of misinformation. Facebook has partnered with a number of organizations to help purge so-called fake news from its platform. Among them are the Atlantic Council, the International Republican Institute (IRI), and the National Democratic Institute (NDI).[64] Twitter has also partnered with the Atlantic Council's Digital Forensic Research Lab and the NDI.[65]

The Atlantic Council is, essentially, an arm of NATO.[66] It is funded by NATO, the US and UK governments, the European Union, major weapons manufacturers, the military, conservative think tanks such as the Charles Koch Institute and the Center for Strategic and International Studies, the National Endowment for Democracy (NED), international banks, Google, Facebook, and Microsoft.[67] On its board of directors and advisory board sit a great many right-wing or far-right establishment characters, including Brent Scowcroft, Michael Chertoff, Condoleezza Rice, Michael Hayden, Madeleine Albright, and Henry Kissinger.[68] The Atlantic Council has published work by John T. Watts in which he argues that the invention of the printing press brought about centuries of "conflict and disruption," and that the "invention of the internet" is having much the same effect.[69] He also suggests that online news organizations should disable their systems that allow user comments, thereby preventing the public from sharing their views with each other about particular news items.[70]

The IRI and NDI are both offshoots of the NED. The NED was created during the Reagan administration with the explicit purpose of spreading US government propaganda and interfering with the affairs of other countries.[71] On the board of the NED sit Victoria Nuland and Elliott Abrams, both known for their interventionist policies that have wreaked havoc on foreign populations from Ukraine to Nicaragua.[72] The board of the IRI includes senators Marco Rubio and Lindsey Graham, virulent supporters of foreign meddling, with the former playing a vanguard role in the attempted coup and propaganda efforts currently directed at Venezuela.[73] The IRI's former chairman was the now-deceased senator John McCain, who seemingly wanted to bomb half the globe, and who once cheerily sang into a microphone, "It's that old Beach Boys song, 'Bomb Iran? Bomb bomb bomb . . .'"[74] The NDI's current chairperson is Madeleine Albright, who, as secretary of state under president Bill Clinton, was questioned by CBS journalist Lesley Stahl about the deaths of 500,000 Iraqi children caused by US sanctions, and notoriously responded, "we think the price is worth it."[75]

Facebook's third-party fact-checkers include Check Your Fact and PolitiFact, and it previously partnered with the now-defunct and unabashedly neoconservative publication the *Weekly Standard*.[76] Check Your Fact is wholly owned by the Daily Caller, a right-wing news organization cofounded by Fox News host Tucker Carlson.[77] The Daily Caller has regularly published false news, offensive content, and propaganda.[78] Facebook censored an article by ThinkProgress after the *Weekly Standard* declared it to be fake news.[79] The Think-Progress article was widely defended as accurate, leading to the speculation that it was censored simply because of the *Weekly Standard*'s political orientation.[80] Like the Daily Caller, the *Weekly Standard* had been known to publish falsehoods.[81] For instance, the *Weekly Standard* was instrumental in selling the Bush regime's lie that Saddam Hussein was connected to Al Qaeda, helping to pave the way for war with Iraq.[82] And PolitiFact has been known to maintain the position that particular partisan claims are true, long after major news outlets have declared them to be false.[83]

As an internal measure for combating fake news, Facebook has been hiring tens of thousands of employees as fact-checkers. These zealous censors now number more than 30,000 and make up the largest contingent of Facebook employees.[84] According to Monika Bickert, head of global policy management at Facebook, they include "former intelligence and law-enforcement officials and prosecutors who worked in the area of counterterrorism."[85] As put by Samidh Chakrabarti, product manager of civic engagement at Facebook, "We basically have some of the best intelligence analysts from around the world."[86] Those at the helm of Facebook are a veritable who's who in the revolving door between government and corporations. The head of Facebook security, Nathaniel Gleicher, was formerly Obama's National Security Council director for cybersecurity policy.[87] Additionally, Gleicher is a senior associate at the hawkish think tank the Center for Strategic and International Studies.[88] Facebook recently hired Jennifer Newstead as their general counsel.[89] Newstead was a coauthor of the USA PATRIOT Act and has defended unilateral US sanctions against Iran under the Trump administration.[90] Joel Kaplan, Facebook's vice president of global public policy, served as the White House deputy chief of staff for policy under George W. Bush.[91]

Kaplan has argued the Daily Caller and Breitbart should be promoted on Facebook the same way as other major news outlets.[92] Facebook's vice president of global affairs and communications is former British deputy prime minister Nick Clegg, a proponent of neoliberal politics and austerity measures.[93]

Other shadowy organizations that are working to censor content online include the German Marshall Fund. Jamie Fly is a senior fellow and director of the Future of Geopolitics and Asia programs at the German Marshall Fund.[94] He was the executive director of the aggressively interventionist, now defunct, Foreign Policy Initiative (FPI), whose board of directors included Bill Kristol and Robert Kagan, former founders of the Project for a New American Century.[95] Fly left the FPI to work as an advisor to Senator Marco Rubio.[96] He has been an ardent supporter of censorship on social media platforms, appearing often in the media to express such views.[97] As he stated to Jeb Sprague, visiting faculty at the University of California, Santa Barbara, "we are just starting to push back. Just this last week Facebook began starting to take down sites. So this is just the beginning."[98]

The Alliance for Securing Democracy (ASD) is a project of the German Marshall Fund, which itself receives funding from the US government and NATO.[99] The ASD has been a chief instigator of anti-Russian sentiment. The ASD receives additional funding from Pierre Omidyar, the founder of eBay.[100] Omidyar funds a number of groups and media organizations that work to influence politics and massage public perception globally, including the stoking of anti-Russian sentiment.[101] The Intercept, an ostensibly anti-war, progressive publication, is primarily funded by Omidyar. Despite claims of editorial freedom and independence, the Intercept may not be the independent news outlet it purports to be, given its intimate connections to pro-war, right-wing organizations, journalistic slant, and delayed publication of a key document provided by whistleblower Edward Snowden.[102] Omidyar is one of the funders of the International Fact-Checking Network, the organization that certifies Facebook's fact-checkers such as Check Your Fact and PolitiFact.[103] On the "team" at ASD is Jamie Fly, as well as Laura Rosenberger, who worked for the State Department and the White House's National Security Council.[104] ASD's advisory council includes Michael Chertoff, Bill Kristol, John

Podesta, and Michael Morell, as well as former intelligence officers and State Department officials.[105] ASD is responsible for creating the Hamilton 68 Dashboard, for which Omidyar provided funding.[106] The Hamilton 68 Dashboard, currently offline and awaiting the "new and improved" 2.0 version, is a tool that serves to make the public aware of social media accounts and websites that purportedly peddle Russian disinformation.[107] Its lack of usefulness and accuracy has led to disavowal of the service by some of those behind it, as well as calls of "bullshit" by some commentators.[108] New Knowledge is linked to the Hamilton 68 Dashboard by way of Jonathon Morgan, who is the CEO of New Knowledge as well as a co-creator of Hamilton 68.[109] Morgan was responsible for creating an army of fake Russian bots to help elect Democratic candidate Doug Jones in Alabama's 2017 Senate race.[110]

Finally, there is FireEye, a cybersecurity firm that has received funds from In-Q-Tel, an investment arm of the CIA, and through its leadership has ties to military partners and weapons manufacturers such as Lockheed Martin, Mandiant, and Aegis Research Corporation.[111] Its CEO, Kevin Mandia, has testified to Congress about the alleged Russian disinformation campaign during the 2016 presidential election.[112] FireEye published a report on the topic shortly thereafter.[113] Christopher Porter, their chief intelligence strategist, is also a senior fellow at the Atlantic Council.[114]

So how has all this fake news and election interference hype played out in practice on the social media and tech giants' platforms? They have been engaging in a brazen, wholesale process of censorship via deplatforming and de-ranking of dissident, counterhegemonic, and alternative media voices, from the libertarian Right to the anarchist Left. This has often been conducted under the amorphous and nebulous accusation of "coordinated inauthentic behavior," or sometimes with no rationale given at all, with no follow-up provided to those individuals and groups who have been disappeared.[115] The following is just a sampling of censorship activity carried out by the tech and social media giants:

▸ On October 11, 2018, more than 800 accounts were deplatformed on Facebook and Twitter. Included in this purge were

Anti-Media, Cop Block, Counter Current News, Filming Cops, the Free Thought Project, Police the Police, and RT America correspondent Rachel Blevins. Twitter simultaneously suspended many of the accounts of these pages and their editors. The combined following of the pages purged was in the tens of millions. The focus of the content in these purged accounts was opposition to police brutality and war, with criticism of US domestic and foreign policy.[116]

▶ On October 1, 2018, Twitter banned the posting of hacked materials to its site.[117] This includes materials brought to public attention by whistleblowers.

▶ Instagram, a subsidiary of Facebook, suspended the accounts of several Iranian government officials, including the Supreme Leader Ayatollah Khamenei.[118]

▶ Days before the Spanish general election, Facebook-owned WhatsApp shut down the channel of Podemos, one of Spain's leftist political parties. The channel had 50,000 members.[119]

▶ Iranian government–funded TV news channels Press TV and Spanish-language HispanTV were disabled without warning on Google platforms, including YouTube and Gmail.[120]

▶ Following a day of tweets urging global support for her son and in defense of free speech, Julian Assange's mother had her Twitter account suspended. Twitter provided no explanation to Christine Assange for its actions.[121]

▶ Twitter suspended the accounts of the Venezuelan Consulate in Vancouver, Canada, the Venezuelan Ministry of Popular Power for Women, the Ministry of Popular Power for Education, and the Ministry of Popular Power for Petroleum, as well as the accounts of Venezuelan media outlets *El Correo del Orinoco*, *Diario Vea*, and ViVe Televisión. Meanwhile, Twitter verified the account of Juan Guaidó, self-anointed president of Venezuela and leader of a US-organized and -funded coup.[122]

▶ Twice in 2018, Facebook shut down the page of respected Venezuelan news outlet teleSUR English.[123] Each time, its account was only reinstated after public outcry.

▶ On August 9, 2018, Venezuelanalysis, an independent, reader-supported news website endorsed by figures such as Noam

Chomsky and John Pilger, had its account removed by Facebook. The account was restored after public outcry.[124]

▶ Thousands of accounts in support of Nicolás Maduro, the democratically elected president of Venezuela, have been banned by Twitter.[125]

▶ On February 15, 2019, Facebook deplatformed the pages for BackThen, In the Now, Soapbox, and Waste-Ed, all produced by Maffick Media. This was done after CNN ran a report on Maffick Media that was instigated by the Alliance for Securing Democracy.[126]

▶ Facebook, in coordination with the Israeli and US governments, has shut down the accounts of prominent Palestinian political parties, activists, and news organizations.[127]

▶ YouTube, a Google subsidiary, has been censoring content it deems "controversial," including work produced by Abby Martin, a respected and prolific journalist and presenter.[128]

▶ Facebook removed ads placed on its platform by US presidential hopeful Elizabeth Warren that called for the break-up of big tech companies.[129]

▶ On the same day that Julian Assange was arrested, Facebook removed the page of Rafael Correa, the former president of Ecuador. In 2012, Correa had granted Assange asylum in the Ecuadorian embassy in London.[130]

▶ Facebook, Twitter, and Google have removed hundreds of accounts, pages, and channels based upon information provided to them by FireEye. Many of the accounts were left-wing and held views critical of the United States and its Middle Eastern allies.[131]

Many accounts and pages have often been banned simultaneously by different giant tech platforms—for example, the profiles, shows, and channels of Alex Jones. In August 2018 Jones was removed from Facebook, Apple, Spotify, and YouTube within the same week.[132] This has led to speculation that the social media giants are working in concert with one another.

A recent operation by the name of "NewsGuard" has emerged that resembles PropOrNot in its intentions and aims, though with more sophisticated, subtle, and potentially nefarious tactics. NewsGuard bills itself as a company that can solve the woes of the social media giants and the unsuspecting public by alerting us to fake news and misinformation. They have gone as far as embedding themselves in academic conferences, promoting their services as a tool for critical media literacy educators.[133] Their product is a web browser plugin that alerts the reader, via a color-coded rating system, as to the veracity and trustworthiness of online news sources. A green icon is a trustworthy site, whereas a red icon is untrustworthy.[134] They are striving for their app to be integrated into social media platforms, and to run by default on all computers and phones, whether public or private, in the United States and Europe.[135] The app is already standard on the Microsoft Edge phone browser, and Microsoft has agreed to include the app on future products, such as, potentially, the Windows 10 operating system.[136] Hawaii is using NewsGuard in all its public libraries across the state.[137]

But who are the people behind NewsGuard? Some of the very same characters who have already been mentioned in this chapter, of course. On the advisory board for NewsGuard sit Michael Hayden, Tom Ridge, and Richard Stengel.[138] Michael Hayden is the former director of the National Security Agency, and during his tenure he vigorously defended the agency's illegal spying on Americans.[139] He is also former head of the CIA, a member of the Council on Foreign Relations, and a principal at the Chertoff Group,[140] the security firm run by Michael Chertoff, the former US secretary of homeland security and coauthor of the USA PATRIOT Act.[141] Both Chertoff and Hayden sit on the board of the Atlantic Council.[142] Tom Ridge, the first secretary of homeland security, is famous for his color-coded terror alert system which helped keep Americans in a compliant state of fear.[143] It's not surprising that NewsGuard uses a similar color-coded system. Richard Stengel is former editor of *Time* magazine, under secretary of state for public diplomacy and public affairs under Obama, and currently a distinguished fellow with the Atlantic Council's Digital Forensic Research Lab.[144] Stengel declared his support for propaganda in a public forum hosted by the Council on Foreign Relations, stating nonchalantly, "My old job at the State Department was what people used to joke [call] the chief propagandist job. I'm not against propaganda, every country does it and they have to do it to their own population and I don't necessarily think it's that awful."[145] Finally, there is the co-CEO of NewsGuard, Louis Gordon Crovitz. Crovitz has edited and contributed to books for such neoconservative think tanks as the American Enterprise Institute and the Heritage Foundation.[146] As a journalist, Crovitz has an appalling record of spreading misinformation and falsehoods.[147] These include "fantastically false claims about the origins of the internet,"[148] and a "misleading and error-filled column about NSA surveillance."[149]

As with the other censorious initiatives profiled in this chapter, NewsGuard doesn't seem as concerned with eliminating fake news as it does with discrediting news sources that are critical of Western political and economic elites. For example, NewsGuard gives WikiLeaks a red rating, in part, they claim, because the organization does not correct their errors. Yet the rationale is plainly nonsensical, given the fact that WikiLeaks has never published anything false or incorrect.[150] NewsGuard's summary for their red rating of WikiLeaks runs as follows: "A publisher of confidential documents, often acquired from leakers and hackers. WikiLeaks published hacked emails, traced to the Kremlin, that hurt Democrats ahead of the 2016 presidential election."[151] They also give red ratings to the Russian outlet RT and the excellent alternative news website MintPress News. However, they give Fox News and Voice of America, the former a largely discredited organization and the latter an explicit outlet of US propaganda, green ratings. The Daily Caller and the now defunct *Weekly Standard* both also receive green ratings.

The gushing support given to NewsGuard by the corporate media is indicative of their support for this type of soft censorship, and contributes to the suspicion that initiatives like NewsGuard are specifically designed to protect and promote corporate media interests.[152] Another product by NewsGuard, BrandGuard, seems similarly ominous for producers of alternative news and dissenting content.[153] Companies can sign up for BrandGuard to prevent their advertisements from appearing on any of the sites that NewsGuard has flagged as red. While many alternative news organizations rely on direct reader and listener support rather than advertising, outlets that depend to any degree on advertising dollars may find important sources of revenue suddenly choked off in the wake of initiatives like BrandGuard, putting their organizations at risk.

PROPPING UP THE MANUFACTURERS OF CONSENT

Censorship, deplatforming, and de-ranking counterhegemonic content and alternative news, while simultaneously promoting more "authoritative" (i.e., corporate news) content, has so far proven insufficient for the tech and social media giants. They wish to financially and ideologically reestablish the corporate press's dominance as the manufacturers of public opinion and consent, and as the gatekeepers of information to which the public has access, in addition to recapturing advertising profits by limiting audience access to alternative media sources.

The Google News Initiative is a partnership between Google, the *Financial Times*, Gannett, the *New York Times*, the *Washington Post*, Stanford University, the Poynter Institute, and many other organizations.[154] This 300-million-dollar project aims to "stem" the tide of what these companies regard as fake news, disinformation, and misinformation and to promote "trustworthy" and "authoritative" content—essentially, themselves.[155] Another goal is to facilitate payment to corporate news sources that charge for content, thereby increasing their audiences and revenues.[156] Report for America (RFA) and Google News Lab are working in conjunction to hire more than one thousand journalists all over the United States.[157] The costs for employing these journalists will be shared: RFA will cover 50 percent, while newsrooms and local donors will pay 25 percent each.[158] Google happens to be RFA's largest donor, making them the de facto paymaster behind this venture.[159] A look at the advisory board of the RFA will reveal the presence of individuals who currently hold, or previously held, positions with the Charles Koch Institute, Fox News, CBS News, ABC News, the *Wall Street Journal*, NPR, Twitter, and the *New York Times*.[160]

Not wanting to be outdone by Google, Facebook has set aside $90 million to produce "trustworthy" and "informative" news programming in collaboration with corporate news giants Fox News, CNN, ABC News, and Univision.[161] These shows, which stream on Facebook's new "Watch" feature, includes hosts such as Anderson Cooper of CNN, Fox's Shepard Smith, and Jorge Ramos of Univision.[162] Of these, Facebook is giving preferential treatment to Fox News, which is the only network to have a show featured on "Watch" every day of the week.[163] Apparently, Facebook thinks Fox News is so trustworthy that they should be featured front and center. Tellingly, advertising revenue will be shared by participating partners.[164]

WHY THE MOVE TO REESTABLISH DISCOURSE CONTROL?

> *While the internet has brought about a revolution in people's ability to educate themselves and others, the resulting democratic phenomenon has shaken existing establishments to their core. Google, Facebook and their Chinese equivalents, who are socially, logistically and financially integrated with existing elites, have moved to re-establish discourse control. This is not simply a corrective action. Undetectable mass social influence powered by artificial intelligence is an existential threat to humanity.*
>
> —Julian Assange[165]

Polls show that trust in corporate media and government are at all-time lows. The corporate press has lost much of its credibility and revenues in the 21st century.[166] Newspapers and TV broadcasters are seeing a massive decline in readership and viewers while people of all age groups, particularly the young, increasingly turn to the internet for news.[167] A 2018 Gallup poll found that only 28 percent of Americans feel that corporate mainstream media work to support democracy, while the majority, 84 percent, believe news media is "critical" or "very important" to democracy.[168] The Pew Research Center has found that only 18 percent of Americans have "a lot" of trust in the corporate media, while 74 percent perceive them as biased.[169] A Harvard-Harris poll found that 65 percent of Americans believe the corporate media is generally untrustworthy.[170] The Edelman Trust Barometer has found that overall public trust in US institutions has fallen more precipitously than in any of the 28 countries surveyed. Additionally, disaggregating for trust among the "informed public" puts the United States at the bottom of their list.[171] Pew has found that the US public's trust in government is near an all-time low, at only 17 percent.[172] The public is unambiguously tired of endless wars and has frequently demonstrated its desire to put a halt to catastrophic foreign interventions.[173]

As the internet has grown in reach and dominance over other media forms, so has its potential as a source of diverse and demo-cratic communication, allowing for many voices to express a mul-titude of opinions, concerns, and grievances. In many ways, it has become our new digital public sphere or square; however imperfect some might find it to be, it at least provides a voice for the hitherto voiceless. Through their engagement with each other on the internet, and with alternative sources of information, the public has become increasingly aware of the ways the corporate media and politicians commit acts of omission, obfuscate, distort, mislead, and sometimes tell outright lies about happenings in the world. The corporate media has at times been forced to admit its mistakes and misinforma-tion after the alternative news media has published detailed factual accounts of events.[174]

The public has used the internet and social media as a tool to organize themselves and act against a number of oppressive and destructive forces in the United States and around the world. 2018, for instance, witnessed a decades-high number of labor strikes in the United States, led mostly by teachers who work under deplorable con-ditions.[175] As of this writing, the Yellow Vest protests continue to rage in France. The power of the internet and of social media has been crucial to these recent movements, and the lesson has not been lost on those in the halls of power. The US Army War College has written, "The implications of social media and the rapid spread of informa-tion (and disinformation) in a highly digital city can be profound . . . Here in the United States, the release of videos showing killings by police has led to significant protests and political movements."[176] The Department of Homeland Security is currently working to compile a database of "social media influencers" that can track global news sources and social media, in real-time, and translate from more than one hundred languages, the online activities of those they might perceive as a threat.[177] Those in power believe that we shouldn't be privy to police killings and other state crimes and misdeeds. These should instead be hushed, they feel, and, as much as possible, kept out of view. This is the exact same logic behind the censoring of alternative media sources that are critical of state and corporate actors.

In the minds of economic and political elites, the problem with alternative, independent, and certain foreign news sources is that they cover, inter alia, issues such as class struggle, inequality, racism, environmental degradation and collapse, democratic and civil liberties shortcomings, brutality and murder committed by state actors both domestically and abroad, illegal wars, war crimes, illegal surveillance, and corporate and political malfeasance in all its forms. In sum, alternative media exposes and lays bare for all to see the bankruptcy and perversions of the capitalist system and those who foist it upon us. This is not merely objectionable to those in power, it is unacceptable to them. Alternative news media serve to discredit and make illegitimate the very foundations upon which establishment authority rests alongside that authority's methods for accumulating and maintaining vast wealth.

Perhaps the most threatening developments for those in power are any signs that capitalism is falling out of favor with the public. Polls show that Americans, especially young adults, are increasingly disillusioned with capitalism and are turning to alternatives.[178] The government, corporations, and the corporate media—or we can just call them "ruling elites"—have lost their monopoly control over the narrative and they desperately want it back by whatever undemocratic means they may find at their disposal. They are working zealously to eliminate any resistance to their rule.

Historically, the economic and political elite have used methods both overt and insidiously covert to clutch onto their position of power, and the present moment is no exception to this trend. As this chapter has demonstrated, the government and organizations funded by it, the tech and social media giants, and the corporate news conglomerates are working diligently to extinguish alternative and independent news, as well as certain international news sources' presence online. Concomitant with this are several other disturbing and related trends. The corporate media and politicians have attempted to discredit legitimate social movements such as Black Lives Matter, the Yellow Vest movement, and even progressive politicians like Tulsi Gabbard and Jill Stein as being associated in some way with Russians.[179] Network neutrality in the United States has been eliminated, a victory for telecommunications firms who wish to entirely privatize the internet. Meanwhile, the European Parliament has recently passed the Directive on Copyright in the Digital Single Market, which many prominent scholars, advocacy organizations, and human rights experts are saying will lead to widespread censorship.[180]

Journalists are facing increasing threats to their lives and livelihoods, and are being scapegoated and characterized as the enemy of the people for doing their jobs. Whistleblowers, instead of being celebrated for revealing the sinister machinations of our governments, are being unjustly jailed or forced into exile—consider the unwarranted charges filed against, and imprisonment of, Chelsea Manning and Julian Assange for exposing US war crimes,[181] as well as Edward Snowden's forced exile for revealing the extent of surveillance being carried out illegally by the US government.[182] Worldwide we are seeing a move toward authoritarianism and tyranny in the forms of neoliberal fascism, proto-fascism, and violent white nationalism. This constitutes a concerted and full-frontal assault against freedom of expression and our ability to resist oppression and express our dissatisfaction with the currently existing state of affairs. These retrograde and reactionary politics and forces must be confronted and defeated. Our freedom and whatever shreds of democracy still remain depend upon it.

The authors would like to acknowledge that this chapter would not have been possible without the groundbreaking journalism and research conducted by the alternative news media organizations and media watchdog groups cited herein. We encourage you to donate to them so that they may continue their excellent work. We would also like to express our gratitude to Mickey Huff and Michael Tencer, whose feedback on this chapter has been invaluable.

EMIL MARMOL is a PhD candidate at the University of Toronto/Ontario Institute for Studies in Education (OISE). As an interdisciplinary scholar with experience in professional film and radio production, he has published on critical media literacy,

Cuban society, the impact of neoliberalism on higher education, repression of Latina/os in education, standardized testing, labor struggles, and film. He is currently writing his doctoral thesis as an autoethnography/testimonio about growing up as the son of Latino immigrants in Orange County, California.

LEE MAGER, PHD, is Saw Swee Hock Southeast Asia Centre Manager at the London School of Economics and Political Science (LSE). He earned his doctorate from the LSE Department of Sociology in 2016; his thesis analyzed the communicative construction of problem/solution discourses among online conspiracy theory communities, anchored in Alberto Melucci's conceptual framework of collective action, to address the question of whether conspiracy theory is an inherently disabling interpretation of power. More recently his interest has been in the state- and media-sponsored conspiracy theory now referred to as "Russiagate."

Notes

1. G.M. Gilbert, *Nuremberg Diary* (New York: Da Capo Press, 1995 [first published by Farrar, Straus in 1947]), 278–79.
2. Jeremy Scahill, "Inside America's Dirty Wars: How Three US Citizens were Killed by Their Own Government in the Space of One Month in 2011," *The Nation*, April 24, 2013, https://www.thenation.com/article/inside-americas-dirty-wars.
3. Thomas Frank, "The Hysteria over Russian Bots has Reached New Levels," *The Guardian*, February 23, 2018, https://www.theguardian.com/commentisfree/2018/feb/23/russian-bots-us-election-coup-d-etat.
4. Mike Whitney, "Obama Backs Down on Crimea," *CounterPunch*, March 18, 2014, https://www.counterpunch.org/2014/03/18/obama-backs-down-on-crimea.
5. Lauren McCauley, "Clearing Russia from Blame, German Intelligence Says Rebels Downed Flight MH17," Common Dreams, October 20, 2014, https://www.commondreams.org/news/2014/10/20/clearing-russia-blame-german-intelligence-says-rebels-downed-flight-mh17.
6. Craig Murray, "Pure: Ten Points I Just Can't Believe about the Official Skripal Narrative," *Craig Murray* blog, March 7, 2019, https://www.craigmurray.org.uk/archives/2019/03/pure-ten-points-i-just-cant-believe-about-the-official-skripal-narrative.
7. Joe Concha, "'Concussion' Pathologist Says Clinton May have been Poisoned," The Hill, September 13, 2016, https://thehill.com/blogs/ballot-box/295688-concussion-pathologist-says-clinton-may-have-been-poisoned.
8. Paul Jay, "Is Russian 'Meddling' an Attack on America?—RAI with Stephen Cohen," The Real News Network, April 16, 2019, https://therealnews.com/stories/is-russian-meddling-an-attack-on-america-rai-with-stephen-cohen.
9. Robert Parry, "New 'Group Think' for War with Syria/Russia," Consortium News, October 5, 2016, https://consortiumnews.com/2016/10/05/new-group-think-for-war-with-syriarussia.
10. Robert Parry, "Russia-gate Spreads to Europe," Consortium News, November 16, 2017, https://consortiumnews.com/2017/11/16/russia-gate-spreads-to-europe/.
11. Derek R. Ford, "US Sovereignty Must Not be Defended: Critical Education Against Russiagate," *Educational Philosophy and Theory*, Vol. 51 No. 1 (2019): 14–17.
12. Robert Parry, "Russia-gate's Litany of Corrections," Consortium News, December 11, 2017, https://consortiumnews.com/2017/12/11/russia-gates-litany-of-corrections; CTVNews.ca Staff, "Exclusive: IP Address at Ontario Power Utility Linked to Alleged Russian Hacking," CTV News, January 3, 2017, updated January 4, 2017, https://www.ctvnews.ca/canada/exclusive-ip-address-at-ontario-power-utility-linked-to-alleged-russian-hacking-1.3226290.

13. "Whales Trained by Russia's Military May be Harassing Fishermen from NATO Ally Norway," CBS News, April 29, 2019, https://www.cbsnews.com/news/whale-norway-arctic-beluga-maybe-trained-russia-military-norwegian-fisherman/.

14. For an excellent chronology of Russiagate from 2016, see Matt Taibbi, "It's Official: Russiagate is This Generation's WMD," Untitledgate, March 23, 2019, https://taibbi.substack.com/p/russiagate-is-wmd-times-a-million. For a list of some of the possible causes of Russiagate, see Stephen F. Cohen, "How Did Russiagate Begin? Why Barr's Investigation is Important and Should be Encouraged," The Nation, May 30, 2019, https://www.thenation.com/article/how-did-russiagate-begin/.

15. Chloe Watson, "The Key Moments from Mark Zuckerberg's Testimony to Congress," The Guardian, April 11, 2018, https://www.theguardian.com/technology/2018/apr/11/mark-zuckerbergs-testimony-to-congress-the-key-moments.

16. Glenn Greenwald, "Robert Mueller Did Not Merely Reject the Trump-Russia Conspiracy Theories. He Obliterated Them," The Intercept, April 18, 2019, https://theintercept.com/2019/04/18/robert-mueller-did-not-merely-reject-the-trumprussia-conspiracy-theories-he-obliterated-them/; Aaron Maté, "The Mueller Report Indicts the Trump-Russia Conspiracy Theory," The Nation, April 26, 2019, https://www.thenation.com/article/russiagate-trump-mueller-report-no-collusion.

17. Brian L. Keeley, "Of Conspiracy Theories," The Journal of Philosophy, Vol. 96 No. 3 (March 1999): 109–126.

18. For a composite definition of alternative news media, see Emil Marmol, "Alternative Media as Critical Pedagogical Intervention Against Neoliberalism and Racism," Democratic Communiqué, Vol. 27 No. 2 (2018): 24–34; and Emil Marmol, "Nine Key Insights for a Robust and Holistic Critical News Media Literacy," Education for Democracy 2.0: Changing Frames of Media Literacy, eds. Michael Hoechsmann, Paul R. Carr, and Gina Thésée (Brill/Sense Publishers (in press)).

19. Daniel Lazare, "Censoring Facebook Censors Us All," Truthdig, November 29, 2018, https://www.truthdig.com/articles/censoring-facebook-censors-us-all; Aaron Maté, "New Studies Show Pundits are Wrong about Russian Social-Media Involvement in US Politics," The Nation, December 28, 2018, https://www.thenation.com/article/russiagate-elections-interference.

20. Max Blumenthal, "McCarthyism Inc.: Hyping the Russian Threat to Undermine Free Speech," Truthdig, November 13, 2017, https://www.truthdig.com/articles/mccarthyism-inc-hyping-russian-threat-undermine-free-speech.

21. Gareth Porter, "33 Trillion More Reasons Why the New York Times Gets It Wrong on Russiagate," Consortium News, November 2, 2018, https://consortiumnews.com/2018/11/02/33-trillion-more-reasons-why-the-new-york-times-gets-it-wrong-on-russia-gate.

22. Maté, "New Studies Show Pundits are Wrong About Russian Social-Media Involvement"; Blumenthal, "McCarthyism Inc."

23. Porter, "33 Trillion More Reasons."

24. Ibid.

25. Blumenthal, "McCarthyism Inc."

26. Julianne Tveten, "How the 'Fake News' Scare is Marginalizing the Left," In These Times, October 11, 2017, http://inthesetimes.com/article/20596/fake-news-left-facebook-twitter-tech-companies.

27. Philip Bump, "There's Still Little Evidence that Russia's 2016 Social Media Efforts Did Much of Anything," Washington Post, December 28, 2017, https://www.washingtonpost.com/news/politics/wp/2017/12/28/theres-still-little-evidence-that-russias-2016-social-media-efforts-did-much-of-anything.

28. Blumenthal, "McCarthyism Inc."

29. Maté, "New Studies Show Pundits are Wrong About Russian Social-Media Involvement."

30. Ibid.

31. Stephen Lendman, "US Definition of a Russian Agent, Asset or Troll. Rep. Tulsi Gabbard, Candidate for the Presidency," Global Research: Centre for Research on Globalization, February 6,

2019, https://www.globalresearch.ca/us-definition-of-a-russian-agent-asset-or-troll-rep-tulsi-gabbard-candidate-for-the-presidency/5667683.

32. Maté, "New Studies Show Pundits are Wrong About Russian Social-Media Involvement."

33. "Facebook Reports Fourth Quarter and Full Year 2016 Results," PR Newswire, February 1, 2017, https://s21.q4cdn.com/399680738/files/doc_financials/2016/Q4/Facebook-Reports-Fourth-Quarter-and-Full-Year-2016-Results.pdf; Joe Lauria, "How Russia-gate Rationalized Censorship," Consortium News, January 29, 2019, https://consortiumnews.com/2019/01/29/how-russia-gate-rationalizes-censorship.

34. Nick Penzenstadler, Brad Heath, and Jessica Guynn, "We Read Every One of the 3,517 Facebook Ads Bought by Russians. Here's What We Found," USA Today, May 11, 2018, updated May 13, 2018, https://www.usatoday.com/story/news/2018/05/11/what-we-found-facebook-ads-russians-accused-election-meddling/602319002/.

35. Maté, "New Studies Show Pundits are Wrong About Russian Social-Media Involvement."

36. Eleanor Goldfield, "From Russia, with Absurdity," Truthdig, February 25, 2018, https://www.truthdig.com/articles/from-russia-with-absurdity.

37. Ibid.; Maté, "New Studies Show Pundits are Wrong About Russian Social-Media Involvement."

38. Amy Goodman with Masha Gessen, "Masha Gessen: Did a Russian Troll Farm's Inflammatory Posts Really Sway the 2016 Election for Trump?" Democracy Now!, February 23, 2018, https://www.democracynow.org/2018/2/23/masha_gessen_did_a_russian_troll.

39. Scott Shane and Sheera Frenkel, "Russian 2016 Influence Operation Targeted African-Americans on Social Media," New York Times, December 17, 2018, https://www.nytimes.com/2018/12/17/us/politics/russia-2016-influence-campaign.html.

40. Though we firmly believe this to be an uncontroversial claim given the evidence and analysis provided in this chapter, we feel it would be fair to provide an article that notes the continuing need for vigilant skepticism of all governments, including Russia's, even in light of the Russiagate non-scandal fizzling out: Paul Street, "The Double Russia Conspiracy Trap," CounterPunch, April 27, 2018, https://www.counterpunch.org/2018/04/27/the-double-russia-conspiracy-trap/.

41. Lauria, "How Russia-gate Rationalized Censorship."

42. Matt Taibbi, "The 'Washington Post' 'Blacklist' Story is Shameful and Disgusting," Rolling Stone, November 28, 2016, https://www.rollingstone.com/politics/politics-features/the-washington-post-blacklist-story-is-shameful-and-disgusting-115978; Pam Martens and Russ Martens, "Timberg's Tale: Washington Post Reporter Spreads Blacklist of Independent Journalist Sites," CounterPunch, December 2, 2016, https://www.counterpunch.org/2016/12/02/timbergs-tale-washington-post-reporter-spreads-blacklist-of-independent-journalist-sites; Ben Norton and Glenn Greenwald, "Washington Post Disgracefully Promotes a McCarthyite Blacklist from a New, Hidden, and Very Shady Group," The Intercept, November 26, 2016, https://theintercept.com/2016/11/26/washington-post-disgracefully-promotes-a-mccarthyite-blacklist-from-a-new-hidden-and-very-shady-group; Max Blumenthal, "Washington Post Promotes Shadowy Website that Accuses 200 Publications of Being Russian Propaganda Plants," AlterNet, November 25, 2016, https://www.alternet.org/2016/11/washington-post-promotes-shadowy-website-accuses-200-publications-russian-propaganda-plants.

43. Taibbi, "The 'Washington Post' 'Blacklist' Story"; Norton and Greenwald, "Washington Post Disgracefully Promotes a McCarthyite Blacklist."

44. Norton and Greenwald, "Washington Post Disgracefully Promotes a McCarthyite Blacklist." See also Nolan Higdon and Mickey Huff, with student writers and researchers, "Post-Truth Dystopia: Fake News, Alternative Facts, and the Ongoing War on Reality—Junk Food News and News Abuse for 2016–17," in Censored 2018: Press Freedoms in a "Post-Truth" World, eds. Andy Lee Roth and Mickey Huff with Project Censored (New York: Seven Stories Press, 2017), 107–138, 127.

45. Tom Mills, The BBC: Myth of a Public Service (London: Verso Books, 2016); David Edwards and David Cromwell, Propaganda Blitz: How the Corporate Media Distort Reality (London: Pluto Press, 2018).

46. Norton and Greenwald, "Washington Post Disgracefully Promotes a McCarthyite Blacklist."

47. Blumenthal, "McCarthyism Inc."; Andre Damon, "Facebook and Google Outline Unprecedented Mass Censorship at US Senate Hearing," World Socialist Web Site, January 18, 2018, https://www.wsws.org/en/articles/2018/01/18/cens-j18.html.

48. Clint Watts's contributor profile can be found at the Foreign Policy Research Institute website, https://www.fpri.org/contributor/clint-watts/ [accessed June 11, 2019].

49. Matt Taibbi, "Russiagate and the New Blacklist," Common Dreams, March 6, 2018, https://www.commondreams.org/views/2018/03/06/russiagate-and-new-blacklist.

50. Andre Damon, "Pages Purged by Facebook were on Blacklist Promoted by Washington Post," World Socialist Web Site, October 13, 2018, https://www.wsws.org/en/articles/2018/10/13/cens-o13.html.

51. Andre Damon, "The 'New Cold War,' Censorship, and the Future of the Internet," World Socialist Web Site, October 17, 2018, https://www.wsws.org/en/articles/2018/10/17/pers-o17.html; Daisuke Wakabayashi, "As Google Fights Fake News, Voices on the Margins Raise Alarm," New York Times, September 26, 2017, https://www.nytimes.com/2017/09/26/technology/google-search-bias-claims.html.

52. Ben Gomes, "Our Latest Quality Improvements for Search," The Keyword blog (Google), April 25, 2017, https://www.blog.google/products/search/our-latest-quality-improvements-search; David North, "An Open Letter to Google: Stop the Censorship of the Internet! Stop the Political Blacklisting of the World Socialist Web Site!" World Socialist Web Site, August 25, 2017, https://www.wsws.org/en/articles/2017/08/25/pers-a25.html.

53. Gomes, "Our Latest Quality Improvements for Search."

54. Ibid.; North, "An Open Letter to Google."

55. Gomes, "Our Latest Quality Improvements for Search."

56. Damon, "Pages Purged by Facebook were on Blacklist"; Andre Damon and Niles Niemuth, "New Google Algorithm Restricts Access to Left-Wing, Progressive Web Sites," World Socialist Web Site, July 27, 2017, https://www.wsws.org/en/articles/2017/07/27/goog-j27.html; Andre Damon, "Google Escalates Blacklisting of Left-Wing Web Sites and Journalists," World Socialist Web Site, October 20, 2017, https://www.wsws.org/en/articles/2017/10/20/goog-o20.html; C.J. Hopkins, "Who's Afraid of Corporate COINTELPRO?" CounterPunch, November 3, 2017, https://www.counterpunch.org/2017/11/03/whos-afraid-of-corporate-cointelpro; Chris Hedges, "The Silencing of Dissent," Truthdig, September 17, 2017, https://www.truthdig.com/articles/the-silencing-of-dissent; Editors, "Your Up-to-Date Guide to Avoiding Internet Censorship," Monthly Review Online, August 26, 2017, https://mronline.org/2017/08/26/your-up-to-date-guide-to-avoiding-internet-censorship/.

57. Alan MacLeod, "That Facebook Will Turn to Censoring the Left Isn't a Worry—It's a Reality," Fairness & Accuracy In Reporting, August 22, 2018, https://fair.org/home/that-facebook-will-turn-to-censoring-the-left-isnt-a-worry-its-a-reality.

58. Kari Paul and Jim Waterson, "Facebook Bans Alex Jones, Milo Yiannopoulos and Other Far-Right Figures," The Guardian, May 2, 2019, https://www.theguardian.com/technology/2019/may/02/facebook-ban-alex-jones-milo-yiannopoulos.

59. Allum Bokhari, "'The Good Censor': Leaked Google Briefing Admits Abandonment of Free Speech for 'Safety and Civility,'" Breitbart, October 9, 2018, https://www.breitbart.com/tech/2018/10/09/the-good-censor-leaked-google-briefing-admits-abandonment-of-free-speech-for-safety-and-civility; Allum Bokhari, "The Good Censor—Google Leak," Scribd, undated [posted October 2018], https://www.scribd.com/document/390521673/The-Good-Censor-GOOGLE-LEAK [accessed May 12, 2019].

60. Bokhari, "The Good Censor—Google Leak."

61. Ibid.

62. Ibid.

63. Ibid.

64. Alan MacLeod, "Facebook's New Propaganda Partners," Fairness & Accuracy In Reporting, September 25, 2018, https://fair.org/home/facebooks-new-propaganda-partners; David Archuleta Jr., "Facebook Allows Governments to Decide What to Censor," CounterPunch,

November 9, 2018, https://www.counterpunch.org/2018/11/09/facebook-allows-govern-ments-to-decide-what-to-censor.

65. Carey Wedler, "How I Became a Casualty in the Facebook-Twitter Social Media Purges," The Mind Unleashed, April 8, 2019, https://themindunleashed.com/2019/04/facebook-twitter-social-media-purges.html; "Values: Elections Integrity," Twitter, undated, https://about.twitter.com/en_us/values/elections-integrity.html#partnerships [accessed May 12, 2019].

66. Kevin Reed, "Facebook's Partnership with the Atlantic Council," World Socialist Web Site, September 8, 2018, https://www.wsws.org/en/articles/2018/09/08/atla-s08.html.

67. Funders of the Atlantic Council are listed on its website: https://www.atlanticcouncil.org/support/supporters [accessed May 12, 2019].

68. The Atlantic Council's website also lists its Board of Directors and Advisory Board, at https://www.atlanticcouncil.org/about/board-of-directors and https://www.atlanticcouncil.org/about/international-advisory-board [both accessed May 12, 2019].

69. Andre Damon, "The US Military's Vision for State Censorship," World Socialist Web Site, October 5, 2018, https://www.wsws.org/en/articles/2018/10/05/pers-005.html.

70. Ibid.

71. MacLeod, "Facebook's New Propaganda Partners"; Archuleta, "Facebook Allows Governments to Decide What to Censor"; William Blum, "Trojan Horse: The National Endowment for Democracy," WilliamBlum.org, undated, https://williamblum.com/chapters/rogue-state/trojan-horse-the-national-endowment-for-democracy [accessed May 12, 2019].

72. The National Endowment for Democracy's website lists its Board of Directors, at https://www.ned.org/about/board-of-directors [accessed May 12, 2019].

73. The International Republican Institute's website lists its Board of Directors, at https://www.iri.org/who-we-are/board-of-directors [accessed May 12, 2019].

74. Tim Murphy and Tasneem Raja, "Map: All the Countries John McCain Has Wanted to Attack," Mother Jones, September 6, 2013, https://www.motherjones.com/politics/2013/09/john-mccain-world-attack-map-syria.

75. Rahul Mahajan, "'We Think the Price is Worth It,'" Fairness & Accuracy In Reporting, November 1, 2001, https://fair.org/extra/we-think-the-price-is-worth-it.

76. "Fact-Checking on Facebook: What Publishers Should Know," Facebook, undated, https://www.facebook.com/help/publisher/182222309230722 [accessed May 12, 2019].

77. Sam Levin, "Facebook Teams with Rightwing Daily Caller in Factchecking Program," The Guardian, April 17, 2019, https://www.theguardian.com/technology/2019/apr/17/facebook-teams-with-rightwing-daily-caller-in-factchecking-program; Paola Rosa-Aquino, "The Koch Brothers are Funding Facebook's Newest Fact-Checking Partner," Grist, April 29, 2019, https://grist.org/article/the-koch-brothers-are-funding-facebooks-newest-fact-checking-partner.

78. Levin, "Facebook Teams with Rightwing Daily Caller"; Rosa-Aquino, "The Koch Brothers are Funding Facebook's Newest."

79. Amy Goodman, with Ian Millhiser and Dahlia Lithwick, "Facebook Censors a ThinkProgress Story on Kavanaugh after a Conservative Site Calls It 'Fake News,'" Democracy Now!, September 17, 2018, https://www.democracynow.org/2018/9/17/facebook_censors_a_think-progress_story_on; Jake Johnson, "Facebook Condemned for Empowering Right-Wing Magazine to 'Drive Liberal News Outlets into the Ground,'" Common Dreams, September 14, 2018, https://www.commondreams.org/news/2018/09/14/facebook-condemned-empow-ering-right-wing-magazine-drive-liberal-news-outlets-ground.

80. Goodman, with Millhiser and Lithwick, "Facebook Censors"; Johnson, "Facebook Condemned."

81. Johnson, "Facebook Condemned."

82. Jim Naureckas, "Advocate of Saddam/Al Qaeda Conspiracy Will Save Us from Fake News," Fairness & Accuracy In Reporting, March 28, 2017, https://fair.org/home/advocate-of-sad-damal-qaeda-conspiracy-will-save-us-from-fake-news/.

83. Parry, "Russia-gate's Litany of Corrections"; Robert Parry, "Russia-gate Breeds 'Establishment McCarthyism,'" Consortium News, October 26, 2017, https://consortiumnews.com/2017/10/26/russia-gate-breeds-establishment-mccarthyism.

84. Nicholas Thompson and Fred Vogelstein, "15 Months of Fresh Hell Inside Facebook," Wired, April 16, 2019, https://www.wired.com/story/facebook-mark-zuckerberg-15-months-of-fresh-hell; Andre Damon, "Facebook: The Global Censor," World Socialist Web Site, December 29, 2018, https://www.wsws.org/en/articles/2018/12/29/pers-d29.html.

85. Damon, "Facebook and Google Outline Unprecedented Mass Censorship."

86. Andre Damon, "As Social Opposition Mounts, Silicon Valley and Washington Step Up Internet Censorship," World Socialist Web Site, September 5, 2018, https://www.wsws.org/en/articles/2018/09/05/pers-s05.html.

87. Alexander Rubinstein, "Facebook's Troll Hunter in Chief Nathaniel Gleicher Tied to Neocon Think Tank," MintPress News, February 1, 2019, https://www.mintpressnews.com/facebooks-troll-hunter-in-chief-nathaniel-gleicher-tied-to-neocon-think-tank/254583.

88. See Nathaniel Gleicher's profile on the Center for Strategic and International Studies (CSIS) website, at https://www.csis.org/people/nathaniel-j-gleicher [accessed June 11, 2019].

89. Whitney Webb, "More Gov't Hooks in Social Media: Facebook Hires Patriot Act Co-Author While Trump Jawbones Twitter CEO," MintPress News, April 24, 2019, https://www.mintpressnews.com/more-govt-hooks-in-social-media-facebook-hires-patriot-act-co-author-while-trump-jawbones-twitter-ceo/257795; Eoin Higgins, "Facebook's Hire of Patriot Act Co-Author Raises Questions on Company's Commitment to Privacy," Common Dreams, April 24, 2019, https://www.commondreams.org/news/2019/04/24/facebooks-hire-patriot-act-co-author-raises-questions-companys-commitment-privacy.

90. Whitney Webb, "More Gov't Hooks in Social Media."

91. Thompson and Vogelstein, "15 Months of Fresh Hell Inside Facebook."

92. Ibid.

93. Joe Mount, "Facebook Hires Former British Deputy Prime Minister Nick Clegg," World Socialist Web Site, November 16, 2018, https://www.wsws.org/en/articles/2018/11/16/clegn16.html.

94. Max Blumenthal and Jeb Sprague, "Facebook Censorship of Alternative Media 'Just the Beginning,' Says Top Neocon Insider," The Grayzone, October 23, 2018, https://thegrayzone.com/2018/10/23/facebook-censorship-of-alternative-media-just-the-beginning-says-top-neocon-insider.

95. Ibid.; "Foreign Policy Initiative," Right Web, July 25, 2017, https://rightweb.irc-online.org/profile/foreign_policy_initiative/.

96. Blumenthal and Sprague, "Facebook Censorship of Alternative Media."

97. Ibid.

98. Ibid.

99. Dan Cohen, "Senate Report on Russian Interference was Written by Disinformation Warriors behind Alabama 'False Flag Operation,'" The Grayzone, December 25, 2018, https://thegrayzone.com/2018/12/25/senate-report-on-russian-interference-was-written-by-disinformation-warriors-behind-alabama-false-flag-operation; Andy Thompson, "Alleging 'Russian Influence,' Facebook Bans Left-Wing Pages," World Socialist Web Site, February 20, 2019, https://www.wsws.org/en/articles/2019/02/20/cens-f20.html.

100. Alexander Rubinstein and Max Blumenthal, "How One of America's Premier Data Monarchs is Funding a Global Information War and Shaping the Media Landscape," MintPress News, February 18, 2019, https://www.mintpressnews.com/ebay-founder-pierre-omidyar-is-funding-a-global-media-information-war/255199.

101. Ibid.

102. Whitney Webb, "Omidyar's Intercept Teams Up with War-Propaganda Firm Bellingcat," MintPress News, October 8, 2018, https://www.mintpressnews.com/omidyars-intercept-teams-up-with-war-propaganda-firm-bellingcat/250477/.

103. Manjunath Kiran, "Who Checks the Fact-Checkers? Facebook Leaves Verification to Groups Funded by Soros, US Congress," RT, April 27, 2019, updated April 29, 2019, https://www.

rt.com/news/457713-facebook-fact-checkers-soros-funding; Rubinstein and Blumenthal, "How One of America's Premier Data Monarchs is Funding"; Alexander Rubinstein and Max Blumenthal, "Pierre Omidyar's Funding of Pro-Regime-Change Networks and Partnerships with CIA Cutouts," MintPress News, February 20, 2019, https://www.mintpressnews.com/pierre-omidyar-funding-of-pro-regime-change-networks-and-partnerships-with-cia-cutouts/255337.

104. See Laura Rosenberger's profile on the Alliance for Securing Democracy (ASD) website, at https://securingdemocracy.gmfus.org/about-us/team [accessed June 11, 2019].

105. The ASD's website lists its Advisory Council, at https://securingdemocracy.gmfus.org/about-us/advisory-council.

106. Rubinstein and Blumenthal, "Pierre Omidyar's Funding of Pro-Regime-Change Networks."

107. Laura Rosenberger and J.M. Berger, "Hamilton 68: A New Tool to Track Russian Disinformation on Twitter," Alliance for Securing Democracy, August 2, 2017, https://securingdemocracy.gmfus.org/hamilton-68-a-new-tool-to-track-russian-disinformation-on-twitter.

108. Adam Johnson, "Media Warn of 'Russian Bots'—Despite Primary Source's Disavowal," Fairness & Accuracy In Reporting, April 5, 2018, https://fair.org/home/media-warn-of-russian-bots-despite-primary-sources-disavowal; Blumenthal, "McCarthyism Inc."

109. Rubinstein and Blumenthal, "How One of America's Premier Data Monarchs is Funding."

110. Ibid.

111. Rubinstein, "Facebook's Troll Hunter in Chief." See Kevin Mandia's profile on the FireEye website, at https://www.fireeye.com/company/leadership.html, alongside the rest of FireEye's Board of Directors [accessed May 12, 2019].

112. Kevin Reed, "What is FireEye?" World Socialist Web Site, August 29, 2018, https://www.wsws.org/en/articles/2018/08/29/feye-a29.html.

113. Ibid.

114. See Christopher Porter's profile on the FireEye website, at https://www.fireeye.com/content/fireeye-summit/en_US/learn/speakers/christopher-porter.html [accessed May 12, 2019].

115. Nathaniel Gleicher, "Coordinated Inauthentic Behavior Explained," Newsroom blog (Facebook), December 6, 2018, https://newsroom.fb.com/news/2018/12/inside-feed-coordinated-inauthentic-behavior/.

116. Jake Johnson, "Facebook Accused of 'Full-Frontal Suppression of Dissent' after Independent Media Swept Up in Mass Purge," Common Dreams, October 12, 2018, https://www.commondreams.org/news/2018/10/12/facebook-accused-full-frontal-suppression-dissent-after-independent-media-swept-mass; Ben Norton, "Facebook Erases Hundreds of Alternative Media Pages in Mass Purge," The Real News Network, October 18, 2018, https://therealnews.com/stories/facebook-erases-hundreds-of-alternative-media-pages-in-mass-purge-1-2; Glen Ford, "Facebook is Not Your Friend," Black Agenda Report, October 18, 2018, https://blackagendareport.com/facebook-not-your-friend; Damon, "Pages Purged by Facebook"; Whitney Webb, "Facebook Purges US-Based Independent Media for Political Disinformation," MintPress News, October 12, 2018, https://www.mintpressnews.com/facebook-purges-independent-us-media-for-political-disinformation/250659; Caitlin Johnstone, "Internet Censorship Just Took an Unprecedented Leap Forward, and Hardly Anyone Noticed," Caitlin Johnstone blog, October 13, 2018, https://caitlinjohnstone.com/2018/10/13/internet-censorship-just-took-an-unprecedented-leap-forward-and-hardly-anyone-noticed.

117. Catalin Cimpanu, "Twitter Bans Distribution of Hacked Materials ahead of US Midterm Elections," ZDNet, October 2, 2018, https://www.zdnet.com/article/twitter-bans-distribution-of-hacked-materials-ahead-of-us-midterm-elections.

118. Ben Norton, "Instagram Acts as Arm of US Govt, Bans Top Iranian Officials after IRGC 'Terrorist' Designation," The Grayzone, April 18, 2019, https://thegrayzone.com/2019/04/18/instagram-us-bans-iranian-officials-irgc-terrorist.

119. Dado Ruvic, "WhatsApp Blocks Channel of Spanish Podemos Party Days before Election," RT, April 24, 2019, updated April 25, 2019, https://www.rt.com/news/457465-whatsapp-blocked-podemos-spain-elections.

120. Alexander Rubinstein, "With US on the Warpath, Iran's Press TV the Latest Target for Google's Political Censorship," MintPress News, April 22, 2019, https://www.mintpressnews.com/with-us-on-the-warpath-irans-press-tv-the-latest-target-for-google-political-censorship/257682.

121. Joe Lauria, "Twitter Restricts Account of Julian Assange's Mother," Consortium News, March 19, 2019, https://consortiumnews.com/2019/03/19/twitter-restricts-account-of-julian-assanges-mother.

122. See the tweet by the Venezuelan Consulate in Vancouver upon having its Twitter account restored: https://twitter.com/ConsuladoVenVan/status/1124007340766826497; and "'Another Arm of the War Machine': Twitter Users Angered over Blue Tick for Guaido Account," RT, May 2, 2019, updated May 3, 2019, https://www.rt.com/news/458183-venezuela-twitter-suspend-verified-guaido/.

123. Jessica Corbett, "'Deeply Disturbing': For Second Time This Year, Facebook Suspends Left-Leaning teleSUR English without Explanation," Common Dreams, August 14, 2018, https://www.commondreams.org/news/2018/08/14/deeply-disturbing-second-time-year-facebook-suspends-left-leaning-telesur-english.

124. MacLeod, "That Facebook Will Turn to Censoring the Left."

125. "Twitter Takes Down Hundreds of Accounts Linked to Venezuela Amid US Calls for Regime Change," RT, February 1, 2019, updated February 2, 2019, https://www.rt.com/news/450320-twitter-venezuela-accounts-removed.

126. Thompson, "Alleging 'Russian Influence.'"

127. Glenn Greenwald, "Facebook Says It is Deleting Accounts at the Direction of the U.S. and Israeli Governments," The Intercept, December 30, 2017, https://theintercept.com/2017/12/30/facebook-says-it-is-deleting-accounts-at-the-direction-of-the-u-s-and-israeli-governments.

128. "Abby Martin Interview Critical of Israel is Blocked by YouTube in 28 Countries," RT, April 6, 2018, https://www.rt.com/usa/423341-abby-martin-israel-youtube-blocked/; Whitney Webb, "YouTube Moves to Censor 'Controversial' Content—Brings ADL On Board as Flagger," MintPress News, August 7, 2017, https://www.mintpressnews.com/youtube-censor-controversial-content-adl-flagger/230530.

129. Jake Johnson, "With Blocked Ads Proving Her Point, Warren Says Facebook Shouldn't Have Power to Decide What Is and Isn't Allowed for 'Robust Debate,'" Common Dreams, March 12, 2019, https://www.commondreams.org/news/2019/03/12/blocked-ads-proving-her-point-warren-says-facebook-shouldnt-have-power-decide-what.

130. Elias Marat, "Facebook Removes Page of Ecuador's Former President on Same Day as Assange's Arrest," The Mind Unleashed, April 11, 2019, https://themindunleashed.com/2019/04/facebook-removes-rafael-correa-page.html.

131. Reed, "What is FireEye?"

132. Alex Hern, "Facebook, Apple, YouTube and Spotify Ban Infowars' Alex Jones," The Guardian, August 6, 2018, https://www.theguardian.com/technology/2018/aug/06/apple-removes-podcasts-infowars-alex-jones.

133. Nolan Higdon and Ben Boyington, "Has Media Literacy been Hijacked?" Project Censored, March 19, 2019, https://www.projectcensored.org/has-media-literacy-been-hijacked.

134. NewsGuard's website is at https://www.newsguardtech.com [accessed May 12, 2019].

135. Whitney Webb, "How a NeoCon-Backed 'Fact Checker' Plans to Wage War on Independent Media," MintPress News, January 9, 2019, https://www.mintpressnews.com/newsguard-neocon-backed-fact-checker-plans-to-wage-war-on-independent-media/253687/; Whitney Webb, "Newsguard Turns to EU to Push Controversial Ratings System on Tech Companies, Smears MintPress as 'Secretly Supported' by Russia," MintPress News, January 30, 2019, https://www.mintpressnews.com/newsguard-european-union/254453/.

136. Webb, "How a NeoCon-Backed 'Fact Checker' Plans to Wage War."

137. Ibid.

138. NewsGuard's website lists its Advisory Board, at https://www.newsguardtech.com/our-advisory-board [accessed June 11, 2019].

139. James Risen, "The Biggest Secret: My Life as a New York Times Reporter in the Shadow of the War on Terror," The Intercept, January 3, 2018, https://theintercept.com/2018/01/03/my-life-as-a-new-york-times-reporter-in-the-shadow-of-the-war-on-terror.

140. See Michael Hayden's profile on the Chertoff Group website, at https://www.chertoffgroup.com/team/michael-hayden [accessed June 11, 2019]. The Council on Foreign Relations website lists its members, at https://www.cfr.org/membership/roster [accessed June 11, 2019].

141. Gregory T. Nojeim, "ACLU Says Bush Choice for Homeland Security Head Worrisome; Chertoff Played Key Role in Formulating Controversial 9/11 Policies," American Civil Liberties Union (ACLU), January 11, 2005, https://www.aclu.org/news/aclu-says-bush-choice-homeland-security-head-worrisome-chertoff-played-key-role-formulating.

142. The Atlantic Council website lists its Board of Directors, at https://www.atlanticcouncil.org/about/board-of-directors [accessed June 11, 2019].

143. Taibbi, "Russiagate and the New Blacklist."

144. "Richard Stengel Named Distinguished Fellow with the Atlantic Council's Digital Forensic Research Lab," Atlantic Council, February 14, 2018, https://www.atlanticcouncil.org/news/press-releases/richard-stengel-named-distinguished-fellow-with-the-atlantic-council-s-digital-forensic-research-lab.

145. "'Every Country Does It': Ex-US Under Secretary of State Backs Propaganda Use," RT, May 27, 2018, updated May 28, 2018, https://www.rt.com/news/427967-richard-stengel-propaganda-talk.

146. Webb, "How a NeoCon-Backed 'Fact Checker' Plans to Wage War."

147. Ibid.

148. Mike Masnick, "WSJ Still Hasn't Corrected Its Bogus Internet Revisionist Story, As Vint Cerf & Xerox Both Claim the Story is Wrong," Techdirt, July 26, 2012, https://www.techdirt.com/articles/20120726/03471619840/wsj-still-hasnt-corrected-its-bogus-internet-revisionist-story-as-vint-cerf-xerox-both-claim-story-is-wrong.shtml.

149. Trevor Timm, "Wall Street Journal Columnist Repeatedly Gets His Facts Wrong about NSA Surveillance," Electronic Frontier Foundation, November 27, 2013, https://www.eff.org/deeplinks/2013/11/wall-street-journal-columnist-gordon-crovitz-repeatedly-gets-his-facts-wrong-about.

150. Craig Murray, "How Wikileaks Keeps Its 100% Accuracy Record," Craig Murray blog, January 12, 2017, https://www.craigmurray.org.uk/archives/2017/01/wikileaks-keeps-100-accuracy-record.

151. The quote found in-text is from the authors' personal use of NewsGuard. A similarly worded screenshot of NewsGuard's warning about WikiLeaks can be found in the article "Guarding You from the News: NewsGuard Warns Against Reading WikiLeaks," Sputnik News, January 15, 2019, https://sputniknews.com/analysis/201901151071476951-NewsGuard-Warns-Against-Reading-WikiLeaks (accessed May 12, 2019).

152. Webb, "How a NeoCon-Backed 'Fact Checker' Plans to Wage War."

153. Ibid.

154. Elliott Gabriel, "Google and Corporate News Giants Forge New Alliance to Defeat Independent Journalism," MintPress News, March 23, 2018, https://www.mintpressnews.com/google-and-corporate-news-giants-forge-alliance-to-defeat-independent-journalism/239475; Philipp Schindler, "The Google News Initiative: Building a Stronger Future for News," The Keyword blog (Google), March 20, 2018, https://www.blog.google/outreach-initiatives/google-news-initiative/announcing-google-news-initiative.

155. Schlindler, "The Google News Initiative."

156. Ibid.

157. See the Report for America (RFA) website at https://www.reportforamerica.org [accessed May 12, 2019].

158. "Tyler Durden," "Why is Google Hiring 1,000 Journalists to Flood Newsrooms around America?" Zero Hedge, September 18, 2017, https://www.zerohedge.com/news/2017-09-18/why-google-hiring-1000-journalists-flood-newsrooms-around-america.

159. Ibid.

160. The RFA website lists its Advisory Board, at https://www.reportforamerica.org/advisoryboard [accessed June 11, 2019].

161. Elliott Gabriel, "Don't Call It Fake News! Facebook to Fully Fund Streaming Mainstream News Shows," MintPress News, June 8, 2018, https://www.mintpressnews.com/dont-call-it-fake-news-facebook-to-fully-fund-streaming-mainstream-news-shows/243580.

162. Ibid.

163. Jake Johnson, "Confirming Progressive Fears, Facebook's 'Trustworthy' News Project is Chock-Full of Fox News," Common Dreams, July 12, 2018, https://www.commondreams.org/news/2018/07/12/confirming-progressive-fears-facebooks-trustworthy-news-project-chock-full-fox-news.

164. Gabriel, "Don't Call It Fake News!"

165. Assange, as quoted by Andre Damon, in the World Socialist Web Site webinar "Organizing Resistance to Internet Censorship," January 16, 2018. See Andre Damon, David North, and Chris Hedges, "Full Transcript: 'Organizing Resistance to Internet Censorship,'" World Socialist Web Site, January 25, 2018, https://www.wsws.org/en/articles/2018/01/25/webi-j25.html.

166. Robert W. McChesney and John Nichols, *The Death and Life of American Journalism: The Media Revolution that Will Begin the World Again*, updated ed. (New York: Nation Books, 2011). See also Art Swift, "Americans' Trust in Mass Media Sinks to New Low," Gallup, September 14, 2016, https://news.gallup.com/poll/195542/americans-trust-mass-media-sinks-new-low.aspx.

167. Elisa Shearer, "Social Media Outpaces Print Newspapers in the U.S. as a News Source," Pew Research Center, December 10, 2018, https://www.pewresearch.org/fact-tank/2018/12/10/social-media-outpaces-print-newspapers-in-the-u-s-as-a-news-source/; Jeffrey Gottfried and Elisa Shearer, "News Use Across Social Media Platforms 2016," Pew Research Center: Journalism and Media, May 26, 2016, https://www.journalism.org/2016/05/26/news-use-across-social-media-platforms-2016/; "How Millennials Get News: Inside the Habits of America's First Digital Generation," Media Insight Project, March 2015, http://www.mediainsight.org/PDFs/Millennials/Millennials%20Report%20FINAL.pdf.

168. See the Gallup report on the poll: Zacc Ritter and Jeffrey M. Jones, "Media Seen as Key to Democracy but Not Supporting It Well," Gallup, January 16, 2018, https://news.gallup.com/poll/225470/media-seen-key-democracy-not-supporting.aspx.

169. Amy Mitchell, Jeffrey Gottfried, Michael Barthel, and Elisa Shearer, "Trust and Accuracy," Pew Research Center: Journalism and Media, July 7, 2016, https://www.journalism.org/2016/07/07/trust-and-accuracy.

170. Jonathan Easley, "Poll: Majority Says Mainstream Media Publishes Fake News," The Hill, May 24, 2017, https://thehill.com/homenews/campaign/334897-poll-majority-says-mainstream-media-publishes-fake-news.

171. Noah Barkin, "Trust in US Institutions Plunges in Trump's First Year," Raw Story, January 22, 2018, https://www.rawstory.com/2018/01/trust-in-us-institutions-plunges-in-trumps-first-year.

172. "Public Trust in Government: 1958–2019," Pew Research Center: U.S. Politics & Policy, April 11, 2019, https://www.people-press.org/2019/04/11/public-trust-in-government-1958-2019.

173. Stephen Miles, "Americans are Sick of Endless War," *The Nation*, June 21, 2018, https://www.thenation.com/article/americans-sick-endless-war/.

174. Whitney Webb, "NY Times Acknowledges Venezuela Opposition as Cause of Aid Fire, Echoing Initial Reports by Alternative Press," MintPress News, March 11, 2019, https://www.mintpressnews.com/ny-times-acknowledges-venezuela-opposition-as-cause-of-aid-fire-echoing-initial-reports-by-alternative-press/256126.

175. Patrick Martin, "Strike Action in the US Hits a 32-Year High," World Socialist Web Site, February 9, 2019, https://www.wsws.org/en/articles/2019/02/09/stri-f09.html.

176. "For an International Coalition to Fight Internet Censorship: An Open Letter from the International Editorial Board of the World Socialist Web Site to Socialist, Anti-War, Left-Wing and Progressive Websites, Organizations and Activists," World Socialist Web Site, January 23, 2018, https://www.wsws.org/en/articles/2018/01/23/pers-j23.html.

177. Michael Snyder, "The Department of Homeland Security Plans to Compile a List of All Bloggers, Journalists and 'Social Media Influencers,'" *End of the American Dream* blog, June 3, 2018, http://endoftheamericandream.com/archives/the-department-of-homeland-security-plans-to-compile-a-list-of-all-bloggers-journalists-and-social-media-influencers; Michelle Kaminsky, "Department of Homeland Security Compiling Database of Journalists and 'Media Influencers,'" *Forbes*, April 6, 2018, https://www.forbes.com/sites/michellefabio/2018/04/06/department-of-homeland-security-compiling-database-of-journalists-and-media-influencers.

178. Frank Newport, "Democrats More Positive about Socialism Than Capitalism," Gallup, August 13, 2018, https://news.gallup.com/poll/240725/democrats-positive-socialism-capitalism.aspx; Peter Moore, "One Third of Millennials View Socialism Favorably," YouGov, May 11, 2015, https://today.yougov.com/topics/politics/articles-reports/2015/05/11/one-third-millennials-like-socialism; Mohamed Younis, "Four in 10 Americans Embrace Some Form of Socialism," Gallup, May 20, 2019, https://news.gallup.com/poll/257639/four-americans-embrace-form-socialism.aspx.

179. Blumenthal, "McCarthyism Inc."; Lendman, "US Definition of a Russian Agent"; Taibbi, "Russiagate and the New Blacklist"; Carol Matlack and Robert Williams, "France to Probe Possible Russian Influence on Yellow Vest Riots," Bloomberg, December 7, 2018, updated December 9, 2018, https://www.bloomberg.com/news/articles/2018-12-08/pro-russia-social-media-takes-aim-at-macron-as-yellow-vests-rage.

180. Jake Johnson, "'Dark Day for Internet Freedom': EU Approves Rules to Create Online Censorship Machine," Common Dreams, March 26, 2019, https://www.commondreams.org/news/2019/03/26/dark-day-internet-freedom-eu-approves-rules-create-online-censorship-machine.

181. "Unraveling the Justice Department's Conspiracy Theory against Julian Assange," Shadowproof, May 29, 2019, https://shadowproof.com/2019/05/29/unravel-justice-department-conspiracy-theory-julian-assange/; Janine Jackson, "Chelsea Manning Again Takes Fall for Defending Public's Right to Know," Fairness & Accuracy In Reporting, April 1, 2019, https://fair.org/home/chelsea-manning-again-takes-fall-for-defending-publics-right-to-know/.

182. Peter Hart, "Edward Snowden, Glenn Greenwald and the Courtier Press," Fairness & Accuracy In Reporting, May 13, 2014, https://fair.org/home/edward-snowden-glenn-greenwald-and-the-courtier-press/.

CHAPTER 9

Our Collective Crisis and Constructive Journalism— Growing the Good and Possible

Kenn Burrows, Amber Yang, and Bethany Surface

The only war that matters is the war against the imagination

—Diane di Prima[1]

Welcome to our collective crisis. The signs are everywhere in a fragmented society incapable of civil dialogue and unable to solve its growing problems. Our shared crisis is twofold—first, a crisis of social disconnection; and second, a crisis of impaired imagination. Both are fed, in part, by a third crisis unleashed by the digital revolution and problem-focused news.

Medical experts cite loneliness and isolation as the primary public health problem in the United States.[2] This is driven in part by the "shallow ties" of the digital age, with the average Facebook user having 338 friends yet feeling more alone than ever.[3] Many are drowning in the busyness of digital life while isolating themselves through social media and online entertainment. A May 2018 survey of more than 20,000 adults revealed that most Americans are lonely, with 43 percent reporting that they felt isolated from others, with adults aged 18 to 22, known as "Generation Z," comprising the loneliest generation of all.[4]

Furthermore, scientists have identified clear links between loneliness and illness, while noting that social isolation can even alter the human genome. Early human survival depended on communication and cooperation; thus, our greatest human need, after food and shelter, is for social connection. This leaves the United States—which highly prizes individuality—clearly at risk.[5] The loneliness epidemic is also impacting other industrialized nations, including South Korea, Japan, and the United Kingdom. In the United Kingdom, a new government position, the Minister of Loneliness, was created to help manage this public health crisis.[6]

We propose that loneliness is not just an individual health problem, but also a societal problem. Our decline in social engagement may impact our abilities to work together to solve collective problems, leaving us feeling helpless and hopeless. Perhaps this diminished creativity is our ultimate crisis—a crisis of imagination. This crisis seems to be driven, in part, by today's media and journalistic practices.

Journalism historically works to expose wrongdoing and generate awareness of possible threats. This fear-based, watchdog role is essential to a democratic society. However, it has led to an overload of news that feeds the evolutionary tendency of "threat awareness," a biological and psychological response known as "negativity bias." The recurrence of natural disasters, human failures, war, terror, and tragedy in the news contributes to a cycle of cynicism and disengagement.

Every crisis at its core is a failure of imagination. Where's the empowering news that highlights human creativity and possibility? In a world gone awry with bad news, we have become passive consumers—instead of creative thinkers reaching out for justice and possibility.

This chapter calls for Constructive Journalism as a creative antidote to an exclusive focus on problem-based news. Constructive Journalism emphasizes our capacity to innovate and generate ideas, and foregrounds our social nature—highlighting community-generated news, solutions-based journalism, and the power of the arts to spark innovative thought and shared (positive) values.

At its best, journalism catalyzes and informs conversations and helps us consider possibilities for a wiser, more creative world. Armed with information, imagination, the willingness to engage one another, and a meaningful cause, we can and will solve the complex, deeply-rooted problems we face.

CRITICAL JOURNALISM informs about threats and public concerns—including critical examination of power inequalities, secrecy, accountability, and fairness/justice.

CONSTRUCTIVE JOURNALISM informs about interactive systems and creative possibilities, reinventing outdated narratives, and catalyzing collaboration and the common good.

THE THREE-FOLD "NEWS CRISIS" AND HOW CONSTRUCTIVE JOURNALISM CAN HELP

According to the Reuters Institute's 2017 "Digital News Report," less than half the population (43 percent) in 36 surveyed countries said they trust the media; in the United States, 38 percent reported actively avoiding the news.[7] The report states, "People cluster to media organizations that fit their belief, and dismiss other outlets. The internet, once thought to open the world up to all the information possible and bring people together, has instead drawn people into their own corners."[8]

Distrust and avoidance of vital news of the world around us threatens not only the future of journalism but also the basis for civil society itself; as Thomas Jefferson wrote, "If a nation expects to be ignorant and free, in a state of civilization, it expects what never was and never will be."[9] To get at the root of the public's distrust for news media, let's take a closer look at this ongoing news crisis:

(1) *Access to responsible news is in decline.* The business model underlying journalism is failing as newsrooms are forced to compete with Google, Facebook, and the digital media revolution. Over this past decade, one in five newspapers have closed—creating an expanding "news desert" of communities without local news coverage. A 2011 Federal Communications Commission report established "news ade-

quacy at 50,000 reporters across the U.S.," but today only 25,000 reporters have jobs, Jessica Cohen reported in a Spring 2019 *Utne Reader* article.[10] Research shows that in the absence of local news coverage there is less civic engagement, less community participation, more misconduct, and the possible emergence of partisan news sites.[11]

(2) *Trust in journalism is at an all-time low.* News media have become more corporate and less likely to challenge the most powerful. The increases in fake news, alternative facts, and weaponized social media seem to have overtaken society, impairing our ability to distinguish truth, connect meaningfully, and act collectively. How then do newsmakers and consumers navigate this post-truth age of media, propaganda, and censorship?

(3) *New media are driving the reinvention of journalism.* In the aftermath of closures of newspapers, and the digital devaluation of journalism—not to mention the rueful effects such developments have had on public trust and engagement—how should the news be gathered and distributed, and what methods and ethics ought to guide the process? Journalism needs more than just a new business model for its long-term survival. Critical Journalism and the news media need to be reinvigorated by incorporating Constructive Journalism as an equal partner in an expanded, integrative model of the "news." We can begin to envision constructive journalistic reforms by reevaluating how our evolutionary inheritance has shaped today's news coverage and our crisis of imagination, and by proposing alternative models to better serve both our needs and the stories covered.

FEAR BIAS IN JOURNALISM AND OPENING TO THE GOOD AND POSSIBLE

Humans evolved to be fearful, since that helped keep our ancestors alive. Our minds and behavior are shaped by threats—real and unreal.

For more than two million years, the human nervous system has evolved to approach rewards or avoid hazards. Consequently, our brain and body generally react more intensely (with more neural activity) to negative stimuli than to positive ones. The amygdala (the brain's alarm system) uses about two-thirds of its neurons to monitor for perceived threats, and it reacts milliseconds faster than the (rational) prefrontal cortex does. This emotional overreaction is called the "amygdala hijack."[12] This fear-based, emotional perspective creates two core perceptual mistakes: overestimating threats and underestimating resources and possibilities.[13]

Journalism is not separate from this reactive orientation to the world. Journalists can improve society by reporting harmful realities as well as helpful realities.[14] However, reporters tend to focus more on the former, and miss reporting the latter. Most news is about what we fear. This constant reporting of possible threats creates a view of the world as mean and dangerous. Furthermore, research shows that negative news overload can lead news consumers to feel depressed, anxious, and helpless. A 2014 study by National Public Radio, the Robert Wood Johnson Foundation, and the Harvard School of Public Health found that 40 percent of those polled said the news is one of their biggest daily stressors.[15] As Anthony Leiserowitz, director of the Yale Program on Climate Change Communication, said, "We call this loosely 'the hope gap,' and it's a serious problem. Perceived threat without efficacy of response is usually a recipe for disengagement or fatalism."[16]

The prospect of people disconnecting from news should worry journalists—but the possibility that relentlessly negative news might actually weaken citizenship is even more troubling.[17] A 2008 study by the Associated Press showed that the prevalence of constant crises in news headlines contributes to a cycle of disengagement—leading to "news fatigue" and "compassion fatigue" as news consumers tune out the news and lose their motivation to help others participating in solving societal problems.[18] In contrast, where's the empowering news that highlights human goodness, creativity, and possibility?

Constructive Journalism: Growing the Good

Constructive Journalism is built, in part, on the principles of positive psychology—the scientific study of the world's innate goodness and the conditions that help individuals and communities heal and thrive. Just as our negativity bias has helped us to survive, *constructive positivity* communicates what is right and trustworthy in the world, providing a signal that our surroundings are safe and that new ways of seeing and understanding are possible.[19]

Constructive Journalism moves the spotlight from victims to creators by employing two types of constructive news, Solutions Journalism and Engagement Journalism.

Solutions Journalism recognizes that people need to sense that problems can be solved, and that we can contribute to those solutions. We need journalism that not only informs but also inspires and activates. Possibility-oriented stories feed our imagination.

Engagement Journalism supports a "narrative of belonging," bridging our differences while inspiring people to come together on matters of shared interest. It brings out the best in us, reducing social isolation and loneliness while emphasizing collective power and common good.

The Integrative News/ Journalism Movement

Integrating **3 essential forms of journalism** (information flow) for a healthy society— using the metaphor of a 3-legged tripod:

Constructive Journalism (possibility-focused)

Critical Journalism (problem-focused) informs us of possible threats... what may harm us, unless attended to.

Solutions Journalism (innovation-focused) highlights design thinking for problem prevention, reduction, or elimination.

Engagement Journalism (greater-good focused) grows the good by awakening connections within and between systems —through expanding public commons, art, storytelling, etc.

Each leg supports and informs the other two.
The camera serves as a metaphor for how we see the world.

(cc) *Kenn Burrows, Amber Yang, and Bethany Surface*

CRITICAL JOURNALISM (FOCUS: PROBLEMS)

News producers and consumers alike need to employ critical thinking skills to navigate the complexity of today's news media, especially to counter propaganda and disinformation campaigns. Critical thinking promotes healthy skepticism of systems of power, including their abuses of power, unaccountability and lack of transparency, and injustices. Critical media literacy is necessary "not only to *engage with the media*, but to engage with society *through the media*."[20] Critical Journalism highlights important public issues by

1) asking key questions (analyzing what's in the frame, and what's left out);

2) using credible resources that include diverse perspectives;

3) supporting awareness of power dynamics within media and culture;

4) considering the message's intended audience; and

5) creating evidence-based interpretations.

Examples:

▶ "How Big Wireless Convinced Us Cell Phones and Wi-Fi are Safe" Researchers compare the telecom industry's public relations tactics to those of Big Tobacco. As with the PR push to conceal tobacco products' proven deleterious effects, the risks of wireless tech are real despite its industry's attempts to obscure them; a Kaiser Permanente study found pregnant women exposed to electromagnetic radiation via cell phones and wireless networks were three times more likely to have miscarriages.[21]

▶ "Despite Promises of ACA, Study Shows Two-Thirds of Personal Bankruptcies Still Caused by Illness and Medical Bills"

The Affordable Care Act has failed to solve the crisis of for-profit healthcare. 530,000 American households continue to see their finances wiped out each year due to medical costs.[22]

SOLUTIONS JOURNALISM (FOCUS: INNOVATION)

Reporting problems is not enough. Journalists have a special role as storytellers, and possibility-oriented storytelling can greatly shape the cultural narrative. Journalists can do this by building on the traditional fact-based questions—who, what, where, when, why, and how—by considering a seventh question: What's possible now?[23] When solutions are underreported, reforms go unrealized. Yet when journalists include solutions in their reporting, they "empower communities and individuals, shift public discourse, and address complex social challenges."[24] People report higher levels of self-efficacy and motivation to take action after being exposed to Solutions Journalism.[25] Similarly, the Institute for Applied Positive Research discovered remarkable results in a study of struggling communities in Detroit. Researchers found that solutions-reporting increased news readers' problem-solving skills by 20 percent.[26] The readers in the study who focused on solutions also reported feeling more energized, less anxious, more connected to community, and more confident that their city was improving.[27]

Three unique practices underlie solutions-oriented journalism: appreciative inquiry, design thinking, and innovation theory. Research in appreciative inquiry shows a direct relationship between what we imagine (possibilities) and what we create.[28] Appreciative inquiry is the act of recognizing and exploring the strengths and capacities of people and organizations. As such, appreciative inquiry involves "a fundamental shift in the overall perspective taken throughout the entire change process to 'see' the wholeness of the human system and to 'inquire' into that system's strengths, possibilities, and successes."[29]

Design thinking and innovation theory help us orient to complex problems and root out how we limit ourselves from seeing game-changing solutions.

Design thinking employs our abilities "to be intuitive, to recognize patterns," and "to construct ideas that have emotional meaning."[30] It emphasizes goals, rather than problems to be solved, because complex problems can be approached in different ways. Coevolution of this problem-solving process leads to strategic insights and a deeper understanding of each issue's context. The following graphic illustrates the design thinking process:[31]

The five phases of the design process:

1	2	3	4	5
DISCOVERY	INTERPRETATION	IDEATION	EXPERIMENTATION	EVOLUTION
I have a challenge.	I learned something.	I see an opportunity.	I have an idea.	I tried something.
How do I approach it?	*How do I interpret it?*	*What do I create?*	*How do I build it?*	*How do I evolve it?*

Innovation theory shows how creative change becomes accepted— and who accepts it. The Rogers Adoption Curve shows how new ideas (solutions) are accepted and adopted, in the order that each group adopts them, and what percentage of the total population each group represents:[32]

Innovators: 2.5 percent (risk-takers who are first to embrace an innovation)

Early Adopters: 13.5 percent (movers and shakers who push innovation into the broader culture)

Early Majority: 34 percent (pragmatists who adopt innovation only after it is proven)

Late Adopters: 34 percent (conservative ones, cautious in embracing new ways)

Laggards: 16 percent (the last group to embrace change, who are often forced to do so)

Innovation theory targets innovators and early adopters in order to develop a critical mass of support, while also fostering media partnerships to educate the public (early majority and late adopters) and reporting ongoing change.

Examples:

▸ "Regenerative Agriculture as 'Next Stage' of Civilization"
   Regenerative agriculture constitutes a world-changing array of practices to rebuild soil, sequester carbon, and increase food production and food quality (nutritional density), with potential to reverse the detrimental effects of climate change within 25 years.[33]
▸ "Eight Use of Force Policies to Prevent Killings by Police"
   Researchers studying 91 of the nation's largest police departments identified eight use of force policies that significantly decrease police violence. Yet only a third of the country's departments implement four or more of these policies. If all eight policies were enforced, police would kill 72 percent fewer people.[34]

ENGAGEMENT JOURNALISM (FOCUS: THE GREATER GOOD)

> *It's time we reassert the human agenda. And we must do so together—not as the individual players we have been led to imagine ourselves to be, but as the team we actually are, Team Human.*
>
> —Douglas Rushkoff[35]

Engagement Journalism reduces the impact of loneliness by awakening a sense of connection (among individuals and within social systems) and by galvanizing the power of collective action. When people are socially engaged, they build collective efficacy—"the capacity of people to act together on matters of common interest."[36] In a fifteen-year study, Felton Earls, a Harvard professor of public health, showed that "collective efficacy" made the greatest difference in the health and well-being of individuals and neighborhoods throughout Chicago, more than wealth, access to healthcare, low crime levels, or any other factor.[37]

However, collective efficacy in our society has diminished steadily as social exclusion and disparities in wealth and income deepen. As this sense of separation builds, a meta-narrative emerges that either supports the breaking of communities (fear, anger, and othering) or the bridging of communities (belonging, empathy, and collective solidarity).[38] The breaking of communities is frequently seen among social organizers, activists, and people who genuinely want an inclusive, caring society, but all too often organizers continue attempting to lead with the same ineffectual approaches of resistance and blame.

john a. powell, director of the Haas Institute for a Fair and Inclusive Society, is a strong voice for social connection. His intention is not to organize around hope or despair but to engage across our differences, and build "deep mutuality"[39]—what we are calling "engagement." Examples of social engagement are everywhere, yet this is "a movement that doesn't know it's a movement."[40]

Engagement Journalism supports social connection and news stories of successful breakthroughs. For example, Movement Journalism, an emerging project in the southern United States, publishes game-changing news stories of people "trying to build collective power and organizing together to make fundamental shifts in the power dynamics of our society."[41] Whether it is communities fighting for public education or activists advocating for the homeless, "deep down it is all the same work. It is building connection where there was no connection, creating relationships where there were no relationships, weaving thick neighborhoods where there were thin neighborhoods."[42]

Engagement Journalism is a powerful force for awakening civic participation and supporting communities in making their own news. Here are five tools that have been used in Engagement Journalism that activists, reporters, and community members can employ to help improve society and its news:

#1: Meditation and Mindful Inquiry

> *Intimate relating begins with the self. It is a toxic fantasy to believe that we can be intimate with others when we have not learned (or are afraid) to be intimate with ourselves.*
>
> —Jerry A. Greenwald[43]

The first step in engagement is deepening and enriching your relationship with yourself. The regular practice of nonjudgmental, present-moment awareness expands our capacity to listen, relate, and connect compassionately to others. Mindful inquiry heals the illusion of separation that keeps us isolated and estranged. Journalists who focus on mindful inquiry promote the development of comfort in uncertainty and the complexity of systemic challenges.

Examples:

▸ "This School Replaced Detention with Meditation. The Results are Stunning"
Schools with mindfulness or yoga programs as substitutes for detention benefit from decreased suspension rates and increased attendance.[44]

▸ "Mindfulness Training Reduces Stress and Anger in Police"
Research shows that Mindfulness-Based Resilience Training significantly reduces law enforcement professionals' stress and anger. Practicing mindfulness offers a new set of skills to help police de-escalate volatile situations, improve community relations, and better handle the demands of their jobs.[45]

#2: Public Space and Collective Gathering

Shared places (such as parks, town squares, trails, nature centers, and libraries) belong to everyone. Strengthening civic commons counteracts gentrification and crime, lays groundwork for economic and social opportunity, and breaks down stark boundaries (for example, rich versus poor, or black versus white). News that highlights the value of the "Commons" is essential to our shared future.

Examples:

- ▶ "UK's Largest 'Disco Soup' Attracts 1,000 People to London Market" Disco Soup is a collaborative, celebratory movement to address the global issue of food waste.[46]
- ▶ "Digital Justice: Internet Co-ops Resist Net Neutrality Rollbacks" More than 300 electric cooperatives are building their own internet. Neighborhoods aim to build shared tools and educate their communities on digital literacy.[47]

#3: Power of the Arts

> *The task of the artist . . . is to make the revolution irresistible.*
>
> —Toni Cade Bambara[48]

Art (including film, music, dance, and poetry) shapes the world by helping activists and community leaders become social catalysts, finding meaning in conflict, illness, and loss, and awakening and informing a slumbering humanity. Constructive journalists use art to bring stories off the page and into our lives—using art-infused reporting to highlight social issues. "Digital technology and increased competition have led journalists to employ more creative techniques to capture viewers' attention, including multimedia storytelling, stylized visuals, and interactive techniques to create a more personal and emotional experience."[49]

Examples:

- ▸ "Focusing on Arts and Humanities to Develop Well-Rounded Physicians"
  In the stressful field of medicine, arts and humanities help medical students form deeper connections with patients, maintain joy in medical practice, and develop empathy and resiliency.[50]
- ▸ "How Jazz Helped Fuel the Civil Rights Movement"
  Jazz promoted integration and social justice, and it "provided a culture in which the collective and the individual were inextricable."[51]

#4: The Power of Play and Humor

> *Play is nothing less than the creation of the human we are meant to be. . . . We play to heal, not to defend, and in doing so create authentic playgrounds, time/places of safety and love, where everyone is included. We are beginners, allowing ourselves to touch and be touched by the wonder and mystery of the world. We feel our belonging.*
>
> —O. Fred Donaldson[52]

Mammals, including humans, learn best by exploring and playing. Play is essential to social-emotional intelligence, creative living, and complex problem-solving. Play and humor have a long history of helping activists speak truth to power while also awakening community awareness of the common good. Currently, many of us get our "news" from *The Daily Show*, or a mix of late-night television hosts who combine play, humor, and political commentary.

Examples:

▶ "Study Finds Play and Cognitive Skills in Kindergarten Predict Civic Engagement in Later Life"
Through play, school children learn to cooperate, share, and encourage each other's curiosity and imagination, leading to the development of working memory and cognitive flexibility, which are fundamental skills for later civic engagement.[53]

▶ "How Comedy Makes Us Better People"
Humor can validate shared experiences, promote flexible thinking, and reframe situations.[54]

#5: Storytelling, Symbol, and Metaphor

Storytelling is fundamental to human experience. Stories touch people on an experiential level. That's where change occurs. We make sense and give meaning to our lives through stories, metaphors, and symbols. The new journalist understands that people need more than information. She/he will work with the community to be a force for good through positive storytelling.

Examples:

▶ "How Storytelling Can Improve Business Communication and Transform Workplaces"
"The quality of connection that results from storytelling is deeper, more lasting, more resonant, and therefore qualitatively more powerful than other means of communication."[55]

▶ "From Negative Biases to Positive News: Resetting and Reframing News Consumption for a Better Life and a Better World"
Constructive stories do five things to transform conflicts into possibilities: "expand the mind, storm the brain, change the question, tell the story right, and move the world."[56]

CONCLUSION

A crisis occurs when the old world isn't working, and the new one hasn't been born yet. This new world will not be created by old thinking and strategies, but rather by how we make meaning of our human condition and the greater good as it emerges. Constructive Journalism—that is, the combined strength of Solutions Journalism and Engagement Journalism, alongside Critical Journalism—reminds us that "facts" are not enough. We are just awakening to the profound significance of the creative process that is driving evolution, and the emerging role of "possibility journalism" in leading this revolution.

KENN BURROWS has been an educator and consultant for more than 30 years, teaching holistic health studies at San Francisco State University since 1991. He is founder and director of the Holistic Health Learning Center, a unique interdisciplinary library and community action center at the university. He is also a member of the executive board of Media Freedom Foundation, which oversees Project Censored, a national effort to educate the public about media literacy, the importance of independent news, and the common good. He also serves as faculty advisor to Project Censored's San Francisco State University affiliate.

AMBER YANG (BA, Psychology; minor, Holistic Health) has served as co-president of Project Censored's San Francisco State University affiliate. She has been an educator for the San Francisco Unified School District as a paraprofessional for at-risk students with trauma and intensive emotional needs, and has extensive experience teaching yoga and mindfulness to youth. She is now pursuing a master's degree in organization development at Sonoma State University.

BETHANY SURFACE graduated from San Francisco State University with a bachelor's degree in psychology and a minor in holistic health. While attending the university, she was co-president of the Project Censored affiliate club for two years, where she researched and published numerous stories for the Project, planned and hosted community teach-ins on campus, and appeared on radio shows and at community events for Project Censored. She spent the last three years working as a personal consultant in the cannabis industry, combining the knowledge of her studies with the critical media literacy skills gained from working with Project Censored. She is currently studying and teaching yoga with her community, and is studying to become a yoga therapist and Ayurvedic practitioner.

Notes

1. Diane di Prima, "Rant (Revolutionary Letter #75)," *Revolutionary Letters*, 5th ed. (San Francisco: Last Gasp of San Francisco, 2007), 103–106, 104.

2. Emily Holland, "The Government's Role in Combating Loneliness," *Wall Street Journal*, September 12, 2017, https://www.wsj.com/articles/the-governments-role-in-combating-loneliness-1505268240.

3. Steven Mazie, "Do You Have Too Many Facebook Friends?" Big Think, October 9, 2014, https://bigthink.com/praxis/do-you-have-too-many-facebook-friends.

4. Ellie Polack, "New Cigna Study Reveals Loneliness at Epidemic Levels in America," Cigna, May 1, 2018, https://www.cigna.com/newsroom/news-releases/2018/new-cigna-study-reveals-loneliness-at-epidemic-levels-in-america.

5. Amy Ellis Nutt, "Loneliness Grows from Individual Ache to Public Health Hazard," *Washington Post*, January 31, 2016, https://www.washingtonpost.com/national/health-science/loneliness-grows-from-individual-ache-to-public-health-hazard/2016/01/31/cf246c56-ba20-11e5-99f3-184bc379b12d_story.html.

6. Dan Hancox, "Why Countries Worldwide are Watching How the UK's Newest Minister is Handling the Loneliness Crisis," Shareable, March 26, 2019, https://www.shareable.net/why-countries-worldwide-are-watching-how-the-uks-newest-minister-is-handling-the-loneliness-crisis/.

7. Nic Newman with Richard Fletcher, Antonis Kalogeropoulos, David A.L. Levy, and Rasmus Kleis Nielsen, "Reuters Institute: Digital News Report 2017," Reuters Institute for the Study of Journalism, March 2019, http://www.reuterscommunity.com/wp-content/uploads/2019/03/risj-digital-news-report-2017.pdf, 29.

8. Ibid.

9. Letter from Thomas Jefferson to Charles Yancey, January 6, 1816, printed in *The Papers of Thomas Jefferson: Retirement Series*, Vol. 9, ed. J. Jefferson Looney (Princeton: Princeton University Press, 2013), 331.

10. Jessica Cohen, "Education in the News Wasteland," *Utne Reader*, Spring 2019, https://www.utne.com/media/education-in-the-news-wasteland-zm0z19szhoe.

11. Ibid.

12. Daniel Goleman, *Emotional Intelligence: Why It Can Matter More Than IQ* (New York: Bantam Books, 2005).

13. Rick Hanson with Richard Mendius, *Buddha's Brain: The Practical Neuroscience of Happiness, Love, and Wisdom* (Oakland, California: New Harbinger Publications, 2009).

14. Solutions Journalism, "Ten Reasons Why We Need Solutions Journalism," The Whole Story (Medium), November 10, 2016, https://thewholestory.solutionsjournalism.org/ten-reasons-why-we-need-solutions-journalism-a4b29c663086.

15. NPR, Robert Wood Johnson Foundation, and Harvard School of Public Health, "The Burden of Stress in America," Public Opinion Poll Series, July 2014, https://www.rwjf.org/content/dam/farm/reports/surveys_and_polls/2014/rwjf414295.

16. Christopher Reeve, "News and the Negativity Bias: What the Research Says," The Whole Story (Medium), November 10, 2016, https://thewholestory.solutionsjournalism.org/news-and-the-negativity-bias-what-the-research-says-78a0bca05b11.

17. Ibid.

18. Ibid.

19. Martin Seligman, "The New Era of Positive Psychology," TED Talk video, February 2004, https://www.ted.com/talks/martin_seligman_on_the_state_of_psychology.

20. Sonia Livingstone, professor of social psychology at the London School of Economics, quoted in Akshat Rathi, "We Get the Journalism We Deserve," Quartz, February 17, 2019, https://qz.com/1552503/media-literacy-is-crucial-to-help-sustain-high-quality-journalism.

21. John Michael Dulalas, Bethany Surface, Kamila Janik, Shannon Cowley, Kenn Burrows, and Rob Williams, "How Big Wireless Convinced Us Cell Phones and Wi-Fi are Safe," in *Censored*

2019: Fighting the Fake News Invasion, eds. Mickey Huff and Andy Lee Roth with Project Censored (New York: Seven Stories Press, 2018), 48–52, https://www.projectcensored.org/4-how-big-wireless-convinced-us-cell-phones-and-wi-fi-are-safe/.

22. Julia Conley, "Despite Promises of ACA, Study Shows Two-Thirds of Personal Bankruptcies Still Caused by Illness and Medical Bills," Common Dreams, February 7, 2019, https://www.commondreams.org/news/2019/02/07/despite-promises-aca-study-shows-two-thirds-personal-bankruptcies-still-caused.

23. Peggy Holman, "Journalism for Navigating Uncertainty: The Possibility Principle," Journalism That Matters, September 18, 2013, http://journalismthatmatters.org/blog/2013/09/18/the-possibility-principle/.

24. Lindsay Green-Barber, "What We Know (And Don't) about the Impact of Solutions Journalism," The Whole Story (Medium), October 8, 2018, https://thewholestory.solutionsjournalism.org/what-we-know-and-dont-about-the-impact-of-solutions-journalism-61ae0c4a0890.

25. Ibid.

26. Michelle Gielan, Brent Furl, Jodie Jackson, the Solutions Journalism Network, and the Detroit Free Press, "Solution-focused News Increases Optimism, Empowerment and Connectedness to Community," Institute for Applied Positive Research, March 2017, http://michellegielan.com/wp-content/uploads/2017/03/Solution-focused-News.pdf.

27. Ibid, 4.

28. "Introduction to Appreciative Inquiry," Appreciative Inquiry Commons, undated, https://appreciativeinquiry.champlain.edu/learn/appreciative-inquiry-introduction/ [accessed May 14, 2019].

29. Ibid.

30. Tim Brown and Jocelyn Wyatt, "Design Thinking for Social Innovation," Stanford Social Innovation Review, Winter 2010, https://ssir.org/articles/entry/design_thinking_for_social_innovation.

31. "Design Thinking and Social Innovation Overview," Elon University, undated, https://blogs.elon.edu/innovationstudio/design-thinking-and-social-innovation-overview/ [accessed April 24, 2019].

32. John-Pierre Maeli, "The Rogers Adoption Curve & How You Spread New Ideas Throughout Culture," The Political Informer (Medium), May 6, 2016, https://medium.com/the-political-informer/the-rogers-adoption-curve-how-you-spread-new-ideas-throughout-culture-d848462fcd24.

33. Amber Yang and Kenn Burrows, "Regenerative Agriculture as 'Next Stage' of Civilization," in *Censored 2019*, 57–58, https://www.projectcensored.org/7-regenerative-agriculture-as-next-stage-of-civilization/.

34. Malcolm Pinson and Kenn Burrows, "Eight Use of Force Policies to Prevent Killings by Police," in *Censored 2018: Press Freedoms in a "Post-Truth" World*, eds. Andy Lee Roth and Mickey Huff with Project Censored (New York: Seven Stories Press, 2017), 96–98, https://www.projectcensored.org/24-eight-use-force-policies-prevent-killings-police/.

35. Douglas Rushkoff, *Team Human* (New York: W.W. Norton & Company, 2019), 7.

36. Tom Borrup, "5 Ways Arts Projects Can Improve Struggling Communities," Project for Public Spaces, January 1, 2009, https://www.pps.org/article/artsprojects.

37. Ibid.

38. john a. powell, "Co-Creating Alternative Spaces to Heal," Haas Institute for a Fair and Inclusive Society, October 22, 2017, video uploaded to YouTube on November 20, 2017, https://www.youtube.com/watch?v=d3gNspcW7Z8.

39. UpFront, "Could Increasing Housing Density Alleviate the Bay Area's Affordability Crisis? Plus: The Othering and Belonging Conference Kicks Off April 9–10—We Spend the Hour with john a. powell" (audio recording), KPFA, April 3, 2019, https://kpfa.org/episode/upfront-april-3-2019/.

40. "The Relationalist Manifesto," Weave: The Social Fabric Project, Aspen Institute, February 2019, https://assets.aspeninstitute.org/content/uploads/2019/02/Weave-Relationalist-Manifesto.pdf.

41. Christine Schmidt, "A Survey of Independent Media in the South Asks If 'Movement Journalism' Can Help Newsrooms Better Cover Social Justice Strife," Nieman Lab, August 14, 2017, https://www.niemanlab.org/2017/08/a-survey-of-independent-media-in-the-south-asks-if-movement-journalism-can-help-newsrooms-better-cover-social-justice-strife/.

42. "The Relationalist Manifesto" (Weave: The Social Fabric Project).

43. Jerry A. Greenwald, *Creative Intimacy: How to Break the Patterns That Poison Your Relationships* (New York: Penguin, 1987 [first published by Simon & Schuster in 1975]), 42.

44. James Gaines, "This School Replaced Detention with Meditation. The Results are Stunning," Upworthy, September 22, 2016, https://www.upworthy.com/this-school-replaced-detention-with-meditation-the-results-are-stunning.

45. Jenn Director Knudsen, "Mindfulness Reduces Stress and Anger in Police," Greater Good Magazine, August 1, 2016, https://greatergood.berkeley.edu/article/item/mindfulness_reduces_stress_and_anger_in_police.

46. Nadia Khomami, "UK's Largest 'Disco Soup' Attracts 1,000 People to London Market," *The Guardian*, September 15, 2017, https://www.theguardian.com/environment/2017/sep/15/uks-largest-disco-soup-attracts-1000-people-to-london-market.

47. Amber Yang and Kenn Burrows, "Digital Justice: Internet Co-ops Resist Net Neutrality Rollbacks," in *Censored 2019*, 71–73, https://www.projectcensored.org/15-digital-justice-internet-co-ops-resist-net-neutrality-rollbacks/.

48. Kay Bonetti, "An Interview with Toni Cade Bambara" (1982), in *Conversations with Toni Cade Bambara*, ed. Thabiti Lewis (Jackson: University Press of Mississippi, 2012), 35–47, 35.

49. Michael Blanding, "Journalism and Art: Complementary and Collaborative Storytelling," Nieman Storyboard, March 28, 2016, https://niemanstoryboard.org/stories/journalism-and-art-complementary-and-collaborative-storytelling/.

50. Eris Heim, "Focusing on Arts and Humanities to Develop Well-Rounded Physicians," Project Censored, April 3, 2018, https://www.projectcensored.org/focusing-arts-humanities-develop-well-rounded-physicians/.

51. Michael Verity, "Jazz and the Civil Rights Movement," LiveAbout (formerly at ThoughtCo), May 31, 2017, updated July 15, 2018, https://www.liveabout.com/jazz-and-the-civil-rights-movement-2039542.

52. O. Fred Donaldson, "Playing by Heart," Touch the Future, undated, https://ttfuture.org/academy/o-fred-donaldson/o-fred-donaldson [accessed May 14, 2019].

53. "Study Finds Play and Cognitive Skills in Kindergarten Predict Civic Engagement in Later Life," NYU Steinhardt News (New York University), January 10, 2017, https://steinhardt.nyu.edu/site/ataglance/2017/01/study-finds-play-and-cognitive-skills-in-kindergarten-predict-civic-engagement-in-later-life.html.

54. Mary O'Hara, "How Comedy Makes Us Better People," BBC Future (BBC), August 30, 2016, http://www.bbc.com/future/story/20160829-how-laughter-makes-us-better-people.

55. Kathy Caprino, "How Storytelling Can Improve Business Communication and Transform Workplaces," *Forbes*, March 23, 2018, https://www.forbes.com/sites/kathycaprino/2018/03/23/how-storytelling-can-improve-business-communication-and-transform-workplaces.

56. Henry Edwards, "From Negative Biases to Positive News: Resetting and Reframing News Consumption for a Better Life and a Better World," Master's Thesis, University of Pennsylvania, August 1, 2017, uploaded August 15, 2017, https://repository.upenn.edu/cgi/viewcontent.cgi?article=1126&context=mapp_capstone.

Acknowledgments

Andy Lee Roth and Mickey Huff

The researching and writing of each *Censored* yearbook is always a team effort. We are grateful to everyone who helped us down the rabbit hole and back again to complete *Censored 2020*.

This book represents the collective efforts of so many talented and committed people, including the courageous journalists who report on vital issues beyond the pale of the corporate press and the independent news outlets that make these reports available to the public; the faculty evaluators and student researchers at the Project's college and university affiliate campuses who help us to cover the increasingly extensive networked news commons; the authors who contributed chapters and sections to *Censored 2020*, inspiring us with challenging questions and new perspectives; and our international panel of judges who ensure that each year's Top 25 list includes only the best, most significant validated independent news stories.

We are once again blessed to work with an extraordinary editor, Michael Tencer. His deep knowledge, keen eyes, and crisp editing enhanced every page in this book. He also suggested the subtitle for this year's book, Through the Looking Glass. We are thankful, too, for the continued friendship of our previous editor, Veronica Liu, who is always there for counsel when we need her.

At Seven Stories Press in New York, we thank Dan Simon, publisher and editorial director; Jon Gilbert, operations director; Ruth Weiner, publicity director; Allison Paller, publicist; Sanina Clark, assistant editor; Lauren Hooker, editor; Noah Kumin, academic and web manager; Stewart Cauley, art director; Elena Watson, managing editor; Anastasia Damaskou, publicity assistant; Silvia Stramenga, rights director and editor of foreign literature; and interns Maya Chessen, Victoria Nebolsin, Sarah Paraszczak, and Dror Cohen—all of whom have our respect and gratitude for their commitment to publishing the Project's research.

We were so enthralled with last year's cover art that we asked the artist, Anson Stevens-Bollen, to return for *Censored 2020*. He did not disappoint with his dystopic rendering of the wonderland landscape of the Trump era. We also thank Khalil Bendib, whose cartoons again grace our book with his wit and wisdom.

The Media Freedom Foundation board of directors, whose members are identified below, help to sustain Project Censored and its mission by providing invaluable counsel and crucial organizational structure. We also thank past director and president Peter Phillips, who continues to be an active supporter of the Project's work and overall mission.

The Project's mission benefits from the resolute guidance and deep insights of our webmaster, Adam Armstrong. In addition to making sure the Project's research and reports remain accessible to our global audience, Adam oversees the production of the Project's online video series, as well as our radio broadcast and podcast of *The Project Censored Show* and the *Along the Line* podcast, plus he maintains the operation of our Patreon page.

We thank Christopher Oscar and Doug Hecker of Hole in the Media Productions for their ongoing support of the Project, especially by working with and inspiring a new generation of documentary filmmakers. During the past year, Media Freedom Foundation board member Nolan Higdon and his student interns have partnered with Abby Martin of *The Empire Files* to begin editing and production of a new Project Censored documentary on fake news. We are especially grateful to Richard and Janet Oscar for their generous support of the forthcoming documentary.

We are grateful to the friends and supporters of *The Project Censored Show* as we embark on our ninth year of broadcasting. We thank senior producer Anthony Fest and our live broadcast engineers at KPFA Pacifica Radio, as well as associate producer and videographer Dennis Murphy at KPCA in Petaluma. Mickey Huff continues as executive producer and host of the program, along with new cohost Chase Palmieri. We also wish to thank everyone who supports the overlapping missions of Project Censored and Pacifica, including Bob Baldock and Ken Preston, for their work on public events with us last year, and the 50 stations from Hawaii to New England that air the program each week. We also welcome the new *Along the Line* podcast team—including hosts Nolan Higdon, Nicholas Baham III, and Aimee Casey, with producer Janice Domingo—who have, as of this writing, produced more than 30 episodes.

We are grateful to the people who have hosted Project Censored events or helped to spread the word about the Project's mission this past year, including Susan Rahman and her students at the College of Marin, as well as the Students for Social Justice club, the Associated Students of College of Marin, and vice president Jonathan Eldridge, for hosting the Project's Media Freedom Summit 2.0: Critical Media Literacy for Social Justice, in October 2018; John Bertucci, videographer/producer Dennis Murphy, Rob Tomaszewski, and everyone at Petaluma Community Access Television (and KPCA radio); John Crowley and the Aqus community; Jen Jensen, Larry Figueroa, and the crew at Lagunitas Brewing Company; Chase and Marco Palmieri and family at Risibisi; Raymond Lawrason and all at Copperfield's Books; Grace Rajendran, events producer, and Nancy Nordquist at University Book Store in Seattle; Mike McCormick of KODX 96.9 FM Seattle; Kevin Herbert at Common Cents; James Preston Allen, Paul Rosenberg, and Terelle Jerricks with the team at *Random Lengths News* in San Pedro, California, as well as the Association of Alternative Newsmedia (AAN); Margli and Phil Auclair, Rick Sterling, and everyone at the Mount Diablo Peace and Justice Center in Lafayette; the Petaluma Progressives, and all those at the Peace and Justice Center of Sonoma County; the Sociology Social Justice and Activism Club at Sonoma State University; the Pacific Sociological Association, which continues to highlight the Project's work on critical media literacy at its annual meetings; the Society of Professional Journalists, Northern California chapter, for honoring our work this past year at the James Madison Freedom of Information Awards for education; Cass Davis in Moscow, Idaho; Jason Houk and Wes Brain at KSKQ, and all the folks behind Independent Media Week, including Kathleen Gamer at Southern Oregon University in Ashland, Oregon; Steve Macek at North Central College, and our allies in the Union for Democratic Communications; Mark Crispin Miller at New York University; Marc Pilisuk; Davey D and Hard Knock Radio; Abby Martin of *The Empire Files* and Media Roots; Mnar Muhawesh and the team at MintPress News, including Alan MacLeod, Whitney Webb, and

Alexander Rubinstein; Eleanor Goldfield of *Act Out!*; Kevin Gosztola and Rania Khalek at Shadowproof and the *Unauthorized Disclosure* podcast; The Real News Network in Baltimore, Maryland; Lee Camp and *Redacted Tonight*; Krish Mohan; Sharyl Attkisson of *Full Measure*; Arlene Engelhardt and Mary Glenney, hosts of *From a Woman's Point of View*; Eric Draitser and *CounterPunch Radio*; Dave Lindorff of *This Can't Be Happening*; Bill Bigelow (Rethinking Schools), Deborah Menkart (Teaching for Change), and everyone involved in the Zinn Education Project; James Tracy and everyone at the Howard Zinn Book Fair in San Francisco; historian Peter Kuznick at American University; John Barbour; J.P. Sottile (the Newsvandal); Michael Welch of *The Global Research News Hour*; Esty Dinur of *A Public Affair* on WORT FM in Madison, Wisconsin; Ian Trottier with *Discussions of Truth*; Malcolm Fleschner with *The Young Turks*; Theresa Mitchell of *Presswatch* on KBOO community radio in Portland, Oregon; Jon Gold; John Collins of St. Lawrence University and the team at Weave News; Chase Palmieri, Jared Fesler, and all at Credder.com; Betsy Gomez and everyone involved in the Banned Books Week Coalition, including Christopher Finan and all those at the National Coalition Against Censorship and the American Library Association's Office for Intellectual Freedom; Ralph Nader and the Center for Study of Responsive Law; and Peter Ludes, Hektor Haarkötter, Daniel Müller, and Marlene Nunnendorf at the German Initiative on News Enlightenment—each of whom helps the Project to reach a broader audience.

We continue to be grateful for our relationships with the Action Coalition for Media Education (ACME) and the Union for Democratic Communications (UDC), with whom we collaborate in hosting conferences that address critical media literacy and higher education. In November 2019, Project Censored and the UDC will collaborate to present a conference focused on mass communication and transnational empire, honoring the legacy of the late Herbert Schiller. We thank everyone working at the hosting institution, California State University, East Bay, including especially chair of communication Mary Cardaras, departmental analyst Katherine M. Daval-Santos, faculty members Grant Kien and Nolan Higdon, as well as Brian Dolber, Rob Carley, Steve Macek, and all on the UDC steering committee.

At Diablo Valley College, Mickey thanks Lisa Martin and History

Department cochairs Matthew Powell and Melissa Jacobson, as well as John Corbally, Bridgitte Schaffer, Carmina Quirarte-Amador, Greg Tilles, Katie Graham, Mary Ann Irwin, Marcelle Levine, Adam Bessie, Mark Akiyama, Jacob Van Vleet, Steve Johnson, Jeremy Cloward, Amer Araim and the Model United Nations club, John Kropf, Ted Blair, Scott MacDougall, Dorrie Mazzone, Toni Fannin, and Adam Perry; Albert Ponce, Sangha Niyogi, and Terence Elliott, along with everyone involved in the Social Justice Studies program; English and Social Sciences dean Obed Vazquez; and the vice president of student services, Newin Orante. Mickey also thanks current and former teaching and research assistants and Project interns including Troy Patton, Sierra Kaul, Elsa Denis, Katy Nguyen, Katia Elias, and Dasha Bukovskaya. At California State University, East Bay, Mickey specifically thanks Danuta Sawka and the chair, Mary Cardaras, in the Department of Communication.

Nolan Higdon, the Project's critical media literacy officer, thanks the following students and interns for their work on the Project's next documentary film: Eduardo Gonzalez, Kestutis Rushing, Scout Gottfried, Daniel McGuire, Chelsea Corby, Sage Healy, Claudia Bistrain, Tourie Boswell, Eliza Otto, Justin Mutch, Gabriel Cox, Michael Stepp, Tera Thompson-Garner, Janice Domingo, Caitlyn Harper, Ryan Edmonson, and Jessica Irrera.

Mickey would also like to thank all of his students for the inspiration they provide, as they are a constant reminder of the possibilities of the future and how privileged we are as educators to have such an amazing role in contributing to the public sphere.

Vital financial support from donors sustains the Project. This year, we are especially thankful to Margli and Phil Auclair, Tony Barrett, Jeanie Bates, Sandra Cioppa, James Coleman, Dwain A. Deets, Jan De Deka, Martha Fleischman, Michael Hansen, Neil Joseph, Sheldon Levy, Robert Manning, James March, Sandra Maurer, Harry Mersmann, David Nelson, Christopher Oscar, Richard and Janet Oscar, Allison Reilly, Lynn and Leonard Riepenhoff, John and Lyn Roth, T.M. Scruggs, Bill Simon, Mark Squire, Elaine Wellin, Derrick West and Laurie Dawson, David Winkler, Timothy Wolf, and Montgomery Zukowski.

With sadness, we recognize the passing in March 2019 of one of the Project's longtime supporters, a pioneering mind and contributor to humanitarianism, Ralph Metzner. He will be missed, but the spirit of his work expanding human and eco-consciousness lives on.

We also acknowledge the loss of journalist and activist Bruce A. Dixon. From his time with the Black Panthers and writing for the Black Commentator internet magazine to his cofounding of the Black Agenda Report where he was the managing editor, Dixon fought for social justice and racial equality by "comforting the afflicted and afflicting the comfortable." His voice will be greatly missed.

Mickey thanks his family, especially his wife, Meg, for her amazing work and counsel, and their children, for patience, moral support, and often much-needed comic relief. Andy thanks Liz Boyd for encouragement and inspiration.

Finally, we thank you, our readers, who continue to cherish a truly free press. Together, we make a difference.

MEDIA FREEDOM FOUNDATION/PROJECT CENSORED BOARD OF DIRECTORS

PROJECT CENSORED 2018–19 JUDGES

ROBIN ANDERSEN. Professor of Communication and Media Studies, Fordham University. She has written dozens of scholarly articles and is author or coauthor of four books, including *A Century of Media, A Century of War* (2006), winner of the Alpha Sigma Nu Book Award. She recently published *The Routledge Companion to Media and Humanitarian Action* (2017), and *HBO's* Treme *and the Stories of the Storm: From New Orleans as Disaster Myth to Groundbreaking Television* (2017). Writes media criticism and commentary for the media watch group Fairness & Accuracy In Reporting (FAIR), The Vision Machine, and the *Antenna* blog.

JULIE ANDRZEJEWSKI. Professor Emeritus, St. Cloud State University. Served as director of the Social Responsibility master's program, and president of the faculty union. Publications include *Social Justice, Peace, and Environmental Education* (coedited, 2009) and, most recently, a book chapter, "The Roots of the Sixth Mass Extinction" (2017). She is currently co-chair of Indivisible Tacoma.

OLIVER BOYD-BARRETT. Professor Emeritus of Media and Communications, Bowling Green State University and California State Polytechnic University, Pomona. Publications include *The International News Agencies* (1980), *Contra-flow in Global News: International and Regional News Exchange Mechanisms* (1992), *The Globalization of News* (1998), *Media in Global Context* (2009), *News Agencies in the Turbulent Era of the Internet* (2010), *Hollywood and the CIA: Cinema, Defense, and Subversion* (2011), *Media Imperialism* (2015), and *Western Mainstream Media and the Ukraine Crisis* (2017).

KENN BURROWS. Faculty member at the Institute for Holistic Health Studies, Department of Health Education, San Francisco State University. Founder and director of the Holistic Health Learning Center and producer of the biennial conference, Future of Health Care.

ERNESTO CARMONA. Journalist and writer. Chief correspondent, teleSUR Chile. Director, Santiago Circle of Journalists. President of the Investigation Commission on Attacks Against Journalists, Latin American Federation of Journalists (CIAP-FELAP).

ELLIOT D. COHEN. Professor of Philosophy and chair of the Humanities Department, Indian River State College. Editor and founder of the *International Journal of Applied Philosophy*. Recent books include *Making Peace with Imperfection* (2019), *Counseling Ethics for the 21st Century* (2018), *Logic-Based Therapy and Everyday Emotions* (2016), and *Technology of Oppression: Preserving Freedom and Dignity in an Age of Mass, Warrantless Surveillance* (2014).

GEOFF DAVIDIAN. Investigative reporter, war correspondent, legal affairs analyst, editor, photojournalist, data analyst, educator, and media captain for Wisconsin gubernatorial candidate Mike McCabe. Founding publisher and editor of the *Putnam Pit, Milwaukee Press,* and ShorewoodNewsroom. Contributor to Reuters, magazines, newspapers, and online publications.

ROBERT HACKETT. Professor Emeritus of Communication, Simon Fraser University, Vancouver. Cofounder of NewsWatch Canada (1993), Media Democracy Days (2001), and OpenMedia.ca (2007). Publications include *Remaking Media: The Struggle to Democratize Public Communication* (with W.K. Carroll, 2006) and *Journalism and Climate Crisis: Public Engagement, Media Alternatives* (with S. Forde, S. Gunster, and K. Foxwell-Norton, 2017). He blogs at rabble.ca.

KEVIN HOWLEY. Professor of Media Studies, DePauw University. His work has appeared in the *Journal of Radio Studies, Journalism: Theory, Practice and Criticism, Social Movement Studies,* and *Television and New Media.* He is the author of *Community Media: People, Places, and Communication Technologies* (2005), and editor of *Understanding Community Media* (2010) and *Media Interventions* (2013). His latest book is *Drones: Media Discourse and the Public Imagination* (2018).

NICHOLAS JOHNSON.* Author, *How to Talk Back to Your Television Set* (1970) and nine additional titles, including *Columns of Democracy* (2018) and *Catfish Solution* (2019). Commissioner, Federal Communications Commission (1966–1973). Former media and cyber law professor, University of Iowa College of Law. More online at nicholasjohnson.org.

CHARLES L. KLOTZER. Founder, editor, and publisher emeritus of *St. Louis Journalism Review* and *FOCUS/Midwest*. The *St. Louis Journalism Review* has been transferred to Southern Illinois University, Carbondale, and is now the *Gateway Journalism Review*. Klotzer remains active at the *Review*.

NANCY KRANICH. Lecturer, School of Communication and Information, and special projects librarian, Rutgers University. Past president of the American Library Association (ALA), and convener of the ALA Center for Civic Life. Author of *Libraries and Democracy: The Cornerstones of Liberty* (2001) and "Libraries: Reuniting the Divided States of America" (2017).

DEEPA KUMAR. Associate Professor of Journalism and Media Studies, Rutgers University. Author of *Outside the Box: Corporate*

Media, Globalization, and the UPS Strike (2007) and *Islamophobia and the Politics of Empire* (2012). Currently working on a book on the cultural politics of the war on terror.

MARTIN LEE. Investigative journalist and author. Cofounder of Fairness & Accuracy In Reporting, and former editor of FAIR's magazine, *Extra!*. Director of Project CBD, a medical science information nonprofit. Author of *Smoke Signals: A Social History of Marijuana—Medical, Recreational, and Scientific* (2012), *The Beast Reawakens: Fascism's Resurgence from Hitler's Spymasters to Today's Neo-Nazi Groups and Right-Wing Extremists* (2000), and *Acid Dreams: The Complete Social History of LSD: The CIA, the Sixties, and Beyond* (with B. Shlain, 1985).

PETER LUDES. Professor of Mass Communication, Jacobs University, Bremen, 2002–2017. Visiting Professor at the University of Cologne, 2018–2021. Founder of the German Initiative on News Enlightenment (1997) at the University of Siegen (Project Censored, Germany). Recent publications include *Brutalisierung und Banalisierung Asoziale und soziale Netze* (Brutalization and Banalization in Asocial and Social Networks) (Springer Essentials, 2018) and "Distorted Knowledge and Repressive Power," in *Media, Ideology and Hegemony*, ed. Savaş Çoban (Brill, 2018).

WILLIAM LUTZ. Professor Emeritus of English, Rutgers University. Former editor of the *Quarterly Review of Doublespeak*. Author of *Doublespeak: From Revenue Enhancement to Terminal Living: How Government, Business, Advertisers, and Others Use Language to Deceive You* (1989), *The Cambridge Thesaurus of American English* (1994), *The New Doublespeak: Why No One Knows What Anyone's Saying Anymore* (1996), and *Doublespeak Defined* (1999).

CONCHA MATEOS. Professor of Journalism, Department of Communication Sciences, Universidad Rey Juan Carlos, Spain. Journalist for radio, television, and political organizations in Spain and Latin America. Coordinator for Project Censored research in Europe and Latin America.

MARK CRISPIN MILLER. Professor of Media, Culture, and Communication, Steinhardt School of Culture, Education, and Human Development, New York University. Author, editor, and activist.

DANIEL MÜLLER. Head of the Postgraduate Academy at the University of Siegen, in Germany. Researcher and educator in journalism and mass communication studies and history at public universities for many years. Has published extensively on media history, media–minority relations in Germany, and on nationality policies and ethnic relations of the Soviet Union and the post-Soviet successor states, particularly in the Caucasus. Jury member of the German Initiative on News Enlightenment.

JACK L. NELSON.* Distinguished Professor Emeritus, Graduate School of Education, Rutgers University. Former member, Committee on Academic Freedom and Tenure, American Association of University Professors. Recipient, Academic Freedom Award, National Council for Social Studies. Author of 17 books, including *Critical Issues in Education: Dialogues and Dialectics*, 8th ed. (with S. Palonsky and M.R. McCarthy, 2013), *Human Impact of Natural Disasters* (with V.O. Pang and W.R. Fernekes, 2010), and about 200 articles.

PETER PHILLIPS. Professor of Political Sociology, Sonoma State University, since 1994. Director, Project Censored, 1996–2010. President, Media Freedom Foundation, 2010–2016. Editor or coeditor of 14 editions of *Censored*. Coeditor (with Dennis Loo) of *Impeach the President: The Case Against Bush and Cheney* (Seven Stories Press, 2006). Author of *Giants: The Global Power Elite* (Seven Stories Press, 2018), as well as four chapters in recent *Censored* yearbooks.

T.M. SCRUGGS. Professor Emeritus (and token ethnomusicologist), University of Iowa. Published in print, audio, and/or video format, on Central American, Cuban, and Venezuelan music and dance and US jazz. Involvement with community radio in Nicaragua, Venezuela, and the United States, including the Pacifica National Board. Executive producer, The Real News Network (2010–2019). Has served on the board of Truthout.org since 2012.

NANCY SNOW. Pax Mundi Professor of Public Diplomacy, Kyoto University of Foreign Studies, Japan. Professor Emeritus of Communications, California State University, Fullerton. Fellow, Temple University, Japan, Institute of Contemporary Asian Studies. Author or editor of 12 books, including *The SAGE Handbook of Propaganda*

(2020) and a new edition of *The Routledge Handbook of Public Diplomacy* (with Nicholas J. Cull, 2020).

PAUL STREET. Researcher, award-winning journalist, historian, author, and speaker. Author of seven books to date: *Empire and Inequality: America and the World Since 9/11* (2004); *Segregated Schools: Educational Apartheid in Post–Civil Rights America* (2005); *Racial Oppression in the Global Metropolis: A Living Black Chicago History* (2007); *Barack Obama and the Future of American Politics* (2009); *The Empire's New Clothes: Barack Obama in the Real World of Power* (2010); *Crashing the Tea Party: Mass Media and the Campaign to Remake American Politics*, with Anthony R. DiMaggio (2011); and *They Rule: The 1% vs. Democracy* (2014). He writes regularly for Truthdig and *CounterPunch*.

SHEILA RABB WEIDENFELD.* Emmy Award–winning television producer. Former press secretary to Betty Ford and special assistant to the President; author, *First Lady's Lady*. President of DC Productions Ltd. Creator of snippetsofwisdom.com. Director of community relations of Phyto Management LLC and Maryland Cultivation and Processing LLC.

ROB WILLIAMS. Founding president of the Action Coalition for Media Education (ACME). Teaches media, communications, global studies, and journalism at the University of Vermont and Champlain College. Author of numerous articles on critical media literacy education. Publisher of the Vermont Independent online news journal. Coeditor of *Media Education for a Digital Generation* (with J. Frechette, 2016) and *Most Likely to Secede* (with R. Miller, 2013), about the Vermont independence movement.

*Indicates having been a Project Censored judge since our founding in 1976.

HOW TO SUPPORT PROJECT CENSORED

NOMINATE A STORY

To nominate a *Censored* story, send us a copy of the article and include the name of the source publication, the date that the article appeared, and the page number. For news stories published on the internet, forward the URL to mickey@projectcensored.org or andy@projectcensored.org. The deadline for nominating *Censored* stories is March 15 of each year.

Criteria for Project Censored news story nominations:

1) A censored news story reports information that the public has a right and a need to know, but to which the public has had limited access.

2) The news story is recent, having been first reported no later than one year ago. For *Censored 2020* the Top 25 list includes stories reported between April 2018 and March 2019. Thus, stories submitted for *Censored 2021* should be no older than April 2019.

3) The story has clearly defined concepts and solid, verifiable documentation. The story's claims should be supported by evidence—the more controversial the claims, the stronger the evidence necessary.

4) The news story has been published, either electronically or in print, in a publicly circulated newspaper, journal, magazine, newsletter, or similar publication from either a domestic or foreign source.

MAKE A TAX-DEDUCTIBLE DONATION

Project Censored is supported by the Media Freedom Foundation, a 501(c)(3) nonprofit organization. We depend on tax-deductible donations to continue our work. To support our efforts on behalf of independent journalism and freedom of information, send checks to the address below or donate online at projectcensored.org. You can also make monthly donations through our Patreon account at patreon.com/projectcensored. Your generous donations help us to oppose news censorship and promote media literacy.

Media Freedom Foundation
PO Box 750940
Petaluma, CA 94975
mickey@projectcensored.org
andy@projectcensored.org
Phone: (707) 241-4596

ABOUT THE EDITORS

ANDY LEE ROTH is the associate director of Project Censored and coeditor of nine previous editions of the *Censored* yearbook. He coordinates the Project's Validated Independent News program. His research, on topics ranging from ritual to broadcast news interviews to communities organizing for parklands, has been published in such journals as the *International Journal of Press/Politics*; *Social Studies of Science*; *Media, Culture & Society*; *City & Community*; and *Sociological Theory*. He earned a PhD in sociology at the University of California, Los Angeles, and a BA in sociology and anthropology at Haverford College. He has taught courses in sociology at Citrus College, Pomona College, Sonoma State University, the College of Marin, and Bard College, and now lives in Seattle with his sweetheart and their two wonderful cats.

MICKEY HUFF is the current director of Project Censored and president of the nonprofit Media Freedom Foundation. He has edited or coedited 11 annual volumes of *Censored* and has contributed numerous chapters to them, dating back to 2008. His most recent book, coauthored with Nolan Higdon, is *United States of Distraction: Media Manipulation in Post-Truth America (and what we can do about it)* (City Lights Publishers Open Media Series, August 2019). Additionally, he has coauthored several chapters on media and propaganda for scholarly publications. Huff received the Beverly Kees Educator Award as part of the 2019 James Madison Freedom of Information Awards from the Society of Professional Journalists, Northern California. He is currently professor of social science and history at Diablo Valley College in the San Francisco Bay Area, where he is cochair of the History Department. He is also a lecturer in communications at California State University, East Bay, and has taught sociology of media at Sonoma State University. Huff is executive producer and cohost of *The Project Censored Show*, a weekly syndicated public affairs program founded in 2010, which is produced for the historic studios of KPFA Pacifica Radio in Berkeley, California, and broadcast on more than 50 community radio stations across the United States.

Huff currently serves on the editorial board for the journal *Secrecy and Society* and for the past several years has worked with the American Library Association, the National Coalition Against Censorship, and the Banned Books Week Coalition. He is one of the founding members of the Global Critical Media Literacy Project and also serves on the advisory board regarding matters of critical media literacy at Credder.com. He is a longtime musician and composer, and resides with his family in Sonoma County, California.

For more information about the editors, to invite them to speak at your school or in your community, or to conduct interviews, please visit projectcensored.org.

Index

Baime, Jacob, 65, 66
Bambara, Toni Cade, 267
Baptist Church, 92–94, 192
Barcus, Austin, 41–43
Baron, Marty, 226
Barr, William, 85
Basu, Nandita, 54
Batamaloo, Srinagar, Jammu and Kashmir, 177, 178
Bayou Bridge Pipeline, 57, 148
BBC (television and radio network), 68, 226, 227
The Beach Boys (music group), 230
Belkin, Aaron, 200
Bendib, Khalil, 5, 27, 34, 42, 66, 75, 90, 111, 116, 123, 225
Benjamin, Medea, 108
Benjamin, Walter, 106
Berkeley, CA, 48
Bernhardt, David, 59, 60
Bessie, Adam, 8, 159–71
Bickert, Monika, 231
Billingsley, Lloyd, 112
bin Salman, Mohammad, 5
Bing (internet browser), 228
BishopAccountability.org, 97
Black Agenda Report, 226
Black Lives Matter movement, 242
Black Power movement, 58
Blado, Andrea, 23–25
Blevins, Rachel, 234
Block, Joshua, 198, 201
Blumenthal, Max, 48, 49, 67, 79n30
Bogota Declaration (COICA), 31
Boko Haram, 64
Bolsonaro, Jair, 31, 32
Boorstin, Daniel, 166
Border Patrol (US), 111
Boston, MA, 117
Bowman, Tom, 107
Boy George (musician), 98
Boycott, Divestment and Sanctions movement (BDS), 65–67
BP (oil and gas company), 55, 60
Bradbury, Alexandra, 8, 135, 149–52
Brand New Congress (US political action committee), 119
BrandGuard (NewsGuard product), 237, 238
Braun, Ashley, 8, 135, 146–49
Brazil, xi, 29, 31, 32, 186, 213
Break Free from Fossil Fuels campaign, 56, 57

Breitbart (Far-Right media website), 232
Breitburg, Denise, 55
Brennan Center for Justice, 56
Brexit, 222
Britain, see United Kingdom
Brown, Cyntoia, 37–40
Brunei, 186, 213
Buckingham Palace, 87
Buffalo, NY, 150
Bureau of Justice Statistics (US), 61
Burger King (fast food company), 55
Burrows, Kenn, 3, 10, 19, 50–53, 255–73
Burton, Susan, 38
Bush, George W., 28, 231
Butina, Maria, 222
Butler, Allison, 63, 64
BuzzFeed, 85, 208
By Invitation Only, 195, 215n31
Bynum, Anne, 43
California, 16, 17, 19, 49, 69–72, 151, 162, 180
California Department of Justice, 69–71
California Division of Juvenile Justice, 71
The California Report (radio show), 72
California State University, San Bernardino, 208
Cameroon, 63
Camp Fire (2018), 8, 166, 170
Canary Mission (anti-Palestine website), 66
cancer, 45, 51, 147
capitalism, 18, 75–77, 115, 118, 120, 241
Capitol Hill, Washington, DC, 108, 125
Cardi B (musician), 86, 89, 91
Cardona Castillo, Bayron, 110
Cargill (food, finance, and technology corporation), 54
Cargo torture center, Srinagar, Jammu and Kashmir, 176
Caribbean, 68
Carlson, Carolyn S., 138
Carlson, Tucker, 88, 112, 231
Carroll, Lewis, 1–3, 10–12, 13n8
Cassell, Heather, 214n8
Catholic Church, 92, 97–99
CBS (television network), 230
CBS News, 36, 37, 42, 52, 55, 238
CBS This Morning, 98
censorship, xi, 15, 103, 133, 135, 186, 187
government, 26–30, 65–67, 91, 173
impact on democracy, xiii, 8, 23–29, 77n8, 96, 119, 122, 127, 152, 178, 179, 222, 223, 241, 242

in the service of fighting "fake news," xii, 9, 79n30, 223, 225, 228, 229, 231–33, 235, 237, 238, 242
of independent media, 28–30, 65–67, 79n30, 223, 225–28, 232–35, 237, 238, 241
of journalists, 6, 23–25, 78n22
public information officers, 8, 134–38
social media, 9, 25–30, 152, 154, 225, 226, 229, 231, 258
Center for American Politics Studies, 239
Center for American Women and Politics, 115
Center for Biological Diversity, 33, 59
Center for Economic and Policy Research, 63
Center for Strategic and International Studies, 230, 231, 248n88
Center for the Study of Hate and Extremism, 208
Center on Juvenile and Criminal Justice, 70–72
Centers for Disease Control and Prevention (CDC) (US), 135
Central America, 7, 41, 104, 107, 109–111, 113, 114
Central Intelligence Agency (CIA) (US), 27, 233, 236
Central Reserve Police Force (India), 175
Central Valley, CA, 8
centrism, 105, 118, 120, 128n5
Cephus, Kulture Kiari, 89
Chakrabarti, Samidh, 231
Charles Koch Institute, 230, 238
Charlotte, NC, 215n28
Charlottesville, VA, 48
Chattanooga, TN, 204
Chávez, Hugo, 29
Chechnya (federal subject of Russia), 186
Check Your Fact, 231, 232
Cheeni Chowk, Anantnag, Jammu and Kashmir, 175
Chen, Victor Tan, 74, 75
Chertoff, Michael, 230, 232, 236
Chertoff Group, 236, 251n140
Chevron, 27
Chicago, IL, 151, 158n30, 208, 265
Chicago Tribune, 59
children, *see* young people
China, 53, 108, 155, 173, 239
Chomsky, Noam, 187, 234, 235
Christchurch, New Zealand, 94

Christianity, 203, 204, *see also* Baptist Church; Catholic Church
Chuck E. Cheese's (restaurant chain), 163, 170
Cisco (technology conglomerate), 53
City College of San Francisco, 33, 72
civil rights, 56, 62, 67, 69–71, 93, 140, 141, *see also* surveillance
media coverage of organizations, 188, 190, 191, 198, 199, 202
Civil Rights movement, 93, 268
civilians, 4, 174, 176, 178, 179
Clapper, James, 4
class, 72–75, 95, 96, 111, 216n35, 119–21, 225, 241, 265, *see also* inequality
Clegg, Nick, 232
climate change, 1, 7, 31–34, 55–58, 86–88, 118, 119, 133, 134
solutions to, 67, 68, 146, 147, 259, 264
Clinton, Bill, 230
Clinton, Hillary, 90, 144, 222, 224
CNBC (television network), 75
CNN (television network), 29, 30, 36, 37, 53, 61, 63, 78n22, 83n94, 105, 118, 134, 235, 238, 239
Coast Guard (US), 200
Cobb, Frank I., 78n12
Code Pink (anti-war organization), 108
Cohen, Elliot D., 48–50
Cohen, Jessica, 258
Cohen, Michael, 86
Cohen, Roger, 107
Cohen, William, 85–102
COINTELPRO (FBI program), 58
College of Marin, 7, 45, 55, 69
College of Western Idaho, 58, 60
Collins, John, 7, 103–131
Colombia, 31
Colorado, 151
Colorado Springs Independent, 189, 215n28
Columbia University, 23, 36
Columbian Chemicals, 155
Combs, James E., 153
Comiti, Paul, 173
Commentator Accountability Project, 211
Common Dreams, 16, 27–29, 31, 32, 228
Community Coalition for Real Meals, 73
Compass Group (food service company), 73
Condé Nast, 89
Congress (US), 4, 7, 28, 39, 49, 58, 104, 114–20, 191, 199, 212, 223, 233
conservatism, 9, 27, 31, 32, 44, 66, 67, 111–13,

Kopf, Daniel, 61–63
KQED (radio and television stations), 72
Kreidie, Gabrielle, 65–67
Kremlin, 30, 79n30, 223, 237
Krishnan, Ramya, 24, 25
Kristof, Nicholas, 113
Kristol, Bill, 232
Krystofiak, Thom, 56
Ku Klux Klan, 116
Kyle, Grace, 85–102
labor, 8, 40, 72–75, 133, 155, 178, 240
   and felon disenfranchisement, 61–63
   and "right-to-work" laws, 151
   forced, 35–37, *see also* slavery
   journalism, 18, 135, 149–52
Labor Notes, 8, 133, 135, 149–52, 158n30
Lambda Legal, 191
land rights, 31, 32
Language: A Key Mechanism of Control, 155
Lanier, Jaron, 169
Larsen, Carl, 203
Las Vegas, NV, 168
Lash, Alyssa, 63, 64
Latinx peoples, 62, 69, 70, 89–91, 109–112, 117, 234
Lauria, Joe, 225
law enforcement, 1, 16, 23, 41, 42, 57, 64, 69–71, 108, 110, 136, 138, 175, 177, 179, 208, 214, 234, 240, 241, 264, 266
Lay, Carol, 154
Lazare, Sarah, 57, 58
Le Guin, Ursula K., 164
Leadership Conference on Civil and Human Rights, 192
Leaving Neverland, 97, 98
Lebanon, 65
The Left Hand of Darkness, 164
legislation, 5, 41, 70, 73–75, 111, 114, 117–20, 133, 152, 180, 191, 202, 204, 209, 231
   and lobbying efforts, 60, 65–67, 133
   criminal justice, 37–40, 43, 44, 61–63
   digital oversight, xi, 77, 145, 231
   environmental, 33, 34, 57–60, 137, 146
   foreign policy (US), 25–30, 46, 49, 66, 67, 119, 155, 227, 232, 234
   labor, 36, 61–63, 150, 151
   LGBTQ-related, 185, 187, 197–202, 205, 206, 212
Leiserowitz, Anthony, 259
Levi, Jennifer, 201
Levinson, Jennifer, 32–34, 72–74

LexisNexis, 21
LGBTQ issues, 114, 187, 190, *see also* transgender issues
   "bathroom bills," 9, 197, 198, 202, 206, 208, 212
   homophobia, 2, 9, 186, 188, 205, 208–211, 214n19
   marriage equality, 185, 189, 203, 205, 211, 215n21
   treatment by the military, 188, 189, 191, 199–201, 204, 206, 208, 212, 215n32
   treatment in the media, 9, 18, 185, 186, 188, 189, 192–97, 205–207, 210–13, 215nn28, 30
Li, Sydney, 76
liberalism, 28, 104, 113–15, 228, 229, 233, 235, *see also* Democratic Party (US)
Liberty and the News, 15, 19
Library of Congress (US), 142
Libya, 48
Lincoln, Bruce, 104
Line of Control, Jammu and Kashmir, 178
Lippmann, Walter, 15, 16, 19, 77n8, 78n12
Lisitsa, Valentina, 79n30
Lockheed Martin, 233
Log Cabin Republicans, 185
Loki, Reynard, 54
London, UK, 5, 46, 87, 235, 267
López, Victoria, 157n16
Los Angeles, CA, 48
Los Angeles Times, 188, 189, 192, 197, 199, 201, 202, 209, 211, 212, 215n30
Louisiana, 7, 57, 60, 61, 92, 93, 148
Louisiana Purchase (1803), 148
Lussier, Caroline, 63, 64
Lynch, Lisa, 65–67, 76, 77
MacDonald, Ian R., 60, 61
Macek, Steve, 7, 25–30, 37–40, 43, 44, 133–58
"The Machine Stops," 8, 164, 165
MacLeod, Alan, 28, 29
Macron, Emmanuel, 95
Macy's (department store chain), 150
Madison, WI, 215n28
Madonna (musician), 98
Maduro, Nicolás, 235
Maffick Media, 29, 30, 235
Mager, Lee, 9, 221–53
Magram, Jonas, 56
Mahoney, Michelle, 58–61
Malaysia Airlines Flight MH17, 222

Maldives, 68
Males, Mike, 69–71
Mali, 63
Mandia, Kevin, 233, 249n111
Mandiant (cybersecurity firm), 233
Manning, Chelsea, 4–6, 242
Manufacturing Consent, 187
Maoist International Movement, 155
Marcetic, Branko, 105
Marine Corps (US), 200
Marion County, FL, 202
Markle, Meghan, 7, 86–88
Marmol, Emil, 9, 221–53
Martin, Abby, 235
Martin, Christopher R., 135
Martin, Shania, 85–102
Masood (pseudonym), 174
mass shootings, 69, 70, 94, 185
Massachusetts, 116, 119
Massachusetts Institute of Technology
    (MIT), 165
May, Adam, 67, 68
Mayorga, Diana, 72–74
McCain, John, 7, 104–108, 230
McCarthy, Joseph, 226
McCarthy, Kevin, 111
McConnell, Mitch, 90, 111, 125
McCutcheon, Jody, 52
McDonald's (fast food company), 54, 55
McKibben, Bill, 56
#MeToo movement, 99, 117, 120–22,
    124–26
media, *see also* journalism; Junk Food News;
    Media Democracy in Action; News
    Abuse
    as fourth estate, 4, 91
    corporate 1, 2, 4, 7, 11, 12, 86, 92–94,
        100, 135, 149–51, 173, 179
    coverage of celebrity gossip, 7, 39,
        85–89, 91–100
    coverage of LGBTQ issues, 9, 185, 186,
        188, 189, 192–95, 205, 206, 208,
        211–13
    coverage of Top 25 News Stories, 3,
        6, 16, 29, 30, 32–34, 36, 37, 39,
        40, 42–44, 46, 48, 50, 52, 53, 55,
        58–60, 63, 64, 68, 71–75, 77, 133
    News Abuse, 103–109, 113, 115, 116,
        118–20, 126, 127, 134, 135
    propaganda, 152–55, 221–26, 237–42
    framing, 34, 98, 103, 113, 126, 133, 187,
        269

"guidelines," 24, 25
    independent, 2, 3, 6, 11, 12, 16–18, 21,
        91, 104, 133, 135, 240, 244n18, 257,
        258, *see also* Validated Independ-
        ent News
    censorship of, 28–30, 65–67,
        79n30, 223, 225–28, 232–35,
        237, 238, 241
    coverage of LGBTQ issues, 9, 186,
        189, 192–97, 205–207, 210,
        212, 215nn28, 30
    coverage of Top 25 News Stories, 26,
        28–30, 32, 33, 37, 44, 60, 74
    press freedom, xii, 4, 5, 18, 23–25,
        see also Constitution (US), First
        Amendment; free speech; surveil-
        lance, of journalists
    sensationalist, 7, 85, 93, 94, 96–98,
        186, 208, 209, 215
    social, *see* social media
    standing, 187, 190–96, 215n31, 216n42
    trust in, 15, 16, 21, 223, 228, 229, 236,
        238–40, 257, 258, 260
Media Democracy in Action, 7, 8, 133–58
Media Manipulation Initiative (MMI), 143,
    145
Media Matters for America, 228
Medicare, 119, 151
Mehraj, Irfan, 173, 179, 181
Mehtar, Juweria, 85–102
Mellon Initiative for Undergraduate
    Research in the Arts and Humani-
    ties, 153
Mendoza, Citlali, 71, 72
Merck (pharmaceutical company), 46
Metahistory, 114
Mexico, 31, 109, 111
Michaels, Samantha, 71
Michigan, 116
Microsoft, 228, 230, 236
Microsoft Edge (mobile internet browser),
    236
Middle East, 46, 235
Mighty Earth (environmental organization),
    54, 55
Migos (music group), 89
migrants, *see* immigration
Mikulka, Justin, 146–48
military, 4, 8, 9, 27, 28, 47–50, 106–108,
    133, 142, 155, 173, 177, 179
    treatment of LGBTQ people, 188, 189,
        191, 199–201, 204, 206, 208, 212,

215n32
militias, 48–50, 64, 174
millennials, 29, 74, 75, 114, 239, 241, 255
millimeter waves (MMW), 51, 52
mindfulness, 10, 266
Ministry of Agriculture, Livestock, and Supply (Brazil), 32
Ministry of Popular Power for Education (Venezuela), 234
Ministry of Popular Power for Petroleum (Venezuela), 234
Ministry of Popular Power for Women (Venezuela), 234
Ministry of Strategic Affairs (Israel), 66
Minnesota, 57, 116, 203
MintPress News, 29, 30, 48–50, 228, 237
miscarriage, 43, 44, 87, 261
Misoprostol (pharmaceutical drug), 90
Mississippi, 43
Moore, Roy, 205
Morell, Michael, 233
Morgan, Jana, 7, 103–131
Morgan, Jonathon, 233
Morning Edition (radio show), 107
Morones, Enrique, 112
Mortensen, Brent, 23–25
Mother Jones, 37, 39, 71
Motherboard (Vice), 46, 48
Mount Pleasant Baptist Church, 92, 94
Mountain Xpress, 215n28
Movement for Black Lives, 67
M'Panya, Mutombo, 61–63
Ms. Magazine, 43, 44
MSNBC (television network), 50, 105
Mueller, Robert, 223
Mueller Report, 25
Mugler, Thierry, 94, 95
Mulla, Mariya, 85–102
Murdoch, Rupert, 123
Nadler, Anthony, 8, 134, 143–46
Naked Capitalism (media blog), 226
National Advocates for Pregnant Women, 44
National Archives and Records Administration (NARA) (US), 139–42
National Center for Transgender Equality, 191, 197, 198
National Center for Youth Law, 199
National Coalition of Anti-Violence Programs, 186
National Crime Victimization Survey (US), 186

National Democratic Institute (NDI) (US), 26, 28, 29, 230
National Endowment for Democracy (NED) (US), 28, 29, 230, 247n72
National Former Prisoner Survey (US), 61
National Geographic, 55, 59
National Institutes of Health (US), 53
National Marine Fisheries Service (US), 59
National Security Agency (NSA) (US), 4, 141, 236, 237
National Security Council (US), 231, 232
national security letters (NSLs) (US), 24, 25, 78n20
Nature Communications (journal), 68
Navy (US), 27, 200
Naylor, Carla, 85–102
Nazism, 48–50, *see also* fascism; white supremacists
NBC News, xii, 29, 40
Nebraska, 53
neoliberalism, 6, 115, 119, 120, 232, 242
Nevada, 39
Neverland Ranch, 97
New Humanitarian (media website), 63
New Jersey, 53
New Knowledge ("information integrity" organization), xii, 233
New Orleans, LA, 215n28
New Scientist (journal), 67
New York, NY, 46, 78n12
New York State, 40, 116
New York Times, xii, 4, 27, 32, 34, 36, 39, 42, 44, 68, 75, 77, 96, 98, 105, 107, 109, 113, 115, 119, 121–25, 131n56, 134, 137, 188, 189, 192, 199–202, 204, 208, 209, 211, 212, 214n19, 215nn21, 29, 30, 217n53, 225, 226, 229, 238
The New Yorker, 131n55, 229
News Abuse, 3, 7, 103–131
News Corp, 123
NewsGuard ("information integrity" organization), 235–37, 250nn134, 138, 251n151
NewsHour (television show), 195
Newstead, Jennifer, 231
Newsweek (magazine), 61
Nguyen, Thanh, 60, 61
Nicaragua, 29, 230
Niger, 64
Nigeria, 63, 64
Nightline (television show), 195
Nimmo, Ben, 30, 79n30

Nimmo, Dan, 153
No Longer Newsworthy, 135
North America, 104, 109
North Atlantic Treaty Organization (NATO), 26, 222, 227, 230, 232
North Carolina, 151, 198
North Central College, 26, 37, 43
North Dakota, 57, 148
North Korea, 35, 36
"Northern Triangle" (Central America), 104, 109, 110, 112, 114
Norway, 222
Notre-Dame Cathedral, 7, 86, 92–94
Nozier, Fabrice, 76, 77
NPR (National Public Radio), 72, 105, 107, 115, 117, 226, 238, 259
Nuland, Victoria, 230
Obama, Barack, 9, 24, 47, 185, 197, 202, 203, 231, 236
Obergefell v. Hodges, 189, 205
Ocasio-Cortez, Alexandria, 116–20
Ochoa, Gilda L., v
Office of Refugee Resettlement (ORR) (US), 42
Offset (musician), 89
Ohio, 147
oil and gas industry, 3, 8, 16, 27, 32–34, 55–58, 60, 61, 95, 96, 135, 141, 146–48
Oil Change International, 33, 34
Oklahoma, 53, 57, 151
Omar, Ilhan, 116, 119, 120
Omidyar, Pierre, 232, 233
Oneschuk, Andrew, 50
Ontario, Canada, 222
Operation Earnest Voice (US military campaign), 155
Orange County Register, 63
Oregon, 151
Orient XXI (media website), 65
Orlando, Florida, 185
Orwell, George, xi, 10, 176, 182n21, 229
Oxfam International, 64
Oxford English Dictionary, 109
Pacific Ocean, 58, 59
Pacific Standard, 61
Page, Carter, 25, 78n22
Pakistan, 8, 173, 174, 176, 178, 179
Palestine, 65, 114, 119, 235
Palominos, Angel, 41–43
Paltrow, Lynn, 43
Paradise, CA, 8, 160, 164
Parenteau, Marc, 8, 159–71

Paris, France, 92, 93
Paris climate agreement, 32
Parliament Square, London, 87
Parvez, Khurram, 176
Pasadena Star-News, 63
patents, 46, 47
Patrick, Dan, 202
Patton, Troy, 25–30
PayPal, 76
PBS (television network), 195
Pekow, Charles, 58, 59
Pelosi, Nancy, 86, 118
Pence, Mike, 9, 185
Pennsylvania, 57, 147
Pentagon (US), 46–48, 50, 107, 202
The Pentagon Papers, 6
People (magazine), 87
Peraza, Steve, 7, 103–131
Perkins, Tony, 9, 192, 203–205, 211
Pew Research Center, 239, 240
pharmaceutical industry, 45, 46
Phillips, Peter, 23–32, 53–55, 104
Pilger, John, 235
Planned Parenthood, 44
Plautz, Jason, 52
Podemos (political party, Spain), 234
Podesta, John, 232, 233
police, *see* law enforcement
Police the Police (police accountability organization), 234
PolitiFact, 231, 232
Pope Francis, 97, 98
Popular Science (journal), 59
Porter, Christopher, 233, 249n114
Postman, Neil, 161
Post-Traumatic Stress Disorder (PTSD), 177
poverty, 8, 110
Powell, Andrea, 40
powell, john a., 265
Poynter Institute, 238
Press Colony, Srinagar, Kashmir, 180
Press TV (television network), 234
Pressley, Ayanna, 116–20
Prigozhin, Yevgeny V., 225
Prince Harry, Duke of Sussex, 7, 86, 87
prison, 3, 4, 17, 42, 57, 106, 111, 203, 242
    children in, 71, 72
    labor, 35, 61–63
    women in, 37–40, 43, 44, 91
Prison Policy Initiative, 61–63
Project Censored, xii, xiii, 6, 7, 11, 12, 16, 18, 21, 22, 48, 77n7, 78nn15–17, 81n68,

245n40
Rutgers University, 115
Ryzdak, Jan, 180
"Safe Harbor" law (New York State), 40
Safechuck, James, 97, 99
Sahara Desert, 109
Said, Edward, 103, 126, 127
Salt Lake City, UT, 215n28
Salt Lake City Weekly, 215n28
Samiec, Jaidene, 37–40
San Diego, CA, 93
San Francisco, CA, 8, 72, 161
San Francisco State University, 50
Sanders, Sarah Huckabee, 116
Sanders, Topher, 43
Sandinista National Liberation Front, 29
Sanofi (pharmaceutical company), 45
Saudi Arabia, 66, 67
schools, 6, 72–74, 120, 124, 136, 149, 151,
    175, 192, *see also* education
    engagement journalism in, 264,
        266–69
    policing in, 16, 19, 69–71
    transphobia in, 195, 197–204
Schüll, Natasha Dow, 168
Schwartz, Aria, 85–102
Science (journal), 54
Scott, Ben, 143
Scowcroft, Brent, 230
Screenwise Meter (Google mobile app and
    web extension), 76
Seattle, WA, 150
Secrets of a Successful Organizer, 150
Self (online magazine), 89
Senate (US), 106, 108, 114, 121, 122, 125,
    126, 205, 224, 233
Senate Armed Services Committee (US),
    108
Senate Intelligence Committee (US), 227
Senate Judiciary Committee (US), 123
Sessions, Jeff, 42, 205, 209
sex trafficking, 6, 17, 35–40
sexism, 2, 120, 121, 185, 186, 189, 199, 200,
    203–205, *see also* transgender issues
sexual harassment and assault, 3, 17, 117,
    176, *see also* #MeToo movement; sex
    trafficking
    and Brett Kavanaugh confirmation
        hearings, 120–26
    and criminalization of victims, 6,
        36–40
    of children, 3, 37, 39–43, 97–99

Shadowproof, 29
Sheikh, Nazir Ahmad, 174
Shilling, Ian, 79n30
Shopping Our Way to Safety, 167
Sigrist, Jonathan, 28
Silicon Valley, CA, 8, 134, 143
Singh, Hari, 178
Singh, Lakhvir, 85–102
Singh, Multani Veer, 174
Skinner, Haley, 85–102
Skripal, Sergei and Yulia, 222
Slate (media website), 28, 78n26
slavery, 35–38, *see also* forced labor; sex
    trafficking
Slick, Grace Wing, 85
Slobodnik, Kyle, 71, 72
Smart Cities Dive (media website), 52
Smith, Ashley, 107
Smith, Shepard, 239
Smithsonian (journal), 68
Smithsonian Environmental Research
    Center, 54
Smollett, Jussie, 186, 208, 209
Snow, Izzy, 7, 85–102
Snowden, Edward, 4, 232, 242
"Soapbox" (video channel), 29, 235
social media, 2, 8, 12, 92, 93, 117, 159, 166,
    168–70, 179, *see also* Facebook; Insta-
        gram; internet; Twitter; YouTube
    bots, 79n30, 152–55, 222, 233
    censorship, 9, 25–30, 152, 154, 225, 226,
        229, 231, 258
    Russian disinformation on, 134, 143–45,
        223, 224, 229
    sockpuppets, 152–55
    surveillance, 3, 46–48
    trolls, 152, 222, 225
Social Security (US), 77
Society of Professional Journalists, 8, 133,
    134, 136, 138
Sodexo (food service company), 73
Solomon, Norman, 105
Somalia, 48, 114
Sonoma State University, 23, 26, 31, 41, 53,
    61, 67, 71
Sontag, Susan, 160
the South (US), 265
South America, 111
South Carolina, 86, 151
South Korea, 256
Southern Baptist Convention, 192
Southern California News Group, 63

representation in the media, 189,
194–96, 198, 208, 210
transphobia, 186, 201, 204, 205,
209–211
Transportation Security Administration
(TSA) (US), 139
Trinity University, 153
"triple-A" region, 31, 32
A Troublemaker's Handbook, 2, 150
Trout, Kelly, 33
True Detective (television show), 94
Truman, Harry S., 199
Trump, Donald, 4, 17, 25, 47, 48, 67, 73, 86,
92, 106, 114, 123, 222–24, 231
and the LGBTQ community, 9, 185,
186, 189, 191, 197–204, 208,
212, 213, 214n8, 216n32, 217n53,
218nn71, 74
and the media, 5, 11, 24, 103, 105
antipathy towards women, 44, 90, 91,
115–18, 126
environmental policy, 33, 34, 58–60
immigration policy, 1, 111–13
Truthdig, 226
Truthout, 54, 226, 228
Tubbs Fire (2017), 163
Tulkoff, Lindsey, 138
Turkey, 28
TV Meter (Google television and internet
monitor), 76
Twitter (social media company), 1, 2, 47,
95, 125, 152, 179, 215n32, 217n53, 224,
227, 229, 230, 233–35, 238, 250n122
Tyson Foods, 54
Uber (transportation company), 75
Ukraine, 48–50, 79n30, 230
undocumented persons, 36, 42, 91, *see also*
immigration
unemployment, 61–63, 75, *see also* labor
United Arab Emirates (UAE), 66, 67
United Caucuses of Rank-and-File Educa-
tors, 151
United Kingdom (UK), 5, 79n30, 86–88,
97, 99, 109, 178, 222, 227, 230, 232,
256
United Nations (UN), 34, 37, 39, 173, 178,
180
Biodiversity Conference, 31
Development Programme, 64
Human Rights Council, 177
International Labour Organization, 35
Office on Drugs and Crime, 39

United States farm bill (2018), 73
United States foreign policy, 25–30, 46, 49,
66, 67, 119, 155, 227, 232, 234
United States–Mexico–Canada Agreement
(USMCA), 209, 210, 212
University of California, Los Angeles
(UCLA), 194, 195, 216n37
University of California, Santa Barbara, 232
University of California, Santa Cruz, 68
University of Cantabria, 68
University of Massachusetts, 61
University of Massachusetts Amherst, 63
University of Ottawa, 49
University of Vermont, 35, 46, 74
University of Waterloo, 54
University of Westminster, 180
Univision (television network), 238, 239
UPS (United Parcel Service), 149
U.S. News & World Report, 117
US Newsstream (database), 189, 209
USA PATRIOT Act, 231, 236
USA Today, 43, 59, 63, 68, 75, 105, 109,
115, 117
Utne Reader, 258
Validated Independent News (VIN), 21,
78n16
Vancouver, Canada, 234
Vatican City, 97
Venezuela, 28, 29, 234, 235
Venezuelan Consulate (Vancouver, Canada),
234, 250n122
Venezuelanalysis, 28, 29, 234
Vermont, 222
Veterans for Peace (anti-war organization),
108
Victoria, Texas, 93
Vietnam, 106–108
ViVe Televisión, 234
Voice of America (radio network), 237
Walk Free Foundation, 35, 36
Wall Street, NY, 147
Wall Street Journal, 105, 107, 115, 120–26,
189, 192, 200, 201, 203, 209, 211, 212,
215n30, 217n53, 226, 229, 238
Walmart, 54, 55
Wani, Burhan, 179, 180
war, xii, 4, 6, 28, 106–108, 110, 173, 231,
232, 234, 240–42, 255, 256, *see also*
military; weapons
Cold War, 26, 221, 222
World War I, 5, 78n12
World War II, 188